Y0-BVO-721

# Psychological metaphysics

The research literature on causal attribution and social cognition generally consists of many fascinating but fragmented and superficial phenomena. These can only be understood as an organised whole by elucidating the fundamental psychological assumptions on which they depend. *Psychological Metaphysics* is an exploration of the most basic and important assumptions in the psychological construction of reality, with the aim of showing what they are, how they originate, and what they are there for.

Peter A. White proposes that people basically understand causation in terms of stable, specific powers of things operating to produce effects under suitable conditions. This underpins an analysis of people's understanding of causal processes in the physical word and of human action, which makes a radical break with the Heiderian tradition.

*Psychological Metaphysics* suggests that causal attribution is in the service of the person's practical concerns and any interest in accuracy or understanding is subservient to this. A notion of regularity in the world is of no more than minor importance in causal attribution, and social cognition is not so much a matter of cognitive mechanisms or processes but more of cultural ways of thinking imposed upon tacit, unquestioned, universal assumptions.

*Psychological Metaphysics* incorporates not only research and theory in social cognition and developmental psychology, but also philosophy and the history of ideas. It will be challenging to everyone interested in how we try to understand the world.

**Peter A. White** is a Lecturer in Psychology at the University of Wales College of Cardiff.

# International Library of Psychology

# Psychological metaphysics

Peter A. White

BF
323
.S63
W48
1993
West

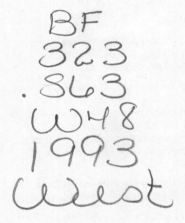

London and New York

First published in 1993
by Routledge
11 New Fetter Lane, London EC4P 4EE

Simultaneously published in the USA and Canada
by Routledge
29 West 35th Street, New York, NY 10001

© 1993 Peter A. White

Typeset in Times by LaserScript, Mitcham, Surrey
Printed and bound in Great Britain by
T.J. Press (Padstow) Ltd., Padstow, Cornwall

All rights reserved. No part of this book may be reprinted
or reproduced or utilized in any form or by any
electronic, mechanical, or other means, now known or
hereafter invented, including photocopying and
recording, or in any information storage or retrieval
system, without permission in writing from the
publishers.

*British Library Cataloguing in Publication Data*
A catalogue record for this book is available from the British Library.

*Library of Congress Cataloging in Publication Data*
White, Peter A. (Peter Anthony), 1954–
    Psychological metaphysics / Peter A. White
    p. cm. – (International library of psychology)
    Includes bibliographical references and index.
    1. Social Perception – Philosophy. 2. Metaphysics – Psychological
    aspects. 3. Knowledge, Sociology of. 4. Attribution (Psychology)
    5. Concepts. I. Title. II. Series.
    BF323.S63.W48                                                    1993
    150′.1 – dc20                                              92-24480
                                                                    CIP

ISBN 0–415–08331–1

For Sara

# Contents

# Figures and tables

**FIGURES**

**TABLES**

# Preface

In his book, *Great Scientific Experiments*, Rom Harré wrote: 'Psychology is the most conservative of all scientific specialisms' (p. 148). I don't know if he was right or not, but his remark has stayed with me for years, because it evokes an image so opposed to what I aimed for and still aim for in my work. Surely science must be radical, revolutionary, endlessly self-critical? Surely any scientist would be more excited by things which overturn orthodox belief than by things which reinforce it? Isn't it *good* for ideas to go beyond the available evidence? I thought this was the essence of science, and Rom's comment shocked me a little in its suggestion that psychology does not generally share these values.

I have no prescription for the best way to do research in psychology. There are things that are better avoided, perhaps, but as far as I can see it is up to each individual to use their talents according to their own judgement of what is best. For me this has meant an inclination towards ideas, innovation, synthesis on as broad a scale as I can manage. I have no talent for analytical thought nor for the design of experiments, the traditional strengths of research in psychology. But I cannot escape the feeling that ideas are more important than anything, that to have as many ideas as possible, no matter if some of them turn out to be nonsense, can only be beneficial to science. I get frustrated with the perpetual demand of journal editors that ideas be supported by research findings before they can be published. This seems counter-productive; not only that, but it places on the researcher the burden of being good at both having ideas and designing experiments. If the idea is published, then people who are better than its progenitor at experimental design all have the opportunity to test it. If it is not, that opportunity is denied to them, and science is the poorer for it.

The wonderful thing about science is that what one creates cannot be arbitrary, but is constrained by the great aim of improving upon whatever has been done before. It seems to me that research in psychology is often practised as if progress meant the steady accumulation of knowledge, indisputable findings, or understanding. I tend to see it more in negative terms: for me, the progress of science involves the breaking down of illusions about reality, escape from wrong ideas. Thus, the promulgation of ideas is an essential component in a critical dialectic: ideas, criticism, more ideas, criticism of those, and so on. Research findings play a role in both components of this dialectic: they give force to criticism, they help to shape and refine ideas.

This is only a personal notion, not a philosophy of science. But it helps to explain why I have moved in the direction of metaphysics. The desire to break down illusions, to find out what is wrong with what we believe, has led me deeper and deeper into the foundations on which those beliefs are constructed. It seems to me that it is only by exposing the foundations that what is wrong with beliefs can be revealed. It seems to me also that, with the foundations still buried, we as researchers are doomed to flounder in a morass of superficial phenomena, the interconnections among which remain hidden from us.

One reason for writing a book is that it permits a synthesis of ideas on a scale impossible for any journal article. Indeed, the almost universal requirement for articles to report research findings has meant that ideas can only be presented in isolation, and with little basis in reasoning. Thus, we end up with a great number of fragments, and progress in research means developing variations and extensions on individual fragments, not tying numbers of them together. In the work that I present in this book, I have deliberately aimed for a coherent synthesis on as broad a scale as possible: not just a lot of ideas, but a lot of ideas organised into a pattern that makes sense to me on a large scale. With luck, the whole pattern will be worth more than the sum of the individual ideas.

I want to emphasise that this book is only a stage in the development of my ideas. I do not regard it as a finished article, but I recognise that the desire to go on improving something has no logical end, that one is never satisfied with what one has done so far. I don't think it is helpful to hide things away in a drawer just because they are not perfect. A published book gives an impression of absoluteness: these things in my mind are not absolute, and I certainly hope that in years to come I shall change my mind about them, or at least see them differently. What I present here is only how I see things now.

I have been the recipient of much good fortune and kindness over the years: I could easily never have been a psychologist at all, but for accident and luck and the help of many people. I owe most to the Psychology Department at Nottingham University and its long-time Head, Professor Ian Howarth. When I was an undergraduate, the department allowed me to transfer to psychology from philosophy, and my love of psychology was fostered by the people who taught me there, perhaps especially Geoffrey Stephenson and Dave Wood. When I returned to Nottingham on sabbatical in 1988, the department generously gave me space for the months I was there, and I am particularly grateful to Geoff Underwood for the facilities he provided. The earliest drafts of this book were written there. I would also like to express my gratitude to David Clarke. David was my co-supervisor at Oxford, and our many lunchtime conversations were an important source of intellectual stimulation for me. He also treated me with unfailing selflessness which I am afraid I did nothing to deserve. His work, I believe, has not received as much attention as it merits. I owe a great deal to many other people, and I can only briefly mention those who are chief among my debts:

Michael Argyle, Derek Blackman, Mike Corballis, Rick Crandall, Rom Harré, Peter Kelvin, Mansur Lalljee, Tom Shultz, and all my friends both in Britain and in New Zealand. Finally, I am deeply grateful to David Stonestreet and Routledge for giving me the chance to publish my peculiar ideas.

# Chapter 1

# Introduction to psychological metaphysics

Consider the whole multifarious conglomerate of beliefs, judgements, concepts, and so on, cultural, sub-cultural, personal, stable or transient, that make up a person's understanding of the world and all that is in it. Could this bewildering diversity have any overall organisation, giving a place to every element within it? It could and does: it is an organisation that can be comprehended by elucidating its most fundamental components, for those are the things, more than anything else, that determine the pattern into which all of the elements in the organisation fall. Not only that, but every judgement, inference, and attribution is made in the light of that organisation, and in a way that depends on the fundamental components of that organisation. Thus, to understand social cognition, it is necessary to understand those fundamental components, how they come to be, and how they shape the pattern of elements which they underpin. Common sense is not a formless mass of bits and pieces: it is an integrated, structured, hierarchically organised whole, and the kind of whole it is makes a difference to everything an individual does.

My primary concern in this book, therefore, is to reach down to the most fundamental levels of that organisation, to show how an understanding of social cognition can be built up from there. This investigation corresponds roughly to the branch of philosophy called metaphysics. In philosophy, metaphysics is concerned with questions about the most fundamental features of reality. For example, what, more fundamentally than anything else, is the world made of? What are the most basic categories or kinds of thing that exist in the world? What is the nature of causation (Campbell 1976; Carr 1987)? We can treat inference, judgement, behaviour, and common sense in general as if they had a metaphysical foundation, meaning that the things that go on in them imply presuppositions about the basic nature of the world. To give a trivial example, taking it for granted that the pot plant now sitting on my desk is the same one that I observed sitting in the same place yesterday implies the acceptance of at least one metaphysical postulate (to do with continuity of existence across a gap between observations).[1]

Although nothing is constant in the world but change, and although no one can step into the same river twice, we can only orientate ourselves in reality by adopting constant reference points as bases for our more specific and variable hypotheses, beliefs, judgements, and interpretations. The function of a set of constant reference points is fulfilled by the psychological equivalent of meta-physical postulates: these are the axioms of the psychological construction of reality, the things which depend on nothing else in that construction, but on the set of which all else depends.

That being so, we cannot hope to understand any aspect of social cognition without elucidating its metaphysical underpinning. This in turn implies a need to explain psychological metaphysics: to explain, that is, why our construction of reality is founded on these assumptions rather than those, how they originate, what they do for us. The traditional focus of social cognition research has been on processes, processes of causal attribution, attitude change, impression formation, and so on. Here, the focus is more, though not exclusively, on concepts, or on things that function as concepts. It is the basic concepts of social cognition that determine the range of processes available to people: those processes are cultural, sub-cultural, and personal variants on universal conceptual themes. This book therefore seeks to elucidate and explain the basic metaphysical themes of the psychological construction of reality. A number of key questions can be identified.

1  What are the metaphysical assumptions in the psychological construction of reality, how do they originate, and what are they there for? The whole book is an attempt to answer these questions, but the third of them receives special attention in Chapter 2.
2  What is it that makes a metaphysical assumption basic to the construction of reality? Essentially, this is a question about the main organising principle of the psychological construction of reality, and is the special topic of Chapter 3.
3  How are the observable phenomena of social cognition, and perhaps social interaction in general, grounded in psychological metaphysics? A full treat-ment of this would have to address all the topics of social cognition, and perhaps all of social psychology. This is well beyond the scope of one book, but selected topics are considered in later chapters of this book.

Before I put off people who might find things of interest and relevance in this book, let me highlight the topic of causal attribution, because part of the purpose of this book is to propose a fundamental and radical alternative approach to causal attribution as a replacement for the one that has held sway since the publication of Heider's book (1958). The negative side of this is that many important things that Heider said about causal attribution are wrong. People are not naïve scientists. The internal/external distinction is not basic to causal attribution. Every causal attribution theory that owed something to Heider's approach, parti-cularly to his emphasis on regularity or covariation information, is fundamentally on the wrong track: in fact, to twist the metaphor a little, all such theories are up a side alley that leads nowhere. The positive side is the postulation of an alternative basis for understanding causal attribution. In this, causal attribution is carried out in the service of practical concerns. The distinction between action and more deterministically caused events and behaviour is important. The theoretical basis is no longer regularity or covariation but a concept of the causal relation as generative, and as involving the operation of causal powers of things. The use of regularity information, whether sampled from the environment or from memory, is only a minor issue. Causal attribution forms only part of this book, but it is an important part, none the less.

My journey into psychological metaphysics began with an analysis of work by Nisbett and Wilson (1977), and a brief summary of this analysis may help to introduce the topic. Nisbett and Wilson (1977) proposed a complex hypothesis about verbal reports of factors influencing mental processes, such as processes of judgement and choice. In their words, the hypothesis involves two related propositions: 'There may be little or no direct access to higher order cognitive processes' (p. 231); and 'The accuracy of verbal reports is generally so poor as to suggest that any introspective access that may exist is not sufficient to produce generally correct or reliable reports' (p. 233). In principle, evidence of the inaccuracy of these 'causal' reports counts as evidence for lack of 'access to' (or awareness of) the relevant mental processes, although this proposition is qualified in practice by several methodological factors (White 1988b). Their proposal, then, relates a proposition about 'introspective access' to a proposition about verbal report accuracy.

How do metaphysical issues come into this? Let us suppose, for the sake of argument, that there are two dichotomies: verbalisable/non-verbalisable, and introspectively accessible/non-introspectively accessible. Logically, this gives us four possible categories of things:

1  Introspectively accessible and verbalisable.
2  Introspectively accessible and not verbalisable.
3  Not introspectively accessible and verbalisable.
4  Not introspectively accessible and not verbalisable.

Under this supposition, the metaphysical assumption underlying the Nisbett and Wilson hypothesis is that only two categories are possible in fact, numbers 1 and 4 (and, following from this, their hypothesis is that all mental processes fall under category 4). This illustrates a general point that metaphysical assumptions imply the a priori rejection of certain logical possibilities. Part of my critique of their hypothesis (White 1986, 1988b) has been that we have no good reason to rule out numbers 2 and 3 a priori. Indeed, even the critics of the Nisbett and Wilson proposal wrote as if they implicitly accepted that only 1 and 4 were possible, and the argument mainly concerned how much and what among mental activity might fall into number 1.[2]

In order to be complete as a scientific theory, their account, and indeed any scientific proposal, hypothesis, and so on, should include the metaphysical assumptions on which the hypothesis depends, explicitly and clearly. If readers share the implicit metaphysical postulates underlying the hypothesis, then accepting the hypothesis as it is presented is merely sloppy thinking: if readers do not, then they will find the hypothesis incomprehensible. Both possibilities should be avoided, and this entails making the metaphysical underpinning explicit. Of course, this argument of mine itself depends on certain assumptions: for example, the metaphysical assumption that verbalisable/non-verbalisable and introspectively accessible/non-introspectively accessible are dichotomies rather than continua, and the methodological assumption that there are no factors such as memory that may give a wrong impression of the true state of affairs. But these assumptions do not undermine the role of the argument as an illustration.[3]

A second illustration will help to emphasise the importance of metaphysical assumptions in science. One of the earliest and most influential theories of causal attribution is that proposed by Kelley (1967). According to this theory, people use the covariation principle – that is, the principle that the cause of an effect is that thing which covaries with the effect – to make causal inferences from information organised along each of three dimensions. Although now past its prime (Hewstone 1989; White 1989a) the influence of this theory on research into causal attribution has been immense. Despite this, Kelley's model depends upon an implicit metaphysical assumption which, although of fundamental importance, has received little attention.

The assumption is revealed by the fact that the method is universal: there is no behaviour or kind of behaviour for which it would not, in principle, be considered appropriate. This implies that there are no differences of any importance between different behaviours, as far as use of the method is concerned. 'Ralph trips over Joan's feet while dancing' is not different in any way that matters from 'Jane makes a bid at an auction' or 'John lets go of the scalding hot kettle'. It makes no difference whether the behaviour is voluntary or involuntary, freely chosen or coerced, deliberate or accidental. This implication is never discussed in Kelley's published articles, but it is there all the same. It might, of course, turn out that the implication is correct (though I shall be arguing that it is not), but that would still not justify a failure to discuss it.

This is important because the validity of the model depends upon the correctness of the metaphysical assumption: if all behaviours are not the same, as far as causal attribution is concerned, then Kelley's model cannot be valid as a universal method for causal attribution. This is why it is important to investigate fundamental assumptions. They are the most basic delimiters of social cognition, and no account of processes can be complete without statements of the assumptions on which the processes depend. Processes follow assumptions, not vice versa. Every hypothesis about a process carries and depends upon metaphysical assumptions. The problem of metaphysics is a particularly insidious one for social cognition: hypotheses make sense to us because we share with their formulators, and with the rest of society, the metaphysical assumptions on which they depend. That is, we take those assumptions for granted, and it is hard for us to think about the things that we take for granted: they underpin and shape our thoughts, but form no part of them. Yet this is what we must try to do. To quote Collingwood (1940): 'In low-grade or unscientific thinking we hardly know that we are making any presuppositions at all' (p. 34). And: 'The birth of science, in other words the establishment of orderly thinking, is also the birth of metaphysics. As long as either lives the other lives; if either dies the other must die with it' (p. 41).

If the elucidation of metaphysical assumptions is important to science, it is crucial to the scientific attempt to investigate common sense and social cognition. Despite this, the topic is rarely aired in social psychology. The most sustained discourse I can find is by Fletcher (1984). He began by listing some 'shared fundamental assumptions':

> that the world exists independently of our perception of it, that the causal relationships that have held in the past will continue to operate in the future, that other people possess states of conscious awareness, that we are the same person from day to day, and that people are sentient, self-aware creatures capable of self-control (unlike rocks and other inanimate objects).
>
> (Fletcher 1984: 204)

Fletcher argued that beliefs of this sort have two characteristic features: first, that there is 'virtually unanimous agreement within Western cultures' (p. 204) concerning them, and in fact that they may be universal, and secondly that they are 'tacitly held and are almost never questioned, justified, or even articulated' (p. 204). The metaphysical assumption I encountered in the work of Nisbett and Wilson and their critics evidently possesses both of these features. Fletcher also went on to argue that beliefs of this sort are 'implicitly present in scientific theories' (p. 205), and he commented, 'I believe there is a very strong presumption that psychological theories should embrace this class of fundamental commonsense assumptions' (p. 206). The word 'embrace' was chosen with care, because he thought that theories that reject any of these assumptions 'invariably become embroiled in intractable difficulties' (p. 205). His reason for thinking this was that the assumptions 'seem to be a necessary component of our attempt to maintain a coherent, intelligible, and plausible view of the world' (p. 205), and, if we start to doubt them, 'one's whole basis for rational action will vanish, and the world will turn into a buzzing chaos' (p. 205).

This is perhaps a statement of faith rather than a compelling argument. When I questioned the metaphysical assumption in the Nisbett and Wilson proposal I did not find that the world became more chaotic: on the contrary, I felt less deluded about reality. And, to take up Fletcher's own example, the common-sense universalistic concept of time that was abolished in the special theory of relativity, faces the really intractable difficulty that it is wrong and therefore must be rejected. My own statement of faith, for what it may be worth, is that the progress of science has consisted of a laborious journey away from the wrong fundamental assumptions of common sense. The physics of motion provides an excellent example of this (cf. McCloskey 1983). What Fletcher's comment reveals is not that the fundamental assumptions of common sense must be true, but that the whole of our construction of reality would fall to pieces without them. True or false, they are of absolutely fundamental and universal importance to us.

Fletcher contrasted the category of implicit and universal fundamental assumptions with two other broad categories of common sense. First, common sense as a set of cultural maxims and shared beliefs. These are usually explicitly known and relativistic. Second, common sense as a shared way of thinking. Here Fletcher had in mind cognitive processes, and cited Nisbett and Ross (1980) and Ross (1977) in this connection. Shared ways of thinking, Fletcher suggested, are generally tacit and relativistic.

The study of social cognition has been dominated by research into the latter category (Fiske and Taylor 1991), although there has been research on cultural beliefs and shared maxims (Furnham 1988). It is, however, almost impossible to find any work on shared fundamental assumptions – though it may be that Heider (1958) was attempting to venture into this territory. Thus, investigation of beliefs and processes in social cognition is proceeding without consideration of the fundamental assumptions on which all such things depend. Fundamental assumptions do not strictly determine how processes operate, but they do delimit a range of possible processes, in that processes which imply assumptions contrary to those actually held by people will not be used. Furthermore, such assumptions are not merely silent partners in mental activity: when we make a causal inference, for example, we are employing our concept of what a cause is, and in this sense our basic assumptions maintain an active presence in our mental activity. As Taylor (1974) wrote: 'We all use our metaphysical principles, whether we think of them or not, or are even capable of thinking of them' (p. 39).

Every belief, every inference, every judgement depends upon metaphysical assumptions: the most important job for someone constructing a theory of lay belief, inference, and/or judgement is to make explicit those metaphysical assumptions, to clarify the role they play in holding reality together in people's psychological construction of it. In many cases, it is the metaphysics that can give power and generality to a theory of lay inference. In all cases, making them explicit is necessary for completeness of theory. I hope in what follows to demonstrate this.

It may be objected that some of the claims about what is most basic in the psychological construction of reality are so obviously true as to be unworthy of comment. I agree that some of them are obvious: it is bound to be a feature of those things that are most basic in the psychological construction of reality that they appear obviously true when pointed out. This is because, as Fletcher (1984) said, they are things that are taken for granted, taken as axiomatic, by everyone. But this does not mean that we can afford to take obvious things for granted in science. In the first place, mistaking what is obvious for what is true is the fallacy of naïve realism: it seems obvious that the Sun goes round the Earth, but taking this obvious thing for granted held up the progress of astronomy for centuries. In the second place, those things that are both obvious and true are not thereby trivial or unworthy of scientific explanation. It is obvious to everyone that the night sky is dark, but this is a far from trivial fact because, as stated in Olbers' paradox, it should not be, and a satisfactory explanation for the darkness of the night sky has only been found this century.

Two cautionary points should be made about psychological metaphysics. First, the metaphysical presuppositions in common sense may never have been the subject of attentive deliberation by most people. It is not likely that people start by deliberately laying down a set of metaphysical postulates and then thoughtfully build up their understanding of reality from those. The metaphysical postulates constitute a foundation of assumptions that are implicit in thought and belief and talk about any part of reality, rather than deliberately put there as a starting-point for it.

Secondly, there is a distinction in philosophy between 'knowing that' and 'knowing how' (for example, Ayer 1956). For instance, the skills of piano playing could be described in terms of 'knowing that' – knowing that this note is middle C, that hitting it just so hard makes just so loud a sound, that a crotchet is twice as long as a quaver, and so on. But although this could work as a (laboured) description, knowing how to play the piano is arguably a different *type* of thing from its possible complete description in terms of 'knowing that'. So it may be for psychological metaphysics: it is like the most basic operating guide to reality, the knowing how of the construction of reality in perception, inference, and so forth. I am tending to describe this metaphysics *as if* it were a set of knowing thats, because that is the only way I can describe it at all, but while the knowing hows of psychological metaphysics may imply the kind of knowing that which I describe here, it must not be forgotten that knowing hows may be what they partly or even wholly are. The investigation of psychological metaphysics is not unduly hampered by keeping an open mind on this. No doubt the fundamental axioms of the psychological construction of reality can be accurately represented as propositions, and probably accurately expressed verbally: but it is how they function that matters, not whether or not they are 'really' propositions.

In respect of this caveat, let me lay down some terminology for the rest of the book. Any single component in the psychological construction of reality will be referred to as an 'element', for the sake of leaving open the question of whether it is a proposition or not. Following Kenny (1989), an element can have either or both of two types of attitude. One type of attitude is a truth value (for example, held to be true, false, uncertain, and so on), and if the truth value is true then the element is or functions as a belief. The other type of attitude is an evaluation, essentially in terms of good versus bad, whether this be nice/nasty, pleasant/unpleasant, desirable/undesirable, or other variations on that theme. Both types of attitude are dependent on the element (Chapter 3 explains what 'dependent' means).

Readers can expect to encounter a good deal of philosophy in what follows. Several times in the past people have expressed the opinion that my work is philosophy rather than psychology, and for this reason I feel compelled to make some clear statements on the subject.[4] My work here is purely psychology. If it makes use of things in philosophy, this is simply for scientific psychological purposes. A psychological theory that makes use of mathematics does not thereby become part of mathematics and stop being psychology: for exactly the same reason a psychological theory that makes use of philosophy does not thereby become part of philosophy and stop being psychology. On the contrary, philosophy can, through its conceptual rigour, be of great assistance to the construction of theories in psychology, just as mathematics can through its exactness. Conceptual analysis is an important ingredient in the study of social cognition. The use of terms in scientific propositions without proper conceptual analysis can only result in ambiguity and misunderstanding, and the study of social cognition is much the poorer for ignoring this. I am sorry if readers feel uncomfortable with philosophy, but I do not regard this as a good reason for leaving it out.

One fundamental difference between philosophy and psychology (or any science) is that the methods of enquiry used in philosophy are essentially rational and employ criteria such as logical coherence, imaginability, intelligibility, and freedom from ambiguity, whereas the methods used in psychology are essentially empirical and employ criteria concerned with the status of evidence. Philosophy and psychology therefore engage in enquiries of different kinds, and the superficial resemblance of the questions asked in each should not be allowed to disguise their basic differences. We could no more design an experiment to test a philosophical notion than we could establish the truth or falsity of a psychological hypothesis by logic alone. Everything I propose in the course of this enquiry is in principle subject to test by empirical methods and not by rationalist methods. It is therefore science, not philosophy.

Much of what follows is concerned with causal processing. Philosophical theories of causation are a part of metaphysics because metaphysical doctrines place limitations on the kinds of theory of causation that go with them, and correspondingly theories of causation invariably imply metaphysical presuppositions. For example, in phenomenalism the basic particulars, meaning the basic things of which reality is made, are sense-impressions, so phenomenalism is compatible only with theories of causation that deal in relations between sense-impressions. For the same reason, causal processing is inextricably intertwined with psychological metaphysics, particularly in its direct relation to one of the basic categories of psychological metaphysics (to be elucidated later), and causal processing can only be understood when explicitly placed in its metaphysical context. Everything that happens (and perhaps also some things that are not events or happenings) can be subject to causal processing, can be seen as caused, whether by human free will, mechanistic efficient causation, or act of God or gods. For this reason causal processing, of which causal attributions for human behaviour constitute a part, has a greater importance than its treatment in psychology hitherto would suggest.

To summarise the general stance of the book, then: all the beliefs a person has about the world, or all things they have that function as beliefs, fall into an organised arrangement which I tend to call 'the psychological construction of reality'. The basis of this organised arrangement consists of a set of axioms, metaphysical assumptions, on which everything else in the construction depends. To understand any judgement, inference, or attribution, it is therefore necessary to elucidate the metaphysical assumptions that underpin it, and more generally its place in the psychological construction of reality.

This immediately raises questions about the nature of the organisation. What is it for a belief or a judgement to depend on something else? What is it for something to be basic to the construction of reality? These questions are dealt with in Chapter 3. Following that the exploration of psychological metaphysics begins. First comes elucidation of the most basic distinction in the construction of reality, that between being and happening. The nature of being in the psychological construction of reality is then analysed. The nature of happening relates to causation, and a major part of the book explores the basic concept of causation that people possess, and attempts to explain its origin, and the development of causal understanding. Following this treatment of general psychological metaphysics I proceed to two main sub-categories of the psychological construction of reality, one concerned with events in the physical universe (that is, events other than those involving human behaviour), and the other concerned with the minds of human beings and their actions.

Inferences, judgements, and indeed metaphysical assumptions are not made for no reason at all, but because they serve some function or functions for the person who makes them. Thus, we cannot hope to understand psychological metaphysics, let alone inference and judgement, without discovering the general functions that such things serve. Research on social inference, causal attribution, and so on, is generally interpreted within a specific assumption that the functions served by social cognition are quasi-scientific; that is, that people seek to understand, predict, and control reality as best they can, and use inference and judgement in the service of those ends. In this book a different assumption is made about the functions of social cognition, and since this assumption permeates much of what follows it is necessary to start by considering it. This, then, is the topic of the next chapter.

## NOTES

1  The use of the term 'metaphysics' to denote these topics is a historical accident. Aristotle wrote a book called *Physics*, and then followed it with a book concerned with what is fundamental to reality. Since the Greek prefix 'meta-' means 'after', and since this book came after the *Physics*, it was referred to as *Meta-physics*, and this became the term for those topics that happened to be treated in that book.

2  In fact I would claim that numbers 2 and 3 are both possible. A good example of no. 3 is the phenomenon of 'blindsight' (Weiskrantz *et al.* 1974), in which a subject who underwent complete unilateral ablation of the visual cortex with resultant hemianopia was able to make accurate verbal identifications of visual stimuli which he claimed not to be able to perceive. An example of no. 2 would be my impression of the qualities of a pianist's interpretation of a sonata, which I cannot verbalise because I cannot adequately translate it into verbal code. Anyone who has struggled to answer a question such as 'What does it taste like?' (such as about some novel variety of cheese) will have experienced the same kind of problem. But, for the sake of clarity, I am not arguing about whether numbers 2 and 3 ever occur, but whether there is any justification for rejecting them a priori.

3   Of course there is more to the metaphysics of the Nisbett and Wilson proposal than just this (Shanker 1991; White 1988b). I have just selected one point for illustrative purposes.
4   Since I wrote that, it has happened again. A journal editor decided that an article I submitted was not appropriate for his journal on the grounds that it was primarily a philosophical discussion. This was incorrect. The article borrowed some conceptual analysis of the term 'disposition' from philosophy, but the focus was clearly on the scientific relevance of this. One cannot formulate a clearly articulated theory or hypothesis without conceptual analysis. For this reason, deliberately to exclude papers that offer conceptual analysis from publication in social psychology journals is profoundly unscientific. Social psychology cannot become a science merely by discovering processes. Analysis of concepts, not only to ascertain their logical status but also in the interests of rigorous terminology, is a prerequisite for science, not a philosophical irrelevance. Papers that offer the service of performing conceptual analysis must be published, if they are good enough, in places where researchers can see them, and that means the mainstream social psychological journals.

# Part 1

# General psychological metaphysics

# Chapter 2

# Practical concerns and lay judgement

The theme of this chapter is that the study of lay inference and judgement has been profoundly biased by an assumption that the preoccupations, fundamental categories and concepts, and even the tools and methods of professional scientists in their work are similar to those of ordinary people, if not exactly the same. This assumption has affected researchers' ideas of what it is to be rational in social judgement and inference, of what people are trying to do when they make judgements and inferences, and of the kinds of topics and issues that are worth investigating, to the detriment of our understanding of lay judgement and inference. I propose a different idea of the function of social judgement and inference, different fundamental categories of judgement, and a different conceptual approach to the study of lay judgement.

I begin by outlining the dominant conceptualisation of lay people in the field of lay judgement, inference, and attribution.

## THE LAY-SCIENTIST ORIENTATION

Under this orientation people are seen as naïve scientists or psychologists. This view is associated with Kelly (1955), but in the areas of social inference and causal attribution it is the similar view of Heider (1958) that has been more influential. Heider began his chapter on the naïve analysis of action, which laid the foundations of the subject known as attribution theory, with this statement: 'It is an important principle of common-sense psychology, as it is of scientific theory in general, that man grasps reality, and can predict and control it, by referring transient and variable behaviour to relatively unchanging underlying conditions, the so-called dispositional properties of his world' (p. 79). This statement implies a belief that the main activities of human beings are grasping, predicting, and controlling reality, and that ordinary people strive to do this in ways that are basically like those of scientists.

A relatively pure exemplification of this view is to be found in Kelley's (1967, 1972a, 1973) multiple observation model of causal attribution. According to this theory, people make causal attributions by a method based on Heider's (1958) covariation principle, which loosely resembles several philosophical methods

(White 1990): to explain some effect, people sample occasions along three independent dimensions and identify as the cause of the effect the factor that covaries with it across the occasions sampled. Heider (1958) had argued that this data pattern was 'fundamental in the determination of attribution' (p. 152), and he also referred to Mill's (1843/1967) method of difference as a basic tool of the naïve psychologist (p. 68). The main assumption in Kelley's model was that people strive to make the most *accurate* causal attribution possible ('grasping' reality), and that they do this by a naïve version of a normative tool of causal inference in science, analysis of variance. Kelley's (1972b) causal schema model was a later development based on the same principles.

The lay-scientist orientation does not depend on the idea that people use empirical methods of causal inference: Nisbett and Ross (1980) introduced their book as portraying people as

> intuitive scientists who are gifted and generally successful, but whose attempts to understand, predict, and control events in the social sphere are seriously compromised by specific inferential shortcomings. In part, these shortcomings reflect people's failure to use the normative principles and inferential tools that guide formal scientific inquiry. They also reflect people's readiness to apply more simplistic inferential strategies beyond their appropriate limits.
>
> (Nisbett and Ross 1980: 3)

In this quotation and the rest of their introduction, the main principles of their version of the lay-scientist analogy can be discerned.

First, the main goals of inference and judgement for the lay person are to understand, predict, and control events in the social sphere. These three activities are also the main goals of professional scientists, though not necessarily in the social sphere, and it is this alleged similarity that is taken as justifying the analogy between lay inference and scientific inference.

Secondly, the normative principles and inferential tools that guide formal scientific enquiry provide the standards against which lay inference is properly assessed, as do securely established facts. This is the scientific model of rationality: to be irrational is to make an inference that is inaccurate, or to use an inferential device that is inappropriate, by the normative standards of science.

Thirdly, the natural kinds of judgement that people engage in correspond to the kinds of judgement in professional science. Nisbett and Ross devoted a chapter to each of these: taking in information, covariation assessment, causal analysis, prediction, and the maintenance and testing of theories, beliefs, and hypotheses.

Fourthly, under the lay-scientist analogy, errors and biases identified by use of the normative standards of science tend to be explained in a novel way: they arise from defects in the machinery of judgement and inference (Miller and Ross 1975; Ross 1977). These are usually called 'cognitive biases'. They include what Nisbett and Ross referred to as the application of 'more simplistic inferential strategies beyond their appropriate limits' (1980: 3). Examples of this would be inappropriate uses of the representativeness and availability heuristics (Kahneman and Tversky 1972, 1973; Tversky and Kahneman 1973). The extreme view is that all errors can be interpreted as effects of cognitive biases, but many writers have defended the traditional 'motivational' interpretation of at least some biases, and the nearest thing to a consensus at present is that both 'cognitive' and 'motivational' biases may influence judgement (for example, Harvey and Weary 1984). The word 'motivational' is used because the source of the bias is not just emotion but some specific motivation such as the desire to preserve or enhance self-esteem. The debate has been critically analysed in a useful way by Tetlock and Levi (1982).

In recent years the emphasis has changed a little. The lay scientist has now become a cognitive miser (Taylor 1981; Fiske and Taylor 1991). The cognitive miser is an information processor of limited capacity who, because of the limits on processing capacity, adopts strategies that simplify complex problems, sacrificing accuracy for adequacy in the interests of efficiency. Fiske and Taylor (1991) described the latest version of this view as the motivated tactician, which is a way of saying that motivational factors in inference are now regarded as more important than they were ten years ago. Thus far the emphasis has shifted: motivational factors are not regarded as merely sources of bias, but also as principles guiding choice of cognitive strategy. The major features of the model as described above, however, have not changed: people are not thought to aim for accuracy at all costs, but scientifically optimal judgement is still the standard for assessing rationality.

## THE PRACTICAL CONCERNS MODEL

The key feature of this approach is that social judgement and inference and causal attribution of all kinds take place in a context of the contemporary practical concerns of the person making them: all judgements, inferences, and attributions are in the service of those concerns, and are made in order to contribute to them. This leads to a profoundly different view of judgement and so on, which can be usefully explicated by addressing each of the four listed features of the lay-scientist conception.

The first point: the primary aims of lay judgement and inference are not understanding, prediction, or control *per se*, but to make the best possible and most appropriate contribution to the practical concerns of the judge at the time. This implies a shift of emphasis, away from scientific or factual accuracy of judgement, away from method or process of judgement, and towards its *function*.

Science and lay inference differ fundamentally with respect to the kinds of question with which they deal. Gorovitz (1965) argued that in ordinary life a causal inference involves the identification of a single causal factor that differentiates the occasion in question from some standard chosen for comparison, specifically consisting of occasions on which the effect in question does not occur (see Hesslow 1988, for a similar argument). By contrast, he argued that the scientific account would differentiate the case in question from not just one standard but from all possible standards for comparison, and that this account would be a conjunction of all determining factors.

An example will show, however, that Gorovitz's argument is not entirely correct. Suppose, for example, that I am engaged in causal processing of Paul's liking for a painting he sees in the art gallery (from McArthur 1972). A scientific account of this, in Gorovitz's terms, would have to include a treatise on the history of art and another on Paul's individuating characteristics, at least: anything less would be incomplete in its listing of determining factors. Clearly, people never do anything like this. But neither do scientists: what this example reveals is a fundamental difference between the scientific and psychological approaches to inference. The tendency in science is to divide the world up into things and types of thing that allow the most parsimonious generalisations to be established, without taking anything for granted.

This more nearly reflects the difference between scientific and lay inference identified by Hart and Honoré (1959). In science, the usual aim is to establish causal generalisations of nomothetic character, to explain *types* of occurrence (Hart and Honoré 1959). For this, observation of multiple occasions is essential, and in consequence summary data from multiple observations, such as patterns of covariation, are indispensable. But in ordinary life the usual aim is to explain single occurrences, particular events, and the methods of science, with their emphasis on sampling and generalisation, are not well suited to this kind of explanation.

In short, Paul's liking for a painting is not a well-formed scientific problem because it does not represent a way of dividing up reality that admits of a parsimonious account. The tendency of ordinary people is to divide up reality in ways that reflect discrete practical concerns, and this is a different way of dividing things up. The metaphysics of the psychological construction of reality is different from the metaphysics of science *because* it reflects this different way of dividing things up: it is an *as if* metaphysics, a functional metaphysics, rather than a deliberated system of thought because it emerges out of the primary importance of practical concerns.

The ordinary person is therefore able to give some sort of account of Paul's liking for the painting because the practical concerns in respect of which this account is constructed determine the selection among the possible relevant factors that will be made. That is, practical concerns narrow down causal processing (and inference in general) by demarcating useful from useless parts of the potential full analysis. For instance, if Jane is a student of art and Paul is her teacher, she may seek some answer that helps her in her education, such as how this painter successfully handled some problem of composition. Or if Jane is playing some kind of one-upmanship game with Paul, she will seek an answer that helps her to score points off him by ridiculing his taste. And, as I shall argue in Chapter 6, practical concerns determine the type of causal question asked, and the process or method used to make a causal attribution is then constrained by the requirement to provide something that answers the question posed. Thus, process or method is purely in the service of function, and cannot be considered apart from function.

The primary aim of lay judgement and inference is to make the optimal contribution to the contemporary practical concerns of the judge. This implies that some process of judgement or inference occurs when there is some practical concern (or more than one) to which it is judged capable of contributing in some appropriate way, and that the type of process used is the one that best contributes to that practical concern, whatever it be. In respect of the latter, one can envisage the practical concern leading to the formulation of an implicit or explicit question, and the type of process used is constrained by the practical requirement to provide something that counts as an answer to the question posed. In Chapter 6 I shall develop this argument in its application to the asking of causal questions, but the principle applies to any form of judgement. The use of judgement and inference to understand, predict, or control, when they occur at all, is not an end in itself but occurs only when it is judged to be in the best interests of the individual's practical concerns.

It is not possible to specify in a general way what practical concerns are, except that they relate to the individual's attempts to cope with events in social reality, to deal with problems, achieve goals, avoid personally unpleasant or harmful effects, and so on. They can be global and stable, such as a career ambition that may require a lifetime's work to accomplish, specific and transient, such as crossing a busy road as quickly as possible without being run over, and important or trivial, such as deciding which of two flavoured drinks to have.

The second point: the standards against which lay judgement and inference are properly assessed are not provided by known facts or normative principles or proper use of valid inferential and judgemental tools of the kinds that guide scientific enquiry. Under the practical concerns orientation, the standard by which judgements and inferences should be evaluated is that of the extent to which they succeed in contributing in some appropriate or intended way to the individual's practical concerns at the time of judgement; that is, the extent to which they serve the function for which they were intended. Inferences and judgements that are evaluated as inaccurate by the standards of scientific propriety or correctness may none the less be optimally rational by the standards of practical concerns.

Two caveats must be borne in mind here. First, this is not to espouse any kind of epistemological relativism. This argument does not dispute that there are true facts and scientifically correct judgements, whether anyone knows what they are or not, or that there are optimal scientific procedures for the discovery of true facts and the making of correct judgements, whether anyone knows what those procedures are or not. What it disputes is the claim implicit in the lay scientist analogy that those things constitute the proper standards of rationality in ordinary life, the standards to which people aspire in making judgements and inferences.

The second caveat is that the practical concerns model does not assert that people have no interest in understanding at all. It asserts only that understanding is not the *primary* goal of inference and judgement. Frequently, no doubt, the standards of science and practical concerns coincide: when they do, under-standing – that is to say, making correct or scientifically optimal judgements and inferences – becomes the goal of lay judgement and inference. But it does not thereby become the primary goal: it is a subsidiary goal, something that merely happens to be desirable on that occasion for the sake of its potential contribution to practical concerns. Practical concerns set the primary goals of inference and judgement; understanding does not.

The test for this is to see what happens when the standards of practical concerns and those set by the lay-scientist model diverge. Under the lay-scientist model, understanding is the primary goal, and people should therefore still aim for the standards set by the lay-scientist model, even if they behave like cognitive misers in their striving in that direction. Under the practical concerns model, people should aim for the standards set by their practical concerns, and the standards of science no longer count for anything.

A simple example will serve to make the point. Suppose two cars are involved in a minor road accident. Clearly, an objective account of the causation of the accident could be given, even if no one is quite sure how to construct it. Under the lay-scientist model, the drivers should share the aim of discovering this objective, true account. Under the practical concerns model, each may still desire to give an account of the causation of the accident, but the account they construct is designed to make an optimal contribution to their respective practical concerns. Let us say these concerns are that each desires that the other should pay for the damage caused. This means that for each driver the goal is to construct a causal account in which the other takes most or all of the responsibility for causing the accident. This, by the standards of practical concerns, is the rational thing to do: the drivers may end up with defective understanding of the causation of the accident, but this is of no interest to either of them. On the contrary, in this case the search for understanding would be irrational, in that it would militate against the practical concerns of the individuals involved.

If researchers wish to investigate how good people are at judgement and inference, where goodness is defined by the standards set by practical concerns, they are up against a considerable problem. There is no universal definition of standards: one can only assess how good an inference is by ascertaining the practical concerns in respect of which that particular inference was made. Prac-tical concerns are liable to vary across both individuals and times. This is, however, a matter of vital importance. It is simply no good saying that people are bad at judgement on the grounds that their judgements are defective by scientific standards if those are not the standards to which people were aspiring. We can *only* evaluate lay judgement against the standards that people set for themselves.

The third point: on the question of kinds of judgement, abandoning the lay-scientist analogy takes away the justification for a typology of judgement based on the analogy, and a case could be made for replacing it with a typology based on a classification of distinct practical concerns. I shall take this up in a later chapter. To anticipate, however, two key considerations are worth underlining here.

The first is that the activity of judgement as modelled along the lines of the lay-scientist analogy is exclusively cognitive or intellectual. That is, the criteria to which judgements must answer are based on the true/false distinction (Kenny 1989). Truth criteria are indeed relevant to the quest for understanding, but they are less relevant to, and certainly not the only judgemental criteria appropriate to, the practical concerns orientation. I shall argue later in the book that an account of judgement under the practical concerns approach must incorporate the ways in which lay judgements are assessed by affective criteria; that is, by criteria such as good/bad, pleasant/unpleasant, and liked/disliked (Kenny 1989). These are often the main criteria by which the suitability of a judgement to the judge's practical concerns are assessed.

The second is that research on social judgement has tended to concentrate on relatively effortful processing of large amounts of unfamiliar information presented in unfamiliar ways in the laboratory. The kind of judgement that is typical of the ordinary person is, by contrast, relatively effortless (that is, it is automatic or has a large automatic component), and deals with relatively familiar information in the social context which the judge is used to. It is based on the application of existing beliefs, not the acquisition of new ones. It is, in general, highly skilled.

Consider an analogy. Owls navigate in virtually complete darkness by means of cognitive maps: the faintest of visual clues are helpful for navigational purposes because they can be located in the owl's model of its territory. But the owl only has a cognitive map of its own territory. Place the owl in an unfamiliar environment and it cannot use its cognitive map any more, and as a result appears to be relatively poor at night flying. (This is in fact one good reason for having a territory.) This is the point: it isn't just that people use the same judgemental tools on laboratory tasks and do worse with them; it is that many of their judgemental tools, the equivalent of the owl's cognitive map, simply cannot be used at all in laboratory settings, and people have to fall back on crude, effortful methods which they almost never need to use outside the laboratory. Judgement must be studied in its social context, because it is just not the same anywhere else.

The fourth point: the practical concerns orientation entails a different conceptualisation of the nature of bias in judgement. Under the practical concerns orientation there is no such thing as motivational bias. Motivational factors, however they should be conceptualised, are factors related to practical concerns, and as such their influence on inference and judgement is legitimate. If my main concern is to preserve my self-esteem, then making a causal attribution that best helps me to do that is optimal by the practical concerns standard, and by that standard there is no bias in the process, nor error in the outcome. It is still an open question how many of the observed deviations from scientific standards of inference are due to this type of practical concern: the point here concerns how the hypothetical influence of motivational factors should be conceptualised.

This is not to say that errors and biases in judgement never occur under the practical concerns model, or that people are perfectly rational by the standards of that model. An error in judgement has occurred if the judgement made does not contribute to the practical concerns of the judge at the time as well as a different judgement could have done. The frequency with which errors of this sort occur is unknown, because results of studies of judgement and inference have never been assessed by the practical concerns standard. Kahneman (1991) claimed that 'it is often easy to show that people . . . behave in ways that do not achieve their own goals and do not meet their own standards' (p. 144). No doubt this is true, though Kahneman did not cite any evidence to support his claim. But it has to be said that Kahneman used this claim for an illegitimate purpose: he used it as part of an answer to the criticism that research on judgement has 'unjustly denigrated human reason' (p. 144). Kahneman's claim does not address this criticism, because the criticism concerns the use of scientific standards to assess judgement. It is the use of this standard that leads to the unjust denigration of human reason, because it is the wrong standard. The fact that people make errors by their own standards is absolutely irrelevant to this. The fact that people make errors of one type has nothing to do with the justification, or lack of it, for the claim that they make errors of another type. The unjust denigration of human reason has come from the use of the wrong standard to assess it, from a failure to consider what someone makes a judgement for – that is, the practical concerns that provide the context of judgement, and the function of the judgement in respect of those concerns.

This is not to say that there is no such thing as cognitive bias in judgement. It is to say that the criteria for the identification of such biases are set by practical concerns and not by the normative principles of science. The mechanisms and/or processes by which inferences are made may still be imperfect in terms of their capacity to contribute to practical concerns, but this is a different sort of imperfection from an inability to meet a normative scientific standard. For example, the representativeness heuristic (Kahneman and Tversky 1972, 1973) is considered imperfect by the lay-scientist standard because it often leads to judgements that are inaccurate when compared with those generated by normative judgemental procedures. But it may not be imperfect by the standard of practical concerns if, for example, judgements made with it are made on occasions when speed matters more than scientific accuracy. Likewise, methods considered proper by scientific standards, such as the use of analysis of variance or some rigorous naïve equivalent to make causal attributions, may be a source of cognitive bias in lay inference if they (sometimes) generate causal attributions that do not make the best possible contribution to the attributer's practical concerns at the time. If people do not use such methods, or use them only when they have no choice, this may be the reason.

In general, the lay-scientist orientation leads to a tendency to ask how accurate a judgement or belief is. The practical concerns orientation leads to a tendency to ask what the judgement or belief is for; in other words, what its function is, and how well it fulfils that function. Consider two examples.

The first example is this: Nisbett and Ross (1980) pointed out that culturally shared maxims sometimes contradict one another. To their illustration, 'out of sight, out of mind', and 'absence makes the heart grow fonder', one might add 'actions speak louder than words', and 'the pen is mightier than the sword'. Their complaint was that these contradictions flourish in common sense because there are few rules constraining the applicability of maxims to instances, so that any instance can be taken as a case of, or confirmation of, some maxim or other. The result is a disorganised, haphazard, 'bloated' (p. 119) set of beliefs. The lay-scientist, in other words, is guilty of vagueness and inconsistency.

This complaint, however, overlooks the fact that cultural maxims have social functions and are not part of an attempt to construct a systematic body of knowledge as a scientist might wish to do. The standards of science are absolutely irrelevant to them, and the only standard by which they should be evaluated is the extent to which they succeed in carrying out the function for which they are intended on any given occasion. When we use sayings such as 'absence makes the heart grow fonder', it is not because they give us some quasi-scientific explanation or prediction, or some deeper understanding of the world. They serve no explanatory function. The functions they serve are social and interpersonal: to comfort, to mollify, to negotiate, to excuse, and so on. Their service of these functions is all the justification they need.

I was prompted to write that paragraph by a scene I witnessed in a car park. A man was complaining to his wife about the behaviour of some other people, and his wife said, 'It takes all sorts, darling'. Did it matter to her, at that moment, whether or not this maxim (it takes all sorts to make a world, in full) explained anything, or represented a piece of the truth about the world, or formed part of an organised, systematic collection of beliefs? No, I would say, all that mattered for her was its intended interpersonal function, and it did indeed stop her husband from further complaint. That is all the justification it needed.

To take a second example, that is what stereotypes do, too. It seems to be fashionable now to treat stereotypes as an answer to an information-processing problem: they help us to deal with demands on our processing capacity. Despite their probable inaccuracy, they help us to make quick judgements under conditions of heavy drain on our processing resources (Fiske and Taylor 1991). This may be true, but it is at best only part of the truth. Stereotypes persist because they serve social and interpersonal functions. By this I specifically do not mean that a stereotype of group $X$ helps us in interactions with members of group $X$. It helps, probably, more in interactions with people who are not members of group $X$. It contributes, as any kind of shared knowledge does, to our ability to communicate with others. For example, some people like to tell jokes, and many jokes concern stereotypes, so knowledge of stereotypes helps joke-tellers to tell jokes and listeners to understand them. Such things assist social purposes such as ingratiation, the gaining of friendship or other social rewards, impression management, tension release, and so on. This is why we hold onto a stereotype even though we don't believe it: we may think it false, but it continues to be useful. Its usefulness is the standard by which it should be evaluated: it is not part of a quasi-scientific attempt to build an organised understanding of the world.

To summarise, then: to the four points of the lay-scientist analogy can be contraposed four equivalent points of the practical concerns orientation:

1  The main goal of inference and judgement for the lay person is the optimal contribution to the practical concern(s) in respect of which judgement is occurring. Any interest the lay person might have in scientific accuracy, understanding, prediction, or control is entirely subservient to this primary aim. Truth *per se* does not matter: only usefulness matters.

2  The only standard against which lay inference and judgement can be assessed is that of the extent to which the outcome of judgement makes the best possible contribution to those practical concerns in respect of which judgement is occurring, if there is some objective means of establishing what this would be.

3  The natural kinds of judgement, in so far as there are such things, reflect distinct and recurrent themes in practical concerns.

4  Cognitive biases in judgement can still be identified, but by the standards set by practical concerns, not by those set under the lay-scientist model of rationality. There is no such thing as motivational bias, because motivational factors reflect legitimate practical concerns and it is therefore rational for one's judgement to reflect them.

This, then, is the model of rationality in the context of which the exploration of psychological metaphysics will be carried out. If there were a valid analogy to be made between common-sense inference and science, it would be with practical science or technology, not with theoretical science. But even this analogy is not tenable, because even practical science is primarily concerned with accuracy: the potter wants to find out exactly what the glaze recipe does to the pot, for example, and there is rarely anything to gain by inaccuracy. In everyday life inaccuracy can sometimes be practically advantageous, and for this reason no analogy with science can work.

# Chapter 3

# The nature of basicity in the psychological construction of reality

## DEFINITION OF BASICITY

Investigating psychological metaphysics means accepting the idea that some things are more basic than others in the psychological construction of reality. Any element in that construction can in principle be compared to any other in terms of their relative basicity. Some elements may be basic in an absolute sense, the most basic things of which reality is made in this construction, axioms of the system, in effect. What is it for something to be more or less 'basic'?

According to Campbell (1976) the idea of what is basic in philosophical metaphysics involves three interconnected notions: 'basic particulars are simple, fundamental, and independent. To be simple is to be independent of true parts. To be fundamental is to be independent not only of parts but of every other thing' (p. 31). Those things that are simple can be parts of complex things, but cannot themselves have true parts. Those things that are fundamental do not depend for their existence upon any other things. The type of dependence meant here, according to Campbell (1976), is not causal dependence but logical dependence. For example, the child is causally dependent on its father, but not logically dependent upon him because it could continue to exist if he ceased to be. This logical dependence, then, could be termed existential dependence.

This is basicity in relation to particulars, which are the basic things of which the world is made (see the next chapter for examples). It is not clear, however, that the criterion of simplicity can be applied to other sorts of things, such as categories. Nor can it be readily applied to comparisons between concrete and abstract things. The word that is common to both types of basicity in relation to particulars, however, is 'independence', and there seems no obvious reason why the criterion of independence could not be applied to anything at all. The simplest hypothesis, then, is that what is basic in the psychological construction of reality is whatever is truly independent of everything else in that construction.

In philosophy existential dependence means dependence as a matter of logic. This seems inappropriate to psychological metaphysics because philosophers can imagine states of affairs and relations of existential dependence far removed from anything that could be encountered in everyday experience, so I shall propose a modified criterion of psychological dependence. This I shall call 'imaginary existential dependence', and the test for it is the ability to imagine one thing without another in the world as it is known to the person concerned. This is weaker than strict logical dependence, one possible test for which would be the ability to imagine one thing without another in any possible world: thus, relations that pass the test of imaginary existential dependence may fail the test of strict logical dependence. This is merely a consequence of the fact that the construction of reality by ordinary people is not like the professional activity of philosophers: imaginary existential dependence relates more precisely to what is, after all, a construction of this world with all its contingent features, and not one of all possible worlds.

A, then, is existentially dependent upon B if one cannot imagine A existing or occurring without B (strictly speaking, with B not being the case) in the world as it is (or as it is held to be by the person doing the imagining). This relation entails that B is more basic than A in the psychological construction of reality. If one can imagine A without B, then either B is existentially dependent on A, in which case A is more basic in the construction of reality than B, or the two have no relation of dependence, in which case either could be at any level of the construction of reality, so long as they are not connected by relations of dependence with other things. The most basic elements in the psychological construction of reality are those things that are existentially dependent upon nothing: one cannot imagine this world without those things being so. They are, so to speak, the psychological axioms of the system.

To summarise, I am arguing that people have an organised construction of reality, and my first hypothesis about this is that *imaginary existential dependence is the main structural principle determining the organisation of that construction.* The construction has an indefinite number of levels, and at its foundation are things that are basic in the sense that they are existentially dependent on little or nothing else. This does not imply that there are no other types of relation between elements in the psychological construction of reality. Relations between part and whole, particular and general, rule and instance, category and member, cause and effect, premise and conclusion, clearly do form part of our understanding of the world, and help to give structure and coherence to it. But they are auxiliary rather than fundamental structural determinants: they take their place within a context established by the principle of existential dependence. Existential dependence, then, is primarily responsible for holding reality together in our construction of it: this is fundamental to scientific appreciation of how people deal with and comprehend reality.

I have here described the psychological construction of reality as if all were static. Clearly this is wrong, because parts of the construction themselves can be changed, and the construction has implications for what happens in processing, particularly in judgement and inference. The following two sections treat each of these in turn.

## MAKING CHANGES IN THE CONSTRUCTION OF REALITY

Imaginary existential dependence constrains how the construction of reality can change. The effect of removing some element from the construction of reality depends on its location. Removal of an element entails the removal of all other elements that are existentially dependent upon it. Removal of an element at a relatively basic level of the construction may therefore entail a large amount of change to the construction, whereas removing an element at a relatively super-ficial level entails little or none. Elements can be said to possess a degree of inertia which is proportional to the number of elements existentially dependent upon them: the tendency of an element to endure in the construction of reality is a function of the number of elements that are existentially dependent upon it. The most basic parts of the construction are therefore also those that are most resistant to change.

Where an element is removed and replaced by another (that is, altered to another), the ease of alteration is likewise determined by the number of elements in the construction that are existentially dependent on the original element *and not* existentially dependent on its replacement, because these elements must also be removed (and/or replaced). Small alterations to the construction, where size is measured as the number of elements that have to be changed, are easier to make than big ones.

This is an important feature of existential dependence. What it means is that *people hold onto elements not because of the weight of evidence that supports them but because of the weight of elements that they support.* Changes in elements at relatively fundamental levels of the construction of reality are akin not to normative science in which hypotheses are changed in the light of evidence, but to paradigm shifts or even conversion processes. In common sense, new evidence is always a relatively weak force for change in elements because, by virtue of its newness, it is inevitably at a more superficial level of the construction of reality than the elements with which it is in conflict. That is, being new, it does not yet support anything else in the construction of reality, whereas the elements with which it conflicts probably do. This fact alone means that the elements are liable to survive the evidential assault.

Note that I am still using the term 'element' here. As stated in the introduction, a person can assign a truth value to an element, which is one kind of attitude towards it. If the person holds the element to be true, it counts as a belief. The general effect of holding an element to be true is to increase its resistance to change, because change requires both the element and the attitude to be changed, rather than just the element. But the statements made about change in elements hold in principle regardless of whether the element is held to be true or not. This is because the presence of an element in the construction of reality reflects its function or usefulness, not its status as a claim about reality. Thus, I may not believe the stereotype that red-haired people are quick to anger, but it is an element in my construction of reality none the less, because it subserves various functions in the construction (for example, helps me to understand jokes about red-haired people).

These points are easy to see if we construct a hypothetical model of reality.

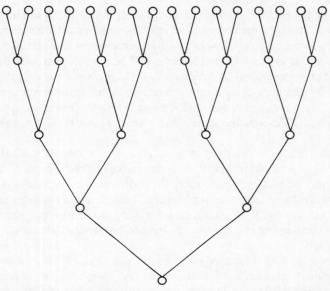

*Figure 3.1* Hypothetical construction of reality showing relations of existential dependence

Figure 3.1 shows a hypothetical construction with a metaphysical axiom represented by the node at the bottom. One node is existentially dependent on another if that node is lower than it in the model *and* a path consisting only of downward-moving lines connects the higher with the lower. Thus, each node at the next-to-bottom level has 14 nodes existentially dependent on it, but is in turn dependent on only one (the metaphysical axiom). In actuality, of course, there would be several metaphysical axioms and their trees would interpenetrate in complex ways. The important point, for present purposes, is that changing or abolishing the content of one node entails changing or abolishing that of all nodes that are existentially dependent on it, or moving them from one part of the construction to another. Thus, the resistance to change of a node can be loosely quantified in terms of the number of other nodes existentially dependent on it. The greater the resistance to change of a node, the less likely it is to be affected by any new information, other things being equal.

Now suppose that some new piece of information is received which violates some element in the model. Suppose, for example, that the element is a stereotype concerning a category, and the new information concerns an instance which has a feature that violates some feature of the stereotype. The preferred means of dealing with this is to make the smallest possible change to the model. Changing the feature of the stereotype is a relatively big change because there may be many nodes in the model that are existentially dependent on the stereotype. These would include not only records of instances that conform to the stereotype but also feelings (for example, negative evaluations of the category) and social functions of the stereotype (such as stored jokes concerning the stereotypical attributes of the category). The stereotype is correspondingly resistant to change.

The smallest change can be achieved by simply tacking on the instance as a sub-category, fitted into the model in such a way that it is existentially dependent on the category of which it is a sub-type, but with nothing existentially dependent on it. Essentially, nothing that is there has to change: just one thing is added. So, other things being equal, this should be the preferred tactic. In the case of stereotypes, there is evidence that this is indeed the preferred method of dealing with stereotype-discrepant information (Johnston and Hewstone 1992). The method can be applied to any kind of element, however, and future research should aim to test the idea in domains of cognition other than stereotypes.

If one element changes for any reason, why should *any* others change? The one overriding reason, according to this analysis, is not that the element is believed to be true, though this does make some difference, but that the element has other elements that are existentially dependent on it: if the element changes, these other elements must change. This does not explain, of course, why any element relatively deep in the structure should ever change: if we could find the answer to this, we could explain why some belief changes are in effect conversion processes (with wholesale changes in belief) and others are mere superficial amendments and additions.

## RELATION TO WORKING MEMORY AND INFERENCE

The things that I have hypothesised about the structure of the construction of reality do not strongly determine operations in working memory, but they set definite constraints on operations. The fundamental constraint is that relations of existential dependence that hold in the construction of reality cannot be violated in operations in working memory. This general constraint has some consequences which I shall elucidate by considering an example of an inference process.

Suppose that we observe person $X$ trying to do action $Y$, and infer from this that $X$ wants to do $Y$. How does one get from a single premise {$X$ is trying to do $Y$} to a conclusion {$X$ wants to do $Y$}? The answer is to introject a second, possibly implicit, premise that enables the conclusion to be drawn by the application of whatever sort of inference rules people employ. In this case the introjected premise will be something like {people who try to do $Y$ want to do $Y$}. Let us assume that it is exactly this.

Now let us map the relations of existential dependence that apply. First, the conjunction of the two premises is existentially dependent upon the conclusion. This may sound the wrong way round, given that the conclusion is inferred from the premises. But in fact it relates to a criterion used to assess the validity of formal logic systems, under which a logic cannot be valid if it is possible using it to derive false conclusions from only true premises. It also relates to the *modus tollens* inference rule, according to which the negation of a conclusion entitles us to infer the negation of its premise: in the present case, if the conclusion were false then by *modus tollens* we could infer that at least one of the premises was false, and this is what is meant by saying that *the conjunction of* the two premises is existentially dependent on the conclusion.

Now suppose that we have unambiguous information that $X$ does not want to do $Y$, thus negating the conclusion. On some occasions people may deal with this by bringing in other information that allows them to treat this as an exception to the rule. But let us assume that they cannot do this, so that one of the premises has to be rejected: which one will they reject?

The answer, following the 'inertia' hypothesis in the previous section, is that the one that is less basic in their construction of reality is more likely to be rejected. This is almost certain to be the explicit premise {$X$ is trying to do $Y$}, because {people who try to do $Y$ want to do $Y$} has existentially dependent upon it a potentially unlimited number of cases of possible relations between trying to do $Y$ and wanting to do $Y$, whereas {$X$ is trying to do $Y$} has very little that is existentially dependent on it.

This leads to a general claim about the manipulation of information in working memory. Where two elements are shown in working memory to be incompatible, or to be in any state such that one of them must be rejected, it is the one that has less that is existentially dependent on it that is more likely to be rejected.

Secondly, the relation between the premises and the conclusion is existentially dependent on each of the three components, the explicit premise, the implicit premise, and the conclusion. The relevant part of this is the dependence of the relation ({$X$ is trying to do $Y$} therefore {$X$ wants to do $Y$}) on the implicit premise {people who try to do $Y$ want to do $Y$}. This relation places a constraint on the sort of operation that is permissible in working memory. One could alter the *instance* without altering the *rule* in the implicit premise: that is, one could come to believe that something is false about the relation in the case of $X$ without ceasing to believe in the general rule. Or one could alter both: one could reject the rule that people who try to do $Y$ want to do $Y$ and reject the inference in the case of $X$. But what is not permissible is to reject the rule but retain the inference. The existential dependence of the inference on the rule means that the inference cannot be maintained if the rule is rejected. This does *not* mean that one could not believe that $X$ both tries and wants to do $Y$: it means specifically that the *inferred relation between* $X$ trying to do $Y$ and $X$ wanting to do $Y$ ceases to exist if the rule ceases to exist.

This asymmetry has the consequence that negative instances (such as instances of people trying to do $Y$ and not wanting to do $Y$) do not necessarily falsify the rule. This consequence applies whenever the instance is existentially dependent on the rule. This appears to contradict the claim just made that rejecting the conclusion necessitates the rejection of one of the premises. But that necessity only applies, as I said, when people cannot bring in other information that allows them to treat the present case as an exception to the rule. That is, it applies only to inference rules to which there are believed to be no possible exceptions. In the trying case, I can find an exception that preserves the rule: $X$ is trying to do $Y$ because someone is pointing a gun at $X$'s head and ordering him or her to do $Y$. So to state the two claims clearly: (1) when one of the premises must be rejected, the less basic is more likely to be rejected; and (2) the instance can be rejected without the rule being rejected, but the rule cannot be rejected without the instance being rejected. These are both processing consequences of the hypotheses about existential dependence.

The problem in many cases is to ascertain relative basicity correctly. Consider the relation between {Socrates is mortal} and {all men are mortal}, assuming that Socrates is a man. Here it seems as though the rule is more basic than the instance: one can imagine a world in which Socrates is mortal but not all men are mortal, but one cannot imagine a world in which all men are mortal and Socrates is not mortal, again assuming that Socrates is a man.

But this is to assess relative basicity by logical rather than by imaginary existential dependence. In imaginary existential dependence, we assess relative basicity in terms of this world as we understand it, not in terms of the possible worlds of logic. Thus, if a rule is sufficiently basic in our construction of the world it serves to constrain the type of instance that people feel able to accept as possible in this world. If my belief that all men are mortal is sufficiently basic in my construction of reality then it takes on a great resistance to change because of the fact that so much else is existentially dependent upon it (under the 'inertia' hypothesis). The effect of this resistance to change is to restrict the imaginability of counter-examples. Because of this, if I had the proposition that all men are mortal at a sufficiently basic level in my construction of reality, I simply would not contemplate Socrates not being mortal as a serious possibility. (This, very simply, is why people do not reason according to the rules of propositional logic: they reason in terms of *this* world, not in terms of possible worlds.) If I seem to have supportive evidence (for example, Socrates speaks to me from beyond the grave in a seance), then I must reinterpret it to avoid rejecting the rule (for example, the medium is a clever fraud). Negative instances, therefore, lead to the rejection of the rule only when the rule is such as to admit no exceptions *and* when the rule is not so basic in the construction of reality as to admit no change.

Being relatively basic does not make an element immune from rejection because it can be assessed against something still more basic. Only the bottom level, the level of axioms of the system, is immune from rejection.

These features of the construction of reality, relations of existential dependence, and the relative resistance to change of basics, yield a kind of operational syntax: they do not determine *how* operations are carried out, and they are not process models in themselves, but they work as a set of rules governing permissible operations on information in working memory. Whatever people have in place of the formal logic systems of philosophers for purposes of inference, it is restricted by its context within this operational syntax of relative basicity.

Having discussed the notion of basicity defined in terms of existential dependence, I now consider its relevance to the study of causal inference, and then briefly also discuss its relevance to kinds of relation other than causal relations.

## EXISTENTIAL DEPENDENCE AND CAUSATION

The notion of existential dependence can be used to draw out a number of vital points for the study of causal inference and attribution.

First, my concept of causation is more basic than any particular causal relation inferred by me because I can imagine that concept of causation being the case even if that inferred causal relation never occurred, but I cannot imagine that particular causal relation occurring if causation as I understand it did not exist. This means that the importance of studying the concept of causation that people possess lies in the fact that this concept is assumed in all instances of causal inference: it works as a basic axiom on which all causal inference is founded, giving meaning to any claim that one thing caused another, and discriminating all causal relations from all other relations. All inferences in social cognition are existentially dependent on certain basic metaphysical assumptions in the psychological construction of reality, meaning assumptions that are existentially dependent on nothing or almost nothing else, and one of my claims is that the basic concept of causation is one of these.

Secondly, a similar point can be made about causal laws. To make this clear, imagine a simple causal law according to which $B$ is always and only caused by $A$. In this case, I can imagine the possibility that the causal law holds but no instance conforming to it ever occurs (for example, because $A$ never occurs), but I cannot imagine occurrences such that $B$ is always and only caused by $A$ without the causal law being true. The former is merely odd, but the latter is a contradiction. Thus, ideas that people have about causal laws are more basic in the psychological construction of reality than any instance conforming to one of those ideas.

Thirdly, in particular instances of inferred causal relations, the inferred relation is, in a relatively trivial sense, existentially dependent on the things related by it. Consider a particular instance of $A$ causing $B$. I can imagine $A$ occurring and $B$ occurring without $A$ causing $B$ (for instance, because different causal laws hold) but I cannot imagine $A$ causing $B$ without both $A$ occurring and $B$ occurring. Consideration of the logic of this reveals that any relation (not just causal relations) is existentially dependent on the things related by it. In the psychological construction of reality, individual things are always more basic than the relations between them.

Fourthly, it is important to distinguish, however, between a particular inferred relation and the general concept of a causal relation. In a particular instance where both $A$ and $B$ occur, any particular relation that pertains between them is existentially dependent on the occurrence of each of them, but the general concept of the causal relation is not, because it transcends the instance in question. On the other hand, the concept of the causal relation *is* existentially dependent on some notion of the things that can be involved in a causal relation; namely, the kinds of thing that can be causes, and the kinds of thing that can be effects. It follows that a full understanding of causal inference requires that we discover people's fundamental assumptions about both the types of thing that exist (that is, the basic categories of the psychological construction of reality) and the nature of the things that fall into those basic types (for example, the basic particulars – see the next chapter).

For example, we might find that people divide the world into enduring particular substances, transient events, and abstractions, that they believe the basic particulars of which substances are made are atoms, and that causal relations can only be mechanical interactions between atoms (a loosely Newtonian view). If true, this tells us something of vital importance about causal inference, which is that people will never infer causal relations between abstractions: any valid observation that they do this will falsify that hypothesis. I am using this purely for illustrative purposes, and in fact I shall be arguing that the actual assumptions about basic categories and basic particulars are different from these. My point here is simply that we cannot study causal inference without identifying the fundamental assumptions that exist about each of these things, because (1) the basic concept of causation is existentially dependent on them and (2) for that reason they delimit the sorts of thing that will be identified as possible causes and effects.

Fifthly, combining some of these points, any individual inferred causal relation is existentially dependent on the basic concept of causation, on any causal law of which it is considered to be an instance, and on the particular things or events involved in the causal relation. The effect, however, is not existentially dependent on its cause: the child can outlive its father, as already stated. Both are at the same level of the psychological construction of reality.

## EXISTENTIAL DEPENDENCE AND OTHER KINDS OF RELATION

Existential dependence is not confined in application to causal relations, although those form the main topic of this book. It applies just as well to category–member relations, for example. I can imagine the world having birds but no robins, but I cannot imagine the world having robins but no birds (this fits strict logical dependence as well). Superordinate categories are therefore at a more basic level of the psychological construction of reality than the categories that are members of them, not because of the category–member relation *per se*, but because of imaginary existential dependence. This relates to the mental activity typologies investigated by Rips and Conrad (1989): for example, if, as their results suggest, people regard remembering as a type of thinking, then thinking is at a more basic level of their psychological construction of reality than remembering is.

Partonomic relations are less straightforward. I can imagine myself existing without my finger, but I can also imagine my finger existing without me (odd, but not contradictory). This seems to imply that I am not more basic in my construction of reality than my finger, and I want to reject that apparent implication. My finger would not have existed if I had never existed, but equally the child would not have existed if its father had never existed, and this does not imply existential dependence.

There is, however, at least one property of my finger that is existentially dependent on me: the finger depends on me for all of its functions. I, on the other hand, do not depend on my finger for all of my functions, but only for those that cannot be done except with that finger. This type of asymmetry does not occur in the father–son relation. To express this more precisely, my finger's functions are existentially dependent on me (and not just on me, but also on my finger being its proper part of me). This is the sense in which I want to claim that my finger is less basic than me in reality as I understand it. This can clearly be seen if we imagine my finger cut off: in such an eventuality, I would no longer want to say that I am more basic than my finger; instead, my finger and I become independent components of reality (that is, independent of each other).

This implies that, in the case of partonomic relations, a thing should be felt to be more basic than one of its parts in the psychological construction of reality if the functions of the part are existentially dependent on the thing and the functions of the thing are entirely or mostly independent of the part. I judge that I am more basic than my finger, but I am less confident of saying that I am more basic than my brain – and I can imagine that anyone's judgement on this would depend on what they thought on the mind–body problem. The partonomic relations among mental activities studied by Rips and Conrad (1989) are not of the same kind as the me–finger relation, because judging that, for example, thinking is a part of remembering does not imply that that is *all* that thinking is: it can be a part of remembering *and* can occur apart from remembering, whereas my finger's functions are a part of my functioning and nothing else. The existential dependence that my finger's functions have on its being its proper part of me is of a kind that applies only to parts that never occur other than in their relation to the whole of which they are a part.

A general point implicit in the foregoing is that existential dependence is not a feature only of physical objects. The examples used above have involved applying existential dependence to relations and to functions as well as to objects. Existential dependence should be applicable to anything that might feature in the psychological construction of reality, if it is to qualify as the structural principle determining that construction.

## DEFINITION OF RESEARCH PROBLEMS IN PSYCHOLOGY

One reason for looking at structural principles in the psychological construction of reality is that they provide a means of identifying distinct research problems in the study of judgement, inference, and any higher-order processes that use information about reality.

While one remains at what might be called the level of surface phenomena, individual actions, inferences, judgements, explanations, and so on, it is not always clear how to categorise phenomena into distinct research problems. For example, could one say that 'how people answer why questions' is a distinct research problem? Possibly, but there are many ways of answering 'why' questions, some involving reference to causal relations, some reference to things quite unconnected with causation, and it is not obvious a priori that these different things belong within the same theoretical account. Moreover, causal inferences or attributions need not occur only in response to 'why' questions, so this categorisation may exclude things that should be included in the same theoretical account with causal inferences in response to 'why' questions. It is not even certain, a priori, that it is right to regard causal attribution as a distinct research problem, given the variety of phenomena that tend to be treated under that heading (for example, Harvey and Weary 1984; Hewstone 1989).

My claim here is that the psychological construction of reality provides a means of resolving problems of this sort and identifying distinct research problems in this general area of psychology. Distinct research problems are defined by those things that are at or near the most basic levels of the construction of reality.

To give an example, I shall be proposing later that people have a particular basic concept of causation. The point for present purposes is not the nature of this concept but the fact that it is located at a relatively basic level of the model of reality. Consider the surface level, the myriad of explanations, answers to 'why' questions, causal attributions and inferences, and so on, of which one might wish to give a theoretical account. Trying to identify distinct research problems while looking only at this surface level is like trying to construct a picture of a tree from knowledge only of where all the individual twigs end. Obviously it is not clear from this information alone how the twigs fall into meaningful groups (such as all those growing from one branch rather than another). But by tracing routes down through relations of existential dependence to basic level concepts, the meaningful groupings can be ascertained. The research problem of causation, for instance, is defined as covering all and only those surface phenomena that are existentially dependent on the basic concept of causation. That is, it covers all and only those events, processes, and so on, in which the basic concept of causation is involved.

Because at the level of surface phenomena relations of existential dependence interpenetrate (that is, a surface level phenomenon may be existentially dependent on more than one basic level thing), one can identify all of the basic research problems on which some phenomenon is existentially dependent, and understand the phenomenon in terms of the interactions between the things involved. For example (adapted from Ross 1977), suppose I explain to someone that Sally bought a certain house because it was in a secluded part of the country. There may be many things going on in this explanation, so to give a proper account of the explanation it is necessary first to trace the network of existential dependencies down to basic concepts. In part the explanation may be dependent on the basic concept of causation; in part perhaps (I am guessing) on some basic principle of informativeness in conversation; and in part perhaps on other things too. Understanding the explanation involves ascertaining upon what it is existentially dependent. Basic theories concern these basic level concepts and how they operate. Less basic theoretical accounts deal with what I shall call 'interrelation problems' which concern how basic-level concepts interact or interrelate at the surface level.

Likewise, sub-categories of research problems are identified by the conjunctions between basic-level concepts. Suppose that the basic concept of causation is as I shall describe it. Suppose also that there is a basic level categorical distinction between human beings (and all about them) and all other physical creation. Then there are sub-categories of research problem definable as causation in the human realm and causation in the remainder-of-physical realm. These are sub-problems because they are related by the basic problem of causation. At the surface level some phenomena may involve both of these, in which case an account can also be given of how they interrelate at the surface level. Thus, all and only surface-level phenomena that are existentially dependent on both the basic concept of causation and the human category fall into the human causation research problem.

The foregoing argument yields three types of research problem: basic research problems, sub-categories of research problems, and interrelation problems. There are at least two other possible types. One is what might be called false or illusory research problems: this consists of problems that are defined with respect to some apparent surface feature which does not relate in any straightforward way to basic level problems. The 'why' question problem discussed earlier is an example of this: it includes bits of the causation problem and bits of other problems, but it also excludes bits of the causation problem, and for this reason it cannot be the subject of a clear, comprehensive, and coherent theoretical account.

The other possible category consists of applied problems. These are research topics that relate to some particular real world problem. They have a clear definition in terms of the surface phenomena that fall into them, but the claim that I would make about them is that they are invariably either interrelation problems or false problems. This is part of the reason why it is usually difficult to generalise from the results of research on an applied problem to anything else: interrelations are always less general in extent than the basic concepts on which they are existentially dependent, and unless the provenance of the applied problem in terms of basic level concepts can be ascertained, even the limited generalisability that may be possible will remain unknown.

## THE PLACE OF PSYCHOLOGICAL METAPHYSICS IN PSYCHOLOGY

Metaphysical postulates form the basis of the psychological construction of reality. By this is meant that everything else in the construction of reality is existentially dependent upon some or all of these metaphysical postulates. They exert an organising influence on the elements in other, less basic levels of the construction of reality. Relations of existential dependence in this construction cannot be violated in processing, and this means that all processing takes place within a framework of metaphysical assumptions.

No metaphysical assumption can be rejected in processing without the consequent rejection of everything in the construction of reality that is existentially dependent upon that assumption. Where some element (for example, a conclusion to an inference process) is incompatible with a metaphysical assumption in the construction of reality, it is the element rather than the assumption that will be rejected, because of the amount that is existentially dependent on that assumption. Because metaphysical assumptions are so basic and taken for granted, they may often take the role of implicit, introjected premises in the most automatic inference processes. Everything in our interpretation of reality and of the things that go on around us is ultimately dependent on the metaphysical bases of our construction of reality. These bases hold reality together for us.

The importance of thinking in terms of existential dependence, then, is that it is a way of making explicit the metaphysical assumptions on which theories and hypotheses depend. This is essential to science.

# Chapter 4

# Foundations
## Basic categories and basic particulars

My aim in this chapter is to set down the metaphysical foundation of the psychological construction of reality. This foundation consists of basic categories and basic particulars, each of which is treated in turn. The psychological explanation for the basic categories proposed follows; this involves a hypothesis about the temporal integration function of iconic processing. Everything in the psychological construction of reality is existentially dependent upon these assumptions about basic categories and particulars. Elucidating them is therefore not only important for its own sake but also a necessary precursor to any investigation of elements at other levels of that construction. This means, for example, that basic categories and particulars must be considered before any investigation of the basic understanding of causation can proceed: the assumptions people have about these things serve to delimit the range of theories of causation that are possible in the construction of reality, and how causation is attached to events by people.

## BASIC CATEGORIES

One of the activities of metaphysics is the elucidation of basic categories. Basic categories are the fundamental *kinds* of thing of which the world is made, or 'the basic divisions which our thought and talk about reality entail' (Carr 1987: 2). As such, basic categories form part of the foundations of the psychological construction of reality: ascertaining what the basic categories of this construction are yields the most general, overall organisation of the construction, the most general definition of clear research problems. This is not to say that psychologically basic categories necessarily match those to be found in any philosophical theory: they are not the products of ratiocination but have a psychological origin, which I shall attempt to elucidate in a later section. But in the absence of psychological theories about basic categories, philosophy is a useful starting-point for exploration of this problem.

To start, then, I shall take Aristotle's (1963) listing of basic categories, together with his own examples of members of those categories:

1 Substance (a man, a horse).
2 Quantity (four-foot, five-foot).

3 Qualification (white, grammatical).
4 Relative (double, half, larger).
5 Where (in the Lyceum, in the market-place).
6 When (yesterday, last year).
7 Being-in-a-position (is-lying, is-sitting).
8 Having (has-shoes-on, has-armour-on).
9 Doing (cutting, burning).
10 Being-affected (being-cut, being-burnt).

Aristotle did not regard all of these categories as equally basic, as I shall show later. But further consideration suggests that there are three broad categories subsuming these ten. First, the categories of where and when, corresponding to space and time. I do not propose to examine psychological notions of space and time more closely in this work. Philosophers debate the nature of space and time: for example, in Leibniz's cosmology space does not exist, but is a mere appearance representing relations of similarity among monads (see basic particulars). Concepts of the structure of space and time have changed greatly over the centuries (Gurevich 1985). An understanding of spatial relations develops during infancy and does not appear to be present at birth (Piaget 1954); children have difficulty with judgements of the temporal order of events even at 3 years of age (Sophian and Huber 1984). These things suggest that the origins and development of concepts of space and time are an important part of psychological metaphysics. In this book, however, I assume only that people ordinarily regard space and time as literal realities, and that they treat space and time as constituting an arena containing all other existing things. This much is sufficient for the purpose of studying their construction of all other existing things.

Secondly, the categories of substance, quantity, qualification, relative, being-in-a-position, and having, together constitute a category that may be called 'being'. The marks of being are spatial extension and, more particularly, persistence in time. All examples of each of these Aristotelian categories refer to entities or predicates that endure for an appreciable amount of time (the psychological definition of 'appreciable' will be presented in a later section).

Thirdly, the categories of doing and being-affected together constitute a category that may be called 'happening' or 'events'. The mark of happening is transience. This is not to say that what happens cannot persist – for example, a change in a quality is a happening that may set up something, the changed quality, that endures in time – but the happening itself, the setting up of the change, is transient and momentary. As in the case of 'appreciable', the psychological definition of 'transient', of what constitutes an event or happening, will be presented later.

This distinction between being and happening is somewhat similar to the basic distinction drawn by Aristotle between matter and motion. 'Motion' for Aristotle meant not just the movement of a body through space but any transition from potential to actual being, and this includes movement through space because location is one of Aristotle's ten categories (Dijksterhuis 1961). The definition adapted from Aristotle by Santillana (1961) helps to make clear Aristotle's conceptualisation of motion: 'movement is the act of being in potency in so far as it has not reached its full actualisation or unfolding' (p. 217). Aristotle's concepts of matter and motion must both be understood in the context of Aristotle's metaphysics. The being of substances relates to two of the Aristotelian types of cause: formal cause and material cause. That is, an account of the being of a substance must refer to form and matter as basic explanatory devices. 'Form thus makes matter into substance' (Dijksterhuis 1961: 20). Motion or change relates to the other two types of cause. Passive potentiality is the capacity of a substance to be acted on from outside, as in a block of marble being sculpted, and this relates to efficient causation. Active potentiality is the capacity of a substance to develop as it were from the inside, as in an acorn growing into an oak tree, and this relates to final cause.

Now I could adopt as a working hypothesis the idea that the psychological construction of reality embodies exactly the Aristotelian distinction between matter and motion. But this would commit that construction to those other elements of Aristotle's metaphysics just described, because it is those other elements that give meaning to that Aristotelian distinction, and it is far from clear that this would be correct. The distinction I have proposed between being and happening carries less conceptual and historical baggage, and leaves questions about whether people distinguish form and matter as the basic constituents of substances, or have Aristotelian notions of efficient and final causation, for future research to settle. Moreover, the distinction between being and happening can be defined and explained in a simple psychological way, as I shall show later.

I am proposing, then, that, apart from space and time, there are two basic categories of existing things, being and happening, and that these two categories have a psychological origin. This, therefore, is not a philosophical claim, but a claim about the psychological construction of reality. Proposing these categories as basic sets up a research programme involving (1) the elucidation of concepts fundamentally related to these basic categories, and (2) the most basic sub-categories within these categories.

In the following parts of the book I pursue the former. The concepts fundamentally related to being concern the nature of basic particulars – the theory of matter, so to speak. The concepts fundamentally related to happening are those that constitute the basic understanding of causation. This amounts to a claim that, in the psychological construction of reality, every happening is understood as caused. This is not to say that every happening, or even every perceived happening, is subject to causal processing, only that it is implicit in the psychological construction of reality that causal processing would be appropriate to any happening.

The corollary implication is that in the psychological construction of reality causation is not regarded as applicable to being. To be clear about this, a concept of causation can be applied to commencement or cessation of being (creation, alteration, destruction, and so on), because these are happenings, but *not* to something merely continuing to be as it is. The persistence of sameness in things is not ordinarily a problem in the psychological construction of reality (except when it violates an expectation that some change was going to occur, but such an expectation can be left out of account for the time being because it is not based on belief about the intrinsic nature of being), but is taken for granted as a natural feature of the category of being. Things continue as they are *unless* something involving causation makes them otherwise. This is the *natural inertia of being.*

Again, this is not universally accepted in philosophy, and the persistence of material particulars is widely regarded as a problem. Emmet (1984) dealt with it in terms of immanent causation (White 1990); and in radical empiricism the persistence of a material particular is interpreted as a construction of the human mind based on the similarity of successive logically independent sense-impressions (Hume 1739/1978). But I take it as uncontroversial that the persistence that marks being is an unquestioned metaphysical assumption in the psychological construction of reality.

To summarise, I hypothesise that the basic categories in the psychological construction of reality are these:

1  Space and time
2  Being ————→ basic particulars
3  Happening ————→ causation

The immediate plan is to fill out this scheme by elucidating the nature of basic particulars and the basic concept of causation in the psychological construction of reality. The importance of this enterprise is that the whole psychological construction of reality is built upon this basis, in the sense that these work as axioms of the system, and so one cannot understand properly any aspect of that construction or of activities such as inference and judgement without knowing how they stand in relation to the metaphysical bases of the construction. No theory of causal inference, for example, can be complete without reference not only to the basic concept of causation but also to the nature of basic particulars and the psychological distinction between being and happening because, as I argued in the previous chapter, the basic concept of causation is existentially dependent upon both basic categories and basic particulars. Psychological metaphysics delimits the range of things in respect of which causal processing will occur – primarily, to happenings and not to persistence of being. Elucidating psychological metaphysics is therefore essential to the understanding of causal processing.

## THE METAPHYSICS OF BEING: BASIC PARTICULARS

The metaphysics of being can be described as the problem of the nature of basic particulars (Campbell 1976). This is different from the search for basic categories: hypotheses about basic categories may imply particular theories of matter or basic particulars, or vice versa, but the two are logically separable enquiries.

In philosophy, basic particulars are constituents of matter that are fundamental in that there are no other particulars on which their existence depends, and simple, meaning that they have no true parts (Campbell 1976). In psychology, basic particulars are existentially dependent on nothing else in the construction of reality, but it is not clear whether they are required to be absolutely simple: at least, there seem to be no grounds for requiring this to be a criterion of basicity a priori.

Despite the differences between philosophy and psychology, in the absence of psychological theories about the nature of basic particulars in the psychological construction of reality, philosophy provides something to start with. Many hypotheses about the nature of basic particulars have been proposed in philosophy. My plan is to give brief descriptions of five of these, leading to a hypothesis about the nature of basic particulars in the psychological construction of reality. My aim is not to present a comprehensive review of philosophical ideas (many are omitted), nor to evaluate their strengths and weaknesses as philosophy, nor to provide descriptions sufficiently rich and full for purposes of philosophical analysis. Readers interested in these things should refer to textbooks and original sources. The aim is simply to use thumbnail descriptions of a few theories as a way of suggesting hypotheses for this psychological investigation.

First, *substance and quality*. For Aristotle (1965), the basic particulars were primary substances. Primary substances are individual things, such as a man or a horse. Santillana (1961) commented: 'The cat . . . is not made of plain atoms. It is one, continuous, specific substance called 'cat', unique in the scheme [of Nature]' (p. 215). Aristotle distinguished primary substances from secondary substances, which are types such as the class of horses – 'the knowable aspect of [the cat's] essence is "catness", which applies to all cats' (Santillana 1961: 215), and from qualities or universals, which can be present in primary substances (such as colour). Everything is either predicated of or present in a primary substance. Referring back to the list of Aristotle's categories in the preceding chapter, the category of substance is therefore basic and all the other categories are less basic in that they are existentially dependent on primary substances, things that only exist in so far as they are predicated of or present in a primary substance. Campbell (1976) referred to Aristotle's philosophy as 'material concrete particularism'.

Secondly, *atomism*. Atomism can be traced to the Greek philosophers Leucippos and Democritus (Toulmin and Goodfield 1962). They proposed that the basic constituents of the universe were atoms, which were defined as indivisible, impenetrable, indestructible basic entities with no properties of their own. Atoms could interact by collision or by interlocking, and these two types of interaction gave rise to the objects and phenomena of the world. This form of atomism was adopted and developed by Newton, whose atoms exerted forces upon one another in two ways, by impact and by gravitation (Campbell 1976). There are several varieties of atomism, not all of which subscribe to the classical definition of an atom. For example, Russell proposed an atomism of events in which the basic particulars are not concrete and do not endure in time: 'the occurrence, in a small region of space, during a short period of time (that is, over a small space-time interval), of a physical magnitude' (Campbell 1976: 101). Under this scheme, things are made of clusters and chains of events.

Thirdly, *phenomenalism*. In phenomenalism the basic particulars are sense-data or sense-impressions. In the radical empiricist philosophy of Hume (1739/1978), for example, phenomenalism is a kind of atomism in which sense-impressions are the atoms of experience. Sense-impressions are instantaneous time-slices of experience (Harré and Madden 1975), and enduring things are constructions of the mind made of instantaneous 'happenings' in consciousness.

Fourthly, *monads*. Leibniz argued that the only truly simple things were monads, simple mind-like things, all dimly conscious of one another, all set in a non-spatial order. These are far simpler than minds. They are permanent and independent of one another, and active, meaning that they contain within themselves the causes of the changes in inner content through which they pass. 'Close similarities of content among colonies of monads present themselves to *our* consciousness in the form of the cohesive material objects of everyday life' (Campbell 1976: 39). Space is an appearance, a way of representing relations of similarity among monads.

Fifthly, *fields*. Under this view the basic particulars are fields (such as magnetic and gravitational fields) which extend indefinitely in all directions. Material objects represent the interplay of fields. A field is described in terms of its power to affect the course of events. Harré and Madden (1975) associated this view with Leibniz, and quoted him as follows: 'The substance of things itself consists in the force of acting and being acted upon' (Harré and Madden 1975: 168). They also said that Priestley claimed that matter *was* a set of powers and nothing more.

These are only five among many theories, but they suffice for present purposes. Before making hypotheses about the basic particulars in the psychological construction of reality, it is necessary to distinguish psychologically basic particulars from what I shall call theoretical knowledge. Someone who has read about contemporary physics, for example, may come to believe that atoms or quarks or fields are the fundamental constituents of things. But this is not the same as saying that that person's construction of reality is founded upon atoms or quarks or fields as basic particulars. As I explained in the introduction, the metaphysical assumptions underpinning the psychological construction of reality are not adopted as the result of ratiocination, or reading about physics, but develop, as it were, during the course of, and quite likely at an early stage of, experience.

It would be wrong to exclude theoretical knowledge from the psychological construction of reality altogether: a schema for a chair, for example, might contain the information that it has four legs, is good for sitting on, and is made of atoms. This would not imply that the metaphysical basis of the construction of the reality that includes chairs is atomism, or even anything logically compatible with atomism. One could take 'made of atoms' out of the schema for a chair without seriously impairing our understanding of chairs. The metaphysical basis of the construction of reality, by contrast, is that which underlies schemas for objects, in the sense that if it were taken away our comprehension of reality would be seriously debilitated.

Bearing this in mind, I would hypothesise that the notion of basic particulars in the psychological construction of reality resembles Aristotle's notion of primary substances more nearly than any of the other theories listed. Our understanding of a chair, to continue the example, is founded on notions very like those of primary substance and quality. A chair is a thing, in our understanding spatially extended, distinct, enduring in time, and existing in objective reality and independently of our sense-impressions. It has qualities, and those qualities do not just make the chair what it is, but depend on it for their existence. We do not ordinarily regard any of these statements about chairs as problematic: we take them for granted in our dealings with chairs. Although we may come to believe that chairs are made of atoms, this belief is a kind of optional extra, and its absence or removal would not entail any fundamental alteration to our understanding of chairs. We do not feel a necessity to understand a chair in terms of its atomic structure, to explain why it does not fall apart into its component atoms (or other constituents) or why it continues to exist without perceptible change in its qualities. We understand that a chair can have parts (for example, the pieces of wood, nails, and glue from which it was made), but the description and understanding of those parts does not in common sense involve a move to a level of description more basic than that of primary substance and quality.

It might be possible to argue that the structure of language supports the claim that people have a substance-quality theory of matter: in language primary substances are denoted by nouns and qualities by adjectives, and the being/happening distinction is captured by the distinction between nouns and verbs. Certainly the structure of language is not incompatible with a substance-quality metaphysics, but arguments from the structure of language to the construction of reality are beset by problems with which I am not qualified to deal, and I shall do no more than note the possibility of developing an argument along those lines.

A thought experiment may help to reveal something of the matter theory of common sense. Imagine a wooden foot-ruler, of the sort common in schools. The ruler is lying on a desk. Now imagine that you push one end of it with your finger, causing it to move along the desk a little. I expect most people would think that the end of the ruler furthest from your finger would move at exactly the same instant as the end you push with your finger – the whole ruler moves together, as it were. In fact, the judgement of exact simultaneity is wrong. The influence of your finger's push is propagated along the ruler at the speed of light, so the movement of the far end begins slightly later than the movement of the near end. This means that the ruler undergoes a slight relativistic distortion of shape – it becomes slightly shorter in the direction of the push.

Of course, a foot-ruler is too short for the relativistic change of shape and the delay to be detectable, so let us carry out the same thought experiment with a ruler one light-year long. Here I expect that people unfamiliar with relativity will still tend to regard the movements of the two ends of the ruler as simultaneous, and even those who have a nodding acquaintance with relativity may be surprised to learn that the movement of the far end, assuming the movement could be propagated that far at all, would not begin until at least one year after the near end was pushed. This answer, I suspect, is not intuitively obvious, though it is a natural consequence of the theory of relativity, which limits all propagation to the speed of light, and of the fact that the ruler is made of atoms and molecules. What this reveals, I would argue, is that we have a natural idea of objects as solid: the substance of a ruler is solid wood, and even though we can learn through education that in fact it is made of atoms, this learning does not lead us to reject the substance theory of matter that is at the base of our psychological construction of reality. We hold it to be in the nature of a truly solid substance that merely pushing it does not cause a change of shape: it moves all together, without distortion. For us, the material world (excluding liquids and gases, and allowing for properties such as elasticity) is made of things like this.

The distinctive effect of the primary substance metaphysics is that we tend to think of things and objects as more solid, more distinct from one another, more self-contained, more static or passively maintained than they actually are. We naturally treat a waterfall as a primary substance, a candle flame, a cloud. None of these is solid in the sense of being impenetrable: each of them is a loose agglomeration of particles (or gas). The structure of a waterfall or a candle flame is dynamically maintained, not static: waterfalls and candle flames are not things at all, but processes (Laszlo 1972). Are there any instances where we think of something as less solid and self-contained than it is? The metaphysics of primary substances has significant consequences for our conceptualisation of mental activity: these will be explored in Part 3 of this book.

The other theories listed rule themselves out by containing important ingredients that are clearly objectionable to common sense. Phenomenalism is ruled out because it does not take the persistence of objects as axiomatic. Monads are ruled out because in this theory the actual reality of space is denied. Fields are ruled out because in this theory no fundamental distinction is made between forces and objects. The argument I would make about atomism is that it is ruled out on psychological grounds, because atoms form no part of experience, such as perception: they are an ingredient of reality that can be understood as such *only* indirectly by being hypothesised, inferred, read about, and so on. That is, they can only enter the psychological construction of reality as theoretical knowledge, and I have already argued that theoretical knowledge cannot be basic to the psychological construction of reality.

## THE ABSENCE OF SCEPTICISM FROM COMMON SENSE

In considering why the other four theories do not succeed in modelling the psychological construction of reality, perhaps the most general point on which they all fail is in not representing appearances. That is, they go beyond what is apparent in perception. The primary substance theory is consistent with a naïve realist stance on perception. In saying this I am not trying to argue that people have a theory of perception, but that they understand the world as if they had such a theory, and naïve realism is the theory that captures the nature of their understanding.

Ayer (1956: 37) listed four main types of sceptical belief:

'Any inference from past to future is illegitimate.'

'It is to be doubted whether the exercise of sense-perception can in any circumstances whatever afford proof of the existence of physical objects.'

[There is no warrant for supposing that memory is ever to be trusted: the doubt which the sceptic raises is] 'whether we can ever be justified in inferring from present experiences to past events'.

[The thoughts and feelings of others are] 'behind a barrier which it is impossible that one should ever penetrate'.

Of course people entertain doubts about things from time to time: what we see can be misleading when, for example, a stick half immersed in water appears bent; memories are not always trustworthy; there is no such thing as a dead cert in a horse-race; and one can wonder how often people mean what they say. But having doubts of these kinds is very far from adopting a thorough-going scepticism about knowledge of the world, or about the trustworthiness of subjective impressions of it. The world of the psychological construction of reality is one in which perception generally affords an accurate picture of reality, so much so that secondary qualities such as colour are naturally thought of as belonging to objects and seen by us, rather than as constructions of the human mind. It is one in which objects are as they seem and naturally endure unless and until acted on in some way, in which memory is usually a faithful record of past events, in which other people are more or less comprehensible and more or less like ourselves as we believe ourselves to be, and in which whatever causal and other laws hold naturally continue into the future.

The naïve realism of this construction can be explained as a consequence of the practical concerns orientation: there is no philosophical position less practical than scepticism, and once you have painted yourself into the philosophical corner of solipsism there is no point in doing anything at all. One might as well suppose that reality is as it appears to be except when there are good practical reasons for treating it otherwise. This is not a novel observation. Heider (1958) wrote about implicit and partly unverbalisable assumptions that people make about the conditions which make it possible for one person to recognise what another is perceiving. Fundamental among these was that the other person is living in the same world as us and perceiving roughly what we would perceive from their position. He in turn quoted Asch (1952):

We start with the bare observation that a number of persons will in a given situation perceive objects and happenings within it in a similar way and that their modes of action in the situation will also have a basic similarity. The tree that I see others see too; what I hear they hear.

(Asch 1952: 128)

Thus, a tendency to naïve realism is essential for interpersonal perception and relations.

This brief digression into naïve realism is not without psychological implications. The status of memory in the psychological construction of reality is very different from the point of view of cognitive psychology, for example, under which recalled memories are constructed from stored information rather than literal records of past events, and this may have significant implications; for instance, in evaluation of eyewitness testimony. But my main purpose in raising it here is to point out its relation to the primary substance metaphysics of the psychological construction of reality. Alternatives such as atomism are ruled out, before any other reason, by their incompatibility with the very literal naïve realism of that construction, in which nothing unobservable can be basic.

Returning to the list of basic categories in the psychological construction of reality, we can now use our hypothesis about basic particulars to fill out one part of it:

1  Space and time
2  Being ———————→ primary substances having qualities
3  Happening ———————→ causation

In addition to qualities, of course, the other Aristotelian categories of being can also be predicated upon primary substances, but the question of whether these categorical distinctions – for example, between quantity and relative – are anywhere near as basic in the psychological construction of reality as that between substance and the set of other categories of being, has no clear answer at the moment. The term 'having' in the list denotes the fact that qualities and the other categories of being are in the psychological construction of reality existentially dependent upon primary substances, which are the basic nature of being.

It still remains to fill in the list with the basic concept of causation, and this will be the topic of the next two chapters. But the list as it is now has important implications for the basic concept of causation. I argued earlier that theories of causation are related to other parts of metaphysics inasmuch as metaphysical doctrines delimit ranges of theories of causation with which they can be compatible. Whatever basic concept of causation exists in the psychological construction of reality, therefore, it must be one that works in terms of the basic category of being, one that is compatible with the primary substance theory of matter.

This is a significant step to take. There are two dominant approaches to the analysis of causation in philosophy. One is what might be called event causation, under which the only cause of an event can be another event. The usual justification for this, apart from its traditional association with radical empiricism, is that a cause is required to be a sufficient condition for its effect. This means that the cause cannot be present when its effect does not occur and, since the effect is an event and therefore transient, the cause must also be transient and therefore an event. The other approach can be called 'object causation' and is exemplified by Aristotelian causation. Under this approach the causes of events are enduring substances or, to be precise, enduring properties of substances, usually referred to as powers. Theorists of object causation usually evade the requirement of sufficiency by postulating that a substance only produces an effect under suitable conditions, which are allowed to be transient.

The postulation of a psychological metaphysics in which the basic particulars are enduring substances therefore entails a theory of object causation, not event causation. This entailment does not function as a firm commitment, of course, but rather as a criterion for falsification of the primary substance metaphysics. That is, if research shows that people operate with a model of event causation and not object causation, it follows that enduring substances cannot be the basic particulars in the psychological construction of reality. None the less, the theory of causation to be proposed here is a model of object causation, founded on the primary substance metaphysics. As we shall see, this is profoundly different from the analysis of causation implicit in traditional psychological theories of causal attribution.

## THE PSYCHOLOGICAL DISTINCTION BETWEEN BEING AND HAPPENING

What, psychologically, distinguishes an event from something that is not an event, happening from being in the terminology I have been using? Since I have claimed that happening relates to causation and being to material particulars, this is in effect to ask what, most basically, engages causal processing? The phrase 'most basically' is important here because I shall argue later that exceptions to the theory I am proposing can arise during development. The most basic distinction is the one to be found at the developmental origin of causal processing.

Consider an example of a sequence, which I am borrowing from Salmon (1984). A boy hits a baseball with a bat; the ball flies through the air and smashes a window. Most people, I think, would regard a causal connection as being involved in two parts of this sequence: the hitting of the ball by the boy with the bat; and the breaking of the window by the ball. I elucidate their understanding of these two things in later chapters.

The problematic part of the sequence is the flight of the ball. Few people, except under interrogation from a psychologist, would engage in causal processing of the flight of the ball, or regard it as in need of explanation. It does need to be explained, of course, and in science the explanation is provided by, among other things, the laws of gravitation. But for ordinary people the curved trajectory of the ball is simply a natural occurrence. Whatever most basically marks an event, psychologically, the curved trajectory of a ball in flight does not have it. We can now ask what distinguishes the flight of a ball from all events.

I have claimed that the basic theory of matter in common sense is the doctrine of primary substances with qualities. One could therefore suggest that an event is a change in at least one predicate of a primary substance. This will not do, because in the case of the baseball its property of spatial location is changing, and moreover the change is not a simple one, being a parabolic trajectory rather than a straight line. So not all changes in predicates are processed causally. One could maintain that spatial location is a peculiar kind of predicate, at least psychologically, and that all changes of other kinds of quality are causally processed. But it is clear that some changes of spatial location, such as the change brought about when the ball is hit by the bat in the first place, *are* processed causally, so whatever may be the case for other types of quality it is still necessary to elucidate the psychological distinction between changes in spatial location that are processed causally and those that are not.

A second approximation might be that an event is a departure from what is expected or normal or familiar. On this definition the trajectory of the ball is not an event because it is entirely familiar and expected on the basis of our experience with objects in the gravitational field of Earth. But this definition excludes too many things. Things that are expected, normal, and familiar often are processed causally: examples will be discussed in the chapter on the causal powers theory. In the baseball example, it is quite possible for an observer to expect the ball to smash the window as soon as it becomes apparent that a collision will take place, and for the observer to expect this on the basis of long familiarity with balls and windows, but having that expectation and that familiarity would not prevent the observer from processing causally the smashing of the window by the ball.

In its flight through the air, the ball is undergoing change in its property of spatial location. But that change is gradual and continuous, rather than abrupt and discontinuous. On the other hand, if, partway through its flight, the ball suddenly turned left, we would certainly seek some explanation if none was apparent, and would causally process the turning left if some possible cause was apparent (such as striking an object in its path). This leads to the suggestion that what matters is not change in a property of a thing *per se,* but change in the *amount or type* of change that is occurring. Let me give an exact definition. An event is *a sudden change in the amount or type of change in some property of a substance.* Change in amount of change can be from some change to more or less, from no change to some change, or from some change to none (that is, suddenly ceasing to change is an event under this definition).

The key term here is 'sudden'. This also needs to be defined and I propose to do this by reference to iconic processing. Iconic processing is the perceptual processing of information held in a large-capacity store for brief amounts of time: information usually decays to the limited capacity of working memory within about 250 milliseconds (Haber 1983a). Although iconic processing as such is visual information processing, there is some evidence for analogous auditory processing (Kintsch 1970; Anderson 1980). Several authors (see commentary on Haber 1983a) have argued that one function of iconic processing is temporal integration; that is, the integration of input information temporally separated by no more than the limit on the duration of some piece of information in iconic processing (about 250 ms). A change in amount or type of change, then, is sudden if it is (1) above the perceptual threshold of detection and (2) within the time-span of iconic processing. This means, in effect, that sudden change is change detected by or in the temporal integration function of iconic processing.

I am proposing, then, that this definition marks the psychological boundary between being and happening: that is, it is a psychological origin for the basic metaphysical distinction in the psychological construction of reality between being and happening. Obviously, some things that are processed causally do not fit this definition of an event: the fall of the Roman Empire can be cited as an example. I argue later that these exceptions emerge in an orderly way during development, in ways involving grafting onto existing concepts and ways of processing. The main argument for the definition of the being/happening distinction in terms of iconic processing, however, is a developmental one: this is taken up at the start of the chapter on the origins and development of causal processing.

# Chapter 5

# Why regularity information is not basic to causal understanding

The history of the mainstream of attribution theory and research since Heider has been dominated by covariation and other types of regularity information. Most of the major theories of causal attribution in psychology have involved regularity information of some kind (Cheng and Novick 1990; Einhorn and Hogarth 1986; Forsterling 1989; Heider 1958; Hewstone and Jaspars 1987; Hilton and Slugoski 1986; Jones and Davis 1965 – specifically the idea of non-common effects; Kelley 1967, 1972a, 1972b, 1973; Shanks and Dickinson 1987), and large numbers of often-cited studies have looked at the relation between covariation information of some sort and causal attribution (see, for example, Hewstone 1989; Ross and Fletcher 1985; Fincham 1983; White 1988a). So great has this dominance been that Ross and Fletcher (1985) commented that covariation is 'the sine qua non of causal inference' (p. 83), in an argument that factors like salience and resemblance depend upon the basic cue of covariation, as far as their role in causal attribution is concerned. The point of this statement is to emphasise, not just that people like to use covariation or regularity information for causal attribution, but that it is basic, essential, to their causal attribution processes.

This point is important, because it is widely acknowledged now that many things other than or additional to regularity information have a place in causal attribution. Causal attributions are affected by theories, beliefs, and expectations and not just by content-free mechanisms for handling input information (for example, Kulik 1983; Abelson and Lalljee 1988). The importance of stimulus factors unconnected with regularity, such as salience (Fiske and Taylor 1991), is also recognised. Moreover, existing beliefs affect not only causal attribution but also the perception of covariation, upon which, classically, causal attribution is supposed to depend (Chapman 1967; Hamilton 1979; Fiske and Taylor 1991). These lines of research might lead one to infer that covariation has already been relegated from its former place of eminence in our understanding of causal attribution. This is not the case, however.

In the first place, although it is accepted that people use theories and beliefs in causal attribution, in some accounts the theories and beliefs that people use to make causal attributions are supposed to be, or to be based on, regularity. For example, Kelley (1972b) defined a causal schema as an assumed pattern of data in a complete analysis of variance framework. This clearly identifies it as a regularity-based device, only regularity stored in the head rather than sampled from the environment. Thus, evidence for the use of theories and beliefs in causal attribution is not necessarily evidence against regularity or covariation. Secondly, the presumed importance of regularity does not depend on the claim that nothing else affects causal attribution; it is a matter of what is supposed to be fundamental or basic to causal attribution, the ground on which theories and accounts of causal attribution are erected. Evidence that other factors affect causal attribution in no way counts against the idea that regularity is basic to causal attribution. It is the presumption that regularity is important in the sense of being fundamental to causal attribution that is contested here.

The main purpose of this chapter, then, is to argue against the idea that regularity (or covariation) is basic or essential to causal attribution, and to argue instead that regularity information has no more than a supporting role to play in causal attribution. After an introductory section listing the types of regularity information, the main body of the chapter organises the arguments under two main headings, arguing that people are not naïve regularity theorists, and that regularity information is neither necessary nor sufficient for causal attribution. The following chapters lay out an alternative theoretical approach to causal attribution, and analyse the place that regularity information occupies under that alternative.

## THE TYPES OF REGULARITY INFORMATION

In the broadest sense, regularity information is any kind of information covering multiple occurrences and/or non-occurrences of what are taken to be the same (kind of) effect. Thus, information about only a single occasion, and information about multiple occasions covering effects not categorised together or considered similar, do not count as regularity information. In philosophy, several types of regularity information have been described, either as concepts of causation or as methods of causal inference, and some of these have been used in psychology as a basis for theories or hypotheses about how people actually make causal inferences. The list of theories and ideas under each type is not exhaustive, but concentrates on those that have been most influential in psychology.

First, *constant conjunction or empirical association*. The most influential theory of this type was proposed by Hume (1739/1978). Hume's main definition of cause is 'an object precedent and contiguous to another, and where all the objects resembling the former are plac'd in like relation of precedency and contiguity to those objects, that resemble the latter' (1739/1978: 170). This definition combines the notion of constant conjunction with spatial and temporal contiguity and regular temporal priority. Although no existing psychological theory resembles this definition exactly, Einhorn and Hogarth (1986) incorporated all the elements of the definition into their account of judging probable cause, along with other theoretical notions, and there have been many studies of the development of children's use of these 'Humean' cues (Fincham 1983; Sedlak and Kurtz 1981; Shultz and Kestenbaum 1985; White 1988a).

Most of these studies have treated the cues as if they were rules used by the perceiver as a means of inferring causation. Although psychologically legitimate, this is not how they were intended by Hume. His argument was that the impression of a causal relation emerged from repeated experiences of independent entities going together: it was, in essence, an associative theory. For this reason, the most nearly Humean account to be found in the psychological literature is probably that of Shanks and Dickinson (1987). In their account, causal judgement is determined by associative processes; that is to say, processes which yield an impression of the strength of association between an event and one or more possible causes. Their approach may have much to offer the study of causal attribution, but the authors themselves were careful to mark out the limits on its scope: it does not apply to judgements based on narrative or abstract representations, to causal perception of the sort studied by Michotte (1963), or to the use of beliefs and prior knowledge for causal attribution.

John Stuart Mill wrote a great deal about causation, but it is his methodological principles of causal inference (1843/1967) that have had the most influence on psychology. These are based on the constant conjunction notion of causation, and are methodological rather than theoretical in the sense of prescribing how causal analysis should be done, and not necessarily how people actually do it. Here three are listed:

1  The method of agreement. 'If two or more instances of the phenomenon under investigation have only one circumstance in common, the circumstance in which alone all the instances agree, is the cause (or effect) of the given phenomenon' (Mill 1843/1967: 255).
2  The method of difference. 'If an instance in which the phenomenon under investigation occurs, and an instance in which it does not occur, have every circumstance in common save one, that occurring only in the former, the circumstance in which alone the two instances differ, is the effect, or the cause, or a necessary part of the cause of the phenomenon' (p. 256).
3  The joint method of agreement and difference (also called the indirect method of difference). 'If two or more instances in which the phenomenon occurs have only one circumstance in common, while two or more instances in which it does not occur have nothing in common save the absence of that circumstance; the circumstance in which alone the two sets of instances differ, is the effect, or cause, or a necessary part of the cause, of the phenomenon' (p. 259).

These methods have been influential in psychology. For example, Heider (1958) proposed that people use the method of difference to distinguish between perceiver, object, and circumstances as possible causal factors (pp. 68–9). He also proposed that people use the covariation principle, 'that condition will be held responsible for an effect which is present when the effect is present and which is absent when the effect is absent' (p. 152), in his analysis of the attribution of enjoyment. He stated that this was the data pattern fundamental in the determination of attribution, and that it underlies Mill's methods, though it may be seen to resemble the joint method of agreement and difference more closely than the others given here. The covariation principle later formed the basis for Kelley's (1967, 1972a, 1973) multiple observation model of attribution. The use of covariation information in causal inference has also been extensively investigated (for example, Ruble and Rholes 1981; Schustack and Sternberg 1981; Siegler 1975).

Secondly, *conditional relations*. In philosophy, conditional theories of causation are treated as a branch of regularity theories. The following are some of the types of conditional relation:

1 Necessary conditions. According to Mill (1843/1967), a cause is the whole set of necessary conditions jointly sufficient for the occurrence of an effect.
2 Sufficient conditions. Several philosophers have proposed that a cause is a sufficient condition for its effect (Sosa 1975). Statements about necessary conditions imply statements about sufficient conditions, and vice versa: if $A$ is a sufficient condition for $B$, then $B$ is a necessary condition for $A$. This shows that conditional relations are not relations of temporal priority. According to Carr (1987), Hume's constant conjunction formula amounts to a sufficient condition definition of a cause.
3 Necessary and sufficient conditions – proposed as a definition of efficient causation by Galileo, according to Bunge (1963).
4 INUS conditions. An INUS condition is defined as an Insufficient but Necessary part of a scenario that is Unnecessary but Sufficient for an effect to occur (Mackie 1965, 1974, 1975; White 1990).
5 Abnormal or differentiating conditions. These are methodological principles according to which a cause is 'essentially something which interferes with or intervenes in the course of events which would normally take place' (Hart and Honoré 1974: 224), or something which differentiates the occasion in question from some appropriate standard chosen for comparison (Gorovitz 1965). Both of these qualify as regularity notions because of their dependence upon some analysis of what usually or normally happens, and because they do not stipulate necessity in the causal relation.

References to all of these can be found in the psychological literature. To deal with cases in which the attributer had only a single observation, Kelley (1972b, 1973) proposed that use would be made of a cognitive structure called a causal schema, and both necessary and sufficient conditions figured in the causal schemas that Kelley postulated. Hewstone and Jaspars (1987) reconsidered tests of Kelley's multiple observation model of attribution, and argued that the evidence favoured an account in terms of necessary and sufficient conditions, separately or together. Einhorn and Hogarth (1986) made use of Mackie's INUS condition concept in their eclectic analysis of causal judgement (though it should be noted that their account is not strictly regularity-based, but only uses regularity information along with other cues and concepts). The Hart and Honoré analysis formed the basis for accounts by Fincham and Jaspars (1980) and Hilton and Slugoski (1986), and Hesslow (1988) gave an account of causal selection that resembles Gorovitz's differentiating factor analysis, though it appears to have been an independent creation. There have also been studies of the use of conditional information in causal inference (for example, Schustack and Sternberg 1981; Shultz *et al.* 1981).

Thirdly, *probabilistic relations*. Several philosophers have conducted probabilistic analyses of causation. For example, Suppes (1970) proposed that 'one event is the cause of another if the appearance of the first event is followed with a high probability by the appearance of the second, and there is no third event that we can use to factor out the probability relationship between the first and second events' (p. 10). Suppes' analysis still falls under regularity theory, but constant conjunction has been replaced by probable conjunction (see also Salmon 1984). Probabilistic analyses of causation are methodological and may be applied in problems of research design. They have not yet, however, been used as a basis for a theory or model of causal inference, although the idea of causal inference as a kind of judgement under uncertainty, which might be treated with statistical formulae, has been developed by Einhorn and Hogarth (1986).

## PEOPLE ARE NOT NAÏVE REGULARITY THEORISTS

The simplest psychological hypothesis one could formulate about regularity is that people are naïve regularity theorists as philosophers prescribe. That is, people just gather regularity information and causal inferences and attributions emerge from it in a theory-neutral manner, depending only on the regularity information gathered. One problem with this is that regularity theories might just be wrong, or, even if they are not wrong, have limitations in principle so great that they could not be used for causal analysis. These are philosophical issues, and the subject of much debate (Taylor 1966; Beauchamp 1974; Bhaskar 1975; Salmon 1984; White 1990). It is beyond the scope of this chapter to evaluate the status of regularity theories of causation in philosophy: readers interested in this should turn to the philosophical literature. It could also be argued, however, that regularity-based methods have limitations in fact such that people cannot use them for causal inference, and that in other respects where people could behave as regularity theorists, available evidence shows that they do not. These are psychological issues, and are considered in this section of the chapter. First, here are four respects in which regularity-based methods are not practicable.

### Causal selection

Regularity-based models in the Humean tradition are purely inductive, which means that there is no a priori selection among causal candidates. In an inductive procedure, the number of possible causes of a single effect a priori is therefore effectively infinite. If we are trying to explain why Susan passed the exam, for example, the causal candidates include, a priori, the event that it was raining outside, the event that a person sneezed behind her, the event that a clock in the room was ticking, even the drift of dust motes in the air before her eyes.

At first glance this does not appear to be a problem for actual use of regularity-based procedures, because the idea of a causal relation simply emerges from a record of experiences, for those events that meet the regularity definition. The problem is that an effectively infinite number of candidates requires an effectively infinite amount of information to be gathered about the occasions in question, if the procedure is to work purely inductively. Clearly, people must make a priori selections: only so much information can be stored in memory, and even if people did manage to store information about all possible causes without selection, there would be so many that the use of regularity-based methods to make just one causal attribution would take forever.

This does not mean that regularity-based devices cannot be used. It does mean, however, that people must make compromises with the ideal regularity-based approach if they are to use regularity for causal attribution. Some compromises are made for them, in effect, by processes of perception and attention: for example, the record of experiences may be biased by factors such as salience (Taylor and Fiske 1975). The kind of compromise made by a naïve regularity theorist, however, should be without prejudice as to the kind of thing that might turn out to be a cause of some effect. This means that the range of causal candidates in the record of experiences is still formidable, and it is to be doubted whether people can deal with the problem of causal selection without that kind of prejudice, without any kind of idea as to what sort of thing might be the cause of the effect in question.

## Impracticability of methodological rules

One way around the problem of infinite possible causes is to postulate methodological rules which allow valid identification of causes from a more limited set of information. The rules proposed by Mill (1843/1967) and quoted earlier are examples of these. The problem from the point of view of psychology is that the methodological rules proposed by philosophers as consistent with regularity theories cannot actually be used. This is not a fault, for they were never intended to be practicable. They are methodological only in the sense of prescribing an ideal method: not how causal inference might be done, but how it *ought* to be done. Ideal methods could only be used under ideal conditions. This is apparent in the rules themselves. The method of difference, for example (Mill 1843/1967, quoted above), requires for its use two occasions, identical in every respect except one. As every occasion carries an unlimited number of circumstances this never happens, so, despite Heider's (1958) proposal to the contrary, the rule cannot be used by people for actual causal inference. Practicable methodological rules could of course be derived from regularity notions, but in order to be practicable the precision in the regularity concept used would have to be sacrificed: it is to be doubted whether practicable rules could ever be more than heuristics. Ideal conditions can be approached (if not attained) in the laboratory, which is why some methodological rules can be used as bases for research designs aimed at identifying causes; but for ordinary people outside the laboratory the requisite degree of control over events is impossible to achieve.

## Categorisation/similarity

Regularity theories require multiple instances. This in turn raises the question of what counts as an instance. For example, Hume's (1739/1978) definition, quoted above, depends upon some notion of resemblance. In his methodological rules Mill (1843/1967) referred to instances of a phenomenon (see above). Thus, causal inference under these definitions and rules depends on either similarity judgement or categorisation. How can one say that two instances are in fact the same phenomenon, or that this object resembles another sufficiently and that one does not? Taylor (1966) has made a strong argument that the problem of similarity judgement is fatal to regularity theories in philosophy: it would be a digression to explore that argument here, but it is clear none the less that if people were regularity theorists they would have to make categorisations or similarity judgements before they could make causal attributions. This problem has been obscured by the widespread use in research of stimulus presentations in which phenomena have already been categorised, so that subjects are not required to go through this process. The reality of this problem does not disprove the idea that people are regularity theorists: it just adds to the difficulty of being a regularity theorist, and is one more thing that should be addressed in an adequate regularity-based model of causal processing.

## Limitation to general statements

Strictly speaking, regularity-based methods can only be used to support general statements; that is to say, statements covering multiple instances of a phenomenon. Single occasions can only be analysed as instances of causal regularities or laws of nature: for this reason, the main use of regularity theories in philosophy is now in attempting to define the nature of causal laws (Beauchamp 1974). This means that regularity-based methods are particularly badly suited to causal attributions about single instances. Consider someone interested in a causal question about a single occasion, such as 'Why did Susan fail that examination?' If the attributer were a naïve regularity theorist, they would try to proceed by gathering information about other occasions of failure – Kelley's (1967) ANOVA model represents one way of doing this. The aim of this would be to identify events that exhibit regularity of association with failure. Since there is no one cause of failure, no event would exhibit exact association with failure. But the attributer might still find several that satisfy some less exacting regularity-based criterion: for example, there might be several events, each of which is a sufficient condition for failure, in that failure always occurs whenever any one of them is present.

Now the kind of inference that a naïve regularity theorist might draw from this has the following form: event *A* is a cause of failure. This is a *general* statement. It does not answer the question why Susan failed that one examination in particular. For this an extra inferential step is required. Where event *A* is the only identified cause of failure present on that one occasion, the inference is straightforward, although it still runs the risk that there is some other, hitherto unidentified cause of failure, that was present on the occasion in question. The degree of risk will depend on such things as the range and type of occasions the attributer has sampled. But where more than one identified cause is present, the attributer is unable to make any selection between them. They may of course be right not to do so, since it is possible that all the identified causes did in fact contribute to that one failure, but whether that was so or not cannot be ascertained by use of regularity cues. This is an essential weakness of regularity theories: they are not suited to analysis of individual occurrences. Analysis of individual occurrences requires an extra inferential step from the regularity-based identification of causes which often cannot be taken with the use of regularity cues alone. Thus, if people were naïve regularity theorists, this would pose serious and often insurmountable problems for the making of causal attributions.

The problems described above do not prevent people from being regularity theorists: they show merely that the job of being a regularity theorist is difficult, and requires some compromise with the ideal notion of how a regularity theorist would engage in causal inference. From a psychological point of view, far more damaging to the idea that people are naïve regularity theorists is evidence that, when people have the opportunity to behave as regularity theorists, they behave in other ways incompatible with a regularity-based approach.

## People identify objects as causes

Under regularity theories, from repeated observations of suitable conjunctions of events *A* and *B*, we are supposed to form the idea that event *A* causes event *B*. The cause is identified as event A. This is all that the regularity approach entitles us to do. It is a model of *event* causation (Taylor 1966): the cause of an event can only be another event. It cannot be something that persists, or is presumed to persist, between observations, such as a stable internal disposition. (Hume's use of the word 'object' should not be taken literally here: it is best interpreted as a kind of shorthand for 'object of experience', which is, under radical empiricism, a type of event.)

There are two main reasons for this. One is that to identify an object (or any persisting thing) as a cause would be to go too far beyond the evidence: regularity is supposed to give an idea of a relation between events, but it does not give us any ideas beyond that. The second reason is that attributing an effect to a stable factor or to an object violates the requirement of sufficiency in the causal relation (Taylor 1966). Something that is there all the time cannot be a cause of something that is there only some of the time, because the former is not a sufficient condition for the latter. Any philosopher who wishes to propose a model of object causality, in which an object or a stable feature of an object can be a cause, must find a way to deal with this problem; see Harré and Madden (1975) for an example.

This implies that, if people were truly naïve regularity theorists, they would not make causal attributions for transient effects to stable factors such as personality characteristics, because to do so would be to go too far beyond the evidence *and* would violate the requirement of sufficiency in the causal relation. In attributing an effect to a stable internal cause, people show that they live in a different conceptual world, a world of object causation, not of event causation. They cannot both do this and be naïve regularity theorists.

## People are not purely inductive

As already stated, regularity theories are purely inductive: they specify no concept of what a cause might be, other than that it must be an event. The idea of a causal relation simply arises from a set of observations or experiences possessing certain defining characteristics. If people were regularity theorists they would not actively look for causes, still less direct their search for causes in any definite way. Evidence, therefore, that people do test either specific or naïve hypotheses when making causal attributions (Hansen 1980; Lalljee *et al.* 1984) counts against the idea that people are regularity theorists. This does not rule out a regularity-based account altogether: one could maintain, for example, that the record of experiences provides an empirical basis for hypotheses which then direct processes of causal inference. A regularity theorist, however, ought not to proceed in this way: a causal inference is supposed to emerge from the record of experiences, not to be sought in any directed fashion. Thus, a hypothesis-tester may use regularity information for both formulation and testing of hypotheses, but is not a regularity theorist.

## People do not limit themselves to observables as possible causes

It is not completely accurate to say that there is no a priori selection of candidates at all under regularity theories: not only do such theories require that a cause be an event rather than an object, but they also require that it be observable. The idea of a causal relation can only arise in respect of things actually observed or experienced by the attributer. Dependence on regularity-based cues entails that no causal inference can ever be made to hypothetical, unobserved causes. This means that no behaviour can be attributed to causes strictly internal to a person, such as mental states and dispositions, because no such causes can ever be observed: the only possible exception to this is the case of self-attribution, when the range of internal causal candidates available is delimited by the range of introspection.

This problem was implicitly acknowledged by Kelley (1967) in his multiple observation model. The model is an idealised procedure for identifying one of three causal loci, the actor, the target, and the circumstances or time, as causally responsible for some effect. Such causal loci can be discriminated using regularity cues. The procedure does not, however, identify anything specific about any of the causal loci. Having identified, say, the actor as the cause, the procedure does not tell us what it is about the actor that was causally responsible for the effect. The problem with this is that it does not reflect actual practice: people do not just say that John laughed at the comedian because of something about John, they say he laughed at the comedian because he has an easily tickled sense of humour, or was in a good mood, or something of that sort. Specific attributions to internal characteristics cannot be made using regularity cues, and the fact that they are made shows that something other than regularity information must be involved. Again, this does not mean that people do not use regularity information at all, but it does show that they are not naïve regularity theorists.

## People go beyond what regularity information allows

The ultimate limitation to regularity-based methods is their very dependence on regularity cues. Causal candidates that covary equally with the effect to be explained cannot be discriminated using covariation-based methods. This is a problem in event causation. For example, where event $A$ is the cause of event $B$, event $A$ may have some other effect $C$ which for that reason also covaries exactly with $B$. When this happens, regularity cues cannot be used to distinguish between $A$ and $C$ as possible causes of $B$. Or, for example, event $A$ and event $C$ may be effects of some other cause and covary exactly with each other for that reason: again, under these circumstances, there is no way to tell which of them is the cause of $B$. Regularity theories can cope with this kind of problem in principle (see, for example, Suppes 1970; Einhorn and Hogarth 1986). Indeed, the use of controlled experimental designs in scientific research helps to distinguish between multiple covariates of an effect, *so long as* the covariation of the events involved with one another is not perfect. For ordinary people engaging in causal attribution, however, the degree of control exerted over stimulus conditions in the laboratory is generally impossible to achieve in social reality: thus, the kind of information necessary to distinguish between covariates of an effect cannot usually be obtained.

This might just mean that people only have access to poorly controlled, imperfect, incomplete information about covariates, presumably with detrimental consequences for the accuracy of their causal attributions. Dependence on regularity is, however, a much more serious problem if we allow people to make causal attributions to things that persist over time. It is a commonplace observation of causal attribution research that people make causal attributions to stable internal features of persons such as personality characteristics, ability, and so on. The problem with this is that all stable characteristics of persons covary equally with effects and therefore could not be discriminated using regularity cues even if they could be observed. If we wish to say what it was about a person that was causally responsible for some effect, we must find some other means of doing so. Thus, however people attribute an effect to one stable internal disposition rather than another, they cannot be using regularity cues to do so, because they are making selections among things that covary equally with the effect being explained.

## Summary

To repeat, this list of problems with the idea that people might be naïve regularity theorists is not meant as a critique of regularity theories in philosophy. It is meant only as a set of issues relevant to the idea that people might be naïve regularity theorists. It is clear that this idea cannot be maintained, because: people cannot proceed without making a priori selections among causal candidates; they cannot use the methodological rules prescribed by philosophers; they would need to make similarity judgements or categorisations before making any causal attributions; regularity cues only support general statements, so that an extra inferential step must be negotiated to make a causal attribution about a single instance; people make causal attributions to stable, persisting things; they do not proceed purely inductively; they do not limit themselves to observables as causal candidates; and they make selections among causal candidates that cannot be discriminated using regularity-based methods.

These points destroy the idea that people are pure, naïve regularity theorists. It is still possible, though, that even though people have (sometimes at least) a model of object causation rather than event causation, even though they are hypothesis testers rather than inductivists, even though they do not limit themselves to observables as causal candidates, and even though they (sometimes at least) require the assistance of cues supplementary to regularity (for example, to discriminate between candidate causes all showing equal covariation with an effect), regularity of some kind might be basic to causal attribution. The next section defines what it would be for something to be basic to causal attribution, and considers whether regularity passes this test or not.

## NECESSITY AND SUFFICIENCY

In philosophy it is a requirement of a valid regularity theory that regularity, however defined, be necessary and sufficient for valid inference of causal relation. For example, under Hume's (1739/1978) definition (see above), repeated observation of the conjunction of objects $A$ and $B$, such that $A$ is contiguous and temporally prior to $B$, is necessary and sufficient for the valid inference that $A$ causes $B$. This is a minimal requirement: if there were ever an instance in which $A$ caused $B$ but $A$ did not meet the criteria specified in some regularity theory (violation of necessity), or an instance in which $A$ met the criteria specified in the theory but did not cause $B$ (violation of sufficiency), then the theory must be wrong.

Many philosophers have argued that regularity is not sufficient for inference of a causal generalisation or causal law: under Hume's definition, for example, day would be the cause of night, so clearly some regularities are not causal. Much of the impetus for the development of modern necessity theories of causation has arisen from the need to distinguish causal regularities from accidental regularities (Bunge 1963; Harré and Madden 1975; Bhaskar 1975).

Bhaskar (1975) has argued that not only is regularity not sufficient for a causal law, it is not necessary either. This is part of a complex philosophy of science which cannot be summarised here, but his main claim about regularity is that the real structures and natural mechanisms which form the theoretical content of causal laws transcend the observable facts, which Humean statements are not allowed to do. That is, our statements about causal laws tend to be independent of, and are often out of phase with, actual patterns of events. If Bhaskar is right, regularity is neither necessary nor sufficient for inference of causal relation, and this would be a damning indictment of regularity theories.

In psychology, regularity-based theories of causal inference and attribution are subject to an equivalent requirement. That is, if the intended claim is that our causal inferences, attributions, and causal understanding in general are based on regularity, however defined, then (perceived) regularity must be both necessary and sufficient for causal inference, attribution, and so on. There is ample evidence, however, to show that regularity is neither necessary nor sufficient for causal inference.

## Necessity

The one essential requirement of any regularity-based model or theory of causal inference is that repeated observations are necessary before a causal inference can be made. Causal inference from a single observation should not be possible under a regularity theory. There is evidence that people do make causal inferences from single observations. For example, Michotte (1963) presented stimuli simulating collisions between objects. Two opaque rectangles were visible on a screen. As subjects watched, one rectangle apparently moved towards the other and came into contact with it, whereupon the latter moved off a certain distance in the same direction and more slowly. Michotte found that many subjects perceived a causal relation on their first exposure to this stimulus sequence: they reported perceiving that the first rectangle kicked, pushed, or launched the second. Michotte termed this the 'launching effect'. Subsequent studies have also found that many, though not all, subjects perceive a causal relation on their first exposure to a launching effect sequence (Beasley 1968; Boyle 1960; White 1988a). Several studies have shown that infants younger than 6 months of age seem to perceive launching effect sequences as causal, and in much the way that adults do (Ball 1973; Borton 1979; Leslie 1982; Leslie and Keeble 1987). For example, if the two rectangles remain in contact for longer than about 150 ms, the launching effect disappears and adult observers report that the movements of the two rectangles are unconnected (Michotte 1963). Infants also have been shown to discriminate sequences with no delay from sequences in which the movement of the second rectangle is delayed for a fraction of a second (Leslie 1982).

Causal inferences from single instances can be explained under regularity theories if perceivers assimilate the instance to a stored record of experiences. Thus, it could be argued, perceivers of Michotte's stimuli have a stored record of many mechanical interactions perceived by them in the past, and this stored record underlies causal perception of the launching effect sequence. Even young infants might have had enough exposure to mechanical interactions to use a record of experiences in the interpretation of launching effect stimuli. The main problem with this point of view is that the stimuli used in these experiments do not resemble natural collision sequences very closely. Michotte did not use real collisions between objects, but illusory collisions between what were actually black lines painted on a rotating disc. Leslie used animated films involving images of rectangles. To use a stored record of experiences as a basis for causal perception, perceivers would have to make a link, an analogy in effect, between these stimuli and natural collisions which they only loosely resemble. This is not impossible, of course, but it is hard to see why perceivers should do it, unless they already have the idea that the sequence is a causal one. Why not just see it as a sequence of movements with no causal relation, which is what it is? Seeing the sequence as a causal relation means making an extravagant generalisation from the record of experiences, which, under a regularity-based account, people should not do.

It is doubtful whether research on the launching effect can be really conclusive because generalisation to things that do not closely resemble instances in the record of experiences is merely improbable, not impossible. The crucial case would be causal inference from an instance of a kind for which no record of experience could have been built up. For animals, the research of Garcia and colleagues (Garcia and Koelling 1966; Garcia *et al.* 1968) is relevant. These studies showed that one trial was sufficient for rats to learn an association between food with a distinctive taste and gastrointestinal illness induced by other means some time later. Perhaps rats do not have a concept of cause, but they behaved as if they had learned a causal relation after one trial, that is, in the absence of regularity (and in the absence of temporal contiguity).

As far as humans are concerned, evidence comes from research by Piaget (1954). For example, in observation 132 (reported on p. 238), Jacqueline, aged 8 months, gets the idea (wrongly, in this instance) of a causal connection between a specific movement of hers and a movement of a saucer after one or at most two trials. This is not enough for a record of regularity to be established. On the other hand, Piaget (1954) does have an account of how a causal relation could be inferred from such an instance. The account combines the notions of efficacy and phenomenal contiguity. That is to say, the infant has the experience of efficacy in performing her own action, and the relation between her action and the movement of the saucer has phenomenal contiguity – they go together in the infant's experience, even though they are separate in space. At this stage the infant has little or no appreciation of spatial relations, so phenomenal relations are enough, as far as causal inference is concerned. Under Piaget's account, infants should tend to see their own actions as effective in bringing about anything with which they have a relation of phenomenal contiguity, and Piaget's (1954) observations support this idea.

Piaget has an argument against the Humean approach here. Suppose an infant perceives a causal relation that is in fact entirely independent of his or her own actions: suppose, for example, that the infant observes an adult (Piaget himself in this case) drumming his fingers on a tin box to make a sound. If the infant is a naïve regularity theorist, he or she should get the idea that the drumming of the fingers is the cause of the noise, from repeated observations of the association of the two in conjunction with temporal and spatial contiguity. The test for this is what happens when the adult ceases the activity: if the infant wants the effect to continue, how do they go about making it do so? If they have the idea that the drumming of the fingers is the cause, they should try to act on the cause – for example, by giving the fingers a light push to get them to start again.

In fact nothing like that happened. Piaget reported several observations in which infants aged about 7 months treated the cause, the fingers, as if its action depended on the infant's own action; for example, by striking the hand or shaking it vigorously. In several more cases the infant did not try to act on the cause at all but merely put into operation magical procedures for bringing about effects, such as arching its back, as if these would make the effect happen again. This is contrary to what a regularity-based theory would predict: the infant is not merely learning contingencies, but operating according to a kind of theory under which what makes things happen is its own action. In the cases observed by Piaget, there was not the slightest empirical justification for such an idea. Thus, infants form causal beliefs in the absence of regularity.

Developmental research has also shown that causal inferences are made on the basis of cues that have nothing to do with regularity. These include similarity (Shultz and Ravinsky 1977; Nisbett and Ross 1980; White 1988a) and generative transmission (Shultz 1982a; Shultz, Fisher, Pratt and Rulf 1986).

There is evidence that children in the 5- to 9-year age range can use covariation as a cue to causal inference (Kassin and Pryor 1985; Mendelson and Shultz 1976; Shaklee and Mims 1981; Shultz and Mendelson 1975; Ruble and Rholes 1981; Siegler and Liebert 1974). There are several problems with this evidence, however.

First, several studies have shown that children have difficulty in using co-variation for causal inference (Ruble and Rholes 1981; Shultz and Mendelson 1975; Siegler and Liebert 1974; Siegler 1975). Siegler (1975) showed that children of about 5 years cannot use covariation as a cue when the cause and effect events are separated by more than 5 seconds, and that this is because children of that age cannot detect covariation in the absence of temporal contiguity.

Secondly, some of the supportive evidence can be interpreted in other ways. Ruble and Rholes (1981) argued that covariation information is often confounded with information about mere magnitude of the effect, and that children may be responding to the latter. Children also appear not to use covariation information when to do so would place excessive demands on memory (Shultz, Fisher, Pratt and Rulf 1986). This is particularly important in view of the fact that studies often present covariation information in idealised or packaged form (for example, McArthur 1972; Schustack and Sternberg 1981) because of which the demands placed on memory are less than they would be under more naturalistic conditions.

Thirdly, some studies have set up contests between different cues to causation, and in these covariation generally comes off badly. Mendelson and Shultz (1976) showed that children preferred a causal candidate which had temporal contiguity but did not covary with the effect to be explained over one which covaried with the effect but lacked temporal contiguity with it. Shultz (1982a) showed in a series of studies that children preferred cues to generative transmission over covariation cues, and there is evidence that children and adults prefer generative transmission cues over all other cues to causal inference (Shultz 1982a: study 5; Shultz, Fisher, Pratt and Rulf 1986). This point is the most important, because it shows that not only is regularity information not necessary for causal inference, it is not even the preferred kind of information, at least in these experiments. If regularity was basic to causal inference, these tendencies and preferences would not occur.

In summary, regularity information is not necessary for causal inference or attribution because such inferences are often made from single observations; made on the basis of similarity without regularity, on the basis of temporal contiguity when in conflict with regularity, and on the basis of evidence about generative transmission when in conflict with regularity.

## Sufficiency

Not only is regularity not necessary for causal inference, it is not sufficient for it either. Many patterns that conform to some notion of regularity are not causally interpreted. For example, many of Michotte's (1963) experiments showed that causal perception did not occur for some variations on the basic launching effect sequence. Causal perception did not occur if the second rectangle moved off in a markedly different direction from the first (experiment 35), or if there was a delay of 200 ms between the arrival of the first rectangle and the movement of the second (experiment 29). The problem with this is that Michotte used a small number of observers, each of whom observed each sequence many times. In other words, observers witnessed a large number of trials involving stimuli exhibiting constant conjunction as required under regularity theories. If regularity is basic to causal attribution, those observers should have begun to see the sequence as a causal relation after a certain number of trials. They did not. In the case of the 200 ms delay, it could be argued that the stimuli violate the Humean requirement of temporal contiguity: this objection loses force, however, in the face of evidence that children can make causal inferences connecting events separated by 5 seconds (Siegler and Liebert 1974). In any case, the sequence in which the second rectangle moves off at an angle meets Humean requirements perfectly, and yet it was not perceived as causal.

Not only do people sometimes not interpret regularity as showing causal relation, they often interpret it in other, non-causal ways. For example, regular successions of events are often interpreted as sequential effects of a common cause. Natural phenomena such as day and night and (some) patterns in the weather are good examples. As already stated, the regular succession of day and night satisfy Hume's criteria for a causal relation; but, instead of being interpreted as causes of each other, they are understood as the sequential effects of a natural process, the rotation of the Earth on its axis (or of the Sun around the Earth, if one prefers that theory). Human behaviour provides many similar examples. When a person is applauding, one clap is not interpreted as the cause of the next: the whole sequence is interpreted as due to the inner state of the person, in some way. In walking, one stride is not seen as the cause of the next. Under regularity theories, the events in any such regular sequence should be seen as causes of one another in a chain, not as common effects of a single overriding cause.

This point can be made in a telling fashion by paraphrasing an account of the use of regularity-based cues in causal inference by Einhorn and Hogarth (1986). Einhorn and Hogarth proposed a complex and sophisticated model of causal judgement derived in part from the philosophical work of Hume (1739/1978) and Mackie (1965, 1974). According to Einhorn and Hogarth, causal processing is a matter of using various cues to causality and judgemental devices to arrive at some notion of the probable cause of an event. They gave an example:

> Imagine that a watch face has been hit by a hammer and the glass breaks. How likely was the force of the hammer the cause of the breakage? Because no explicit context is given, an implicitly neutral context is invoked in which the cues-to-causality point strongly to a causal relation; that is, the force of the hammer precedes the breakage in time, there is high covariation between the glass breaking (or not) with the force of solid objects, contiguity in time and space is high, and there is congruity (similarity) between the length and strength of cause and effect. Moreover, it is difficult to discount the causal link because there are few alternatives to consider.
>
> (Einhorn and Hogarth 1986: 4)

If this were a valid account, then satisfaction of the cues listed would be sufficient for causal inference. This is not the case, as can be seen with the example of two consecutive strides in a walk. How likely is it that the first stride was the cause of the second? Assume, as Einhorn and Hogarth did for their example, a neutral context because no extra information is given. In this case, as Einhorn and Hogarth (1986) put it, the cues-to-causality point strongly to a causal relation; that is, the first stride precedes the second in time, there is high co-variation between the occurrence of one stride and the occurrence of the next (moreover, it is possible to observe repeated conjunctions of strides); contiguity in time and space is high, and there is congruity (similarity) between the length and strength of cause and effect (that is, one stride looks very much like the other). In short, the two strides fit the criteria for ascription of a causal relation just as well as the hammer and breaking watch glass do, yet people do not ascribe a causal relation. Thus the cues listed are not sufficient as an account of causal inference.

Other events that satisfy regularity criteria are interpreted in other ways. Consider the saying, 'Red sky at night, shepherd's delight'. Here, a (supposed) regular association of a red sky at night with fine weather the following day is treated as indicative or diagnostic rather than causal. No matter how many regular observations were made of red skies at night followed by good weather the next day, no observer would say that the red sky at night was the cause of the subsequent good weather. It is merely taken as a sign of fine weather to come, not as a cause of it. Such interpretations are not uncommon. The sight of a flashing right indicator on a car is (usually) reliably followed by the car turning right, but no one would claim that the flashing indicator is a cause of the car turning right: it is merely taken as a sign that that is to come.

Many social phenomena exhibit regularity because they are fixed by a set of procedural rules. Regular associations of events of this kind, however, are not interpreted as causal sequences. Things happen in a fixed order in a church service, for example, and can be repeatedly observed to do so, but observers do not interpret this as event $A$ causing event $B$ and so on; instead, they understand the sequence as a ritual, as a social creation that is orderly because it is governed by a set of rules known to all the participants (cf. Harré and Secord 1972). Procedural rules produce regularity among many sorts of occurrence, from trains whose order of running is fixed by a timetable to meals, the order of courses in which is fixed by convention.

Indeed, often just referring to the regularity of things is sufficient for purposes of explanation: an expression like 'that's just the way things are' explains by identifying a natural order or pattern to reality, beyond which there is felt to be no need to go. This kind of reply is used perhaps most often to answer the 'Why?' questions of children, effectively to educate them about the way the world is. It is characteristic, however, of the medieval world view (Tillyard 1943; Lewis 1964), in which everything was seen as part of a static, orderly, all-embracing structure, and to explain was to identify the place of a thing in that structure. Under this view, regularity indicates the nature of the universal order, not causal relation.

To summarise, regularity is often interpreted as non-causal, whether as a sequence governed by an overriding cause, as relating sign or indicator to thing signified, as governed by procedural or other social rules, or as just part of the natural order of things. Philosophers and scientists recognise that some regularities are spurious and do not indicate causation. The point of the sufficiency criterion is that it makes it the job of a good regularity theory to distinguish those regularities that constitute causal relations from those that do not. Likewise, the point of the sufficiency criterion in psychology is that it makes it the job of a regularity-based account of causal inference to distinguish those regularities which people interpret as causal from those which they interpret in other ways. It is important to note that we are not just asking how people distinguish spurious correlations from those that indicate causation: we are asking how they choose between various kinds of causal and non-causal interpretations of regularity. In a sense, the conclusion one could draw from this section is that we do not yet have a regularity-based account that does this. This leaves open the possibility that one might be found in the future. It is hard to see how this could ever be achieved, though: we have seen that the sophisticated set of rules and cues proposed by Einhorn and Hogarth (1986) incorrectly identifies one stride in a walk as the cause of the next, and it is hard to imagine any regularity-based device that would not do the same (Einhorn and Hogarth found it necessary to complete their account with cues and devices not based on regularity). This is no problem for theory-based accounts of causal inference: the distinction between regularities interpreted as causal and those interpreted in other ways is established simply by the particular beliefs people hold. Thus, people believe that a flashing right indicator is a sign and not a cause of turning right because of the content-specific beliefs they possess about driving, not through the application of a sophisticated regularity-based device to their record of experiences. The problem is only to say how the beliefs originated, but this has more to do with socialisation than with regularity.

## THE ABNORMAL CONDITIONS FOCUS MODEL

So far I have concentrated on covariation information. This is only one type of regularity information, but similar problems arise for the use of any type of regularity information for causal inference. To illustrate, I consider a theory of causal processing based on conditional information, the abnormal conditions focus model (Hilton and Slugoski 1986). Part of the purpose of this is to prepare the ground for the causal powers theory of causal processing, the topic of the next chapter.

The basic propositions of the abnormal conditions focus model consist of two criteria for selecting the cause of some effect. The first criterion selects as causal candidates conditions that are necessary for the effect, given the scenario within which the effect occurred. This qualification is important, because many causes are not necessary conditions except in the context of a particular scenario. To use the example that Hilton and Slugoski (1986) used, a faulty rail is not a necessary condition for the derailment of a train, because derailments can occur in the absence of faulty rails, but it may be necessary given other features of the scenario on the occasion in question. This criterion is called the 'counterfactual criterion'.

The second criterion selects from the set of factors identified by the first criterion the condition (or combination of conditions) that is abnormal in the context of the given subject-matter. Hilton and Slugoski (1986) expanded the derailment example as follows: 'In explaining a train derailment, one can refer to any number of necessary conditions but for which the accident would not have occurred, such as the presence of a faulty rail, the weight of the wagons, and the speed at which the train was moving' (p. 76). The faulty rail is selected from these as the cause of the accident because it is the one feature from that set which is abnormal with regard to trains. Abnormality is judged by comparison with a contrast case, consisting in this example of occasions on which trains run normally without going off the rails. This criterion, called the contrastive criterion, was derived by Hilton and Slugoski (1986) from the legal philosophy of Hart and Honoré (1959), where it was put forward as a methodological principle for identifying causes. The contrastive criterion is empirical (and is in effect the identification of a sufficient condition from within the set of scenario-specific necessary conditions) and implies no evaluative judgement, although it does reflect the idea of Hilton and Slugoski (1986) that causal processing occurs in response to departures from some notion of what is usual.

I first discuss the counterfactual criterion. This is a purely empirical criterion, but the problem with it is that it cannot be used in a purely empirical manner. A necessary condition for some occurrence can be identified empirically (within the limits of provability) by seeing whether the effect ever occurs in the absence of some condition. But this test would exclude the faulty rail as a necessary condition for (and possibly the cause of) the derailment because it would be observed that derailments do occur in the absence of faulty rails.

This is why the counterfactual criterion must deal in scenario-specific necessity. But to identify conditions that are necessary given the rest of the scenario, one would have to look at a sufficient sample of other occasions that are identical to the scenario in question *except* for the absence of the condition under investigation. And it would be necessary to do this for every condition in the scenario. The reason for this is that scenarios in which things other than the condition under investigation are different are not the same scenario, and for that reason are not relevant to a test of scenario-specific necessity. In order to establish, for example, that the speed at which the train was moving was a necessary condition (given the scenario) but for which the derailment would not have occurred, we would have to look at other occasions identical to the one in question except for the fact that the train was moving at a different speed. This degree of control over reality is impossible to achieve: even in rigorous experimental designs many factors are randomised or ignored (such as time of day, weather, individuating characteristics of persons involved).

Yet people do have intuitions about necessity, and these intuitions act as guides to the selection of likely causal candidates. It is for exactly this reason that it is not usually thought necessary to control or randomise time of day or weather conditions outside the laboratory when running an experiment in psychology. If the train driver had eaten cornflakes for breakfast that morning, no one would worry about running an empirical test to assess whether this belonged in the set of scenario-specific necessary conditions. And if the driver had never eaten them before, it would be impossible to prove that they were not a scenario-specific necessary condition. One could argue, perhaps, that these intuitions about necessity come from use of the second criterion in the Hilton/Slugoski model, the contrastive criterion. But this criterion would fail to exclude the cornflakes because if we looked at occasions on which the train ran normally we would find that the eating of cornflakes was absent, because the driver had never eaten them before. (To be pedantic, it would not be difficult to imagine breakfasts that no other driver had ever eaten.) It was for exactly this reason that Hilton and Slugoski needed something in their model that would narrow down the field of causal candidates before the contrastive criterion was used.

Where, then, do these intuitions about necessity come from? The solution for which I would argue is that people discriminate between the faulty rail and the cornflakes as potential causes by means of their knowledge of the causal powers of those things. That is, people already know that a faulty rail has the causal power to derail a train, and that the driver's breakfast does not have that power, and they use this knowledge to identify the faulty rail as a likely cause. An anonymous reviewer of White (1989a) commented that people might indeed identify the cornflakes as the cause of the accident if the driver turned out to be allergic to them and drove badly as a result. This possibility actually reinforces my point: the cornflakes become a possible cause of the accident *not* when they are identified as an abnormal condition, which they are in this example regardless of whether the driver is allergic to them or not, but when the possibility is raised that they possess *a specific causal power that could have led to the accident.* With knowledge of this sort, no assessment of conditional relations need be made: indeed, under the present theory conditional statements would be based on causal ones, rather than vice versa. Before developing this argument, I turn to the contrastive criterion.

I have already argued that things that people would not normally consider as possible causes, such as the cornflakes in the derailment example, are often identified as causes by the contrastive criterion. It is also the case that things that *are* causes are sometimes ruled out by it. This happens when a causal mechanism has a realm of applicability that is limited in ways not known to the person using the criterion, and when a cause that would usually produce some effect is sometimes impeded from doing so by other factors. Suppose the effect to be explained is 'Paul likes a painting he sees in the Art Gallery' (from McArthur 1972), and that Paul likes this painting because of its beautiful colouring. If one takes contrast cases of paintings that Paul does not like, one may find that some of these also have colouring that he acknowledges as beautiful, but that he has other reasons for not liking them (for example, 'I don't like any Mannerist paintings'). By use of the contrastive criterion, this would lead to the rejection of the beautiful colouring as an explanation of Paul's liking for the painting, because beautiful colouring is observed to be present on occasions when the effect does not occur. Covariation models such as Kelley's (1967) run into the same problem because, in this example, beautiful colouring and liking do not covary, or at least do so only imperfectly.

One could argue that this sort of problem can be solved if one chooses the right contrast cases. For example, beautiful colouring would not be rejected as a possible cause if the contrast cases consisted specifically of non-Mannerist paintings that Paul does not like (and if there are no other factors that impede the operation of beautiful colouring as a cause). But how does one know that non-Mannerist paintings are the right ones to choose as contrast cases? Generally, how does one decide what contrast cases to choose? In the derailment example, Hilton and Slugoski (1986) chose 'trains', presumably meaning all trains, but in the painting example I chose Paul, rather than all people. This points up the lack of objective procedures for selecting contrast cases.

Under some circumstances selection of contrast cases is dictated by the type and amount of information available. For instance, when the information presented corresponds only to Kelley's (1967) three dimensions of covariation information, selection of contrast cases can only be made from that information, and Hilton and Slugoski (1986) analysed in detail how this would be done under their model. But under other circumstances selection of contrast cases appears arbitrary, and arbitrary choices mean running the risks of rejecting things that *are* causes and failing to reject things that are *not* causes.

Choices become less arbitrary with increasing knowledge. Knowing that Paul doesn't like any Mannerist paintings enables one to select only non-Mannerist paintings as contrast cases. The effect of such knowledge is to reduce the likelihood of rejecting an actual cause. But increasing knowledge does not help us to use the contrastive criterion to reject things that are not causes. In the derailment example, no further knowledge of what happens when trains run normally will help to reject the eating of cornflakes as a possible cause because, being a unique occurrence, it is invariably absent from occasions on which trains run normally. And every scenario has an indefinite number of unique features, none of which can be rejected by the use of contrast cases (such as exact time and date of occurrence, exact direction of driver's gaze, exact number of raindrops falling on the track, and so on). Some people might even argue that all events are unique, and it is only our tendency to categorise different events together that makes us think otherwise (Taylor 1966). Certainly, the idea of something as present on some occasions and absent from others depends on the validity of categorisation, unless it is actually the same thing each time.

It is not only unique occurrences that cannot be rejected by the contrastive criterion but also exact covariates that are not causes. Suppose that Paul always has his hands in his pockets when he likes a painting, and always has his hands out of his pockets when he does not like a painting, and that this is a reaction brought about independently of the bringing about of his liking or disliking. (We can also suppose that it is a quicker response than the liking response, so that an appropriate temporal order is established.) No use of either the abnormal conditions focus model or any covariation-based model could result in the rejection of the hand movement (or location) as a cause of Paul's liking. Empirical criteria for causal inference are perfectly satisfied.

Of course, if people inferred from this pattern of covariation that the hand movement was the cause of Paul's liking or disliking, then this would be strong evidence that they were using some covariation-type approach to causal inference, that they were prepared to consider *any* candidate that met empirical criteria, regardless of its nature as an event or condition. But my intuition that people would not do this, and that they would not seriously consider the hand movement as a cause of the liking, leads me to propose that people will only use covariation information, if at all, when an event or condition has passed some initial test of plausibility as a potential cause of the effect in question. I have already made the claim that this test of plausibility involves a judgement of whether the candidate has the causal power to produce the effect, not an assessment of covariation, but before developing this claim into a theory, I shall detail one final, important problem for regularity-based models.

## THE IMPORTANCE OF A CONCEPT OF THE CAUSAL RELATION

Perhaps the fundamental problem for regularity theories is that they fail to address the question of what it means to say that one thing is the cause of another. Criteria for causal inference such as the contrastive criterion and Kelley's (1967) covariation model are drawn from circumstances extrinsic to the cause: rather than identifying and analysing the actual nature of the causal connection, or rather the concept of the causal connection that exists in common sense, they make use of what may be termed 'symptomatic indicators of causation'. Moreover, since regularity information is neither necessary nor sufficient for causal inference, it follows that the definition of a causal relation must involve something more than reference to regularity (or regularity with its Humean accoutrements of contiguity and temporal priority). There must be a concept of the causal relation, otherwise there would be nothing that serves to distinguish causal relations from relations of any other kind. Such a concept, whatever it is, must be basic to our understanding of causation because it is common and exclusive to all those things identified by us as causal relations. No psychological theory, therefore, can afford to ignore it.

The approach taken in formulating the present theory is, to begin with, an analysis of the causal connection itself, as it is understood in common sense, and to develop an account of causal processing by building out from that. In the present theory, the causal connection as understood in common sense is a generative relation in which effects are produced by the operation of causal powers. To describe this theory is the task of the next chapter.

Since regularity, however defined, is neither necessary nor sufficient for causal inference or attribution, it cannot be basic to causal processing. This is not to say that regularity has nothing to do with causal processing at all. There is considerable evidence that people do, sometimes, interpret regularity as an indicator of causation (White 1988a; Hewstone 1989). Thus, in the next chapter, the exposition of the causal powers theory is supplemented with an account of the role and use of regularity information in causal inference under the causal powers theory.

# Chapter 6

# The causal powers theory of causal processing

Most theories and models of causal attribution and inference in psychology essentially concern a process or method of causal attribution. The classical causal attribution model, Kelley's (1967) multiple observation model, for instance, proposes a set procedure based on the application of the covariation principle to information organised along certain dimensions. All such models fail, however, for the simple reason that no one process is basic to causal processing.[1] Something is basic to causal processing if it is involved in all and only causal processing. Whatever is basic is the thing that makes a process a *causal* attribution or inference process, and not a process of any other kind. Since the evidence shows that there are many different kinds of process in causal processing – compare Michotte (1963) with Siegler and Liebert (1974), for example – no process qualifies as basic to causal processing. To be adequate as a theory, an account must begin by identifying what is basic to causal processing and build up from there. I argue that what is basic to causal processing is not a process but a concept of the causal relation, and I build up a theoretical account from that. I first describe the basic features of the theory and its conceptual foundation. I then outline a typology of causal questions and show how the methods or processes used to make a causal attribution depend on the type of question that has been asked.

The theory is based on a philosophical approach to causation, the theory of powerful particulars (Harré and Madden 1975; Madden and Humber 1974), and I shall begin with a brief sketch of that.

## THE THEORY OF POWERFUL PARTICULARS

The central concept in the philosophical theory proposed by Harré and Madden (1975) is the 'powerful particular'. This is a thing (such as a physical object or a person) with a certain type of property; namely, a power to produce certain sorts of effects. 'Causation always involves a material particular which produces or generates something' (Harré and Madden 1975: 5). Harré and Madden rejected the traditional association of power in philosophy with animism and anthropomorphism, and argued that the causal powers of things are based on the 'chemical, physical, or genetic natures of the entities involved' (p. 5).

Although a causal power is a stable, persisting property of a thing, it only produces an effect under appropriate conditions, termed 'releasing conditions'.[2] One of the examples used by Harré and Madden is the statement 'acid solution can turn logwood solution red'. According to Harré and Madden, this means that acid solution has the causal power to turn logwood solution red. This power, however, will only produce that effect when suitable conditions are met, for example when the two solutions are mixed together. Thus, words like 'igniting', 'exploding', 'bending', 'breaking', and 'crushing' 'are causal verbs expressing the powers that particulars have by virtue of their natures to make certain events occur under specific releasing conditions like scratching, alighting, falling, and submerging' (Madden and Humber 1974: 177). Every instance of causation involves both a causal power and a releasing condition. Releasing conditions include not only stimuli which activate a quiescent particular but also the absence or removal of a constraint, restriction, or interference. For example, the structure of a barn may be held up against the pull of gravity by a centre beam, so that if the centre beam is removed the operation of the power of gravity brings the structure down.

Harré and Madden (1975) also distinguished between *enabling conditions*, the satisfaction of which ensures that a thing or material is in a state of readiness, and *stimulus conditions* [releasing conditions] which bring about a response, on condition that a thing or material is in a state of readiness. Enabling conditions can be intrinsic or extrinsic. The satisfaction of intrinsic enabling conditions 'ensures that a thing or material is of the right nature and in the right state for the exercise of a certain power' (p. 88). For example,

> the presence of an engine is an intrinsic enabling condition for a car to have the power to move and must be included in the specification of what it *is* to be a car. The presence of a driver is an extrinsic condition. A car does not cease to be properly a car when the driver steps out. The actions performed by the driver to set the car in motion are extrinsic stimuli [releasing conditions].
>
> (Harré and Madden 1975: 88; italics in original)

Some of the dispositional properties of things are liabilities rather than powers. These differ from powers only in being capacities to undergo, rather than capacities to do. For example, in saying that copper is malleable, we are ascribing to it the liability to undergo certain sorts of change, such as changes of shape when hit with a hammer.

Under this theory, then, the causal connection is a generative relation in which the cause actually produces or generates an effect, and the generative mechanism is the operation of a causal power of some thing under a specific releasing condition. Harré and Madden (1975) argued that, under this account, causal relations can be directly perceived. The warrant for the perception of causation is on the same level as that for the perception of shape or motion. When we watch someone strike a match, for example, we perceive the causal connection between the striking of the match and its ignition, just as we perceive the shape of the match or its movement.

# THE CAUSAL POWERS THEORY OF CAUSAL PROCESSING

The present theory is based on the idea that the basic concept of causation in the psychological construction of reality resembles that just outlined.

In this theory a distinction is accepted between 'automatic' and 'controlled' processing. This distinction comes from the research of Shiffrin and Schneider (1977), and is characterised mainly in terms of attention (Anderson 1980). Controlled processing is by definition attentive processing, whereas automatic processing does not require attention. Controlled processing is therefore restricted by the limited capacity of working memory, whereas automatic processing does not require what Anderson (1980) referred to as 'subject control', and attempts at intervention in automatic processing may even have a deleterious effect. Controlled processing tends to be associated with activities or parts of activities that are not well learned. As learning proceeds, so the activity tends increasingly to be executed under automatic processing.

One contention in the present theory is that causal processing can be either automatic or controlled, and that much if not most causal processing is automatic. Although related in that they share the same basic concept of the causal connection, automatic and controlled processing operate under different circumstances and in different ways. I shall begin with automatic causal processing.

## Automatic causal processing

The account of automatic causal processing proposed here can best be presented by comparison with an alternative account of causal processing, that by Einhorn and Hogarth (1986).

Einhorn and Hogarth proposed a complex and sophisticated model of causal judgement derived in part from the philosophical work of Hume (1739/1978) and Mackie (1965, 1974). According to Einhorn and Hogarth, causal processing is a matter of using various cues to causality and judgemental devices to arrive at some notion of the probable cause of an event. Let me repeat the illustration I quoted in the last chapter:

> Imagine that a watch face has been hit by a hammer and the glass breaks. How likely was the force of the hammer the cause of the breakage? Because no explicit context is given, an implicitly neutral context is invoked in which the cues-to-causality point strongly to a causal relation; that is, the force of the hammer precedes the breakage in time, there is high covariation between the glass breaking (or not) with the force of solid objects, contiguity in time and space is high, and there is congruity (similarity) between the length and strength of cause and effect. Moreover, it is difficult to discount the causal link because there are few alternatives to consider.
>
> (Einhorn and Hogarth 1986: 4)

I have quoted this example at length to give an impression of the elaborate and deliberative approach to causal judgement that is a feature of the Einhorn and

Hogarth model. My interpretation invokes the notion of a generative relation representing the operation of a causal power of the hammer. Basically, someone who watches the hammer smash the watch glass perceives the causal connection. By this I mean not that they actually and accurately see an actual causal connection, but that causal processing in this case is part of the automatic processes of visual (and perhaps auditory) perception. It does not require attentive deliberation, and it is constructive, interpretive, or inferential to no greater or lesser extent than perception in general is. Such automatic causal processing depends on two things:

1   The basic concept of causation as involving generative mechanisms in which the causal powers of things produce certain effects under certain releasing conditions.
2   More specific beliefs about the causal powers, releasing conditions, liabilities, and effects that pertain on the occasion in question. People become familiar with or acquire beliefs about the causal powers of a large number of things and types of thing, and it is through this familiarity that causal processing of events involving those things becomes automatic. In the case under consideration, causal perception involves the use of beliefs about the causal powers of hammers (and the liabilities of watch glasses). These beliefs are not required to be correct, although of course they could scarcely be used in the processing of stimuli that unambiguously fail to conform to them.

These two types of knowledge are not the subject of attentive deliberation during automatic causal processing. Automatic causal processing occurs when and because beliefs of the sort described can be put to work in perception.

There are two ways of discriminating my account from that given by Einhorn and Hogarth (1986) for the watch-glass scenario. The first is that described in the previous chapter: the Einhorn and Hogarth account fails because event relations that satisfy all of their cues to causality are sometimes not processed causally, as in the example given of two strides in a walk. For the second, imagine that the hammer and watch-glass sequence is recorded on film, and that during playback the film is halted at the frame before the one in which the hammer contacts the watch-glass. Let us assume that, in the film, the hammer is depicted as descending with sufficient force to smash the glass and that, if the film had been allowed to continue, this is what observers would have seen. It seems uncontroversial to me that most people, if asked to say what was about to happen, would reply that the hammer was going to smash the watch glass. The point about this is that people are only able to make this kind of prediction on the basis of pre-existing beliefs about the things involved. They cannot be using empirical cues because, at this stage, the event predicted has not happened and, in consequence, there are no temporal contiguity, spatial contiguity, covariation, similarity, or any other such cues for them to observe. This argument implies that prediction is, sometimes at least, not a likelihood judgement at all (cf. Kahneman *et al.* 1982) but a causal judgement projected into the future; that is, the use of causal beliefs to judge what is going to happen next.

The theory of powerful particulars is a theory about the actual nature of causal relations and includes the claim that actual causal relations can (at least sometimes) be directly perceived. The present theory is about the nature of causal processing by people, the notion of the causal relation in the psychological construction of reality, and does not include the claim that actual causal relations can be directly perceived. Instead, automatic causal processing utilises existing beliefs about causal powers in perception of causal connections. Causal processing will be accurate when those beliefs are accurate, and inaccurate when those beliefs are inaccurate. Causal processing is also more likely to be inaccurate when quality and/or quantity of available relevant information is inadequate. People may also fail to perceive actual causal relations, despite perceiving the things and events involved, if they hold no beliefs about the causal powers of the things involved.

Because no claim is made about direct perception of causation, it is necessary to explain how, under the present theory, people come to understand causation in terms of generative relations and the causal powers of things. This explanation will be given in the account of developmental origins later on (see also White 1988a).

Although I have not mentioned causal relations involving human beings in this section, much human behaviour is also subject to automatic causal processing. Suppose I watch a film in which there is a fist-fight, and I see one actor apparently punch another on the chin, whereupon the latter stumbles backwards. I would claim that automatic causal processing goes on here, in which I see the effect as produced by the causal power of the assailant (or the punch) under the releasing condition of contact with the recipient's chin. My knowledge that the fight was in fact a carefully staged stunt need not prevent this automatic causal processing from occurring.

An important feature of this account is that those things that are identified as causes in automatic causal processing are normal, usual, familiar, or expected occurrences. Abnormal, unusual, unfamiliar, and unexpected occurrences cannot be processed automatically. This means that the abnormal conditions focus model (Hilton and Slugoski 1986) cannot be applied to automatic causal processing, nor can any other theory in which what is identified as a cause is always some sort of departure from what is usual or expected. This does not merely limit the scope of the model: if people basically understood causation in terms of abnormal conditions, then this understanding should apply to and delimit all causal processing. The occurrence of causal processing to which the model cannot be applied means that the abnormal conditions idea cannot be the basic concept of causation. At best, it is part of what may go on in controlled causal processing.

## Controlled causal processing

Returning to the watch-glass example, Einhorn and Hogarth (1986) posed what seems like a problem for the automatic causal processing idea: 'Now imagine that the same event occurred during a testing procedure in a watch factory. In this context, the cause of the breakage is more often judged to be a defect in the glass' (p. 4). The problem is that an event that would ordinarily be automatically causally processed as representing the operation of the hammer's causal power is, in this case, interpreted differently. The example may not be well chosen, in that the point of a testing procedure such as they describe is to identify defects in watch glasses. In this case, the smashing of the watch glass would by definition indicate a defect in the watch glass: it would be a criterial indicator of defects.

But the problem does not depend on the example. Automatic causal processing, almost by definition, deals with events that are familiar, normal, or expected. Einhorn and Hogarth (1986) argued that causal reasoning occurs in response to events that are abnormal, unusual, or unexpected (p. 5). This is different, of course, from arguing that causal reasoning identifies as a cause something that is abnormal, unusual, or unexpected. I would argue that causal reasoning of this kind falls under the heading of controlled causal processing. One problem for views of the sort advocated by Einhorn and Hogarth (1986) is how to define, and how to identify in practice, 'abnormal', 'unusual', and 'unfamiliar' events (Gorovitz 1965). I would propose a psychological solution to this problem of definition: that controlled causal processing occurs only for events that are not or cannot be automatically causally processed (note that I do not say 'all and only'). This includes what we ordinarily think of as violations of expectations, abnormal, unusual, or unfamiliar events, because these are types of events that cannot be automatically processed. That is, what determines whether an event is a candidate for controlled causal processing is not whether it is a violation of expectations (and so on) but whether or not it can be automatically causally processed by some person who observes it.

In automatic causal processing the concepts of causal power and releasing condition are implicit, underlying, but not attended. In controlled causal processing at least one of these is the subject of attentive processing. By this I do not mean that people think, so to speak, this is the causal power and that is the releasing condition. Rather, in controlled causal processing, some thing or event (or combination of things and/or events) is identified as the cause of some event, and the thing identified as the cause may be either a causal power or a releasing condition (or both or, as in the watch-glass example, but probably more rarely, a liability). Whatever is not explicitly identified may remain implicit, which means that there can be elements of automatic causal processing even on occasions when controlled causal processing occurs. What people report as the cause is the whole or part of whatever is identified in controlled, not automatic, causal processing, simply because it is that to which attention is given.

For example, if the interaction between acid and logwood solution were subject to controlled causal processing, then either the causal power of the acid, the act of mixing them together, or the liability of the logwood solution, or all of these, could be identified as the cause. Whatever is so identified will not be anything in the interaction that is automatically causally processed. How the cause is selected from what is not automatically causally processed will be described below. Controlled causal processing does not occur on every occasion when automatic causal processing does not. I propose two rules that delimit or determine the occurrence of controlled causal processing within the set of things not subject to automatic causal processing. My general hypothesis, then, is that controlled causal processing involves the identification of causal candidates that (1) are either causal powers or releasing conditions or liabilities or some combination of these, *and* (2) meet the two rules to be outlined next.

First, controlled causal processing occurs when it is in the interest of some practical concern for it to do so, and such processing is directed by the aim of generating something that best contributes to that practical concern, whatever that concern may be. The practical concern (or concerns) acts in effect through the posing of an implicit or explicit causal question, and the process of causal attribution is constrained by the practical requirement to provide something that counts as an answer to the question posed. It is this that governs the selection of one or more elements from the full potential causal account of some effect. I shall consider the types of causal question later in this chapter.

Secondly, applicability of an existing causal belief: every belief about a causal power is a belief about the sort of effect that can be produced by operation of that causal power. This means that every effect delimits a range of causal powers believed by the attributer to be capable of producing an effect of that kind. One or more of these relevant beliefs is then treated as a causal hypothesis or candidate, and the search for information is directed by the aim of testing the hypothesis or the applicability of the candidate. For example, if the effect to be explained is a child's stomach ache, and the attributer has the belief that too much ice cream has the causal power to produce stomach ache, then the attributer will seek to discover whether in fact the child has eaten too much ice cream, this being the condition necessary to render the belief applicable to the instance.

Strictly speaking, things are not quite as simple as this. Logically, an occurrence of an effect only implies a causal power to produce that effect on that occasion, but the range of causal candidates that can be considered is broader than this in several ways. First, people tend to assume that causal powers are stable properties of things (probably by a kind of default assumption that something continues to have the properties it has at some moment unless and until there is good reason to think otherwise). Secondly, beliefs about causal powers may be organised at different levels of categorisation. For example, the causal power to pass exams may be seen as comprised of other, more specific causal powers such as the power to concentrate, the power to recall relevant information, the power to write good English, and so on. Thirdly, beliefs about causal powers may be organised in relation to beliefs about other characteristics of things. Someone may be seen as having a certain causal power by virtue of their possession of some other property; and different causal powers may be related in that they are all seen as being possessed by virtue of the same property.

Existing causal beliefs are also necessarily involved in automatic causal processing, but the point here is that the apparent freedom given to controlled causal processing by the practical concerns criterion is limited by dependence on existing causal beliefs. The only things that a person can identify as causes are things that that person already believes can be causes of the effect in question – either things believed to possess the causal power to produce the effect or releasing conditions appropriate to the operation of some causal power to produce the effect, or liabilities to be affected in that way (except when the person is directly taught a new belief). In addition, the only such beliefs that are candidates on any given occasion are those the applicability of which is not precluded by the available information.

Suppose I am trying to explain why Paul likes a painting he sees in the art gallery. One possible explanation might be that Paul has long been interested in Expressionist art, and this is a famous German Expressionist painting. What determines whether this is generated in controlled causal processing (or accepted by someone to whom it is given) is whether it is one among a set of possibilities already held in memory by the person generating (or receiving) the explanation. The explanation would not be generated, for example, if the attributer had never heard of Expressionism, because this would imply that they had no belief that Expressionism could be causally involved in liking for a painting. In addition, the explanation would not be generated (or accepted) if the attributer (or recipient) believed that this was not an Expressionist painting – in other words, if the available information implied that the belief was not applicable. This criterion limits the attributer's ability to satisfy the practical concerns in respect of which controlled causal processing is occurring. It acts like a reality principle in that it prevents the attributer from generating explanations that optimally satisfy practical concerns but are obviously at variance with what is known to be the case. Explanations that are obviously at variance with the facts will only be generated and accepted when the practical gains of doing so outweigh the potential costs (for example, looking stupid or foolish) of giving such an explanation.

This criterion reveals a further fundamental difference between the types of explanation that are generated or considered proper in science and in common sense. In science things are often explained by reference to some *novel* (that is, newly thought-of) mechanism, model, theory, or other explanatory device. In ordinary life, one explains things by reference to something that is *familiar*, normal, or well-known in other contexts. Reference to something novel, meaning something not held as a causal belief by someone to whom it was given, would not be considered adequate, at least not without additional justification or explanation.

To summarise controlled causal processing:

First, the *when* of controlled causal processing. Controlled causal processing occurs only for events that cannot be or for some reason are not automatically causally processed, and when the current practical concerns of the individual are such that the individual judges that controlled causal processing will contribute to them in some appropriate way.

Secondly, an outcome of controlled causal processing that is adequate for the person who generates it has the following characteristics:

1  It is founded on the general concept of a causal connection as a generative relation representing the operation of a causal power of some thing.
2  It involves the identification of a specific causal power or releasing condition or liability (or some combination of these) as the cause of the effect in question.
3  It is directed by and fulfils the aim of contributing to the practical concerns in respect of which controlled causal processing is occurring, specifically by answering the particular causal question posed in respect of those practical concerns.
4  Whatever is identified as the cause will be something already believed by the individual to be a possible cause of the effect in question, and not precluded by the information available to the individual (whether or not such information is correct).

These are the general conditions of controlled causal processing. As I have already said, every causal inference or attribution can be viewed as an answer to an implicit or explicit question, and the job of the process or method of causal attribution used is to provide something that counts as an answer to the question set. This is an invariable rule because the question set is determined by practical concerns, and it is only something that counts as an answer to the question that has the potential of optimally satisfying those practical concerns. The next step, then, is to develop a typology of causal questions. I show that this typology provides a means of defining the range of application of hypothetical processes and models of causal attribution, thus identifying those that are competitors for the same ground. The typology therefore constitutes an organising framework for the plethora of findings in the causal attribution literature.

## TYPOLOGY OF CAUSAL QUESTIONS

Making a causal attribution can be regarded as generating an answer to an implicit or explicit question. Questions can be of different types. For example, asking 'Why did John laugh at the comedian?' and 'Why do people watch football?' are arguably of different types, in that one refers to a single occasion and the other to multiple occurrences of a phenomenon. The type of question asked makes a difference both to the kind of information that is relevant to answering it and to the kind of thing that can be an answer to it. For example, information about occasions on which neither John nor the comedian was present is unlikely to be regarded as useful to answering 'Why did John laugh at the comedian?' A statement such as 'because Bill likes football' does not answer the question 'Why do people watch football?', because it fails to address the 'people' referred to in the question. This suggests two simple but powerful hypotheses about how people make causal attributions:

1  When people seek more information in order to make a causal attribution, the information they *prefer* is information about the occasion or occasions implicit or explicit in the causal question posed.

2  The basic requirement for causal attribution is identifying something that answers the causal question posed.

The power in these hypotheses depends on knowing what type of causal question is being addressed, and this in turn requires a valid taxonomy of causal questions. Construction of a valid taxonomy or typology is not entirely straight-forward. Typological distinctions that are of importance to philosophers may play no part in lay causal attribution, and while the psychological literature may be a more relevant source of typological distinctions, the importance of these distinctions depends on the validity of the research in which they can be found, and the possibility remains that psychologists have yet to study some aspects of causal attribution that are nevertheless of fundamental importance. It is therefore unavoidable that any typology proposed at present be regarded as provisional and subject to modification in the light of future research. This potential drawback is outweighed, however, by the benefits in terms of the organisation of causal attribution theories that can result from having a typology of causal questions.

I have used the philosophical literature (see White 1990) as a source of principles for the construction of a typology. The principles drawn from this survey are probably not the only ones that may be valid, but they serve adequately for present purposes. Names are provided for the major types identified.

1. Asking a causal question implies that the questioner does not know something about the causal relation in question, and, where the question concerns a single event, this may be any of the three elements of the causal relation: the cause, the effect, and the relation between them. This gives a differentiation between cases where the effect is known and the cause not, cases where the cause is known and the effect not, and cases where two events are both known but the relation between them is not, yielding three types of question:

'What caused this effect?' or 'Why did this happen?' (Single occasion single effect question)
'What effect did this have?' (Single occasion cause question)
'Did this cause that?' (Single occasion connection question)

2. Cases involving single explananda versus cases involving multiple explananda of the same type (that is, multiple occasions) versus cases involving multiple explananda of different types, either on one occasion or more than one. This is a differentiation between four basic types of question:

'What caused this single effect?' (Single occasion single effect question, as above)
'What causes these similar effects?' or 'What causes all effects of this type?' (That is, the former could be a specified subset of the latter.) (Multiple occasion occurrence question)
'What caused all of these things on this occasion?' (Single occasion multiple effect question)

'What caused all these things across these occasions/all occasions/this parti-cular time-span?' (Other ways of delimiting the set may also be possible – for example, 'What caused World War II?') (Multiple occasion various effects question)

3. Within single explananda, comparison versus no comparison. Several types of comparison are possible, but the point of the comparison in each case is the giving of attention to a difference between the event in question and the thing(s) with which it is compared. This being so, any comparison with some definite other thing, whether it be one event or many or just an expectation or prediction, is fundamentally similar in that the causal question concerns the difference observed between the event in question and the comparison. But a comparison can also be made with a record of past events or a state of belief in which things are not clear or definite: for example, either of two outcomes may have seemed equally likely in advance (for example, 'Smith and Jones are equally likely to win the match'), so that when one of the two is realised there may be a need to explain, in effect, what tipped the balance that way. So there are two main types of comparison question.

'Why did this happen?' (Exemplifying questions not involving comparison)
'Why did this happen now when then (one or more other occasions) it did not?' or 'Why did this happen now when that was expected?' (Comparison question)
'Why did $X$ happen when $X$ and $Y$ (etc.) both (all) seemed equally likely beforehand?' (Selection question)

4. Occurrence versus non-occurrence. There are problems of definition with occurrences and non-occurrences. For example, the dog not barking in the night could be called a non-occurrence, but if barking was expected then it could also be construed as the occurrence of a violation of expectations or, more simply, an occurrence of failing to bark. Also, failure could be called an occurrence of failure or a non-occurrence of success. Thus, occurrence and non-occurrence must be defined with respect to a particular event. For some particular event $X$, then, two questions can be set:

'Why did $X$ happen?' (Single occasion single effect question, as above)
'Why did $X$ not happen?' (Single occasion non-occurrence question). If the question implies an expectation that $X$ would happen, then this counts as an example of the comparison question given above.

5. Events versus states of affairs. Questions about states of affairs are probably always questions about how some state of affairs came about or, where what appears to be a state of affairs is actually a process of continual maintenance, what is continually maintaining it. Thus, 'Why does this book have a yellow cover?' is a question about the origination of that state rather than the state itself, and 'Why is the sky blue?' is a question about the active maintenance of a state

of affairs, though the questioner is not required to realise that this is so. The two basic questions for this distinction, then, are:

'Why did this event happen?' (Single occasion single effect question, as above)
'What brought this state about?' *or* 'What maintains this state?' (Single occasion state question).

6. Identification versus discrimination. The distinction here is between cases in which the cause is not known and is being sought, and cases in which more than one possible cause is known to have been present and some kind of selection between the candidates is to be made. This distinction varies in nature according to whether one is explaining a single event or multiple events, because in the case of multiple events some candidate may cause some and not others, so that questions can be asked about what proportion of events in the set, and/or which particular ones, were caused by that candidate and not by others. So:

'What caused $X$?' (Single occasion single effect question, as above)
'Was $X$ caused by $A$ or $B$ (etc.)?' (Single occasion cause discrimination question)
'What proportion of occurrences of $X$ is/was caused by $A$?' *or* 'Which particular occurrences of $X$ from this set were caused by $A$?' (Multiple occasion effect discrimination question)

7. Within multiple occurrences, occurrences only versus non-occurrences only versus both occurrences and non-occurrences.

'How can all (or a given set of) occurrences of $X$ be explained?' (Multiple occasion occurrence question, as above)
'How can all (or a given set of) non-occurrences of $X$ be explained?' (Multiple occasion non-occurrence question) (If this is by comparison with or against a background of one or more occurrences of $X$, then this becomes one of the comparison questions (under no. 3 above))
'How can all (or a given set of) occasions on which $X$ might happen, and whether it did or not, be explained?' (Multiple occasion occurrence and non-occurrence question)

8. Active intervention versus passive obtaining of information. Active intervention reflects the usual place of causal attribution in the current practical concerns of the attributer (White 1984, 1989a). For example, a series of poor performances in a sporting activity may create a practical concern that must be met by direct intervention of some kind. Causal attribution need not be the primary aim, but may have a role to play in dealing with the practical concern. For example, the attributer may try a change of equipment, effectively on the causal hypothesis that equipment may be having an adverse effect on performance. If change in performance (of the desired sort) is observed then causal attribution may be made to the intervention. If no change is observed, then something else may be tried. So:

'If possible cause $A$ is changed (or substituted with $B$ or prevented or introduced), what difference does this make to $X$?' (Intervention question)

This list could be extended, further subdivided, and supplemented by questions of related kinds. One possible extension concerns questions about the action of some cause to prevent the occurrence of some effect, although this could arguably be treated as a subdivision of questions about non-occurrences. Another concerns questions about causal chains and networks, asking, for example, about relations between different causes in the chain (Brickman *et al.* 1975; Kelley 1983). Many subdivisions are possible. For example, questions involving comparisons can be subdivided according to type of comparison: for example, 'Why did $X$ happen at that moment (and no other)?', versus 'Why did $X$ happen to that person (and no other)?', and so on. Questions emphasising different parties to or aspects of an occurrence may also represent possible subdivisions: for instance, borrowing from Ross (1977), 'Why did *John* buy that house?', implying a request for comparison between John and other possible buyers, versus 'Why did John buy *that* house?', implying a request for comparison between the house bought and other houses. Questions of related kinds include questions about conditional relations such as 'On what does the occurrence of $X$ depend?', which is a question about necessary conditions (begging the question of whether people regard causes as necessary conditions, or necessary conditions as causes). In addition, further types can be created by concatenating the types given. For example, concatenating distinctions under the first and second types gives 'What is the whole range of effects of this cause?', or 'What are all the effects that this (type of) cause has?' Concatenating distinctions under the first and sixth types gives 'Did $X$ cause $A$ or $B$?', and so on.

All of the questions given above (apart from those in the previous paragraph) are listed in Table 6.1.

## METHODS AND PROCESSES OF CAUSAL INFERENCE

The types of question differ in both the type of information that is relevant to them and the type of thing that counts as an answer. Compare single occasion single effect questions and comparison questions, for example. A single occasion single effect question could be answered by gathering information about that single occasion and no other, if that information permits identification of a cause by reference to some pre-existing belief (such as a causal schema – Kelley (1972b) – or a causal power). But a comparison question requires the provision of information about the comparison occasions explicit or implicit in the question. As for an answer, the most obvious difference is that the answer to a comparison question may often be a subset of the answer to a single occasion single effect question. For example, if I ask 'Why did the car crash?' and decide that it crashed because the driver was going too fast on an icy road in a car with defective brakes, this is quite compatible with answering a comparison question, 'Why did it crash this time when it has never crashed before?' by referring only

*Table 6.1*  Types of causal questions

A  *Single occasion single effect question.* What caused this (single) effect *or* Why did *X* happen?
B  *Single occasion cause question.* What effect did this have?
C  *Single occasion connection question.* Did this cause that?
D  *Multiple occasion occurrence question.* What causes these similar effects *or* What causes all effects of this type *or* How can all (or a given set of) occurrences of *X* be causally explained?
E  *Single occasion multiple effect question.* What caused all of these things on this occasion?
F  *Multiple occasion various effects question.* What caused all these things across these occasions/ all occasions/ this particular time-span?
G  *Comparison question.* Why did this happen now when then (one or more other occasions) it did not *or* Why did this happen now when that was expected?
H  *Selection question.* Why did *X* happen when *X* and *Y* (etc.) both (all) seemed equally likely beforehand?
I  *Single occasion non-occurrence question.* Why did *X* not happen?
J  *Single occasion state question.* What brought about this state *or* What maintains this state?
K  *Single occasion cause discrimination question.* Was *X* caused by *A* or *B* (etc.)?
L  *Multiple occasion effect discrimination question.* What proportion of occurrences of *X* is/was caused by *A* *or* which occurrences of *X* from this set were caused by *A*?
M  *Multiple occasion non-occurrence question.* How can all (or a given set of) non-occurrences of *X* be explained?
N  *Multiple occasion occurrence and non-occurrence question.* For all (or a given set of) occasions on which *X* might happen, how can its occurrences and non-occurrences across these occasions be causally explained?
O  *Intervention question.* If possible cause *A* is changed (or substituted with *B* or prevented or introduced), what difference does this make to *X*?

to the fact that the brakes had been all right in the past but failed on this occasion. This answer is a selection from the whole causal interpretation of the incident.

Generally, then, people seek information about the occasion or occasions implicit or explicit in the question asked, and the information they seek is that which will allow them to answer the question asked. Essentially, people seek information as a way of making selections from within the range of causal beliefs judged relevant to the effect. The search for something that fits an existing belief is, in effect, a hypothesis-testing procedure.

There is evidence that people do proceed by testing hypotheses (Lalljee *et al.* 1984), but it should be noted that this is not an invariable practice under the present theory. People will not test hypotheses if (1) information available at the time the causal question is posed enables a causal belief to be applied as an answer to the question without further search for information, or (2) cues to causation such as temporal contiguity enable a possible cause to be identified before it is retrieved from memory as a candidate.

In the following sections I deal with multiple occasion and single occasion questions separately, including an extended treatment of the use of regularity information in answering single occasion questions.

## Multiple occasion questions

For multiple occasion questions, as for all causal questions, people should prefer to obtain more information about the occasions implicit or explicit in the question. This includes, of course, sampling from memory as well as from the environment. In the case of comparison questions where the comparison is an expectation, this information should include information about the nature and/or basis of the expectation in question. If people cannot obtain information of the preferred type, then they will proceed with information of whatever less preferred type they can obtain: failure to obtain the ideal type of information need not prevent causal attribution from taking place, although in some cases it may.

The main requirement for causal attribution is identifying something that answers the question posed. This means that there are question-specific constraints on both the thing that will be identified in the answer and the method, process, and so on, used to provide it. For example, identifying a factor common to all occasions implicit or explicit in the question may count as an answer to a multiple occasion occurrence question, but not to a comparison question, because it does not account for the difference between the occasion on which the effect occurred and the other occasions on which it did not. These constraints are most apparent in the case of questions involving reference to more than one occasion.

For multiple occasion occurrence questions, there is a constraint to identify something common to the occurrences of the effect in the question, because identifying something which can account for some of the occurrences and not others does answer the question. For preference, then, the thing identified in the answer is a thing present on all the occasions in question. The question makes no reference to non-occurrences, so there is no constraint concerning the presence or absence of the thing identified on occasions when the effect in question does not occur (nor, indeed, on occasions of occurrence not included in the question, if there are any).

Multiple occasion various effects questions pose special problems in that it is permissible to answer them by identifying more than one independent cause (or set of causes). There is a requirement for each cause to be present on each of the occasions of the effect which it is adduced to explain, so it effectively reduces to one or more multiple occasion effect questions. Answers to these may, of course, be organised into a causal structure of some kind; for example, a branching tree of causal relations stemming from a single occurrence which could be said to be the cause, or at least the initiator, of the whole tree.

Comparison questions address a comparison between one occasion when an effect occurred and others when it did not. Under hypothesis 2 (p. 80), this imposes a constraint to provide something that deals with the comparison and, to meet this demand, the thing identified is virtually compelled to be something present on the occasion in question but absent from all of the comparison occasions. That is, it must be a differentiating factor, a factor that makes the difference. Under this type, the comparison can be an expectation rather than a set of other occasions, but the constraint imposed is essentially the same.

Multiple occasion occurrence and non-occurrence questions impose a constraint to identify something that accounts for both the occurrences and the non-occurrences, and this is virtually compelled to be something that is present when the effect occurs and absent when it does not occur. Clearly, something that is present on both occurrences and non-occurrences of the effect does not account for the difference between them and therefore does not count as an answer to the question.

Multiple occasion non-occurrence questions are essentially similar to multiple occasion occurrence questions in requiring an answer that identifies something common to all the occasions in question; if, however, the question implies comparison with one or more occasions on which the effect in question occurred, then it becomes essentially similar to a comparison question or a multiple occasion occurrence and non-occurrence question, depending on the nature of the comparison in the question.

Multiple occasion effect discrimination questions are different in that they imply that there may be more than one possible cause of the effect in question, and the answer to the question is a proportion or weight or a list which represents the discrimination of one particular possible cause from all others. This requires information about presence and absence of the chosen cause, occurrence and non-occurrence of the effect, and (where this varies) presence and absence of the set of other possible causes of the effect. The third of these is required because, in the case of multiple possible causes, covariation between one possible cause and the effect is a very imperfect guide to causation. Joint presence of cause and effect entitles causal inference if no other possible causes were present on that occasion but not otherwise: if the attributer is to address the problem of discrimination posed in the question, therefore, something more than assessment of covariation is required.

Intervention questions virtually necessitate the use of some sort of differentiating factor analysis, as for comparison questions, because the question implies a comparison between occasions before and after some intervention. But for comparison questions the effect is given and the cause is to be ascertained, whereas for intervention questions the cause is given as the intervention, and it is the effect which is to be ascertained. Thus, the answer to the question should consist of differences identified in effects between occasion(s) following the intervention and occasions prior to it. A more sophisticated intervention question would pose it as a problem in discrimination, since not all changes in the effect following the intervention may be due to the intervention.

The simplest prediction that follows from this is that people should use regularity information in different ways under different circumstances. There is research evidence to support this, as the following examples show.

1   Some studies have found that, when making a causal attribution, people employ evidence about contrast cases; that is to say, cases similar or comparable to the one in question but in which the effect in question did *not* occur (Hilton and Slugoski 1986; McGill 1989). McGill (1989) found that causal attributions varied according to choice of background information in a way consistent with the hypothesis that people were seeking as their explanation some difference between the case in question and the cases in the chosen background.

2   Other studies have found that information about other *occurrences* of the effect in question is given most weight in causal attribution. Schustack and Sternberg (1981) found that information about joint presence of hypothesised cause and effect was given much greater weight than information about non-occurrences of the effect.

3   Other studies have found that covariation between the candidate cause and the effect to be explained is used as a cue to causal inference, though in some cases this may be via inferences about necessary and/or sufficient conditions (Hewstone and Jaspars 1987; McArthur 1972; Mendelson and Shultz 1976; Orvis *et al.* 1975; Shaklee and Mims 1981; Shultz and Mendelson 1975; Siegler 1975; Siegler and Liebert 1974). This evidence, if valid, implies use of information about both occurrences and non-occurrences of the effect, though not necessarily equally weighted.

These different, almost contradictory, tendencies can be interpreted as representing attempts to deal with different types of causal question. People use joint presence information to identify a common factor when they are dealing with a multiple occasion occurrence question. They use contrast cases to identify differentiating factors when they are addressing a comparison question. They use covariation information to identify a covariate or conditional relation when they are dealing with a multiple occasion occurrence and non-occurrence question. This can be seen if we look more closely at some of the studies cited.

In the studies by Schustack and Sternberg (1981), the causal question posed was: 'use the evidence in each problem to determine the likelihood that a particular one of the possible causes, in isolation, leads to the outcome' (p. 106). Subjects addressed this question in respect of a particular causal hypothesis that was specified for them. In experiment 3 this was changed to a predictive judgement, but in other respects the problem was the same. The 'outcome' was not, or not necessarily, a single occurrence but something that might be depicted as happening more than once in the stimulus materials. This, therefore, is a multiple occasion occurrence question. It is not a multiple occasion effect discrimination question because subjects were constrained by the instructions to treat the causal candidate as applying to either all occurrences of the outcome or none. The observed preference for joint presence information (which is consistent with the use of Mill's method of agreement) is a simple consequence of the type of question asked.

By contrast, McGill (1989) set out her studies so that people would treat the causal question, which was usually presented in an ambiguous form, as a comparison question. For example, in her experiment 2 the question was a request to indicate what subjects believed probably caused Bill to yell at the waiter on a single occasion, and she manipulated background information to make a certain kind of comparison appropriate. Some subjects were given information emphasising a comparison between Bill and others, encouraging a reinterpretation of the question as referring to Bill in particular, and others were given information emphasising a comparison between the waiter and other waiters, encouraging a reinterpretation of the question as referring to the waiter in particular. This was associated with predicted differences in the answer given to the causal question. In her experiment 1 the comparison question was virtually explicit: she compared 'Why did you (your best friend) in particular choose this major?' with 'Why did you (your best friend) choose this major in particular?' (p. 192), phrasing which encourages subjects to make a certain kind of comparison.

It follows that theories that postulate the use of a certain kind of regularity information for causal attribution are theories about how people address a certain type of causal question. The ANOVA model (Kelley 1967) is effectively a hypothesis about how people answer multiple occasion occurrence and non-occurrence questions. The abnormal conditions focus model (Hilton and Slugoski 1986) is effectively a hypothesis about how people answer comparison questions. In principle, models, hypotheses, and theories that address different types of question do not compete with one another because they have non-overlapping ranges of application, as defined by the type of causal question they address. In practice, they can still compete with one another under certain circumstances:

1   In cases where the causal question being addressed is ambiguous or unknown (that is, known perhaps to the subject but not to the experimenter). In experiments where the type of causal question asked is not clear, different subjects may elect to answer different types of question, within whatever range of types is permitted by the degree of ambiguity in the instructions. Such ambiguities therefore do not help the testing of hypotheses.

2   In cases where the information available to subjects is limited. This is because the type of question asked determines information *preferences*: where information of a preferred kind is not available, subjects must make use of whatever less preferred information is available. An example is the study by McArthur (1972) in which the causal questions asked were single occasion single effect questions (for example, 'Why did John laugh at the comedian?'). According to the foregoing argument, people prefer more information about the single occasion in question to answer this type of question, but information of that kind was not available to McArthur's subjects. The type of information presented (summary statements of consensus, distinctiveness, and consistency information) allowed several less preferred strategies to be used. This being

so, models and hypotheses with non-overlapping ranges of application (for example, the ANOVA model and the abnormal conditions focus model) can compete against each other *under these circumstances*, as accounts of how McArthur's subjects behaved, and as alternative less preferred strategies for dealing with the problem.

The competition in these cases, however, is a matter of applicability, not validity. Where people cannot tackle a single occasion single effect question with a method suitable for tackling a question of that type, they are forced in effect to recast it as a question of a different type. The issue then is whether they choose to recast it as a comparison question, in which case the abnormal conditions focus model is one possible account of how they answer it, or as a multiple occasion occurrence and non-occurrence question (from which the answer to a single occasion single effect question could plausibly be derived), in which case the ANOVA model is one possible account of how they answer that. Thus, if the evidence from studies like McArthur's favours, for example, the ANOVA model over the abnormal conditions focus model, this is only evidence that subjects chose to recast the causal question as a multiple occasion occurrence and non-occurrence question rather than a comparison question. Such a finding could not be assumed to generalise to attempts to answer other types of question, nor to circumstances under which other types of information were available, nor indeed to other single occasion single effect questions where information of the pre-ferred type for answering questions of that type *is* available.

It was hypothesised above that the basic requirement for causal attribution is identifying something that answers the causal question posed. This requirement reduces the number of possible causes somewhat, but not sufficiently for a specific causal attribution to be made. For example, by use of Kelley's ANOVA model it is possible to rule out, say, the target and the circumstances as causes of the effect, and to say that the effect was due to something about the actor. The problem is that there remain a very large number of stable properties of the actor that could have been responsible for the effect, and because all stable properties of the actor covary equally with the effect covariation cues cannot be used to discriminate between them. This is a limitation inherent to all regularity-based inferential devices, and there are only two ways of dealing with it.

One way is to accept the limitations of the model and adopt a relatively coarse-grained analysis. This was Kelley's strategy: the ANOVA model is limi-ted to the consideration of three causal candidates – actor, target, and circum-stances – and is not concerned with selection within any of these three. The drawback to this is that it does not appear to represent actual practice: almost all causal attributions made in social reality are more specific than regularity-based models alone allow. People don't say that John laughed at the comedian because of something about John: they say he laughed because he has an easily tickled sense of humour (or something of equivalent specificity). The drawback is not limited to Kelley's model but holds for all possible regularity-based models. I showed in the previous chapter that the same problem handicaps the abnormal conditions focus model (Hilton and Slugoski 1986).

The alternative is to find a way of making selections that does not depend upon empirical cues – that is, to use preconceived beliefs. This is the way preferred under the causal powers theory. In principle, the attributer is only concerned with those things that are believed to possess the causal power in question and, having identified one, attributes the effect not just generally to that thing, but specifically to the causal power of that thing (or the property by virtue of which the thing has that causal power).

It should be clear that part of the importance of a taxonomy of causal questions is its use in defining precisely the range of application of a given model or hypothesis of causal attribution; also that such models and hypotheses can only properly be tested in studies (1) setting the appropriate type of causal question, (2) providing the kind of information preferred for answering that type of question, and (3) where the causal question asked is *unambiguously* of a particular type. It is also worth pointing out that some types of causal question have been neglected and provide rich ground for the development of new models and hypotheses. There does not appear to have been any theory or research directed at how people use active intervention to make causal attributions (intervention questions) or how they identify *effects* of some occurrence, rather than causes (single occasion cause questions). These are surely important issues.

The place of regularity information in causal attribution under the causal powers theory, then, is primarily defined by the relation of a particular type of regularity information to a particular type of causal question. Regularity information may still be used, however, to answer questions for which it is not the preferred type when the preferred type is not available. Under such circumstances, regularity information may be used even to answer types of question referring to a single occasion, as I show in the following sections.

**Single occasion questions**

To repeat, when seeking more information for causal attribution, people prefer information about the occasion or occasions implicit or explicit in the causal question posed. This leads to the claim that, for all single occasion questions, the preference is for more information about the single occasion in question. In the case of single occasion single effect questions, this claim is supported by the study reported by White (1989a) in which a single occasion single effect question was posed and 96.9 per cent of questions asked by subjects were requests for more information about the occasion in question.

The aim of information search under a single occasion question is to identify a causal candidate that answers the question posed (hypothesis 2, p. 80) and meets the four general criteria of adequacy outlined above. The search for more information is not random, but directed by some causal hypothesis or hypotheses that the attributer has in mind (White 1989a; Lalljee *et al.* 1984), although people will take and use whatever information is available to them. The nature of the effect defines the causal power that must have operated to bring it about, and this delimits the range of causal hypotheses the attributer will consider. The attributer looks for more information about the occasion in question, in an attempt to identify something that is believed to possess that causal power. (Alternatively, releasing conditions or liabilities may be identified, but the procedure for doing so is essentially the same.)

When this strategy is unsuccessful, gathering more information about the occasion in question can still be used for purposes of causal inference. In this case, the type of information sought consists of cues present in the single occasion in question and treated as valid or at least useful cues to causal inference. These include temporal and spatial contiguity, similarity (Shultz and Ravinsky 1977), and temporal proximity and priority (White 1988a).

When this strategy is unsuccessful, and if the attributer still wishes to find an explanation, then further information must be sought. The search for information is never purely empirical: it is always for the purpose of testing some causal belief or hypothesis, or discriminating between multiple candidates. The closest approach to pure induction in causal inference is the direction of information search by 'naïve hypotheses' (Hansen 1980) about where a possible cause is most likely to be found. Given this, several kinds of information may be sought or considered potentially relevant:

First, information gained by direct teaching or personal research (e.g. over-hearing a conversation, reading a magazine article, etc.).

Secondly, regularity information.

Thirdly, information about occurrences of other effects from the range believed possible for some hypothesised causal power. This becomes relevant where the hypothesised causal power is at a higher level of categorisation than that implied by the effect. For example, where the effect is the smashing of a plate by a hammer and the hypothesised causal power is the power to smash anything fragile, evidence about other sorts of fragile things smashed by the hammer counts as support for the hypothesis.

Suppose a road accident has occurred. Narrowly, this can only mean that the accident was caused by the operation of a causal power to produce road accidents, and the attributer should be searching for something with this power. Less narrowly, road accidents could be seen as just one of a number of effects of a causal power at a higher categorical level. They could also be seen as one of a number of effects due to one or more causal powers possessed by virtue of some other property. Suppose John has the idea that the accident was due to the stupidity of the driver. In his search for further information, any occurrence that can be seen as evidence of stupidity, or more directly of causal powers thought to be possessed by virtue of stupidity, counts as support for the hypothesis: it does not have to be other accidents. If John is asked what 'driver stupidity' means to him, and he replies that it includes running into other cars, jumping red lights, driving too fast, and turning corners without indicating, then evidence about the occurrence of any of these effects (namely, behaviour of these kinds by the driver in question) can be used to support the hypothesis that this accident was caused by driver stupidity. Regularity information concerns only occurrences and non-occurrences of the effect in question. Under the causal powers theory, information about occurrences of any of the known range of effects of the hypothesised causal power can be judged relevant, and this may encompass more than would count as regularity information.

Fourthly, information about things, properties, and so on, believed to be correlated or associated with the hypothesised causal power. Causal powers can be seen as elements in schemas, stereotypes, implicit personality theories and so on, and to this extent information about the presence or occurrence of other elements in the belief structure that contains the hypothesised causal power can be used to support the causal hypothesis, by being interpreted as indirect evidence of the presence of the causal power in question. For example, certain features of the car, such as the state of the bodywork or choice of interior decor, although not believed to be possible causes of accidents, may conform to certain elements of a 'stupid driver' schema and thus, by eliciting that schema, may encourage the attribution of, and to, driver stupidity.

Summarising, then, regularity information will be used to answer a single occasion question when all three of the following conditions hold: (1) the attributer needs to gather more information of some kind; (2) gathering more information about the occasion in question is not possible or has not yielded a causal inference; and (3) the attributer wishes to continue the search for an answer. Then it is one among (at least) four kinds of information that may be sought, and is not necessarily the preferred kind of the four.

*The use of regularity information in answering single occasion questions*

Although regularity information is not preferred for answering single occasion questions, there is considerable evidence that people can use it for that purpose (White 1988a; Hewstone 1989). I shall first discuss the use of regularity information for this purpose in general terms, and then consider the specific use of regularity as an indicator of the relative strength of powers and liabilities.

Suppose Jane wishes to find out whether some food, about which she has no belief at present, has the power to bring about indigestion (more informally, 'I've got indigestion, was it that meal I ate last night?'), and that she is using regularity information to answer the question. Since indigestion can either occur or not occur, and in the presence or absence of the eating of the type of meal in question, four components of regularity information may be available:

1 Occurrences of the effect in the presence of the possible cause.
2 Non-occurrences of the effect in the presence of the possible cause.
3 Occurrences of the effect in the absence of the possible cause.
4 Non-occurrences of the effect in the absence of the possible cause.

It could be argued that the ideal pattern that should obtain if the meal is the cause of the indigestion is perfect correlation between eating/not eating the meal and getting/not getting indigestion. In fact, this perfect pattern could only be expected to obtain where there is known to be one and only one possible cause of the effect in question. The value of each of these types of regularity information is compromised by (1) the possibility of multiple independent causes of the effect and (2) the dependence of a power on the satisfaction of a suitable releasing condition for its operation. These factors affect the use of each type of regularity information.

First, occurrences of the effect in the presence of the possible cause are consistent with the truth of the hypothesis and count as support for it. They are not unambiguous, however, unless it is known that no other thing with the power to bring about the effect was present on the occasion in question. This essentially is Kelley's (1973) discounting principle: the possibility of the presence of other causes of the effect reduces the tendency to attribute the effect to the possible cause in question.

Secondly, non-occurrences of the effect in the presence of the cause look like disconfirming evidence, but in fact they are not. A causal power requires a releasing condition for its operation: even if something has the causal power to produce an effect, it will not do so if no suitable releasing condition is present. This requirement entails that, with a specific exception described in the next paragraph, information about non-occurrences is less useful than information about occurrences when testing hypotheses about causal powers. A non-occurrence of the effect in the presence of the cause could be due either to the falsity of the causal hypothesis or to the fact that no appropriate releasing condition for the hypothesised causal power was met. An occurrence of the effect in the presence of the cause, on the other hand, could not happen unless some adequate releasing condition had been met, and for that reason is less ambiguous.

One obvious means of combating the ambiguity of non-occurrences in the presence of the hypothesised cause is to set up suitable releasing conditions, or to obtain information about occasions on which releasing conditions are known to have been present. In this case the causal hypothesis leads to a definite expectation that the effect will occur, and in this case non-occurrences are just as informative as occurrences. The difficulty of rejecting hypotheses about causal powers on the basis of these events is that it is often hard to be sure that a suitable releasing condition has been met. For example, in testing the hypothesis that a certain meal has the power to cause indigestion, it may be easy enough to set up an apparent releasing condition, eating the meal in question, but if the occurrence of the effect depends not only on that but also on other conditions (such as whether the person is tense or relaxed), then inferring the falsity of the hypothesis from the non-occurrence of the effect may not be correct. The main problem with non-occurrences, then, is in knowing whether suitable releasing conditions have been met. This problem does not arise for occurrences, so when testing hypotheses about causation, people should prefer information about occurrences of the effect in question to non-occurrences.

Thirdly, occurrences of the effect in the absence of the cause do not count against the hypothesis because of the possibility of multiple independent causes. Indigestion may be caused by the meal in question, but other things may also have the causal power to produce indigestion. They do have some relevance, though, as evidence that at least one other thing has the same power. This may be taken as weakening the case for the causal candidate in question, particularly if there is evidence that the other thing was also present on the occasion in question (the discounting principle again).

Fourthly, observing that indigestion does not occur when the meal in question has not been eaten reveals nothing about the causal power of the meal. Such an observation may be taken as strengthening the case for the causal candidate in question by counting against the possibility that other things have the same causal power, but it can only be taken this way when the attributer has no other pre-existing beliefs about possible causes of the effect in question.

Basically, for the third and fourth types of regularity information together, their role is to give an empirical indication of the possibility and likelihood of other causes of the effect in question, and they may therefore have some value in strengthening or weakening the case for the cause in question. It all depends, however, on their judged relevance to the case in question – that is, whether any other possible cause could have been present on that occasion.

For assessing covariation, objectively all cells in a contingency table should be weighted equally. For causal inference according to the covariation principle, the same rule of equal weighting applies. For causal inference under the causal powers theory, however, there is no simple solution to the problem of weighting because of the considerations just elucidated, and often *unequal* weighting is objectively correct. This means that observations that people weight the four types unequally in causal inference (Schustack and Sternberg 1981; Einhorn and Hogarth 1986) are not necessarily evidence of error or bias. They only count as error or bias under a philosophical theory of causation which requires equal weighting, and it is not known whether any theory of this kind is correct (White 1990).

The statements made about the components of regularity information only apply for hypotheses about causal powers believed to be stable properties of things. For causal powers believed to be transient or occasion-specific, regularity information (and indeed any information about other occasions) has little if any relevance. The most that could be expected of regularity information is that it could rule out all possibilities other than some transient causal power by showing that nothing stable has any regular pattern of association with the effect. Regularity information can neither confirm nor disconfirm hypotheses about transient causal powers, which may mean that the possibility that the effect was due to a transient causal power, though impossible to rule out, is usually ignored because of the difficulty of testing it.

These statements only apply to the use of regularity information to ascertain whether a thing has a given causal power or not. They do not apply to its use in assessing relations between powers and liabilities (see the next section), nor to its use in answering other types of causal question, such as questions referring to multiple occasions.

The value and use of regularity information in causal attribution both depend on many factors, and a full account of this dependence would be enormously complex. It is to be doubted, however, whether people ever find themselves in such a position that they can use nothing other than regularity information, except under the artificial constraints of a laboratory study. For one thing, causal attribution for single occasion single effect questions usually occurs for events and occasions in which the attributer is personally involved, which means that a great deal of information about the occasion and the people and things involved in it is likely to be available. In addition, when sampling information from memory, people usually retrieve causal beliefs rather than regularity information. Of course, those causal beliefs may have been derived from information about multiple occurrences: it has already been argued that regularity information is one of several possible sources of causal beliefs. But the beliefs once formed are no longer in the form of regularity information. This is one respect in which the present theory differs from Kelley's causal schema idea. People will sample information about particular occasions and/or summaries in the form of regularity information only when no existing causal belief comes to mind. So, while it is important to discover how people use regularity information, it is at least as important to consider regularity information in its place, that is as just one type of information of no special importance that people may use for causal attribution when they have no choice and along with information of other types.

### Ascertaining the strength of a power or liability

As stated in the introduction, under many circumstances a causal connection can be viewed as a relation between a causal power of one thing and a liability of another. Many statements of causation by ordinary people are properly interpreted as implying, if not stating directly, relations between causal powers and liabilities, or resistances, to put it the other way round. Saying that Susan passed the exam, John laughed at the comedian, or Paul liked the painting he saw in the art gallery, is in each case to specify a relation between a power and a resistance. Susan's power to pass exams was greater than the difficulty of the exam to be passed; the comedian's power to make people laugh was sufficient to evoke John's liability to laugh; the power of the painting to evoke liking was sufficient to evoke Paul's liability to like things. ('Sufficient' is meant here not in the sense of a sufficient condition, but specifically in the sense of a power being sufficiently great to produce an effect, given the liability of the thing in which the effect is produced. It is a matter of strength, not conditionality.) As may be ascertained from the examples, success and failure attribution covers one type of power/resistance relation: that is, all success and failure attributions are power/resistance relations, but not all power/resistance relations are success and failure attributions.

When we are given outcome information, such as 'Susan passed the exam', this is already sufficient for a simple causal interpretation to be constructed. The statement tells us the basic nature of the power involved (Susan's power to pass exams), and that of the liability or resistance (the difficulty of the exam); it also tells us that a releasing condition for the operation of the power was met (Susan sat the exam), and it tells us the relative strengths of the power and the resistance; that is, Susan's power to pass the exam was greater than the difficulty of the exam (ignoring the possible role of other factors). What attributional work needs to be done, then, in respect of this outcome? What we have is a kind of causal frame or schema: while the outcome tells us the relative strengths of the power and the resistance, it does not tell us the absolute strength of either. Other information is needed to fill in these values, and the kind of attributional work we engage in, depends on whether either of these values is filled in or not. We can therefore distinguish three cases.

First, neither value is filled in. In this case, a causal question such as 'Why did Susan pass the exam?' would lead the attributer to infer that something more is needed than what is given in the outcome information, so for the question to be answered one or both of the values must be filled in by gathering more information. The question is then answered by supplying some of the information gathered: for example, 'because she has high ability'.

The role of regularity information in this has been dealt with above. Basically, regularity information is one among a number of types of information that may be used but are not the first preference. Regularity information may be considerably more useful when combined with information about the properties of the sample: for example, information about pass rates on the exam is more useful when accompanied by information about the level of ability of the candidates who sat it.

Regularity information in the form of consensus, consistency, and distinctiveness reveals the strengths of the power and resistance involved. Take 'John laughs at the comedian'. Consensus information reveals the strength of the comedian's power to make people laugh. Low consensus says that the comedian has little power to make people laugh. High consensus says that he or she has a lot. Distinctiveness information reveals the degree of John's liability to be made to laugh. Low distinctiveness says that John is easily made to laugh, high distinctiveness that he is not. (Specifically, it means that he laughed on this occasion *despite* the fact that he is not easily made to laugh.) Consistency information is different in that it reveals whether or not the usual power/ resistance relation is modified by any qualifying factors: high consistency says that it is not, low consistency that it is. These qualifying factors can belong to the circumstances or to either of the people involved (for instance, John is in an unhappy mood), and can identify other powers operating to bring about or prevent relevant effects, or to the absence of some releasing condition for the comedian's power to make either John or people in general laugh.

The powers and liabilities involved can be of variable specificity, however: one can have a liability to be made to laugh by some comedians and not others, and a comedian can have the power to make some people laugh and not others.

The ultimate in this specificity is indicated by the configuration of low consensus, high distinctiveness, high consistency, which can only indicate that the comedian has the power to make John laugh (and hardly anyone else) and John has the liability to be made to laugh by this comedian (and hardly anyone else). The meaning of an attribution to the person, in terms of the specificity of the power or liability identified, varies, therefore, for different configurations of Kelleyan information.

Using this reasoning it is possible to make predictions for each configuration, including the partial configurations used by Orvis *et al.* (1975). The predictions match the results of their two studies rather better than do those generated by Orvis *et al.*, but several models can lay claim to similar success (Hilton and Slugoski 1986; Hewstone and Jaspars 1987; Forsterling 1989) and it is doubtful whether there is much to be gained by continuing this particular debate. The point for present purposes is merely to illustrate one of the roles of regularity information, that of assessing strengths of powers and resistances.

The second case is one where one of the default values is filled. Again, a causal question implies a need to refer to something not present in the information given. For example, if the exam is known or believed to be easy and the question is 'Why did Susan pass the exam?', there is an implication that referring to the ease of the exam does not count as an answer (if the questioner knows how easy the exam is). The interpretation of the causal question in this case depends upon its relation to a default expectation set up by the information possessed. For an exam known to be easy, the default expectation is a pass or high mark; for an exam known to be difficult, the default expectation is a fail or low mark. Where the outcome is anomalous with the default expectation, the causal question is reinterpreted as a comparison question, and the attributer's task is to explain the departure from the default expectation by referring to some differentiating factor. For example, where Susan has passed an exam known to be difficult, the explanation might refer to Susan's egregious ability (that is, her causal power to pass the exam is much greater than some presumed average). Thus, causal attribution to ability or causal power of the candidate in this case is meant to explain the outcome by identifying a factor that differentiates the occasion in question from the average that constitutes the default expectation. Cases of this sort resemble cases of script deviation studied by Hilton and Slugoski (1986), and their abnormal conditions focus model might therefore apply to these cases.

Where the outcome conforms to the default expectation, the attributer must work out why a causal question is being asked: the implication must be that there is something explanation-worthy about the outcome, and to find out what it is more information must be gathered. Again, the preferences discussed earlier come into play here, and the same statements about the relevance of regularity information hold. Essentially, the aim is to find some piece of information against which the outcome does appear anomalous, and then it is the anomaly that will be explained. And again, once this has been achieved, the question is reinterpreted as a comparison question, except that instead of a default expectation there is a specific expectation based on the particular information obtained. For example, if Susan passes an exam known to be easy, and in seeking information that makes this explanation-worthy we discover that Susan has very low ability, this sets up a specific expectation of failure for Susan, and the attributional task is to explain the violation of this expectation. As before, identification of a differentiating factor, possibly through use of abnormal conditions analysis, is the aim.

Also, where one of the values is already filled, outcome information may enable the other to be filled as well. For example, if the exam is known to be very difficult, then a pass implies very high causal power, and this is sufficiently specific for the attributer to fill in the value for the power accordingly.

In the third case, where both values are filled or at least when the relative strength of each is known, there is a clear implication for outcome unless the values are similar. When values are similar, the outcome must be explained by reference to some other factor that, so to speak, tipped the balance. When the outcome is anomalous with respect to the implication, then, as in the previous case, the job of causal attribution is to explain the anomaly, and the same general procedure applies.

We can therefore see three distinct kinds of causal attribution in the foregoing. One is answering a causal question by introducing some new piece of information, such as explaining why Susan passed an exam known to be difficult by referring to her high ability, a fact not previously known about her (answering a single occasion single effect question). The second is the explanation of anomalies, outcomes that violate default or specific expectations or implications of known information (answering a comparison question). The third is explaining an outcome when the strengths of the power and the resistance are judged to be very similar, so that reference to some extra factor is required (also answering a single occasion single effect question, or a selection question). The second and third are both dependent upon having the causal interpretation filled in with values for the causal power and the resistance, which is always the step of primary importance when making a causal attribution about some aspect of a power/resistance relation.

There are basically two ways of dealing with the second and third types of causal attribution. One consists of reference to the causal power believed to be involved, and the other to factors which may affect the operation of that causal power.

First, ways in which the causal power may be invoked in causal attribution depend upon beliefs about the nature of the causal power involved. Some powers may be believed to operate in an all-or-none fashion (either the hammer smashes the plate or it does not); others may be believed to have degrees of activation in operation (people don't always perform to their full potential). Some may be conceived as single powers; others at a higher categorical level may be seen as comprising more than one power. The power to pass exams, for example, may be taken as including ability, concentration, alertness, motivation, knowledge, and so on.

Where the power is believed to have degrees of activation, or is believed to be a collection of powers, then occurrences of the outcome (such as passing the exam) unambiguously indicate that the power was sufficient in relation to the resistance, but non-occurrences are ambiguous. A non-occurrence could mean either that the power was not sufficient in relation to the resistance, or that the power was sufficient but not fully activated, or that the collection of powers was sufficient but only some components of it were activated or not sufficiently so. Thus, when success is expected (because the power to succeed is believed to be sufficiently great in relation to the exam) and failure occurs, these possibilities allow a variety of explanations.

Secondly, operation of the causal power can be affected by two kinds of thing:

1  Presence or absence of releasing conditions.
2  Interference from causal powers of other sorts (that is, powers to produce other kinds of effects) which may facilitate or inhibit the operation of the power in question. For example, failure in an exam may be due to a sprained wrist, interfering with the operation of the power to pass the exam by adversely affecting a power (the power to write) on which the operation of the power to pass exams depends.

When failure is expected and success occurs, either the belief about the power or the liability must be revised or reference must be made to some facilitatory interference.

There is no ducking the complexity of this account. Every event can be seen as caused, and passing an examination, though describable in a single phrase, may involve many events and many causally relevant factors. For familiar parts of social reality, people are likely to have accumulated a considerable array of causally relevant beliefs, and beliefs, moreover, about how different factors interact with one another, forming an extended causal network. Although people may not concern themselves overtly with whether something is a causal power, a releasing condition, or an interfering factor of some kind, these concepts are implicit in the ways in which beliefs are used in the interpretation of events.

## Summary: answers to causal questions and ways of generating them

We are now in a position to enumerate the things that count as answers to each of the causal questions in the list, and these are therefore presented in Table 6.2. Identifying letters correspond to those in Table 6.1. Where the answer given is 'causal power', it is always possible that, under some circumstances, a releasing condition or a liability may also be given as an answer.

It is now possible to list the preferred method of causal attribution for each type of causal question.

*Single occasion single effect questions, single occasion non-occurrence questions, single occasion state questions, and single occasion cause discrimination questions.* First preference: application of existing belief about causal power (and/or releasing condition and/or liability) judged capable of producing the

*Table 6.2* Things that count as answers to causal questions

A Causal power.
B Effect believed possible for causal power in question.
C Yes/no.
D Factor common to all effects in question.
E One or more causal powers.
F Factor or factors common to all occasions in question.
G Differentiating factor.
H Occasion-specific addition to causal structure not known in advance.
I Causal power – presence of power to prevent or absence of power to produce.
J Causal power.
K Choice of one from candidates in question.
L Proportion or weight or list of chosen occurrences.
M Factor common to or factor(s) absent from all occasions in question.
N Covariate.
O Difference identified by comparison of $X$ before and after change.

effect in question. Second preference: gather more information about the occasion in question to test applicability of one or more candidates from the range of causal beliefs defined as relevant by the nature of the effect. Third preference: pose a question of another type, use preferred or appropriate method to generate an answer to that, then deduce answer to single effect question from that.

*Single occasion cause questions.* First preference: application of existing belief about effect judged capable of being produced by the causal power in question. Second preference: gather more information about occasion in question to test applicability of one or more candidates from the range of effects defined as relevant by the nature of the causal power. Third preference: if possible, pose question of another type, use preferred or appropriate method to generate an answer to that, then deduce answer to single effect question from that.

*Single occasion connection questions.* Judge whether the specified effect falls within the range of effects believed possible for the specified cause. If not, then answer 'no'. If it does, then answer 'yes' or test applicability of alternatives using one of the methods given for type *A* and so on, in same order of preference.

*Multiple occasion occurrence questions.* Use some variety of common factor analysis; for example, some practicable approximation to the method of agreement (Mill 1843/1967) to identify one (or more) from the range of causal beliefs defined as relevant by the nature of the effect, that is common to all effects in question.

*Single occasion multiple effect questions.* As for single occasion single effect questions, except that different causal powers may be applied to different effects among those in the question.

*Multiple occasion various effects questions.* As for multiple occasion occurrence questions, except that different causal powers may be applied to different effects among those in the question.

*Comparison questions.* Use of some variety of differentiating factor analysis, for example, the method of difference (Mill 1843/1967; Hilton and Slugoski 1986; Hesslow 1988; McGill 1989; Hart and Honoré 1959; Gorovitz, 1965) to identify one (or more) from the range of causal beliefs defined as relevant by the nature of the effect that is present on the occasion of occurrence and absent from occasions of non-occurrence (or, possibly, absent from the occasion of occurrence and present on occasions of non-occurrence).

*Selection questions.* Gather more information about the occasion in question to identify some occasion-specific addition or amendment to the existing causal interpretation; either information about the presence, absence, operation, or non-operation of elements of that interpretation on the occasion, or information facilitating the formation of one or more new causal beliefs in any of the four ways given earlier.

*Multiple occasion effect discrimination questions.* (1) Where the required answer is a weight or proportion, generate a judgement of weight or proportion by a method such as contingency analysis (Neunaber and Wasserman 1986) or association (Shanks and Dickinson 1987). (2) Where the required answer is a list, pose a single occasion connection question for each occurrence in the set specified in the question, and answer by listing occurrences for which an affirmative answer is given. This may also be a method of generating a weight or proportion.

*Multiple occasion non-occurrence questions.* As for multiple occasion occurrence questions, except that analysis may identify factor(s) absent from all non-occurrences in the set specified in the question.

*Multiple occasion occurrence and non-occurrence questions.* Use of some type of covariation or conditional analysis: for example, some practicable approximation to the joint method of agreement and difference (Mill 1843/1967); the covariation principle (Heider 1958; Kelley 1967, 1972a, 1973; Hewstone and Jaspars 1987) to identify one (or more) from the range of causal beliefs defined as relevant by the nature of the effect that is present on the occasions of occurrence and absent from the occasions of non-occurrence.

*Intervention questions.* Comparison of occasions before and after change to identify differences from the range of effects believed possible for the cause in question. Other causal candidates may optionally be tested, using the same methods and in the same order of preference as for single occasion single effect questions.

I have not been absolutely precise in my specification of methods, because in most if not all cases there are several possibilities. For example, for comparison questions I specified only 'some type of differentiating factor analysis' because there are already at least three alternative accounts in the psychological literature that could apply (McGill 1989; Hesslow 1988; Hilton and Slugoski 1986).

These statements hold for the type of causal question that the attributer is addressing. This is not necessarily the type asked, for example, by an experimenter. It therefore remains possible that the attributer may deal with what the experimenter intended as, say, a multiple occurrence and non-occurrence question by turning it into, say, a comparison question and addressing that. If people prefer to deal with, or are more used to, one type of question over another, then they may often or habitually translate the less preferred type into the more preferred type. There is a need for research on the relative frequencies with which people address causal questions of different types, not least because a theory whose range of application is confined to one type will have no relevance to causal attribution at all if people never actually address causal questions of that type, or always translate them into some other type.

## CONCLUDING REMARKS

### Regularity information and causal inference

If the foregoing account suggests that the use of regularity information in causal attribution is formidably complex and hard to predict, that is a fair reflection of the complexity of any form of causal processing which depends on pre-acquired beliefs. Only a purely inductive empiricist would use a simple universal method for causal inference: as soon as any concession is made to stored information, ideas, strategies, and so on, the effectively unlimited capacity of long-term memory and the potential for developing large numbers of automatic or partly automatic routines for causal processing entail a relatively high degree of sensitivity to features that differentiate one occasion from another. I have tried to identify the factors that are most important in terms of the difference they make to the way in which causal attribution proceeds: but there is no universal recipe for causal attribution, no single and invariable use for regularity information, no set weighting for occurrences or non-occurrences.

The main statements about regularity information in the foregoing can be summarised as follows.

1  The relevance of any type of regularity information to causal attribution depends upon the implicit or explicit type of causal question that is being asked. For some types of causal question, some types of regularity information, and methods of inference utilising those types, are preferred. For other types of causal question, notably those referring to a single occasion, no type of regularity information is preferred.

2  For answering causal questions about single occasions, regularity information is one among (at least) four types of information that may be used for causal processing when (a) the attributer has no single applicable belief *and* (b) cannot gather any more information about the occasion in question or none that renders some belief applicable *and* (c) when the attributer cannot generate a causal candidate by the use of occasion-specific cues such as contiguity; or it will be used when the attributer has one or more causal hypotheses and wishes to test them or discriminate between them in some way additional to gathering more information about the occasion in question.

3  When regularity information is used, the use to which it is put is not inductive but is part of the testing of causal hypotheses.
4  For ascertaining whether some thing or person has a certain causal power or not, the types of covariation information are not weighted equally. The weighting of the types of covariation information depends on whether there is the possibility of multiple independent causes, and on whether anything is known about the presence or absence of releasing conditions (or whether the attributer can set up a releasing condition).
5  When making inferences about relations between powers and resistances (such as ability and task difficulty), regularity information is used in various ways to assess the relative and/or absolute strength of the power or resistance involved.

The emphasis here has been on the role of regularity information in testing causal hypotheses, rather than generating causal inferences. Are there any circumstances under which attributers engage in a purely inductive search for a cause? The foregoing account implies that this would only occur if (1) they had no relevant or applicable causal belief *and* (2) they could not generate one by processes such as deduction or analogical reasoning *and* (3) they have no further information about the occasion in question and no means of obtaining any *and* (4) they have no idea how to direct their search among other occasions (meaning that they have no naïve hypotheses about where a possible cause is most likely to be found – cf. Hansen 1980). Whether this combination of features ever actually occurs is an empirical question, but it does not seem likely. Apart from anything else, it is hard to imagine any situation in which the attributer could not fall back on some kind of analogy ('It may be a Martian, but I'll bet it feels pain just like Earth creatures do').

## Formation of new causal beliefs

The only other use of covariation information is in the formation of new causal beliefs. The attributer's preference is always to make a causal attribution by applying an existing causal belief. Where this preference cannot be satisfied and where the attributer still wishes to make a causal attribution, then some new causal belief is created and applied. There are several ways in which new causal beliefs may be created:

1  By use of basic causal cues of similarity, temporal contiguity, spatial contiguity, and temporal priority of cause over effect (White 1988a; Mendelson and Shultz 1976; Lesser 1977; Shultz and Ravinsky 1977; Sedlak and Kurtz 1981).
2  By direct or indirect teaching or personal research (for example, reading a newspaper article, overhearing a conversation).
3  By other methods of inference such as analogical reasoning (Gick and Holyoak 1980, 1983).

4  By empirical methods such as covariation analysis. In this case, the search for a candidate is not purely inductive but directed by a naïve hypothesis as to where a candidate is most likely to be found (Hansen 1980).

**Practical concerns and causal questions**

Under the present view, type of causal question asked is dominant over both information search and causal attribution process. If this is the case, then it is important to discover what determines the type of causal question asked. The general answer to this is the practical concerns of the attributer at the time (White 1984, 1989a). That is, causal attribution should be viewed as an activity embedded in and conducted for the sake of some practical concern(s) of the attributer, and the point of engaging in causal attribution is to make the optimal contribution to those concerns (whether people always or even often succeed in this is an open question). Practical concerns can be of many different kinds, and can be both general, such as gaining mastery of one's life, or specific, such as avoiding being held liable for an accident.

For example, suppose a child is sent home from school for hitting another child. If the parents have to deal with the upset associated with that particular occurrence, they may ask a single occasion single effect question having to do with what led to the incident in question, and seek to identify occasion-specific factors that fit their beliefs about what makes one child hit another. The teachers, on the other hand, may see the incident as exemplifying a recurrent tendency on the part of the child, with worrying implications for the child's future behaviour, and this may lead them to pose either a multiple occasion occurrence question, seeking to identify some factor common to all of the child's misdemeanours, or an intervention question, seeking to identify some way of putting a stop to the trend. It is likely that differing practical concerns lead the different parties towards different answers to their respective causal questions. It would be a mistake, however, to see either answer as 'wrong' or 'biased', because each may be well suited to the respective practical concerns that led to the particular causal question asked. The giving of different causal attributions for the same event does not indicate that one or more of the causal attributions is in error or biased, only that the parties involved have different practical concerns which lead them to ask different types of causal question.

Practical concerns also lead to other differences in causal attribution, such as differences in definition of a causal field. For example (borrowing from Mackie 1975), suppose a man has developed cancer. The man himself may ask why he got cancer then and at no other time in his life, and find that he was exposed to radiation at his place of work which, he believes, has the causal power to bring about cancer (thus the explanation consists of the identification of a releasing condition for the operation of that power). The factory, on the other hand, may ask why that man got cancer when others who were also exposed to radiation did not, and this may lead them to consider factors that differentiate the afflicted man from the remainder. Both parties have asked comparison questions, but they have defined different causal fields, and this leads them to find different answers. The point to note here is that the definition of the causal field can be seen as determined by the differing practical concerns of the parties involved: for the stricken individual, the hope of being awarded damages; for the factory, the aim of avoiding conviction and costs.

I have already alluded to the fact that explicit causal attributions are usually selections made from a more extensive causal interpretation. The guiding principle of selection is the requirement to provide something that counts as an answer to the question set. When a direct question has been asked of the attributer by someone else, this principle entails giving the questioner information they do not already possess, on the grounds that people don't ask questions to which they already know the answers and that, in consequence, giving them something they already know cannot count as an answer to the question they have posed. This means that there are two factors to do with the questioner that determine the selection made from the causal interpretation.

One is the phrasing of the question. This can act, for example, by delimiting a causal field or by setting up one or more comparison cases (and therefore working as a comparison question). The effects of question phrasing were neatly illustrated by McGill (1989). In her experiment 1, subjects were asked why they or their best friend had chosen their major college subject. Some subjects were asked, 'Why did you (your best friend) in particular choose that major?', and these subjects tended to refer to features of the person, presumably taking up the implication of the question that the questioner desires something that differentiates them from other people who might not have made the same choice. Other subjects were asked, 'Why did you (your best friend) choose that major in particular?', and these subjects tended to refer to features of the major, presumably responding to the implicit request for something that differentiated the chosen major from others that were not chosen.

The other factor is the attributer's beliefs about the questioner's state of knowledge. Suppose that a questioner asks of Sally why she bought a certain house, and that Sally knows that the questioner knows all about the house and nothing about Sally. In this case the practical concern of informativeness demands that Sally respond by telling the questioner something about herself. If the questioner knew all about Sally but nothing about the house, then the practical concern could only be satisfied by telling the questioner something about the house. These selections occur despite the fact that the questioner has not explicitly asked a comparison question, and despite the fact that no causal field or comparison case or cases has been set up. Asking a comparison question, then, is one way of making or eliciting a selection from a causal interpretation, but not the only way.

In these examples the notion of a scientifically correct causal attribution as a standard against which to compare the accuracy of the attributer's answer is not useful, because the scientifically correct answer is too complex (cf. Gorovitz

1965). In the school example, the full explanation for the child's misdemeanour is likely to involve reference to occasion-specific factors, characteristics, and behaviours of the victim, of the offender, of the offender's family, features of the child's life in general, past and present, the school, and broader social and cultural factors, and so on. In the cancer example, the full explanation is likely to involve a host of social, personal, biochemical, genetic, and environmental factors. The notion of a practically optimal answer, however, is not meaningless because such an answer can be, and usually is, comparatively simple. If the victim of the cancer can set and answer a causal question in such a way that the factory appears to have been causally responsible for his illness, then causal attribution has been of maximum service to his practical concern. Similarly, if the factory can set and answer a causal question that appears to rule out events on their premises as a possible cause, then they too have made best possible use of causal attribution in terms of their practical concerns. Practical concerns, then, provide the standard by which causal attributions should be assessed, as well as determining both the type of causal question asked and other aspects of the way in which causal attribution is carried out.

The usual sequence in causal attribution, then, can be summarised as follows: practical concern – posing of causal question – information search – process or method of causal attribution – answer to question posed. In this chapter I have tried to show that consideration of types of causal question provides a powerful organising framework for models and theories of the activities in this sequence.

## NOTES

1   The term 'causal processing' is used for convenience and without prejudice as to the type of theory that may apply at this basic level, and covers causal perception, causal inference, causal attribution, etc.
2   Harré and Madden used both 'stimulus conditions' and 'releasing occasions'. The word 'stimulus' has connotations in psychology which I prefer not to evoke, but both 'releasing conditions' and 'releasing occasions' are suitable terms to use in the context of my theory.

# Chapter 7

# Origins and development of basic causal concepts

The aim of this chapter is to assess the origins and development of the under-standing of causation in infancy. This is crucial to the grounding of the causal powers theory: for a certain concept to be basic to the psychological construction of reality almost certainly means that it is laid down early in life, or there from the start. The research discussed here is also relevant to the origin of the basic concept of action, with which I shall deal in a later chapter.

There is a school of thought according to which causal processing emerges out of the learning of environmental contingencies. But environmental con-tingencies, such as those set up for the study of operant conditioning, consist by definition of relations *between* events, usually between two events. Causal pro-cessing is of just *one* event, and the perception of one event is arguably a psychologically easier task than the learning of a relation between two events. For this reason I would claim that, when environmental contingencies are inter-preted as one event causing another, this represents the grafting of an already existing causal concept onto the perception of contingencies.

I begin by listing some of the limitations to the infant's understanding in the first six months of life.

1  The infant has no concept of objects or object permanence (Piaget 1954).
2  The infant has no concept of self (Piaget 1954).
3  Accordingly, the infant makes no differentiation between self and not-self, or between inner (mental) and outer (physical) realities (Piaget 1954).
4  The infant has no concept of space or spatial relations (Piaget 1954).
5  The infant cannot detect contingencies between events that occur more than 3 seconds apart (Watson 1984). Watson pointed out that this severely limits the development of causal understanding based on environmental contingencies, because most such contingencies to which the infant is exposed, such as those involving its own actions and those of its mother, are usually separated by more than 3 seconds.
6  The causal structure of the infant's world is deficient, compared to the standard set by regularity theories of causation (Watson 1984), because the infant is exposed to frequent violations of sufficiency (for example, partial

reinforcement schedules) and necessity (rewards given freely – that is, not connected with the infant's behaviour).

Despite these limitations, there is evidence from two lines of research that some form of causal processing has begun by the age of 6 months, probably earlier. One comes from research on the 'launching effect' in infants (Michotte 1963; Leslie 1982, 1984; Leslie and Keeble 1987; White 1988a). The other comes from research on efficacy and phenomenal contiguity by Piaget (1954). I shall discuss each in turn.

## THE ICONIC PROCESSING HYPOTHESIS

### Research on the launching effect with infants

Several studies of causal processing carried out on infants have taken as their model Michotte's (1963) research with adult subjects. Michotte presented visual stimuli involving what appeared to be two rectangles, A and B. A moved towards B at constant speed and came into contact with it, whereupon A remained at the point of contact and B moved off in the same direction at constant speed. Adult observers of this usually report that the movement of B is caused by the impact of A upon it, and that A pushes, kicks, or launches B. This is known in English as the 'launching effect'. Michotte reported that the effect was perceived by almost all observers, but he used trained observers who were familiar with the stimuli in most of his studies. Subsequent research has confirmed that many, though not all, adult subjects perceive the launching effect on their first exposure to the stimulus sequence (Boyle 1960; Beasley 1968; White 1988a). Considering that the stimuli were in all cases very imperfect representations of actual mechanical causality (Kassin and Baron 1985), the surprising thing is not that causal perception was not universal but that it occurred at all.

In the first of the studies with infants, Ball (1973) presented trials in which a red object moved behind a screen and a white object emerged from the other side, moving in the same direction. Then the screen was removed. Some infants then saw trials in which the red object collided with the white one, which then moved off in the same direction. This condition was designed to be effectively similar to Michotte's (1963) launching effect procedure. Other infants saw trials that were similar to this except that the two objects did not come into contact. The latter group spent longer visually tracking the display than did infants in the contact group, 'as if they were seeing a new stimulus' (Ball 1973: 11). Ball's youngest group ranged from 9 to 21 weeks, and his oldest group was up to 122 weeks old, but there was no effect of or interaction with age.

Borton (1979) worked with 3-month-old infants. He also compared contact with non-contact groups, but the initial trials consisted of the uninterrupted movement of a single object. Borton measured three types of looking behaviour and found differences between contact and non-contact trials on all three, whereas he found no differences between the contact and single-object trials.

Leslie (1982) presented initial trials consisting of one of three films: (1) a standard launching effect sequence; (2) the same sequence except that A and B remained in contact for about 580 ms before B moved off; or (3) the same as (1) except that A stopped short of B and did not come into contact with it. He then measured dishabituation, in terms of duration of continuous gaze at the stimuli, to test films in which only one component of the movement in the initial films was presented: that is, either A's movement or B's but not both. Dishabituation was considerably greater for infants initially shown launching effect films than for infants shown either of the other initial films. Leslie's younger group ranged from 13 to 24 weeks old. There were no effects of or interactions with age.

Taken together, these studies show that infants respond differently to launching effect trials than they do to trials in which either spatial contiguity or temporal contiguity is violated, just as adults do (Michotte 1963). To what extent, however, do these findings show *causal* perception? One could argue that infants see launching effect trials simply as a single movement, whereas they see spatial and temporal discontiguity trials as two movements. Leslie (1982) pointed out that his findings contradicted this interpretation. His test films, as I have already described, included only a single movement of one of the rectangles. If his infants perceived the launching effect trials as a single movement, therefore, they should have dishabituated *less* to these single-movement test films than should infants shown trials involving two movements. In fact, the opposite happened. This supports the idea that causal perception was occurring among the infants he studied.

Later studies by Leslie have added weight to this interpretation. Leslie (1984) found that infants perceive some kind of internal structure in the launching effect sequence: this was shown by the fact that they dishabituated to a simple reversal of the launching effect sequence (running the film backwards) but not to a reversal of a film of a single object moving. Leslie (1984) asked what kind of internal structure the infants were perceiving. He set up two hypotheses:

1 'Hume would argue that infants will perceive two independent aspects of the event – the spatial contact and the temporal succession of the movements' (Leslie and Keeble 1987: 269).
2 Michotte 'asserts that a causal relation will be registered directly' (Leslie and Keeble 1987: 269).

To distinguish these two hypotheses, Leslie (1984) set up four films:

(a) Direct launching (Michotte's standard launching effect sequence).
(b) Delayed reaction (the standard sequence except that the two rectangles remained in contact for 500 ms before the second one moved off).
(c) Launching without collision (the standard sequence except that the two rectangles were 6 cm apart when at their closest).
(d) Delayed reaction without collision (the standard sequence with both delay and gap).

Adult observers only report perceiving the launching effect under (a) (Michotte 1963), and under hypothesis 2 the same should hold for infants. Leslie pointed out, however, that (a) and (d) contrast with each other in respect of both delay and gap, and so do (b) and (c). So if infants simply encode these features of the sequence, as they should do under hypothesis 1, then they should show as much dishabituation to (c) after training with (b) as they do to (d) after training with (a). Leslie's results favoured hypothesis 2 over hypothesis 1. He also found, however, that each of the four films was discriminable from the others, and that there was nothing special about the direct launching sequence. His results suggested that the sequences are encoded on a single dimension, with (a) at one end, (d) at the other, and (b) and (c) somewhere in the middle. This is a dimension of spatio-temporal continuity. Thus, it is not clear from his results whether infants are discriminating on the basis of perception of causal relation or on the basis of judgement of spatio-temporal continuity.

Leslie and Keeble (1987) set out to distinguish these two possibilities. Their method again was to measure dishabituation to reversals of the films. For film *A*, the launching effect sequence, this would mean reversal of both causal direction *and* spatio-temporal direction: for film *B*, delayed reaction, if this sequence is not perceived as causal, then reversing the film means only reversing the spatio-temporal direction. In this case, if what is special about film *A* is perception of a causal relation, there should be more dishabituation to film *A* than to film *B*. Leslie and Keeble ran two studies and found this result in both of them. This differentiates spatio-temporal from causal features and shows responsiveness to causal features. Moreover, Leslie and Keeble argued, this differentiation cannot be attributed either to better memory for *A* than for *B* or to infants' preference for looking at *A* over *B*.

## Iconic processing

My hypothesis to explain this causal perception in infants makes reference to iconic processing. Iconic store, sometimes called visual sensory memory, is a large capacity store prior to attentive processing in which visual information is held for brief amounts of time (Anderson 1980; Kintsch 1970). The amount of information held decays to the limited capacity of short-term memory, under near-ideal presentation conditions within about 1 second (Anderson 1980; Sperling 1960). Even under these conditions, however, most information has been lost after 300 ms, and the traditional duration of the icon is 250 ms (Haber 1983b).

In his experiments, Sperling (1960) used static, briefly presented displays with blank fields before and after. Critics have observed that this leads to a misleading notion of the icon as a simple register of perceptual input (Haber 1983b). Under normal circumstances the icon is continuously updated by new visual input. As Haber (1983a) expressed it, 'Information of dynamic change rather than a static picture is the proper stimulus for perception' (p. 50). Iconic store is more than just a store of information: various forms of processing of information on the iconic time-scale may take place there. Iconic processing functions operate on material integrated over a span of not more than 250 ms. Several authors have argued, with supporting evidence, that one function of iconic processing is temporal integration (Adelson 1983; Bridgeman and Mayer 1983; Klatzky 1983; Mace and Turvey 1983; Philips 1983; Wilson 1983). This involves the integration or relation of visual information input at different times but not more than about 250 ms apart. This can subserve the detection of change and temporal continuity.

## The iconic processing hypothesis

I have already argued that the psychological definition of an event or happening is given by the temporal limits of the temporal integration function of iconic processing. In the stimuli used by Leslie (1982, 1984) and Leslie and Keeble (1987), however, there are many events, only some of which are discriminated by infants as causal. There is a collision between two rectangles in which the moving rectangle stops and the one that was stationary moves. A solitary moving rectangle stops. A solitary stationary rectangle starts moving. A rectangle moving at uniform speed changes colour. These are all events, meaning that they are or would be detected as such by the temporal integration function of iconic processing. Only the first, however, is perceived causally. What distinguishes it from the others? This is an important question, because adults might identify a cause for any of the other events: causal processing is therefore more restricted in infants than in adults, but the nature of and reason for the restriction may reveal something that is basic, perhaps prototypical, to causal processing by adults.

It cannot be that the infants are able to perceive actual causal connections because the causal connection perceived in this case is illusory: it is simply an animated film or, in Michotte's studies, a piece of equipment involving black lines painted onto a rotating disc. There is no actual causal relation to be perceived. We must therefore look for features of the stimuli which distinguish the launching effect sequence from others.

Let me summarise Michotte's findings on the temporal parameters of the launching effect in his studies with adults. For convenience I shall call the rectangle moving before collision 'A' and the one moving after the collision 'B'.

1  In experiment 29 Michotte (1963) varied the delay between the moment at which A came into contact with B and the moment at which B moved off. At longer time intervals these two movements were seen as independent and not causally related. The perception switched from the launching effect to two unrelated movements when the delay increased from about 100 ms to 150 ms, and the change was complete at the latter interval.
2  For the launching effect to occur, the two objects had to be present simultaneously. B had to be present and stationary for about 115 ms (experiment 6) before A contacted it and it moved. At shorter intervals, the impression was that there was only one object that appeared in continuous movement, and the launching effect did not occur.

3  If *B* was not present initially, *A* disappeared before contacting *B*, and *B* then appeared, already moving, in its usual location (experiment 5), subjects had the impression that there was only one object. They perceived two objects only if the gap between the disappearance of *A* and the appearance of *B* was about 200 ms or more.

In each case we see that the critical duration for the change in perception was less than the traditional duration of the icon, about 250 ms (Haber 1983b). This is consistent with the possibility that the explanation for the temporal limitations on perception of the launching effect is that it is a product of processing on the iconic time-scale. For example, in experiment 29, if the two rectangles were in contact for too long, then the movements of each could not be integrated into the perceptual relation which constitutes the launching effect because the time-scale of temporal integration in iconic processing was not great enough to encompass both of them.

The clue to the role of iconic processing in the launching effect is the fact that perceptual cues are used in the construction of objects. It has been shown that 4-month-old infants use coherence of movement as a cue to object unity (Kellman and Spelke 1983; Kellman *et al.* 1986). This is a relevant observation, because coherence of movement is preserved across the two rectangles in the launching effect sequence used by Leslie (1982, 1984) and Leslie and Keeble (1987). This means, first, that coherence of movement cannot be sufficient for identification of object unity because infants in those studies did not perceive the launching effect sequence as similar to the uninterrupted movement of a single rectangle, which also preserved coherence of movement.

Further light is shed on this by comparison between two of Michotte's experiments. The first, no. 29, is the one already described in which, as the time for which the two rectangles were in contact increased from about 100 ms to about 150 ms, the launching effect was gradually replaced by perception of two unrelated movements. The other experiment, no. 30, involved a single rectangle in uniform motion, except that it paused briefly in the middle of its movement. The duration of the pause was varied. Brief pauses were not perceived as such. The motion of the rectangle was perceived as discontinuous only when the pause duration was at least 84 ms. Subjects perceived a halt on all trials when the pause was at least 168 ms. This pattern is virtually identical to that of the change from the launching effect to perception of two unrelated movements in experiment 29. The perception of a causal relation (in experiment 29) was exactly correlated with the perception of continuity in motion of one object (experiment 30). In fact, from tables IV and VI of Michotte (1963), the correlation between the percentage of trials on which direct launching was reported (experiment 29) and the percentage of trials on which continuity of movement was reported (experiment 30) is +0.95. That between the percentage of trials on which two unrelated movements were reported (experiment 29) and the percentage of trials on which a halt in motion was reported (experiment 30) is +0.98.

Only one difference exists between these two sets of stimuli. Michotte used one rectangle in experiment 30 and two, both clearly perceived as such by observers, in experiment 29. The phrase 'both clearly perceived as such' is important because of the findings from experiments 5 and 6 just reported. When infants are perceiving launching effect stimuli, the two rectangles are clearly separate in space for a sufficient amount of time to be perceived as such. What happens, however, is that the movement properties of one are transferred to the other under the condition of contact between them: continuity of motion is preserved across the collision. (As Michotte put it, causal perception occurs when the movement of one is displaced onto the other.)

Here is the point: the motion continuity and coherence cues conform to the pattern that would normally be taken by the infant as indicating a single object. The other cues indicate two objects. This conflict of cues is what is special about the launching effect sequence, as far as infants are concerned. The conflict between the cues can be interpreted as involving two objects and the transfer of motion properties from one to the other. This is the prototype of a causal relation. Infants are not designed to discriminate causal relations from other events: all we need suppose is that the temporal integration function of iconic processing is functioning in them, and that they use it to detect events, and are sensitive to cues to object unity. The rest follows from this. Nor need we suppose a sophisticated concept of causation: at this stage, no notion of power or efficacy or any such thing need be involved in their perception of the launching effect. *It is merely a transfer of motion properties from one object to another.* This is what distinguishes the launching effect from all other stimuli to which infants in the studies by Leslie (1982, 1984) and Leslie and Keeble (1987) were exposed.

Under this notion, when there is no conflict between object unity cues, no causal relation should be perceived. Therefore, when there is no motion continuity, there should be no causal perception. This is what happens when there is a perceptible temporal gap between the two movements (Michotte 1963: experiment 29; Leslie 1984; Leslie and Keeble 1987) and when there is a perceptible spatial gap between the two movements (Michotte 1963: experiment 30; Leslie 1984; Leslie and Keeble 1987). The launching effect can occur in adults when the two rectangles do not come into contact but only when the gap between them is less than 10 mm at the moment of transfer of motion properties from one to the other. Moreover, in this case the gap was perceived not as a gap but as a medium through which causation is transmitted so that, in a sense, motion continuity is still perceived (Michotte 1963). The launching effect also tends to disappear as the direction of movements of *A* and *B* becomes increasingly dissimilar (Michotte 1963: experiment 35): increasing dissimilarity of direction means increasing dissimilarity of motion properties, *ceteris paribus*.

In cases where there is motion continuity but no conflict with other object unity cues, only one object and no causal relation should be perceived. This happened in experiments 5 and 6 of Michotte (1963), described earlier. In these experiments, observers perceived one object in continuous motion unless *A* and

*B* were both present for at least 115 ms or both absent for at least 200 ms. When the launching effect stimuli are presented under viewing conditions that are degraded in various ways – for example, when observers were asked to fixate a point away from the two rectangles – the launching effect was again replaced by perception of one object in continuous motion (experiments 7, 8, and 9). The effect of the degrading was that observers were no longer able to use other cues to tell where one object ended and another began, so that there was no conflict between these cues.

The iconic processing hypothesis postulates a genesis of causal processing in a relatively low-level visual mechanism. It takes information from lower-level processes of motion perception and deals with the conflict in the cues to object unity. As Leslie and Keeble (1987) argued, a low-level perceptual mechanism is relatively impervious to other information, reasoning, and general knowledge. It is likely to continue throughout life and may therefore be responsible for adult perception of the launching effect. Moreover, the job of such a system is 'to feed central learning systems with descriptions of the environment' (Leslie and Keeble 1987: 286): these descriptions form a basis, a set of assumptions in effect, on which further learning and conceptual development takes place. Thus, when an adult comes to apply higher-order cognitive processes to causal inference and attribution, they are applying those processes to information which may already have been causally structured by lower-level processes in visual perception.

The question remains as to what role this visual mechanism plays in the development of causal understanding. Even if it is the earliest kind of causal processing to be engaged in by the infant, this does not entail that it underlies and shapes all subsequent developments. There could still be an independent origin for the conceptual structures used in much adult causal processing. One clue as to its role, however, comes from a second experiment performed by Leslie (1982). The iconic processing hypothesis does not imply that only instances of mechanical causation will be perceived causally: any event relation that fits the requirements of confinement to the iconic time-span and conflict between object unity cues, such that motion properties are transferred from one object to another, will do. Many events in the infant's environment that conform to these require-ments probably involve human actions. Many, for example, involve human hands manipulating objects in various ways, pushing and pulling, lifting and carrying, depressing and turning, and so on. These actions meet the requirement: the motion of the hand is transferred to the object manipulated without appreciable delay. It is relevant to note that Michotte (1963), found that the launching effect still occurs if *A* continues to move after contacting *B* – cf. also his experiments on the entraining effect; Michotte (1963).

Leslie (1982) performed a relevant experiment. He used two films: one in which a hand entered the field, grasped a Russian doll, and lifted it out of the field; and one in which the same movements of the hand and the doll occurred, but they did not come into contact. Leslie habituated infants as young as 3 months to one of these and then showed them the other one. Both orders of presentation were used, and significant dishabituation occurred in both cases. By contrast, comparing the contact film with a film in which the hand entered from the opposite side of the screen and grasped the doll led to no dishabituation. Leslie did not argue for a causal processing interpretation of these findings, but he did argue that they demonstrated infants' sensitivity to the contiguity relation between a hand and an object that it picks up. It is possible, then, that hand–object relations fall into the set of continuity relations that are formative for causal processing. Too little evidence exists, however, for definite conclusions to be drawn.

## ORIGINS AND DEVELOPMENT OF THE CONCEPTS OF POWER AND GENERATIVE RELATIONS

The research discussed so far may provide a point of origin for a number of components of causal understanding:

1 The link between causal processing and events: at earliest times the only things identified as events are those corresponding to the iconic processing definition of a happening, and at those times evidence suggests that causal processing is occurring for, and perhaps only for, some of those things.
2 Because of the requirement of spatial (or phenomenal) contiguity between the two rectangles in launching effect stimuli, the launching effect may be the starting-point for a concept of a releasing condition (see below).
3 The launching effect may also provide an important step in the generalisation of causal concepts from the infant's experience of its own actions to impersonal causation (also see below).

However, there are some components of the basic concept of causation that cannot be supplied by the launching effect. The only concept of the causal relation that matches the features of launching effect stimuli is a transfer of properties concept, and this manifestly does not resemble the concept of causation that children and adults possess. By the age of 2 years there is strong evidence that children have a concept of the causal relation as generative in nature; that is, as a relation in which the cause actually produces or brings about the effect. The evidence for the generative relation concept comes from a series of studies carried out by Shultz and colleagues (Shultz 1982a; Shultz, Altman *et al.* 1986; Shultz, Fisher *et al.* 1986), and a number of points about these studies are relevant here.

First, in comparative studies, Shultz and colleagues found that cues to generative transmission were reliably preferred by children aged 2–4 years over other cues to causation such as covariation, temporal contiguity, spatial contiguity, similarity, temporal priority, and human intervention. Use of cues to generative transmission appears to be an earlier development than use of the other cues listed.

Secondly, additional evidence for the universality and basicity of the generative relation concept was provided by a cross-cultural study in which subjects from rural parts of Africa used cues to generative transmission in ways similar to those of Shultz's Western-educated subjects (Shultz 1982a).

Thirdly, in one study (Shultz 1982a: study 5), Shultz found that preference for generative transmission cues was equally strong at each of four age levels: 4 years, 8 years, and adult. The lack of an age interaction in a study using both adults and 4-year-olds strongly suggests that the generative relation concept undergoes no fundamental change after the age of 4 years, and is shared by both young children and adults.

In addition, I have argued that people understand causes as causal powers (and, permissibly, as releasing conditions and liabilities). Neither of these concepts, causal powers or the generative relation, can originate in causal processing of launching effect stimuli. This may sound counter-intuitive, since it is obvious to so many adult observers of launching effect stimuli that the first rectangle kicks or pushes the second, an impression which owes a great deal to concepts of powers and generative relations. But we have to imagine an infant who does not possess such concepts, and ask ourselves how they might acquire such concepts from observing launching effect stimuli. The answer is that there is nothing in the stimuli that would give them such concepts: they would only acquire a concept of transfer of properties. Thus, for the origins of these concepts we have to look elsewhere. Here I turn to the second main line of research with infants, that by Piaget (1954).

## Piaget on efficacy and phenomenalism

Piaget's ideas cannot be completely accurate. For example, he wrote, 'at first there is no causality for the child other than his own actions' (1954: 220), but the evidence reviewed earlier (Leslie and Keeble 1987) shows that this is too sweeping. I shall begin, however, with a summary of the developmental sequence of causal understanding in the sensorimotor period according to Piaget.

Piaget proposed six main subdivisions of the sensorimotor period, during which the infant proceeds from a phenomenal world lacking any division between self and other, inner and outer space, objects, spatial relations, or abstract concepts with which to interpret experience, to one in which all of these things have been attained, at least at an elementary level. The development of causal understanding proceeds hand in hand with these general aspects of cognitive development.

### Stages 1 and 2

The origins of causal understanding at these two stages lie with two kinds of experience that Piaget called 'efficacy' and 'phenomenalism'. Of these, efficacy is the more important. Efficacy is an experience that accompanies action, though it is not at all easy to define. Piaget (1954) wrote:

> Whether the nursling at the age of one or two months succeeds in sucking his thumb after having attempted to put it into his mouth or whether his eyes

follow a moving object, he must experience, though in different degrees, the same impression: namely that, without his knowing how a certain action leads to a different result, in other words, that a certain complex of efforts, tension, expectation, desire, etc., is charged with efficacy.

(Piaget 1954: 228)

The feeling of efficacy is located at the point of culmination of the action: the infant does not, however, know how a certain action leads to a certain result. Uzgiris (1984) commented that this places the source of causal understanding at 'the juncture of effort and the resulting outcome' (p. 132). It is the word 'juncture' that is important here, because there is no idea of cause and effect and relation between them: that is, no idea of two things related in a particular way; there is just the *one* thing, the experience of efficacy in the bringing about of things willed or desired.

This alone makes it a strong candidate for an origin of the concept of causation: the origins of concepts are likely to lie with the most simple things, because these are most immediate for the infant. The job of relating two things, or of appreciating a relation between two things in such a way as to yield a concept, is surely more difficult than just appreciating a single common experience. It would therefore be easier to begin cognitive development with a single experience as a basis than with a relation made between two experiences: the latter requires that the infant notice both *and* notice that they go together, which is asking a lot more than noticing the experience of efficacy asks.

Not only that, but there are many possible conceptual relations between two things. Cause and effect is one, but there are also similarity, being a part of (for example, *X* and *Y* are both parts of *Z*), class inclusion, mere temporal succession. Why should any pairs be conceptually marked out as causal, rather than as any of these other types of relation? The Humean answer is that those pairs are marked out as causal which possess regularity of association in time combined with contiguity and regular temporal priority of one member of the pair over the other (Hume 1739/1978). But these features would only appear to give the idea of regular temporal succession. Hume only said that the idea of causation arose out of experiences conforming to this pattern: he did not say how this happened. And without efficacy, it is hard to see how it could happen: without efficacy, there is no idea of anything in the world other than regularity of temporal succession, and this is not a causal idea.

The intriguing thing about efficacy is that it lays the conceptual foundation for the *relation* before the idea of any two things as related in that way emerges. Once the infant starts to relate things, the concept of causation is there as a category of relation already. The infant has only to learn how to use it, that is, to learn rules for assigning some events to the causal relation category and not others.

The other half of the point of origin is phenomenalism, that is to say, the phenomenal contiguity of two events (Piaget and Inhelder 1969). Phenomenal contiguity does not require spatial contiguity. Two events may go together in experience even though there is no spatial relation between them, because at this stage the infant has no appreciation of spatial relations. This means that any two events may possess phenomenal contiguity for the infant: there are no limits on the possibilities, other than those imposed by the limited psychological functioning of the infant, and whatever structuring of experience may occur at this early stage. This in turn means that any two events may be candidates for causal relation: there is no restriction to things that are spatially contiguous, or to things that possess any specific quality or property. At these first two stages, there is only phenomenal contiguity: nothing more conceptually sophisticated is involved.

*Stage 3*

This is the stage of secondary circular reactions: the infant is now able to co-ordinate prehension and vision; for example, directing the movement of its hands while looking at them. According to Piaget (1954), the effect of this accomplishment for development of causal understanding is the dissociation of cause and effect, 'the cause being identified with the effectual purpose and the effect with the phenomena perceived' (p. 233). Thus, the infant understands the efficacy of desire, effort, and purpose, 'in short, the whole dynamism of conscious action' (p. 234).

There is, however, no notion of a causal mechanism other than the mere efficacy of action. Causal understanding is still dominated by phenomenal contiguity, and limited by a failure to appreciate spatial relations. Piaget observed that when a child at this stage achieves an interesting result – for example, by pulling a string – they will tend to repeat the hand movement as if not appreciating the importance of contact with the string, as if the hand movement alone was sufficient to bring about the result. In fact, a gesture which the child learns is efficacious in producing one thing is used as if it were efficacious in producing *anything*: the idea of a specific cause for a given effect has not yet been learned.

So at this stage the notion of efficacy still dominates the concept of the causal relation: cause and effect are dissociated from such things as intention, purpose, desire, and effort on the cause side and the outcome of action on the effect side; but there is no notion of limits on the efficacy of a particular cause, and phenomenal contiguity is enough: any two things that possess phenomenal contiguity can be seen as causally related, given only the experience of efficacy as an accompaniment. Most important, the child's only idea of cause at this stage (7 months) is its own activity: the child attributes all causal efficacy to the dynamism of its own activity.

All of this must be qualified by one further observation, which is that causality by imitation occurs at this stage. As soon as infants have learned how to imitate, they use imitation as a way of bringing about the thing imitated. Piaget argued that this is not fundamentally different from the other causal understanding exhibited at this stage, in that the idea of the cause is still the child's own activity. There is one difference, however, and that is that not just any activity will do: the thing about imitation is that the infant is using a specific activity to bring about a specific effect, and the match between the two matters. So it appears that, in this case at least, there is some appreciation of causal specificity.

It is important to note that repeated experiences are not necessary for the idea of a causal relation at this stage. On p. 238, Piaget (1954) reported that Jacqueline got the idea of a causal relation between her movement and the movement of a saucer after one or at most two experiences of the phenomenal connection. This shows the immediacy of efficacy and phenomenalism: they do away with the excessive cognitive requirements of the Humean approach (namely, the infant is required to keep a register of numerous experiences categorised as being of the same kind, in order to learn as a good Humean would). I reported in Chapter 4 the evidence Piaget (1954) found against the Humean approach at this stage.

## Stage 4

This stage, occurring between 9 and 11 months, is a transitional stage as far as causal development is concerned. The main development is an appreciation of spatial contiguity: efficacy comes to be understood as working only through physical contact with the thing acted upon. The first forms of this are drawing things to oneself and pushing them away.

There may also be some dim appreciation of other centres of causation. For example, when the infant pushes away a spoon bringing medicine to the mouth, Piaget (1954) argued that this is an attempt to prevent what the thing pushed away is going to do, and that this therefore shows understanding that the thing can do something – that is, that it is an independent centre of action. Similarly, when the infant touches the mother's lips to make her start singing again, this shows not only a belief in the importance of physical contact for making something happen, but also an understanding of activity – singing, in this case – that is not their own activity.

According to Piaget there is still no true objectification of causation because the infant has not yet achieved object permanence – this is debatable (Schuberth 1983). But objectification, spatialisation, and the distinction between self and other, or inner and outer worlds, are beginning to emerge.

## Stage 5

There are four main achievements at this stage, about 12 months. First, the infant has now acquired the idea of object permanence, and with this goes a belief that objects can have lasting powers of their own. For example,

> Jacqueline is before me and I blow into her hair. When she wants the game to continue she does not try to act through efficacious gestures nor even, as formerly, to push my arms or lips; she merely places herself in position, head tilted, sure that I will do the rest by myself.
>
> (Piaget 1954: 275)

Piaget claimed that 'the child considers the person of another as an entirely autonomous source of actions' (1954: 276).

Secondly, causal relations are fully spatialised. That is, the child has a full understanding of spatial relationships, such as one thing being on top of another. This enables the use of instruments such as sticks as intermediaries between the child's own action and some other thing acted upon.

Thirdly, the child understands the importance of specificity in the cause; that is, that not just any action that feels efficacious will do to bring about some desired effect. This is important because it marks a transition from causation understood as the omnipotence of mere efficacy to causation understood as the operation of specific powers, each limited in scope.

Fourthly, efficacy and phenomenalism become dissociated. The child now distinguishes between self and everything else, and no longer considers all things as caused by the efficacy of his or her own actions. Other things are independent centres of causal powers. Efficacy becomes confined to the realm of the child's own activity, and is understood as the direct power exerted by his or her own intentions or will on his or her body (Piaget 1954: 287). Phenomenalism becomes the basis for the understanding of physical causality. This dissociation reinforces the distinction between the outer world and the self.

*Stage 6*

The infant at stage 5 is limited in being able to perceive causes but not to 'evoke them when only their effects are given' (Piaget 1954: 293). The accomplishment of stage 6, then, is the capability of representing causality: that is, the child can construct or imagine causes not seen, and can foresee effects by starting from a given cause. As Piaget stated, 'representation is necessary to the concept of the universe as a lasting system of causal connections' (1954: 298); and 'the construction of schemata of a causal kind is completely interconnected with that of space, of objects, and of temporal series' (p. 308). At this point the infant leaves the sensorimotor stage, and it is this capacity that presumably underlies the rapid development of the concepts of intentionality and causation documented by research on young children (Shultz 1980, 1982b).

## Comments

The essence of Piaget's disagreement with the Humean tradition lies with the notion of circular reactions. Under the Humean scheme the infant would be represented as basically passive, with ideas of causation merely arising out of repeated experiences of appropriate kinds, without any reasoning or process of understanding. Circular reactions, on the other hand, are *directed*, having a motive power which tends towards the reproduction of an interesting result. Piaget argued that 'it is always, during the earliest stages, on the occasion of personal activity that causal connections are established' (1954: 311), and his justification for this was that circular reactions show, indeed depend on, some appreciation of the connection between action and result. One cannot direct one's activity in such a way as to aim to reproduce an interesting result if one has no idea of any connection between action and result. The Piagetian infant is active, and discovers causality through action. The key features of secondary circular reactions are efficacy and phenomenal contiguity, and these form the basis for all subsequent development of causal understanding.

Piaget's account of causal understanding is closely tied to the sequence of sensorimotor development proposed by him. The problem with this is that he appears to have underestimated the cognitive capacities of young infants in several respects. For example, there is evidence in favour of the idea of object permanence in infants a few months old, and also for the capacity for representation of absent objects in the first year of life (see Schuberth 1983, for a review). Clearly, an infant cannot have the idea of a stable power of a thing before it has object permanence: but, if it has object permanence when only a few months old, the development of the concept of powers is enabled at an earlier stage than Piaget thought.

Piaget claimed that, in the earliest sensorimotor stages, the infant has no object concept, no differentiation between inner and outer worlds, or self and not-self, no concept of space, no co-ordination of sensory modalities. That set of claims is rather unsatisfactorily grounded in the fact that there is no evidence to the contrary. The methodological problems of research on the conceptual and cognitive accomplishments of infants are so severe that we must beware of underestimating infantile capabilities, just as we must beware of inventing abilities and cognitive mechanisms that are more sophisticated than is strictly necessary to explain the infant's behavioural accomplishments.

A further problem is that Piaget lacked a theory of action, or, to be precise, a theory of infantile action. When writing about the causes of action in infants he referred to such things as desires, intentions, purposes, and effort. Not only is it not clear what any of these things might be, but there is no understanding of how any of them is involved in the production of action, if at all. According to some philosophers – such as Taylor (1966) – none of them is. This is vitally important because it is in the causes of action that the idea of a cause originates, under Piaget's account. Not only that, but whatever cognitive or other processes are involved in the construction of a concept of action, they can only work on information that is available to them about how action is produced. Thus, if the actual producers of action are hidden from these processes, whatever that means, they cannot form the basis of a concept of action.

## THE CONCEPT OF CAUSATION

The basis of the causal powers theory is a concept of causation as involving the operation of causal powers of things to produce or generate effects, under suitable releasing conditions. This concept has three main components: the idea of a power; the generative or productive relation; and the idea of a releasing condition. We can see a possible origin for each of these in Piaget's findings.

### The generative or productive relation

To see the source of this it is necessary to review briefly the main argument against the Humean approach. Hume (1739/1978) proposed that the idea of a causal relation would emerge from repeated experiences of event pairs with characteristics conforming to Hume's definition; namely, contiguity and temporal priority of cause over effect. Hume did not, however, say how the idea of a causal relation would emerge from this, nor indeed why anything at all should emerge from it, let alone the peculiar and specific notion of causation that he acknowledged we possess, involving necessity and efficacy.

Imagine for a moment that the concept of causation is taken away from us, with no other change to us. Ask now, how we would get it back. According to Hume, we would get it back from experiences of events related by regularity, contiguity, and temporal priority. I can imagine how such experiences would give us the idea of regular temporal succession. $X$ follows $Y$, we would say, as in night following day. But it is a substantial conceptual leap from regular temporal succession to causation. There are, a priori, any number of directions in which a leap of that size might take us. Something more than Hume's definition would be needed to direct our leap towards the concept of causation we actually have. With regularity alone, there is no compelling reason why we should ever have an idea more sophisticated than that of regular temporal succession.

The problem is compounded, as far as development is concerned, by the extreme cognitive demands the Humean approach makes on the infant. There are two. The first is the requirement to store large numbers of similar instances from different times in memory, since multiple instances are required for the idea of causation to emerge. The second is the requirement to categorise experiences, since instances must be identified as the same or of the same kind before the notion of regularity can apply. An idea as basic as causation must surely originate in something less cognitively demanding for the infant.

Piaget's account does identify something that meets this requirement. The notion that is captured in the concept of a generative or productive relation is that of efficacy. This, according to Piaget, is experienced by the infant from earliest times. Moreover, efficacy is a feature of a single instance: there is no need for a register of distinct experiences somehow synthesised or summed together, no need for categorisation. In addition, efficacy occurs in a suitable place: the juncture between action and result. According to Piaget, in earliest times the infant does not differentiate action and result, but by stage 3 this differentiation has been made and efficacy then resides in the place one would expect a concept of the causal relation to reside, between cause and effect. Given these features, efficacy appears the ideal candidate as an origin for the notion of a generative relation.

### The concept of a power

The cause of every effect is, at least in part, a power. It is always a power that operates to produce an effect. The concept of power has two noteworthy features. First, it is specific: a given power operates to produce a given kind of effect, or range of effects of similar kinds, varying, for example, in intensity and nothing else. Secondly, it is a stable feature of a thing: that is, powers are not required to be permanently possessed by things but do tend to endure. (The full technical account of this, referring to natures and enabling conditions, can be found in Harré and Madden 1975.)

The concept of a cause (as opposed to that of a causal relation) requires differentiation between cause and effect. According to Piaget, this happens at stage 3 as a result of the development of secondary circular reactions. In this case the cause is located in the infant's action or its immediate precursors (Piaget mentioned such things as desire, purpose, and intention). At stage 3, however, the infant does not appreciate the specificity of the relation between action and result, behaving as if any action accompanied by the experience of efficacy can produce any effect.

The earliest sign of the idea of stability in a power is the tendency to repeat a specific efficacious action: there would be no purpose in repeating a specific action if the infant did not appreciate the *continuation* of its power to bring about the desired effect. Thus the idea of stability in the power is grounded in the tendency to repeat the act. It is not clear where such deliberate repetitions of actions begin, but repetition is clearly observed in secondary circular reactions, which have begun by stage 3. If this is the case, then by stage 3 the infant has part of the idea of a causal power, that of stability.

It is not so clear, however, that the idea of specificity has its source here. It is true that it is just one specific action that is repeated in a secondary circular reaction, but it is also true that at this stage the infant continues to behave as if any action were efficacious in producing any desired result. Thus, if there is an idea of specificity underlying secondary circular reactions, it has not at this stage been generalised to all actions, never mind to all occurrences of any sort. The earliest unequivocal evidence of specificity, according to Piaget's account, comes at stage 5, where the infant has learned that not just any action that feels efficacious will do to produce a desired effect.

Thus, by stage 5, the infant has acquired the two main features of the concept of a power, stability and specificity. This is important because both, under this account, have their source in the infant's experiences of its own action and the results of its actions. This, I would suggest, is vital for generalisation of the power concept to things other than the infant.

### The concept of a releasing condition

The idea of a releasing condition is that a power will operate to produce an effect when, and only when, some suitable condition is satisfied. The hammer only smashes the plate under the releasing condition of forcible contact between them. In this case, as in many cases, the main component of the condition is spatial relation: the hammer will never smash the plate (directly) if the two are never in contact. According to Piaget, at earliest times the infant has no appreciation of spatial relations, but is satisfied with phenomenal contiguity. That is, one thing can be the cause of another if the two occur together in experience, regardless of their spatial relations.

Piaget argued that the infant has begun to master spatial relations by stage 4, appreciating at this stage that mechanical causality requires physical contact. The efficacy of its own action in producing an effect, such as a noise from a rattle, depends upon physical contact between the hand and the rattle: making the appropriate movement is no good if the hand is not in contact with the rattle. This, under Piaget's account, is the first appreciation of the conditionality of powers: although the infant may think that it has the power to produce a certain effect, it begins to understand that it cannot exercise the power unless certain conditions are met.

Having said that, the idea of a releasing condition may be grounded in experiences even earlier than those of the stage 4 infant. Leslie (1984) and Leslie and Keeble (1987) found that infants as young as 4 months (stage 1 or 2 in Piaget's scheme) discriminated between a standard launching effect sequence and one in which there was launching without collision, the two rectangles being 6 cm apart at the moment of transfer of properties from one to the other. The difference between contact and non-contact is already critical to the infant's perception of these sequences. It would be going too far to say that this is evidence for a concept of conditionality in the transfer-of-properties relation. The difference between contact and non-contact, however, may provide a basis from which a concept of conditionality could emerge.

## FURTHER DEVELOPMENT

Under this account, the idea of a generative relation emerges from the experience of efficacy in the juncture between action and result, that of a power from the understanding of reproducibility and specificity of the infant's own actions, and that of a releasing condition from an appreciation of spatial relations, particularly physical contiguity in the case of mechanical causation. This leaves many questions about the development of causal understanding unanswered. Here I briefly consider three, acknowledging that for want of evidence these remarks must be somewhat speculative.

### Generalisation of the generative relations concept

If people come to understand all causal relations as generative in nature, and the generative relations concept has its origin in the experience of efficacy in one's own action, then at some point the infant or child must start to apply the generative relations concept to events which are not accompanied by the experience of efficacy.

According to Piaget, infants have some appreciation that there can be other centres of activity at stage 4. This might indicate that the generative relations concept has been generalised at this stage, but it is not clear that this must be so. When the infant touches its mother's lips to make her sing again, all it needs to understand is that its own action is a way of making a pleasant experience occur again. There is no requirement to understand that the pleasant experience is produced by an independent centre of activity. Perhaps it just happens, as far as the infant is concerned. Similarly, when observing a launching effect sequence, the infant need only understand the relation as involving transfer of properties. No idea of the production of effects is required.

There is no evidence with which to settle this question. The most plausible candidate for generalisation is perception of something as resembling something that the infant does. If the infant has the idea of itself as doing something and having the experience of efficacy in the doing of it, then the simplest interpretation of the same thing done by something other than the infant is that efficacy is involved in the doing of that. The clearest example of such a candidate is imitation, in which the infant is indulging by stage 3. The infant does something, the adult does something, the infant does it again, the adult does it again, and so on. So long as the infant can recognise the similarity between its action and the adult's action, it can use imitation as a way of generalising the concept of the generative relation.

Of course, any recognition of similarity might do. For example, on one occasion the infant might manipulate a rattle manually, and on another occasion the infant might observe an adult doing the same thing. The advantage of imitation, as far as ease of generalisation is concerned, is the temporal proximity of the two similar actions. This increases the likelihood that the infant will put them together in such a way as to make the conceptual leap from one to the other. There is more to be said about the attribution of efficacy to other things in the next section.

## Generalisation of the concept of power

The idea of a power can be seen to emerge in the infant's experience of its own activity *before* the infant shows any clear appreciation of the powers of other things. According to Piaget, the idea that other things have stable powers arrives at stage 5, by which time the infant already has an idea of its own powers. If this developmental sequence is correct as Piaget describes it, then the idea of powers in other things is a straightforward development from the idea of powers in one's own action.

The point is that the production of an effect is a kind of interaction between the powers of one thing and the liabilities of another. In my usual example, the smashing of a plate is an interaction between the power of a hammer and the liability of the plate, and would not occur if the plate did not have the liability to be smashed. A similar relation applies in the case of the infant's actions upon other things. When the infant makes a noise by shaking a rattle, the production of the noise represents an interaction between a power of the infant and a liability of the rattle. Thus, in learning the specificity of the effect, the infant learns about a specific liability of the thing acted upon as well as learning about a specific power of its own. In learning about the reproducibility of the effect (by repeating the action), the infant learns about the stability of the liability: the thing can be made to rattle now – and now – and now – and so on.

The conceptual leap from liability to power is very small. Indeed, in the Harré and Madden (1975) account, liabilities *are* powers, distinguishable only by being passive rather than active. We naturally tend to locate the cause in the active power rather than the passive power, because the effect is an alteration in the thing that has the passive power, not in the thing that has the active power, as the typical case of the hammer and the plate exemplifies. None the less, both the active and the passive power are involved in the production of the effect. Thus, in so far as the infant understands reproducibility and specificity in its own actions, it automatically understands reproducibility and specificity in the phenomena it produces by acting upon objects. This is sufficient to give it the concept of a passive power, a liability, in an object, and it is a short step from there to the notion of an active power in an object.

There may be an even more direct route to the idea of powers in other things. If causal relations are relations between powers of one thing and liabilities of another, then an infant can learn about the powers of other things through personal experiences of being acted upon. Piaget laid great emphasis on the activity of the infant as the key to conceptual development, whereas it might have been a better idea to emphasise *interaction*. For example, when the infant is lifted and carried by an adult, the relation is between the power of the adult to lift and carry the infant and the liability of the infant to be lifted and carried. The infant's awareness of being carried is not, of course, accompanied by the experience of efficacy, because it is not something that the infant does. The presence and absence of the experience of efficacy may therefore be the key to the infant's differentiation of things done by it from things done to it.

Now, just as the infant can learn about the liabilities of other things through the exercise of its own powers, so it can learn about the powers of other things through operations involving its own liabilities. Being carried, identified as not being something the infant does because of the lack of the experience of efficacy, implies the power to carry, but also that that power is not the infant's. The conceptual leap the infant must make is to divorce the concept of a power's operation from the experience of efficacy. Since, according to Piaget, the infant has the idea that other things can have powers by stage 5, this leap must have been made by that stage. It must presumably occur through the effective realisation that such things as being carried have all the marks of a causal relation *except* the experience of efficacy, so that it might as well be understood in the same way.

Once this conceptual leap has been made, the infant has the option of attributing the experience of efficacy to the thing that has the power. The infant can think, in effect, that since the relation has all the characteristics of a causal relation except the experience of efficacy, and it does not have the experience of efficacy because it is not the infant who is exercising the power, it is reasonable to infer that the thing that does exercise the power has the experience of efficacy in exercising the power.

Of course, infants do not reason it out like that. What I have in mind is a rule-based device for inductive generalisation. Recall that, under Piaget's account, at stage 3 the infant indulges in a kind of unconstrained generalisation: a gesture which the infant learns is efficacious in producing one thing is treated as if it were efficacious in producing anything. It is only at stage 5 that the infant grasps the idea of specificity in causal powers. This implies that the infant has learned something about the limits on inductive generalisation. In the case of causal powers a simple limit can be established by using a rule based on the cue of resemblance. Thus a gesture which is efficacious in producing one thing is treated as efficacious in producing all things which have a sufficient degree of resemblance to the first thing; that is, effects of the same kind.

This achievement suggests the possibility that infants at stage 5 may have acquired a general procedure for inductive inference based on the cue of similarity. If so, this device can be used to generate the idea that other centres of power have the experience of efficacy in the exercise of their powers: causal relations so produced resemble causal relations involving the operation of the infant's own powers in every respect except for the experience of efficacy, and therefore fit the rule for inductive generalisation of the concept of efficacy. I propose that such a device is operating in infants by stage 5. It may be logically imperfect, but it would be a valuable tool for learning. Locke and Pennington (1982) have argued that adults show a tendency to make extravagant inductive generalisations in a variety of different ways (see also Nisbett and Ross 1980): what appears excessive in adulthood may be merely a harmless residue of an inferential practice that is vital to cognitive development in infancy and childhood.

Clearly, the same device can be used to generalise other concepts. Inferring the experience of efficacy in other centres of power implies inferring the capacity to have experiences, or consciousness of some sort. Thus the infant may attribute such characteristics to anyone or anything perceived as a centre of power. Animism in the broad sense means simply seeing things as alive, without any particular concept of what it is to be alive. Looft and Bartz (1969) surveyed a wide range of evidence for animistic thought in children, and it is immediately noticeable from this survey that the attribution of life to things is at least associated with, if not determined by, the attribution to those things of powers to do things. The very first quotation they gave from Piaget exemplifies this: the child is quoted as saying that poison is alive because it can kill (Looft and Bartz 1969: 2). Although it is clear that animistic thought is reasonably common among children, in other respects Looft and Bartz (1969) found it hard to draw definite conclusions. For example, although Piaget originally suggested that animistic thought passes through a series of stages, empirical support for this is not strong and other investigators have cast doubt upon the stage notion (for example, Munn 1965).

The presence of animistic thought in children, though, supports the notion that children are generalising experiential features of causation from themselves to other things. One implication of the present approach is that previous researchers may have looked at the wrong angle on the development of animistic thought. Generally, they have concentrated on the range of things that are regarded as being alive: for example, in Piaget's scheme of development, the range begins by being very broad and gradually narrows down through childhood. This is to treat the concept of life as monolithic. If in fact it involves several concepts, of which power and consciousness are two examples, then it becomes possible that these concepts do not all suffer the same fate. For example, while children may become more discriminating in their application of concepts such as consciousness as they grow, they learn nothing which induces them to restrict their application of the power concept. Power is, so to speak, depersonalised during development.

Furthermore, if the power concept is generalised to all causal processing from personal experience, and related concepts are initially generalised along with it, this would provide a simple explanation for the apparent persistence of animistic thought into adulthood. Looft and Bartz (1969) reported considerable evidence for this, and additional evidence comes from studies by Heider and Simmel (1944), Tagiuri (1960), and Michotte (1963). Whether animistic responses in these studies were meant literally or as metaphor hardly matters to the present interpretation: the only reason why people might find animistic metaphors congenial is that they exemplify a way of thinking that 'comes naturally', so to speak. If people really understood the world as being the lifeless, inert world of the mechanistic philosophy, as is sometimes claimed (Bronowski 1951), then they would not find animism congenial as metaphor. Animistic causal thought is further discussed in the chapter on physical causation.

## CAUSAL PROCESSING OF OTHER TYPES OF SINGLE INSTANCES

During development, causal processing is gradually released from the confines of the iconic time-scale, so that children become able to infer causal relations between things separated by several seconds (for example, Siegler 1975; Siegler and Liebert 1974). There are perhaps two types of development here: one is to see an event (by the iconic processing definition) as caused by something temporally separated from it by more than the iconic time-span, and the other is to see as events things that occupy extended periods of time, such as the fall of the Roman Empire. I propose two main ways in which either type of development can occur.

First, as soon as the child has acquired some concept of the causal relation, content-specific beliefs can be grafted onto it. Although a general concept such as the generative relation concept is not sufficient by itself for the development of content-specific beliefs, what it makes possible is the direct teaching of causal beliefs by adults (Kassin and Pryor 1985). Once a child has a general understanding of what it is for one thing to cause another, he or she can acquire a content-specific belief simply by being told, for example, that too much ice cream causes stomach ache. The combination of a general concept and direct teaching of specific instances or rules is sufficient for the rapid proliferation of content-specific beliefs, given only a normal range of experience. These beliefs are beliefs about the causal powers and releasing conditions through which things are brought about, and much adult causal inference consists in the application of these beliefs to particular instances. This is why it is necessary that people acquire some concept of the causal relation: possession only of cues for causal inference without a general concept of causation would not help direct teaching of causal beliefs.

Secondly, causal processing can escape the confines of iconic processing by abstraction of cues corresponding to invariable features of the continuity relation. The motion continuity relation has four invariable features:

1   Temporal contiguity. For example, as already discussed, the launching effect does not occur if $A$ and $B$ remain in contact for longer than 150 ms (Michotte 1963).
2   Spatial contiguity. The launching effect does not occur if the two rectangles do not come into contact, except when the gap is less than 10 mm and is perceived as a medium rather than a gap (Michotte 1963).
3   The continuity relation has a characteristic temporal order. Before contact, $A$ has property $x$ and $B$ does not. Then contact occurs. After contact, $B$ has property $x$ and $A$ either does or does not have it. The property is transferred at the moment of contact.
4   The property or properties involved in the continuity relation is/are similar before and after transfer. This is a defining feature: the property transferred must be roughly the same before and after transfer, otherwise there is no continuity. In Michotte's (1963) experiments, the transferred properties were speed and direction of movement. Increasing dissimilarity between $A$ and $B$ in either of these was associated with decreasing probability of the launching effect occurring.

These four features are present in every case of the continuity relation. Although iconic processing is usually regarded as automatic, the potential for development from that starting-point lies in the possibility of abstracting the four features as cues to causal inference at higher levels and longer time-scales, and with other types of event. Although causal processing most straightforwardly occurs for events possessing all four features, abstraction means that the features can be used as cues to some extent independently of one another. This kind of development can be regarded as due to further use of the similarity-based inductive generalisation device.

Presumably this happens at first for events possessing three of the features (for example, events with spatial contiguity, temporal order, and similarity but not strict temporal contiguity). But there is considerable evidence (reviewed in White 1988a) that each of the four features is used on its own as a cue to causal inference by children aged about 5 years (for instance, Lesser 1977; Mendelson and Shultz 1976; Shultz and Mendelson 1975; Shultz and Ravinsky 1977). Kassin and Baron (1985) suggested that these are 'basic' cues to causal inference. My proposal here, then, is that these four are basic cues because they are features of the sort of event that is the first to be perceived causally. This is, in part, a progress from automatic to controlled causal processing, meaning that abstraction of cues from initially automatically causally processed events makes possible controlled causal processing of events that possess those cues.

It is worth adding that many of the occurrences crucial for the development of the concepts associated with the causal powers theory share the first three of these four features. When an infant manipulates an object with its hand, for example, the relation between action and effect has temporal contiguity, spatial contiguity, and temporal priority of cause over effect. Moreover, in many cases the infant must learn the importance of spatial contiguity for the effect to occur. Similarity is a less common feature of such relations. When an infant shakes a rattle to make a noise, the effect (the noise made) is not similar to the cause (the action of shaking the rattle). Relations such as lifting and carrying do involve similarity, though, in that the spatial displacement of the object lifted is similar to that of the hand that lifts. It may be through actions involving the manipulation of objects that the process of abstraction of these cues, and the development of controlled as opposed to automatic causal processing, emerge.

What I have described in this section is the progressive development of causal processing in terms of its application to things other than motion continuity relations. This means in effect that the definition of 'event' changes through development. In a sense, 'event' can mean anything that is treated as conceptually equivalent to a motion continuity relation in so far as it can be subject to causal processing. Thus, although strictly speaking the fall of the Roman Empire is not an event, it can be treated in causal processing as if it were one. Very likely, anything that can be described with a single verb (such as 'fall') may count as an event for an adult, but this is an issue I shall not be pursuing. It is necessary to make clear, though, that as far as psychological metaphysics is concerned the distinction I have drawn between being and happening in terms of iconic processing is basic, and apparent violations of this in causal processing of things that do not fit the iconic processing definition of an event are later developments, grafted onto the basic concept of causation.

In this chapter I have concentrated on the origins and development of the concept of causation. I have not looked at the development of the concept of action. This must wait until the treatment of action as a topic in its own right later in the book. It is apparent, though, that since the origins of causal concepts lie in the infant's own actions, the concepts of action and causation share a similar ancestry, and the story of their development is in part the story of their differentiation from each other. This is taken up in Chapter 11.

# Part 2

# Psychological metaphysics of the physical world

# Chapter 8

# Fundamental assumptions about the nature of order in the physical world

The following chapters are concerned with the psychological metaphysics of the physical world, which I am defining for convenience as encompassing all events other than human behaviour (and mental activities). Most of what follows is concerned with causal processing of physical events. When we consider that such processing may vary from causal inference for a single occurrence such as the breaking of a pane of glass to notions of universal physical laws, it is evident that causal processing of physical events proceeds on a number of levels, and therefore that the different levels involved should be treated to some extent independently for the development of theory.

Doise (1986) has distinguished four levels of explanation in social psychological studies: intrapersonal, interpersonal, intergroup, and societal. These levels have been used by Hewstone (1989) as a means of categorising and analysing the phenomena of causal attribution. These levels are hierarchically related, and equivalent hierarchical relations of levels are detectable in the psychological construction of the physical world. Hierarchical distinctions, however, are not the only kind that should be made. First, the basic distinction between being and happening spans all hierarchical levels; and, secondly, physical things can be grouped according to different criteria. In the present analysis, I suggest that the criteria of category membership and physical location or grouping provide the main theoretical interest, and this distinction also is made at most of the hierarchical levels identified (the exception being the level of individual things, where criteria of grouping have relevance only to properties of a thing).

What kind of understanding do people have of the nature of order in the universe? Clearly, people do not see the flux of events as chaotic or patternless. People expect that the sun will rise tomorrow, that they will get wet if they stand out in the rain, that spring follows winter, and so on. Events fall into a kind of order, and common sense enshrines things that function as assumptions about the nature of that order. This is a broad question which subsumes many more specific ones. For example, to what extent do people see individual events as part of a pattern representing constant and universal natural laws? Do they see order as imposed on the universe by a deity or as intrinsic to it? Do they see order as reflecting causal laws, or as a fixed and static hierarchy? These questions, although of fundamental importance to the study of common sense, have received virtually no attention in psychology. The history of ideas provides some valuable clues to possible answers.

Two steps can be identified as fundamental to the creation of science. The first, perhaps three centuries prior to the second, appears in the *Iliad*, where the course of events is determined by the characters of the actors and not by fate or the gods (Farrington 1969). The second, apparently originating with Thales, is the idea that the universe and everything in it can be explained by reference to a small number of concepts of a wholly natural sort (Farrington 1944). For the first time, natural phenomena were seen as 'the inevitable working out of natural processes' (Toulmin and Goodfield 1961: 62).

This can be contrasted with belief in the arbitrary fiat of divine will. So long as every event in the universe is seen as caused by a god or gods, there is no need for scientific thinking: if events appear orderly, regular, or predictable, they are so because and only because the gods choose to have things that way, and the gods could at any time choose to make things otherwise, to be unpredictable or capricious. Under such a system of belief, propitiating the gods is more important than understanding the nature of events.

A more revealing contrast can be made with the 'science' practised by, for example, the Babylonians and the Egyptians. The Babylonians in particular were sophisticated in observational astronomy and in arithmetic. They developed an accurate calendar and were able to predict the occurrence of some celestial events such as solar eclipses. Their need for prediction and for a calendar was essentially practical: predicting the course of the seasons is important for agricultural production, for example. But surviving documents yield no evidence of theoretical science: their predictions appear to have been purely empirical. They regarded the celestial bodies as gods, which influenced not just weather and the tides 'but also the health and fortunes of men and of states' (Toulmin and Goodfield 1961: 31).

The Egyptians also had an empirical appreciation of regularities in nature, the most important of which for them was the annual inundation of the Nile, and their discovery that it could be predicted by observations of the heavens. Moreover, the Egyptians were technologically advanced, being accomplished at metal-working, writing and record-keeping, agriculture, pottery, building, glass-making, weaving, ship-building, and carpentry (Farrington 1969). Again, this appears to have been unaccompanied by theoretical science.

The point of these comparisons is to clarify the nature of the advance made by the early Greek thinkers. Theoretical knowledge is not a prerequisite for practical knowledge: the Babylonians, the Egyptians, and the Sumerians all developed sophisticated practical knowledge and technological accomplishments without the aid of theoretical knowledge, even though their techniques sometimes incorporated activities that we would regard as redundant, such as a ritual sacrifice to propitiate the god of the pottery kiln. Furthermore, the Babylonians and the Egyptians held beliefs about regularity in causation (implicit in their practical competence and in their ability to write down recipes, instructions which they knew would lead to a certain outcome), and were able to make accurate predictions, which implies a belief that future events *can* be predicted. These peoples had, therefore, beliefs of a sort about order in the universe. Causal analysis, prediction, and control are not necessarily scientific concerns: scientific thought is not necessary for success in prediction or control.

The advance made by the Greeks was not, therefore, the idea of order in the universe, nor the origination of any of the activities of causal analysis, prediction, or control. It was, rather, the postulation of a particular *kind* of order in the universe, upon which the development of theoretical science depended. This was, in Thales' principle, an order inherent in, natural to, the physical universe, not one imposed upon it by divinity.

Bunge (1963) argued that contemporary science implicitly adheres to a principle of determinacy having two components, which he described as follows: 'the genetic principle (*Nothing springs out of nothing or goes into nothing*) and the principle of lawfulness (*Nothing unconditional, arbitrary, lawless occurs*)' (p. 351, italics in original). The latter in particular is recognisably similar to the principle formulated by Thales. A little later, Democritus had essentially formulated both halves of Bunge's principle: 'Nothing is created out of nothing' (Farrington 1944: 62; Farrington referred to this as the doctrine of the conservation of matter); and 'By necessity were fore-ordained all things that were and are and are to be' (Farrington 1944: 62; Farrington referred to this as the reign of natural law). Order in the universe is natural to the universe, not imposed by the gods; and events in the universe can be explained in terms of a few natural laws, which are omnispatial and omnitemporal in scope. Not only that, but there is a kind of constancy in the operation of causes: if circumstances are unchanged, like causes should produce like results, or, as Bronowski (1951) expressed it: 'that given a definite configuration of wholly material things, there will always follow upon it the same observable event' (p. 45).

The cosmology of Thales appears primitive now, in part because its fundamental component was concrete (water), and in part because it was an attempt to answer what we would now regard as an inappropriate question (according to Collingwood 1945: 29, 'What is the original, unchanging substance which underlies all the changes of the natural world with which we are acquainted?'). Thales' successor Anaximander took a further crucial step in postulating as basic something unseen and abstract, a primary substance underlying and constituting all things. He explained the evolution of the world in terms of autonomous developments from premises which were the initial states of this basic stuff – eternal, infinite in extent, and in circular motion. Here we see the beginnings of the slow progress of science away from dependence upon the familiar for explanation. We see also the emergence of an enduring theme of scientific explanation: the manifest diversity of concrete things and events underlaid by the hidden unity of abstract explanatory devices.

Although some people may still understand order in the universe as god-given, there can be little doubt that most people in the Western world have inherited from the Ionians the idea that order is a purely natural feature of things. In his list of 'shared fundamental assumptions' of common sense, Fletcher (1984) included 'that the causal relationships that have held in the past will continue to hold in the future' (p. 204). Bunge's (1963) principle of determinacy quoted above could also be included, as could Bronowski's (1951) expression of the mechanistic notion of cause: 'that given a definite configuration of wholly material things, there will always follow upon it the same observable event' (p. 45).

Although these assumptions appear fundamental to adults in Western society, they are cultural artefacts and may be acquired only gradually during childhood. They do not exist in societies such as (presumably) pre-Ionian Greece, where people believe that order is created by the gods, and could be suspended or radically altered at any time. A number of studies have shown that the search for general principles as means of explanation develops during childhood. For example, using problems concerning the physical properties of objects, Karmiloff-Smith (1988) found that children at age 5 years were content with a local explanation of each individual phenomenon, and did not seek consistency of explanation across instances. Older children were more likely to search for general explanatory principles. Similar trends have emerged in other areas (Kuhn 1989; Kuhn *et al.* 1988; Klahr and Dunbar 1988). Of course, younger childen must have some appreciation of order and regularity, otherwise they would never have expectations (for example, about when Daddy is due home from work) and would never be surprised. It seems likely, therefore, that notions of order and regularity are basic to the psychological construction of reality, and that the tendencies found in the research just cited owe more to the development of relatively sophisticated domain-specific knowledge, or to difficulties in making the similarity judgement that justifies the application of a general rule to multiple instances.

Underlying the application of general principles to instances is what Bronowski (1951) called the foundation of human thought, the 'ability to order things into likes and unlikes' (p. 28) – that is to say, categorisation. To express this in terms that make it an assumption, that the world consists not just of a large number of individual things but that individual things are of kinds, such that one can make valid statements about all individuals of a kind.

This is a somewhat unsystematic collection of ideas, and I propose to use psychological metaphysics to make it slightly less so. My starting-point is the psychological distinction between being and happening, and it is possible to erect on this a number of fairly basic psychological activities, which enshrine fundamental assumptions about the natural order.

## BEING

First, *primary substances*. As I have already shown, the basic particulars, in other words the basic category under being, are primary substances with properties, defined much as Aristotle defined them. The assumption about natural order enshrined in this is that things (anything that someone would identify as a primary substance) remain as they are unless and until something happens to make them otherwise (the natural inertia and persistence of things). This applies, of course, to the properties of primary substances as well as to the primary substances themselves. The psychological origin lies with processes, presumably mainly perceptual processes, involved in the construction of physical objects and, developmentally, the acquisition of the object concept.

Secondly, *categorisation*. The study of categorisation processes has a long and active history in psychology, and I do not propose to pay further attention to it in this book. The point of relevance here is that the activity of categorisation effectively enshrines the assumption already stated, that the world consists not just of a large number of individual things but that individual things are of kinds, such that one can make valid statements about all individuals of a kind. Moreover, categories belong in ordered hierarchies: for example, 'robin' is a category under a hierarchy of other categories (such as 'birds', 'vertebrates', 'animals', 'living things', and so on). Thus, people have beliefs not only about the categories there are but also about relations between categories at different hierarchical levels. Again, it might seem obvious that categorisation is basic to common sense, but it should not be taken as inevitable. We live in a world where the multifarious phenomena of nature have been classified and ordered by generations of work in science. Before this activity began it was far from obvious that things would end up that way; and indeed when science was already mature, scientists occasionally denied the validity of natural categories. As recently as 1744 Buffon was arguing that there are only individuals in nature and that categories are mere constructions of the human mind (Hankins 1985). Buffon's arguments were hard to defeat because the bases for valid classification of individuals into kinds were not known at that time. Categorisation may be a comparatively abstract and sophisticated activity, but it must be founded on basic psychological functions: the principles of conditioning through reinforcement, for example, depend on the tendency of an organism to treat different individual stimuli as essentially similar, and distinct from other stimuli. The importance of categorisation in social cognition probably owes more to fundamental psychological functions of that sort than it does to scientific ideas.

Thirdly, *situations and natural groupings*. People have ideas about how things characteristically go together, or the things that generally 'belong' in a certain situation or place: for example, the usual contents of a living room, or the constituents of an African savannah landscape. This is a topic that falls under the study of schemas (see chapters in Wyer and Srull 1984), and again I do not propose to go any further with it here. The assumption about natural order enshrined in this is that kinds or categories of thing are not distributed randomly through the world, but exhibit *non-causal regularities* in their associations with one another and general place in the world. We can see this assumption elevated to cosmological status in Greek theories such as the concentric spheres of earth, water, air, and fire postulated by Empedocles and Aristotle (Farrington 1944), and it may be that the furthest extension of this assumption in the psychological construction of reality can be found in beliefs on such a global scale; but it is present in schemas of more local application as in the examples just given, perhaps more commonly. This suggests that ideas about natural groupings and situations may also be ordered in a hierarchy from local to global (for example, the contents of a living room; the rooms to be found in a typical house; the arrangement of houses in a town, as opposed to factories, shops, parks, and so on). If the previous paragraph dealt with common-sense taxonomy, this paragraph could be said to deal with common-sense geography, both human and physical.

## HAPPENING

First, *causal powers*. One could argue that the level that is equivalent to that of primary substances is that of individual happenings or occurrences. But in fact this is not the case: the defining mark of individual happenings is transience, so the level that is truly equivalent to that of primary substances is the level at which the assumption of natural inertia applies, and this is the level of causal powers, because causal powers are properties of primary substances and therefore share in the natural stability that properties of primary substances are generally assumed to possess.

The fundamental assumption is that a given causal power always acts in the same way. This amounts to a tautology in that, if a power suddenly acted in a different way, it would be judged not to be the same power. But it is an important ingredient of the natural order, none the less, because it implies a further assumption that unique occurrences can be seen as of a kind with one another in so far as they are attributable to the same causal power. The point is that a causal power is normally seen as a stable property of a primary substance and therefore capable of producing more than one effect: this beaker of acid, for example, has the power to turn litmus paper pink, and if I dip several pieces of litmus paper into the beaker, each individual instance of a piece turning pink will be interpreted as of a kind with the others in being produced by the same causal power. If one piece turned green, that would be attributed to something else.

Secondly, *kinds of causal power*. This is equivalent to the level of categorisation of primary substances, the assumption being that particular causal powers fall into kinds or categories. For example, any beaker of any kind of acid can be seen as having the same kind of causal power, the power to turn litmus paper pink. Kinds of causal power are probably closely related to categories of thing in the psychological construction of reality. There is also a close relation between causation and categories of primary substances, in that members of some categories may be consistently seen as causes of effects in other categories, so that different categories fall into what may be termed causal hierarchies. This is investigated in Chapter 10.

Thirdly, *natural processes*. I deal with these in the next chapter but for the moment let me say that these are complex causal interpretations of a single effect in the physical world, consistent in general structure but differing in specific content. An example would be the derailment of a train interpreted as caused by subsidence of the land under the rail, making the rail buckle.

Fourthly, *causal networks and structures*. These are investigated in Chapter 10, but for the moment let me say that these are concatenations of individual causal relations (and natural processes) into such possible things as chains, trees, loops, and networks. This is equivalent to the level of hierarchies of natural groupings, and reflects an equivalent assumption that causal relations (and therefore causal powers and kinds of causal power) are not randomly arrayed with respect to one another but fall into regular patterns of association.

Fifthly, *causal laws*. This is what might be called the cosmological level of causal processing, roughly equivalent to the assumption of global organisation of things in the world. The assumption in this is simply that whatever natural causal laws exist are omnispatial and omnitemporal in scope.

The various levels of natural order for being and happening are not unrelated to one another, of course. For example, beliefs about causal structures and networks may arise from or at least be connected with beliefs about natural groupings of things; and beliefs about natural groupings may arise from beliefs about a causal network or structure seen as responsible for their production. Categories may be defined partly in terms of causal powers believed to be shared by all members of the category in question; conversely, the natural extent of a kind of causal power may be set by some predefined category, such that all and only members of the category have or can have that kind of causal power.

Whether there is a place in this scheme for assumptions such as Bunge's (1963) principle of determinacy is not clear. I am trying to shed light on assumptions about the nature of order in the psychological construction of reality by viewing them as reflections of fundamental psychological processes, principally processes involved in the organisation of information in perception and memory: organisation into things, organisation into kinds, organisation into groups, and most fundamentally organisation in terms of the being/happening distinction. Whether the assumptions implicit in the operation of such processes are valid representations of the actual order in nature is beside the point: they are psychological creations, and that is how they should be understood. A diagram to summarise these assumptions about natural order may be of some use: but please note, the diagram does not map relations of existential dependence. The only relation of existential dependence intended to hold in this diagram is that the whole scheme is existentially dependent on the psychological distinction between being and happening. Even then, if this distinction did not exist the various levels identified might still hold, only the contents of each level would have to be changed.

The top level of the diagram consists of a box labelled 'world view'. This includes the level of causal laws, but more especially general conceptions of the nature of order in the universe. For example, the universe may be seen, as the Greeks tended to see it (Collingwood 1945), as an organism endowed with soul

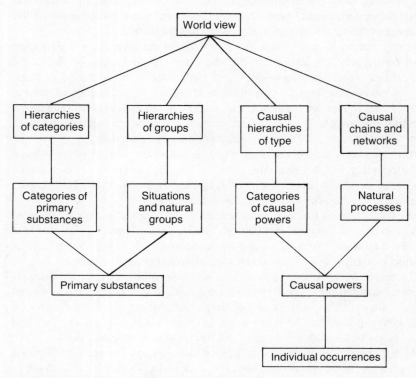

*Figure 8.1* Diagram of levels in the natural order

and will, or, in the post-Newtonian view, as a mechanism, soulless and deterministic. The world view of common sense is investigated in Chapter 10.

In conclusion, the kinds of natural order in the psychological construction of reality are naturally understood as belonging to the world; in other words, as natural in the Ionian sense, not as expressing the will of god or gods, not as merely empirical, violable contingencies. Ideas such as the will of god may be superimposed upon them, but such beliefs should be seen as sophisticated elaborations, not as part of the fundamental assumptions of the psychological construction of reality. The psychological processes that form the foundation for this construction of physical reality are: iconic processing (and its role in the development of causal processing); the object concept (and the processes involved in its acquisition); categorisation; schema-construction. Generally speaking, as we move from bottom to top of the diagram, the role of basic psychological processes becomes less and that of culture becomes greater: that is, a world view is a much more culturally determined creation than is the assumption of the natural inertia of material particulars, for instance. The basic levels set constraints on the range of ideas that may be given by culture in respect of higher levels, and arguably those constraints become less restricting as one ascends the levels. The diagram summarises the levels of enquiry identified above.

# Chapter 9

# Causal relations in the physical world

The exact subject-matter of this chapter is the causal processing of any happening other than what is understood or interpreted by the person doing the causal processing as voluntary human action. This exception is dealt with separately in a later chapter. I use the term 'physical causation' to denote the subject-matter so defined.

The paradigm case of causal perception under the causal powers theory is mechanical causality of the sort studied by Michotte (1963): at its simplest, a mechanical interaction in which a moving object collides with a stationary one, following which the one that was stationary moves. This can be technically described as the power of the initially moving object producing the effect of the initially stationary object moving under the releasing condition of contact between them; the movement of the initially stationary object is the actualisation of its liability to be moved.

The studies of mechanical causality by Michotte (1963) established that causal perception of mechanical interactions conforms closely to the laws of mechanics. This is consistent with the causal powers notion, conforming to a simple principle which governs perception of causal relations. Power is quantifiable, and the more power is put into operation, the bigger the effect it will have, other things being equal. Putting this the other way round, an effect of a given size requires an amount of power for its production that is proportional to its size. For example, greater spatial displacements of a given body require the application of greater force (for example, from collision with another body), other things being equal.

Michotte (1963) also attempted to study qualitative causality, meaning mechanical interactions producing a change in some property different from the active property of the cause, such as change of colour, but on the whole failed to show consistent causal perceptions of such interactions. This may have been due to imperfections in his attempts to simulate qualitative causality, however. It hardly requires demonstrating that people relate the volume of sound produced by a vibrating string in a piano to the amount of force with which the key is struck. The exact limits on perception of this kind of qualitative causality remain to be established by research, but clearly in cases such as the striking of piano keys the power principle applies – more power produces greater effect, in terms this time of amount of noise.

In the case of all-or-nothing effects, the relation of power to effect depends on the idea of a threshold of action (Harré and Madden 1975). If an effect requires a certain amount of power to occur, then an amount of power less than that will not produce the effect. For example, for a window to smash it must be struck with a certain minimum amount of force: if a ball strikes it with less force than that, the window will not break. Any force greater than that minimum will break the window, though of course greater forces may result in greater dispersion of fragments or greater damage.

Causal perception and inference in the case of physical events obviously involves a great deal more than perception of these simple mechanical inter-actions. Consider some examples: lightning strikes; a clock ticks; an oven cooks a meal; a plant grows; a volcano erupts; a snail crawls. This is a diverse collection of events: it hardly seems likely that people understand the causation of all of them in the same way, yet almost nothing is known about how people do understand them. Although there has been research on common-sense under-standing of physical events, this has concentrated on the naïve physics of motion (McCloskey 1983), the use of analogy to model physical processes (Gentner and Gentner 1983), and the development of children's understanding of physical causation (Piaget 1930, 1977). As a preliminary to research on this kind of understanding, two themes stand out as worthy of comment.

## INTERNAL AND EXTERNAL CAUSES

In the psychological metaphysics of mind I argue that Heider's distinction between external and internal causes of behaviour is not basic to causal attri-bution, because it confounds the distinction between action and events deter-ministically produced. In the case of physical causation this distinction does not apply (except metaphorically), so it is possible that in this sphere the internal/external distinction has a better claim to being basic. This being so, we can ask how people understand the operation of internal and external causes of things.

In Aristotle, internal and external causes are conceptualised differently. Internal causes are natural processes, which are autonomous tendencies of a primary substance (whether it be animate or inanimate) towards a mature form, and in which final causes predominate. External causes are conceptualised as interferences in natural processes or natural motion, and are seen more in terms of efficient causation. Natural processes governed by final causes were intended by Aristotle as a solution to a real problem of development: why, for example, should an acorn *have* to develop into an oak tree rather than a beech tree or a horse? Since no answer to this can be found in external conditions, Aristotle proposed an internal tendency for change in a particular direction as part of the nature of a thing.

Emmet (1984) distinguished between immanent and transeunt causation. This can most easily be described in terms used by Johnson (1921). Johnson defined a continuent as a persistent character recognisable over time, and an occurrent as a change in a continuent. Transeunt causation is exemplified by one continuent external to another acting upon it, and immanent causation is exemplified by a change of state within a single continuent. Emmet's view of immanent causation is 'as a mode of functioning internal to a system, and producing change and development over time' (p. 81). This distinction is different from Aristotle's in that the animistic and anthropomorphic content of the Aristotelian version has been abolished.

In both of these accounts, one type of causation can operate independently of the other, but in other theories causation necessarily involves an interaction of some sort, and in these interactions internal and external factors may have different roles. Bunge (1963) argued that external causes, understood as efficient causes, were insufficient as an account of the determination of effects, and that they were better depicted as 'unchainers of inner processes' (p. 197). Bunge gave the example of releasing a taut bowstring, which unchains an inner process that fires an arrow. Causation necessarily involves both the inner process and the external unchainer of it. The theory of powerful particulars (Harré and Madden 1975) offers a similar account.

It is perhaps a weakness of existing causal attribution theory that internal and external causes are conceptualised as interacting statistically, such that each contributes a proportion to the causation of an effect. This is transparent in, for example, the actor/observer differences hypothesis formulated by Jones and Nisbett (1972), where internal and external factors are compared in terms of 'more' and 'less'. It seems more likely that people have qualitatively distinct concepts of the nature of internal and external causes, and the roles they play in a structured account of the origination of effects. It makes no sense to ask *how much* of an oak tree's development is due to its genetic code and *how much* to the nutrition it receives: it only makes sense to ask *how* these factors interact. No doubt people's understanding of the role of internal causes varies greatly according to whether the primary substance in question is a plant growing or a clock ticking. Elucidation of this is an important task for future research. It is relevant to note that children as young as 3 years already know that animals are capable of self-generated movement and inanimate things are not, and have some idea of distinctive internal causes of self-generated movement (Gelman and Kremer 1992).

## CAUSATION IN THE NATURAL AND ARTIFICIAL REALMS

The Aristotelian universe was thoroughly permeated by human-like characteristics. Just as humans seem to have will and purpose, so do natural things. The clearest example of this is natural development, which is explained in terms of final causes, meaning a kind of inner-directedness towards some mature form. Even the stars possessed will, and it was their will that maintained them in their perfect, circular orbits. Whether this is really anthropomorphic thinking can be debated (Richards 1989), but it is not debatable that no sharp line was drawn between humans and other things in the world, as far as the categories of explanation were concerned.

In the Scientific Revolution, the notion of final cause was rejected and the physical universe was modelled solely in terms of efficient causation. 'Matter was essentially passive, inert, uncreative, soulless, and static' (Toulmin and Goodfield 1962: 188). Bronowski (1951) argued that this was the modern view of the world, 'a machine in which whatever happens does so only because something else happened before' (p. 30). An event could be seen as a member of a fully determined causal chain stretching back to the First Cause.

If Bronowski is correct, then in common sense the physical universe is understood in mechanistic terms, and ideas of purpose, will, and so on are restricted in application to human beings, and perhaps a few other animal species. Evidence from psychology, however, suggests that things are not so simple. Consider first a study by Berzonsky (1971). Berzonsky ran structured interviews in which he gave young children various events to explain. He grouped the events into three categories: 'familiar objects' (for example, what makes a clock tick, a car move), 'remote objects' (such as, what makes the wind blow, it thunder), and 'malfunctions' (for instance, what makes airplanes crash, a roof leak). Explanations were coded using two main categories. 'Non-naturalistic' explanations were of roughly Aristotelian or animistic kinds and included 'motivational, finalistic, moral, magical, animistic and dynamic classes' (p. 710). Phenomenistic explanations and references to coincidence were also included here. 'Naturalistic' explanations were roughly mechanistic, 'of a logical or mechanical character . . . related to a given effect in an essentially physical manner' (p. 710).

The results showed that non-naturalistic explanations were most frequent for remote objects, markedly less frequent for familiar objects, and least frequent for malfunctions, while the reverse was the case for naturalistic explanations. Berzonsky interpreted this as an effect of familiarity. Familiarity was, however, confounded with another factor. The nine remote objects were all natural phenomena, as in the examples given. Of the familiar objects, six were artificial (human-made) and three were natural. All four malfunctions concerned artificial objects. Berzonsky did not give separate results for the natural and artificial members of the familiar objects category, nor did he break down his results by object. The results suggest, however, that among young children mechanistic causation is the preferred model of explanation for things that are artificial or literally machines, and that natural phenomena and things are interpreted along lines more reminiscent of Aristotelian thought.

Studies since then have shown that children at age 3 can distinguish between human-made and natural things in a variety of ways (for example, dolls and telephones versus birds and lemons): not only that, but pre-school children have a concept of natural cause, which they can apply reasonably well in the explanation of natural phenomena such as clouds and the sun (Gelman and Kremer

1992). Although children of this age referred to human causes of natural pheno-mena more often than they should have done, Gelman and Kremer argued that 'younger children are artificialistic not because they lack a concept of natural cause. . . . Rather, younger children often lack domain-specific knowledge and are willing to guess on such occasions' (p. 403). And their guesses generally refer to people because they know more about human causes than about causes of other kinds. Evidently young children have a sophisticated understanding of kinds of physical causation, bounded by the limits to their domain-specific knowledge more than by concepts of causation, but it is still not clear to what extent their understanding has an Aristotelian character.

This naturally raises questions about the prevalence of Aristotelian explana-tions among adults. Many studies have shown a propensity of both children and adults for describing inanimate events and occurrences in animistic terms (Bassili 1976; Heider and Simmel 1944; Looft and Bartz 1969; Piaget 1930; Michotte 1963; Tagiuri 1960). One could argue that both adults and children are using animistic terms as metaphors, or that animistic thought is confined to young children and atrophies during development (Piaget 1930); even young children are now thought to be less animistic in their thinking than the Looft and Bartz (1969) review suggested (Gelman and Kremer 1992). But why should people fall into the use of a particular metaphor – as almost all subjects in the study by Heider and Simmel (1944) did – if it is not congenial to their way of thinking? I shall be returning to the possible place of Aristotelian concepts in the common-sense way of thinking about the physical world in the next chapter. For present purposes I shall make some brief comments about animism.

Strictly speaking, 'animism' refers to a tendency to see as alive things that are not. Thus, one can ask how far the concept of life is generalised among creation by adults and by children at various stages of development. The classical picture, derived largely from Piaget's research (Looft and Bartz 1969), is that animistic attributions become less widely applied during development. Thus, at early stages the child attributes life to anything that has the power to do things; then only to things that move; then only to things that move apparently of their own accord; finally, life is restricted to animals and plants. This picture has been critically reviewed by Looft and Bartz (1969); see also Gelman and Kremer (1992). Perhaps the most important points to make about it are that researchers have tended (1) to treat the concept of life as monolithic when it is not, and (2) to treat the attribution of characteristics on which the attribution of life depends as unproblematic when it is not.

First, being alive is one thing; having a faculty of reason and a capacity for choice between actions is something else entirely. There are many things that are exclusive to living creatures without necessarily being possessed by all of them: the capacity for action, consciousness, the capacity for self-movement, powers to do certain kinds of thing, directed change (that is, growth), reproduction, nutri-tion, perception, memory, and so on. Where among these can we find a criterial indicator of life; that is, something possessed by *all and only* living things? It would hardly be surprising if children had some trouble sorting out this problem. But it would be a mistake to suppose that use of a criterion to attribute life to something meant that all characteristics judged exclusive to life were being attributed to that thing (Klingensmith 1953). For example, when a child says that the sun is alive because it gives light, all we can really say is that the child is using that characteristic (or the general category it represents – say, the power to do things) as a criterion for the attribution of life. We cannot say that the child also thinks that the sun can reason, grow, reproduce, remember, or act voluntarily. Thus, the concept of animistic thought hides a host of related but separable research problems. By what criteria do children and adults attribute life to things? How does this change during development? How widely (and how) do they attribute particular characteristics such as consciousness, memory, growth, the capacity for voluntary action, and so forth? How does each of these things change during development?

Secondly, in the Piagetian picture, at one stage the attribution of life is restricted to those things that move spontaneously. This begs the question of how people infer that something is moving spontaneously. Such an inference often depends on having the right theory of how movement is caused. For example, young children sometimes say that the sun moves, because it follows them when they walk (Piaget 1930). Older children, and many adults, of course, believe, or used to believe in times past, that the sun moves because it revolves around the Earth. Whether the movement perceived is illusory or real, the interpretation of it as self-movement is just that, an interpretation, and one that depends on beliefs held by the person in question.

This continues to be a problem for adults because the causes of occurrences are often not obvious. Why does a volcano erupt, for example? For decades or centuries it has sat still and done nothing; now it erupts. No cause is visible. The behaviour of the volcano looks like action in that respect. Thus, if we are still tempted to use self-movement as a criterion for the attribution of life, the animistic metaphor is congenial in application to the volcano. Perhaps this takes us a little closer to understanding why people have different interpretations of causal relations in the natural and artificial realms. In the artificial realm, we generally have theories about the causes of behaviour in machines that relate them to observable events. Thus, a car moves because of what a driver does; a word processor operates in direct response to commands issued by button-press; a light comes on because someone depresses a switch. But no one sees what makes lightning strike, what makes a volcano erupt, or what makes the wind blow. In this respect, the behaviour of natural things looks more like the behaviour of living things than does that of artificial things.

There may not be an absolute divide between natural and artificial things, in terms of people's causal understanding, not least because many artefacts depend for their function on an interaction between nature and artifice – think of a pottery kiln, or a gas light, for example. But it is clear that there is much more to explaining how people understand such things than just animistic tendencies in thought. As for most topics in the psychological metaphysics of the physical world, this is an unjustly neglected research area.

## NATURAL PROCESSES

I now consider the understanding of multiple events with some kind of perceived or inferred sequence or structure. So far, I have argued that psychological metaphysics involves a basic distinction between being and happening, and that happening relates to causation: events, psychologically defined in terms of the iconic time-span, are understood as produced by the operation of a causal power of some primary substance under a specific releasing condition. This would appear to imply that what is identified as the cause of some event in explicit causal inference will always be one or both of the causal power or the releasing condition involved in the event's production. This implication would be false, however, for it would not be hard to think of instances of lay causal inference in which the 'cause' identified is something prior to the production of the event in question. It is not unknown for people to say that the cause of a car accident was the mistake of a mechanic who failed to secure a critical bolt when the car was serviced some hundreds of miles and several days previously. An analysis of that sort would be motivated by a desire to attribute responsibility (perhaps legal liability) to some human individual, but this is not an invariable characteristic of instances of this kind. For example, one could say that a train derailment was caused by a subsidence of the land which made the rails buckle so that the train was thrown off. In this case no human agency is involved, but the thing identified is still prior to the operation of the causal power under the releasing condition that produced the accident.

My initial aim in this section is to extend the causal powers theory of causal processing to account for causal analyses of this sort, and to predict when this sort of causal analysis will occur. This leads on to further consideration of the causal order in reality, as understood in common sense.

For the time being I am keeping to the original definition of event as a change in the amount or type of change in some property of a substance that is above the threshold of detection and within the time-span of the temporal integration function of iconic processing. In perceptual information, events and only events are candidates for causal processing. Since causal processing can be of two sorts, automatic and controlled, this entails that those events that are processed causally also fall into two categories, events that are subject to automatic causal processing and events that are subject to controlled causal processing. It is therefore possible to imagine sequences of events all subject to automatic causal processing.

Consider the example used in the section on defining events and non-events, a boy hitting a baseball with a bat and the ball flying through the air and smashing a window. As I argued in the exposition of the general theory of causal processing, what is explicitly identified as the cause of some effect is whatever is subject to controlled causal processing. My argument here is that what an observer identifies as the cause of the window being smashed (leaving aside practical concerns for the moment) depends upon whether the events in the sequence are subject to automatic or controlled causal processing. The trajectory of the ball between bat and window is not causally processed at all because neither it nor any part of it is an event. The only events in the sequence as described here are the hitting of the ball with the bat and the smashing of the window by the ball.

If the event of the ball smashing the window is subject to controlled causal processing, then what is identified as the cause of the window smashing will be the causal power of the ball and/or the releasing condition of contact with the window and/or the liability of the glass. If the event of the ball smashing the window is entirely automatically causally processed then what is identified explicitly as the cause of the window breaking will be whatever among the events antecedent to that event is subject to controlled causal processing. This will involve reference to the hitting of the baseball by the boy with the bat. Of course, if a person initially automatically causally processes the smashing of the window, this in no way prevents them from processing it (or information about it stored in memory) attentively at some later time, and if this happens then their identification of cause may change. Also, causal analysis will depend on the type of question asked about the event. For example, asking why the ball made contact with the window in the first place is likely to lead to identification of the boy's action as the cause, while asking why, that having happened, the ball smashed the window may lead to the weight or force of the ball being identified, while asking why the window broke that time when on previous occasions it had been struck but survived may lead to identification of some acquired weakness in the glass, or to the unusual force with which the ball was hit. The type of question asked determines, in part, where attention is given, and this of course determines, in part, what among the events is subject to controlled causal processing.

The argument, then, is that causal analysis will lead to the explicit identification of something prior to the production of the event in question as the cause of that event *when* the production of the event in question is entirely automatically causally processed and when, for whatever reason, causal analysis involving controlled causal processing continues. With this segmentation of reality into being (non-events), events subject to automatic causal processing, and events subject to controlled causal processing, the concept of what I call a 'natural process' can be defined as follows: a natural process is change in at least one property of at least one thing and in which there are *either* no events *or* only events that are entirely automatically causally processed. Thus, the trajectory of the baseball is a natural process if the hitting of the ball by the bat and the smashing of the window by the ball are both subject at least in part to controlled causal processing; and the flight of the ball plus the smashing of the window together constitute a natural process if the smashing of the window is automatically causally processed. A natural process is a psychological construction: it is entirely an open question whether it represents any truth about reality.

It follows from this definition that a natural process is bounded at both its beginning and its end by events that are at least partially subject to controlled causal processing: there are three exceptions to this, however.

1  When the end is defined in advance, for example by the type of question asked.
2  A natural process may also be bounded by the moment at which it starts to be, or is no longer, perceived, but this is an exception of no theoretical significance.
3  The bounding of a natural process at its beginning or its end or both by what is understood or interpreted by the person doing the causal processing as a voluntary human action. I shall deal with this in Chapter 11.

The term I use for a boundary to a natural process, at either its beginning or its end, and not including these three classes of exception, is an 'interference'. There is no a priori limit on the duration of a natural process so defined or on the number of events in one.

I can now propose a hypothesis about natural processes. When the production of an event is entirely automatically causally processed and when controlled causal processing continues, what is explicitly identified as the cause of that event is the event[1] (or causal power or releasing condition involved in this event) initiating a natural process of which the event in question marks the termination.

I now compare the foregoing with a different type of analysis of causal structure. This is the INUS condition analysis developed in philosophy by Mackie (1965, 1974). Suppose someone claims that a fire was started by some person dropping a smouldering cigarette butt. In a case of this sort, the dropping of the butt is an ingredient of a scenario that may include, for example, a pile of flammable material near the discarded butt, wooden construction materials, and so on. Mackie argued that the whole scenario is not a necessary condition for a fire because fires can occur under other scenarios. If adequately described, however, it is a sufficient condition for the fire. The discarding of the smouldering butt, on the other hand, is not a sufficient condition for the fire because other conditions, such as the presence of oxygen, are required. But it is a necessary part of the scenario, because the scenario would not have led to a fire without it. So the discarding of the butt is an Insufficient but Necessary part of a scenario that is Unnecessary but Sufficient for a fire to occur. This is an INUS condition, and this is Mackie's concept of a cause.

This is a philosophical theory, but it has been suggested in psychology that this might be part of the way in which lay people analyse causes (Einhorn and Hogarth 1986); Mackie's ideas have also been discussed by Hastie (1983), and by Hilton and Slugoski (1986). Mackie's theory, like Hume's, is a regularity theory of causation, although it deals in statements about conditionality rather than regular co-occurrence or covariation.

I would propose that an account in terms of causal powers and generative relations is closer to the common-sense understanding of this sort of case, specifically one employing the natural process/interference distinction. Essentially, the discarding of the butt is seen as the cause of the fire because it is an initiation of a natural process seen as causally connected to the fire in a way that does not include any other interferences. That is, it is the closest interference to the fire in the causal structure that constitutes someone's causal analysis of the fire scenario.

What is selected as the cause must be an event, as defined earlier. There are in fact no other events in the scenario as described. The presence of oxygen and the pile of flammable material are not chosen as the cause of the fire because they are not events. One could of course imagine other possible events. The initial lighting of the cigarette, for example, might be seen as a necessary condition for the discarding of the smouldering butt (that is, for the fact that the butt is smouldering when it is dropped) but it would not be cited as the *cause* of the fire because the interference that the dropping of the butt represents comes *between* the lighting of the cigarette and the fire.

One could also imagine that, after dropping the butt, the actor leaves the building, slamming the door behind him. This is an event, and it is between the dropping of the butt and the fire in time. But it is not cited as a cause of the fire because we have no existing causal beliefs connecting slamming doors with starting fires. In saying this I am returning to one of the formal characteristics of an adequate causal inference in controlled causal processing: the thing cited as the cause must be something that is already believed to be a possible cause of the effect in question.

Let us suppose that, first, the cigarette sets fire to the pile of flammable materials, and these then set fire to the building. Why is the latter not cited as the cause of the fire? It is an event, but it is not identified as the cause of the fire in controlled causal processing because it is part of a natural process leading from the dropping of the butt to the building being on fire. It is not an interference, as defined above.

This analysis leads to the following statement of the characteristics of that which will be identified as the cause of some event in physical reality in controlled causal processing:

1  It fulfils the aim of contributing to current practical concerns. Specifically, it is something that counts as an answer to an implicit or explicit causal question.
2  It involves the identification of a specific causal power or releasing condition or combination of the two as the cause of the effect (and/or some liability).
3  It will explain by identifying something that is already believed to be a possible cause in principle of the effect in question.
4  Within the above stipulations, it will identify the most recent interference prior to the effect in question, where interference is defined as above.

For the sake of simplicity I have so far been expounding the theoretical account of natural processes and interferences in terms of the strict iconic processing definition of 'event'. In the previous chapter I argued that the concept of an event developed from this original definition, so that things outside the iconic time-span, such as the fall of the Roman Empire, could come to be construed as events. This argument obviously applies to natural processes as well. So, while the definition of a natural process is constant, the sorts of things that may count as natural processes psychologically change during development with change in the way that events are identified. If, for example, one had a concept of the fall of the Roman Empire as a single event, and if that event came to be automatically causally processed, then it could be seen as part of a natural process, under the definition given in this chapter. Thus, natural processes can exist in the psychological construction of reality at any level of generality or abstraction, depending only on where the concept of 'event' can be applied. There is no fundamental difference between natural processes appearing at different levels of generality or abstraction, only difference in the specific events and things included in them.

## Causal propagation

This does not complete the theoretical account of natural processes. I have segregated the stream of natural processes and interferences into events and non-events. All interferences are events, but not all events are interferences. Natural processes can include both events and non-events. Only events are subject to causal processing.

This seems to imply that in the psychological construction of reality causal relations tend to be isolated from each other by the gaps between events. Take the baseball example. Here we have two events processed causally, the hitting of the ball by the boy with the bat, and the smashing of the window by the ball. The events are connected by the natural process of the ball's trajectory through the air. But the trajectory of the ball is not subject to causal processing, so it appears that the two causal relations are isolated from each other, as far as causal processing is concerned. Obviously this is not correct: most people would say that there is some kind of causal relation between the two events. It would not be out of place in ordinary discourse to say that the boy smashed the window by hitting the ball at it, whether intentionally or unintentionally. Clearly, people perceive or infer what may be called causal propagation between the events.

Salmon (1984) treated examples rather like this in his philosophical account which distinguishes causal production from causal propagation. Causal propagation concerns the fact that causal influence can be propagated through time and space, as in the path of the baseball. This is an example of what Salmon called a process, and the defining feature of a causal process is the ability to carry a mark. For example, consider a light pulse travelling from a spotlight to the wall of a planetarium. This is a causal process because it can carry a mark: if a red filter is placed between the spotlight and the wall, the light pulse will be red all the way from the filter to the wall. Now rotate the spotlight: the motion of the spot of light around the wall is not a causal process because it cannot carry a mark. If a red filter is placed in its path, the spot of light will be red when it passes over the filter, but will cease to be red as soon as it moves off the filter.

Salmon gave an account of causal production and propagation based on the spatio-temporal features of mark-carrying. His account, however, does not involve reference to causal powers and releasing conditions. Under the causal powers theory of causal processing, causal propagation involves the acquisition by something of a particular kind of mark, specifically a mark that can serve as a *releasing condition* for a causal power of the thing that acquires it.

The baseball, then, has a causal power which we can define for the sake of the example as the power to smash windows. Obviously this power will not operate when the ball is stationary (unless a window is dropped on it): the operation of the causal power requires some kind of releasing condition. The ultimate releasing condition is contact between the moving ball and the window. But this releasing condition is simply a reflection of the fact that the ball was hit in such a way that it collided with the window. The releasing condition is in effect imparted to the ball by the act of hitting it with the bat, and the ball carries the releasing condition across the intervening time and space.

Really, of course, the releasing condition is a complex thing, involving not just contact between ball and window but also the ball moving with sufficient momentum to smash the window, and the mark carried by the ball has more to do with momentum than with contact. Equally, the property imparted to the ball by the bat is not fixed: for example, the ball can slow down during its flight. But so long as the change does not fit the definition of an event – that is, so long as it is not sudden – then the whole trajectory of the ball will be seen as one natural process, carrying part of the releasing condition for the ball to smash the window.

So the effect of the last interference before the occurrence of some effect to be explained is the origination of part of a releasing condition for the operation of a causal power of a thing, which is acquired as a transient property of the thing involved in the natural process between the interference and the effect to be explained. The thing carries the partial releasing condition through time and space to the site of the effect in question, where the effect is produced by the fulfilment of all that is required of a releasing condition for the operation of the relevant causal power of the thing. I propose that people understand all movement of physical objects in this way: the force of an object in motion is a function of its causal power in relation to mechanical interactions and the acquired releasing conditions represented by its motion properties.

## Natural processes and topistic causal thinking

There is in principle no upper limit on the complexity of natural processes in the psychological construction of reality. Automatic processing and long-term memory are not confined to the limited capacity of short-term memory, so it is possible for perception of and beliefs about complex causal networks to develop. Events that initially require controlled causal processing come, with experience, to be automatically causally processed. Those things that are natural processes in common sense therefore depend to a considerable extent upon the acquisition of beliefs about the things and causal connections involved. There is a tendency for initially isolated causal connections to become increasingly integrated in a complex natural process, so that the structure of events becomes more coherent over time, in the psychological construction of reality.

The corollary of this is that, at an early stage of development, causal beliefs exhibit a topistic character. 'Topism' is a term for a metaphysical doctrine exemplified by some forms of atomism, in which the universe can be likened to a collection of tiny units interacting, units which are logically independent of one another: this can be contrasted with a continuum metaphysics, exemplified by field theory (Toulmin and Goodfield 1962). Topistic causal thinking, then, would be exemplified by a belief that a cause could have some single specific effect; for example, an effect on one unit of matter, without any influence on any other unit. Sacks (1973) gave as an example of a 'mystical' topism the idea of the 'magic bullet' or 'perfect specific', a substance which precisely cures some disease without any other effect on the afflicted organism. My argument here is that topistic causal thinking in common sense does not reflect a topistic or atomistic metaphysics, but rather is a natural feature of causal beliefs at a relatively early stage of development.

Consider a hypothetical example. A particular cereal crop is threatened by a weed. The farmers learn that the weed is the preferred food of a species of beetle not found in their locality. They introduce the beetle with the aim of destroying the weed and protecting their crop. This could be taken as an example of topistic causal thinking. The farmers believe in effect that the introduction of the beetle will have one effect and no other. But this belief does not mean that the farmers adhere to some doctrine of mystical topism. Rather it is at this early stage the only causal belief they have about natural processes involving the beetle, and at this stage it is therefore inevitable that their thinking will exhibit an apparently topistic character.

Now it turns out that the beetle also eats the eggs of a ladybird that is the main predator of several species of insect whose preferred food is the cereal crop. These pests multiply in the absence of their natural enemy and the crop is devastated. Once the people involved discover these facts and become familiar with them, they can develop a more complex picture of natural processes involving the beetle, in which individual causal connections are related in a coherent structure of events. When this happens, their thinking about the beetle no longer seems topistic, not because they have changed philosophies but because they have acquired more beliefs about causal connections and integrated them into a coherent structure of a natural process.

Another hypothetical example can be given from medicine. A drug is discovered which, let us say, cures cancer of the spleen. Early clinical trials are so successful that the drug is dubbed the new magic bullet. Again this need not reflect a topistic philosophy, which is the way in which Sacks (1973) appears to have interpreted this sort of thinking, but simply indicates that no other causal beliefs about the drug yet exist. Longer term trials indicate that the drug has other effects on patients as well, let us say sterility and hair loss. Again, once these are discovered the causal beliefs become articulated into a more complex natural process and the topistic character of the initial causal belief disappears. Of course, if doctors continued to believe in the possibility of a magic bullet in the context of these more complex beliefs, then this *would* be an instance of Sacks' (1973) mystical topism underlying their thinking. But it is important to distinguish topism as an article of faith from topistic causal beliefs as an incidental feature of beliefs about causal processes at an early stage of development.

Sacks (1973) contrasted perfect specifics with panaceas as representatives of contrasting philosophies – mystical topism and mystical holism, respectively. Under the present view, both depend on the natural process/interference distinction. A perfect specific is an imaginary stuff that cancels all and only one particular type of interference in the natural processes of health: a panacea is an imaginary stuff that cancels *all* types of interference in the natural processes of health. Neither affects the natural processes of health in the slightest, except indirectly through their effects on interferences in health.

These examples are less simple than they might appear, in terms of the natural process/interference distinction. The beetle and the drug can each be viewed as an interference in a natural process – the weed/crop interaction, and the development of the cancer, respectively. The beetle and the drug can have this role because they are both novel introductions, events that have to be subject to controlled causal processing at first. They can be initiators of some natural process, but cannot be contained within one, at first. What happens, then, as causal beliefs become more integrated, is that things that began as interferences become ingredients in natural processes. This is part of what happens as they become familiar and switch from controlled to automatic causal processing. What we identify as an interference changes as our familiarity with events increases.

The complication in the farm and disease examples concerns the proper conceptualisation of the weed and the cancer in the psychological construction of reality. They could be viewed initially as interferences in natural processes themselves, the natural processes of farming and the healthy functioning of the body, respectively. Under this view, for example, if one has a set of beliefs about the healthy functioning of bodies, and the body appears to be healthy, then the occurrence of cancer is an unexpected event, an interference in the natural processes of health. Following this, the idea of the natural process involved switches to one of body-with-cancer, and the administration of the drug is viewed as an interference in that.

The problem with this view is that the idea of the cancer as a disruption of the processes of health does not depend on whether it is processed as an interference or as part of some natural process. Health and disease, natural environment and pollution, farm or garden and weed, all seem to fit some notion of natural occurrence and disruption, yet there is clearly something more to this than the psychological definition of natural process and interference in terms of automatic and controlled causal processing.

There appear to be two possible answers to this problem. One can be found in a consideration of the metaphysics of being; that, in effect, the causal order in the psychological construction of reality is determined by the metaphysics of happening *and* by the metaphysics of being. I speculated earlier that the internal/ external distinction might turn out to be of fundamental importance to people's understanding of physical causation. This distinction, however, is existentially dependent on the primary substance metaphysics of matter, and more specifically on the ways in which people identify primary substances: 'internal' means as part of a primary substance, and 'external' means not as part of that primary substance. Following Emmet (1984), we can use the term 'immanent causation' to refer to the production of effects by the operation of a causal power internal to the thing in which the effect is produced, and the term 'transeunt causation' to refer to the production of effects by the operation of a causal power extrinsic to the thing in which the effect is produced.

In the cancer example, then, the human body is a thing or primary substance and the cancer is something that is not a natural part of the body. The cancer, of course, is internal to the body (in the spleen in this case), but despite this it is not part of the concept of the human body and is therefore external ('extrinsic' might be a better term) as a causal influence upon the body. The effects of the cancer on the body can then be distinguished from the normal working of the body as transeunt, rather than immanent, causation, and my hypothesis is that this distinction is embodied in common-sense causal processing.

The farm and weed example appears more contentious because it is debatable whether a farm is a primary substance in the way that a human body is. The conceptual (as opposed to perceptual) identification of primary substances is a psychological problem of great complexity: the farm cannot be identified simply in terms of its physical boundaries, as some primary substances could be, because this would mean the inclusion of things that one might not consider part of the farm, such as birds, visitors' cars, and so on. Likewise, the human body is not identified simply in terms of its boundaries because the cancer lies within those. In addition, the physical boundaries of a farm are in fact impossible to ascertain, including an uncertain amount of air into which the crops grow and an uncertain amount of soil through which their roots extend. Moreover, it has extent in time as well as space, and its physical boundaries are liable to change over time.

For present purposes, though, I am more concerned with the fact that people *have* a concept of a farm than with how they identify one. It is sufficient to observe that people could make decisions about what is and what is not part of the farm, if requested. Now, people might say that the weed is not part of the farm, so that its influence is processed as transeunt causation. In this case it is similar, in its causal conceptualisation, to the cancer.

There is, however, a second way of looking at examples like the cancer and the weed. The difference between health and disease, natural environment and pollution, farm or garden and weed, can be conceptualised in terms of practical concerns. Disease, pollution, and weeds can all be distinguished as things that disrupt the attempt to fulfil some definite set of practical concerns. The person wishes to reman healthy, to do those things that depend on health, and the cancer threatens that; the farmer wishes to produce crops or make a profit, and the weed threatens that. The metaphysics of being need only be minimally involved in this, in that the weed and the cancer are still distinguished as primary substances from the farm and the body: we no longer need to define a farm as a primary substance, only to define the set of the farmer's practical concerns.

The idea of conceptualising interferences in terms of practical concerns has considerable appeal, but it is not enough on its own: the metaphysics of primary substances and the internal/external distinction must also contribute. This can be judged by consideration of a hypothetical example in which the two conflict. Suppose that a factory near the farm emits large quantities of carbon dioxide which promote the growth of the farmer's crop. This causal influence would be seen, under the present theory, as of a kind with the influence of the weed in that it is an influence on the farm from something outside what the farm is thought of as being, even though it facilitates rather than disrupts the practical concerns of the farmer. Whatever the role played by practical concerns, it would appear from this that the distinction between immanent and transeunt causation is important to the causal processing of physical occurrences.

The basicity of this distinction is also apt to encourage topistic causal thinking of certain sorts. Returning to the cancer example, the distinction between the natural processes of the body, conceptualised in terms of immanent causation, and the influence of the cancer, conceptualised in terms of transeunt causation, may be responsible for a feeling of plausibility in the idea of a perfect specific. That is, the idea of a perfect specific may appear plausible because its action can be exactly defined by reference to the basic categorical distinction between transeunt and immanent causation: it affects the events occurring under the transeunt heading and leaves those occurring under the immanent heading untouched. With this possibility, topistic causal thinking may persist even in the context of complex acquired beliefs about natural processes in relation to bodily functioning, because effects of the conceptual distinction between immanent and transeunt causation are psychologically independent of beliefs about natural processes.

## LEVELS IN THE CAUSAL ORDER

I have in this chapter been concerned with the simpler patterns of organisation of causal connections involving physical events:

1 Individual causal connections involving the production of an effect in a thing by the operation upon it of an extrinsic causal power, as in mechanical causation.

2  Individual or multiple causal connections involving the production of one or more effects or a continuous process in a thing by the operation of a causal power intrinsic to it.
3  The relation of non-events and events subject to both automatic and controlled causal processing in coherent sequences called natural processes.

These things lay the foundation for consideration of the broader organisation of causal connections. Three main aspects of this are treated in the next chapter: the sequential structure of causal connections related to one another, particularly whether sequences of causes and effects are organised in linear or cyclic (feedback) structures; relations between things in different domains or categories of physical reality, specifically the kind of hierarchical (or other) relations that obtain between different categories of things; and the world view of common sense.

## NOTE

1  Lest readers think that I have slipped back into a model of event causation, 'event' here means the operation of a causal power in producing an effect.

# Chapter 10

# Causal order in nature

In this chapter I am concerned with the ways in which individual causal connections are organised in relation to one another, conceptually as opposed to the basically perceptual organisation in terms of natural processes. The main questions to be considered are the hierarchical organisation of causal influence across categories of things, tendencies to see causal influence as linear or cyclic, and, in a later section, the world view of common sense.

## CAUSAL CHAINS AND HIERARCHIES IN NATURE

In the absence of psychological research on this topic, my intention is to consider this aspect of the psychological construction of reality in the light of historical precedents. I consider three among the many that could be chosen. These brief summaries are derived from more extensive accounts to be found in Toulmin and Goodfield (1961, 1962), Dijksterhuis (1961), Boas (1962), Farrington (1944), Santillana (1961), Bronowski (1951), Debus (1978), and Laszlo (1972).

### Aristotle

I have already discussed several aspects of Aristotelian thought, including his four types of cause, primary substance metaphysics, and ten basic categories. But the feature of Aristotelian thought that is most relevant to the present investigation is the notion of the world as a one-way causal hierarchy. This is a type of hierarchy in which the seat of control is found at the top level, and causal influence proceeds down the hierarchy but not up. Santillana (1961) commented: 'The underlying image seems to be patriarchal power generating life, type, and order without losing anything of its dominant force' (p. 220). The choice of the words 'patriarchal', 'power', and 'generating' is not accidental: Aristotle understood causation as involving the operation of powers actually producing or generating effects (cf. Harré and Madden 1975), and the patriarchal overtone represents not just the unidirectional nature of the hierarchy but also its essentially anthropomorphic character. The top level of the hierarchy controls what goes on at lower levels in a way that looks very like the exercise of free will, in the sense that it is a causal origin and has no antecedents outside of itself. 'The upper causes rain down, so to speak, constant action and order . . . without being affected by anything below' (Santillana 1961: 220).

## The mechanistic tradition

In very crude terms, the Scientific Revolution saw the abolition of formal and final causes from accounts of the universe, and the triumph of efficient causation. The transformation to mechanicism (the term preferred by Dijksterhuis 1961) was not accomplished overnight: Hooke and Newton, for example, continued to refer to the concept of action and vital spirits (Schaffer 1987), and finalistic concepts persisted in science, particularly physiology, long after the age of Newton. Ultimately, though, the world view of classical mechanicism became thoroughly divorced from the Aristotelian tradition. The natural order of mechanicism is one based on laws of efficient causation, not one based on purposes, patterns, correspondences, symbolism, divine harmonies, or hierarchies (Debus 1978). The behaviour of all bodies could be explained by the laws of mechanics, by causation acting upon a body from outside. 'Matter was essentially passive, inert, uncreative, soulless, and static' (Toulmin and Goodfield 1962: 188). The unfolding of the universe, then, was a set of linear chains or networks or trees of efficient causation, fully deterministic, encompassing every event in the universe, with no element or level being free of causal antecedents.

## Natural systems

The change in world view that came with systems theory is not so much at the level of individual causal connections, which can still be conceptualised in terms of classical efficient causation, but in their organisation: the undifferentiated linear sequences of the classical mechanicist view can be contrasted with the hierarchically organised relations of interdependence that mark the natural systems view (Laszlo 1972). Two features are of particular importance for present purposes. First, sequences of causation in the systems view can exhibit circularity (in the sense of returning to the same point at a different time), thus creating cycles (such as the water cycle) and feedback loops. Feedback loops can be of two kinds: negative feedback, as in a thermostat, where the action of one element in a system initiates – I am using the word 'initiates' very loosely here – a sequence of events leading to the cancellation of the effects of that action, thus actively maintaining an equilibrium; and positive feedback, in which the action of an element initiates a sequence which leads to and perpetuates the action and its consequences, resulting, without interference, in a unidirectional change in the values of at least one parameter towards an extreme value.

The other relevant feature is the notion of a two-way hierarchy of control. Laszlo (1972) envisaged nature as a hierarchy of systems from many simple ones at the bottom to few complex ones at the top. Natural systems link the levels immediately above and below themselves: 'they are wholes in regard to their parts, and parts with regard to higher-level wholes' (p. 67). In terms of causal processes, systems take input from and give output to the levels above and below themselves, so that the hierarchy is two-way and no level has control, in the Aristotelian sense, of the hierarchy as a whole.

## Research in psychology

There are two existing streams of psychological research that are relevant at least to the contest between Aristotelian and mechanistic ideas about physical causation. From the developmental literature come several investigations of children's tendency to interpret natural events animistically (Berzonsky 1971; Looft and Bartz 1969), discussed in previous chapters. There is also a set of studies on students and other adults showing that 'naïve' ideas about motion sometimes follow Newton's laws of motion and sometimes resemble either medieval impetus theories or Aristotelian thought (Kaiser *et al.* 1986; Kaiser, Proffitt, and Anderson 1985; Kaiser, Proffitt, and McCloskey 1985; McCloskey 1983; McCloskey *et al.* 1980; McCloskey *et al.* 1983; Shanon 1976).

These two bodies of research may not be unrelated. Animism and anthropomorphism were ingredients of Aristotle's view of the universe, so that the two sets of findings can be unified under the suggestion that common-sense beliefs about nature retain an influential residue of the long Aristotelian tradition, which has been at most only partly superseded by the mechanistic philosophy and physics of the Scientific Revolution. This possibility is enhanced by findings that adults, too, often use animistic language to describe abstract or mechanical events (Bassili 1976; Heider and Simmel 1944; Michotte 1963). Most striking is the finding reported by Michotte (1963). Michotte used stimuli designed to resemble the oldest cliché of classical physics, collisions between billiard balls, and he found that his subjects' causal perceptions showed excellent agreement with the laws of mechanics. Despite this, his subjects often described what they saw in animistic terms (for example, 'A gives B a kick in the seat of the pants and sends him flying', p. 280).

One way of looking at this is that it represents the possibly atrophying remnant of Aristotelian thinking, which dropped into Western culture during the Middle Ages and has yet to disappear entirely. It is also possible, however, that a developmental psychological interpretation is appropriate. In earlier chapters I have argued that the earliest example of causal perception can be found in infancy in the perception of mechanical causality, specifically in the perception of motion continuity across two objects, where continuity is psychologically defined with reference to the temporal integration function of iconic processing. At some stage not long after this, a concept of causation as involving the generation of events through the operation of powers of things is acquired and becomes imposed upon causal perception of transfers of properties. The power concept originates in the experience of efficacy in the production of action, which means that it tends initially to be associated with other apparent components of willed action: that is, those components become part of the way in which causation in general is understood. During development those animistic components of causal perception and inference are gradually weeded out, so to speak, so that only the power concept remains. It is perhaps for this reason that people retain a fondness for animistic metaphors of the sort observed by Michotte (1963).

The importance of this for the present study is that a one-way Aristotelian hierarchy is essentially an animistic concept, as already described. Whether or not Aristotle's view of nature owes something to fundamental psychological factors which applied to him as well as to us, this developmental hypothesis, and the evidence for animistic ideas and metaphors in causal perception, imply that people should tend to view nature as a one-way causal hierarchy, in which events are generated through the operation of powers attributable to things higher up the hierarchy, culminating in the source of power in the system at whatever lies at the top of the hierarchy. A two-way hierarchy in which no particular level has control (or free will) does not fit this view.

## Studies

I have so far carried out two studies on the psychological construction of causal structures in nature, using the three traditions outlined above as competing hypotheses about the order in those common-sense beliefs. These studies are reported in full elsewhere (White 1992). Here I shall briefly describe the main results.

The two studies used the same method. A set of file cards (84 in the first study, 64 in the second) was laid out on a table. On each card a short sentence was written describing some event or change in the natural world, such as a winter being warmer or colder than usual, the population of a certain species or type of animal or plant increasing or decreasing, and so on. The cards consisted of pairs of opposites or near-opposites, so that for every card describing a change in one direction there was a card describing a change in the opposite direction. Participants were asked to draw out pairs of these cards that they thought were causally related in some way, and to say which was the cause and which was the effect. The experimenter made a note of the choice and the cards were then returned to the table, so that either or both could be used again if the participant wished. There was no limit placed on either time or the number of pairs chosen.

In the first study 25 adult participants produced 1,293 pairs, a mean of 51.72 per participant. In the second study, 25 different adult participants produced 1,346 pairs, a mean of 53.84 per participant.

## Categorical hierarchies

In both studies the cards were designed to fall into various categories. In the first study the categories were the weather, human activities, animals, and plants. A fifth category, physical processes, was also included, but this was a miscellany of different types of thing (including cards referring to the ozone layer, floods, and so on), and will not be discussed here. In the second study temperature, water (rain, clouds, and so on), plant, and animal cards were used.

It is possible to ask, for pairs which relate one category to another, whether there is any overall pattern into which those pairs fall. Specifically, do the pairs fall into an Aristotelian unidirectional hierarchy or into a two-way systems hierarchy? The results of both studies revealed a strong tendency towards a unidirectional hierarchy, shown in Figures 10.1 and 10.2.

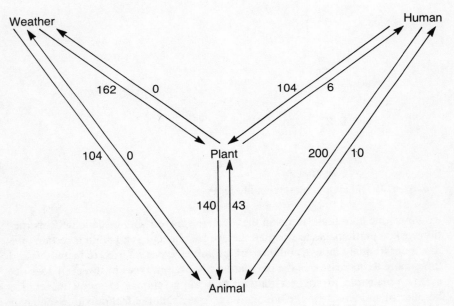

*Figure 10.1* The causal hierarchy, study 1

Figure 10.1 shows a unidirectional causal hierarchy with weather and human at the top, plants in the middle, and animals at the bottom. Weather and human are independent of one another: there are no human–weather links and, perhaps more unexpectedly, only four weather–human links. Causal links that violate the directionality in this hierarchy account for only 5.32 per cent of all pairs, and almost all of these are animal–plant pairs. This pattern is consistent with the Aristotelian model and inconsistent with the systems approach: the latter requires a two-way hierarchy in which no level has absolute control, and the data show that the hierarchy is not two-way to any significant extent.

It is perhaps not surprising to find the weather at the top of a unidirectional hierarchy, but the presence of human activities there is worthy of further comment. The human activities included were deliberately chosen so as to be plausibly affected by the plant and animal events included in the study. For

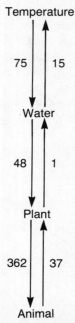

*Figure 10.2* The causal hierarchy, study 2

example, one card read 'farms in the area are sprayed with insecticide' (instructions asked participants to imagine the events as occurring within a certain area of about 50 square miles), and three of the animal cards referred to increases, and three more to decreases, in the population of different types of insect. It does not seem implausible to suggest that farmers might choose to spray insecticide because of an increase in the population of insects, but in fact only one such pair was chosen by any participant. By contrast, there were 19 choices of pairs in which the spraying of insecticide was the cause and a decrease in the insect population was the effect. This is typical of the pattern: human activities were chosen as causes of things to do with plants and animals, but the opposite almost never occurred.

In the second study, the tendency to unidirectionality in the hierarchy was even more pronounced. Again, weather was at the top, plant events in the middle, and animal events at the bottom, and only 3.9 per cent of pairs chosen violated this unidirectionality.

**Causal chains and loops**

Because people were allowed to use each card as many times as they wished, individual pairs could be connected in chains of causal beliefs. Suppose a participant chooses a pair in which card 1 is cause and card 2 is effect. That participant may at some other time choose a pair in which card 2 is the cause and some other card is the effect, making in effect a two-link causal chain. For study 1, with 84 cards, any of the remaining 83 cards may be chosen as the effect. This means that 82 of the possible choices make a linear chain and one (card 1) makes a feedback loop (1–2–1). Longer chains may also be constructed, but the basic principles are the same.

Given that we know how many chains have been produced and how long each chain is, it is possible to calculate how many feedback loops should occur by chance, and to compare this chance expectation with the number actually observed.

In the first study 338 chains were produced. Of these, 337 were linear and 1 was a feedback loop. The number of feedback loops expected by chance is 5.96. This chance expectation is rather small, and this was one reason for decreasing the number of cards from 84 to 64 in the second study: with fewer cards, more and longer chains should be produced.

In the second study, 1,275 chains were produced, of which 1,249 were linear and 26 were feedback loops. The number of loops expected by chance was 75.78. There is no easy way to calculate the statistical significance of the observed departure from chance expectation, but it is clearly a highly improbable result.

A loop of the form card 1–card 2–card 1 is a positive feedback loop. That is, it describes a process which, unless interfered with, will run away to an extreme (for example, total extinction of a species). In nature, states of affairs are often maintained by negative feedback loops (exemplified by the operation of a thermostat). Construction of representations of negative feedback loops is comparatively difficult with this methodology, and requires the use of four cards linked in a particular way. Not surprisingly, therefore, almost all of the loops produced were of the simpler, positive feedback kind. Only one negative feedback loop was produced, and this by a man who had a degree in physics, understood the concept of negative feedback, and deliberately set about constructing such a loop. It would be premature to conclude that most people have no understanding of negative feedback, however: there may be other methods which would make it easier for them to show what understanding they have.

These results show, then, not only that the chains observable in the sets of pairs produced by individual participants tend overwhelmingly to have a linear quality, but that people produce far fewer feedback loops than would be expected by chance.

## Cycles in nature

The items in the second study were designed to investigate the expression of cyclic structures in people's beliefs about natural processes.

First, five of the 64 cards collectively described a simple version of the water cycle. Choice of just five pairs would be sufficient to reproduce the cycle. The water-cycle cards were distinctive among the animal and plant cards: most participants began by choosing one or more water-cycle pairs, which attests to their salience. Despite this, none produced the entire cycle, and only one participant chose even four of the five pairs. The mean number chosen was 1.68. Most participants chose either single pairs or short linear chains of two or three pairs.

Secondly, the animal and plant cards were divided into sub-categories constituting simplified versions of the food chain. One version had three categorical levels (plants, plant-eating animals, and carnivores), and one version had four levels (plants, plant-eating insects, insect-eating animals, and carnivores). The idea was to see whether participants produced causal chains which traversed a complete cycle of one of these food chains. For the three-level food chain this would require a causal chain of at least four pairs, and for the four-level food chain a causal chain of at least six pairs. The traverse of the cycle was not required to be an exact loop, in the sense of ending with the same card with which it began: ending in the same sub-category was sufficient. For example, a chain beginning with a plant item could end with any plant item and still qualify as a traverse of the cycle.

As already stated, 1,275 causal chains were produced in this study, and of these 754 were at least four pairs long. In fact, since many chains were longer than this and the longest contained 13 pairs, this number somewhat underestimates the potential number of complete traverses of the food chain. Despite this, only two of the chains traversed the complete food chain (both involving the three-level chain). There is no easy way to calculate the number expected by chance, but it hardly matters when the number observed is so small.

Taken together, these findings show no evidence for any appreciation of cyclic processes in nature, and reinforce the impression of an overwhelmingly linear construction of causal chains.

## Interpretation

The evidence of these three sets of findings is consistent with a simple model of the common-sense construction of the causal order in natural processes. People do not construct cycles or loops, or a two-way causal hierarchy in the manner of the systems approach. Instead, they understand categories in nature as organised in a unidirectional causal hierarchy, and they understand individual events as related in causal chains which are overwhelmingly linear, more so than would be expected by chance. The categorical hierarchy is consistent with an Aristotelian construction, and the linearity of causal chains is consistent with either an Aristotelian or a mechanist interpretation.

## Causal hierarchies and causal powers

The idea that people understand categories in nature as falling into an Aristotelian one-way hierarchy is consistent with the hypothesis that people understand causal processes in nature as involving the operation of powers of things. The Aristotelian concept of a one-way causal hierarchy requires a notion of causation as the operation of a power as the means by which elements lower down the hierarchy are controlled and directed by those above. The presence of Aristotelian hierarchies in common-sense causal structures is therefore consistent with, and grounded in, the basic concept of causation as involving the operation of powers of things. Indeed, to the extent that the elements at the top of the hierarchy have no causal antecedents to their actions, they are conceived as operating in a way analogous to the operation of free will. The top of the hierarchy 'runs' nature much as human beings run a state through good government. The Greeks were fond of this sort of parallel, and the governance of nature was, to them, a combination of reason and necessity, a kind of natural or divine justice. Santillana (1961) quoted Aristotle as saying that nature refuses to be badly administered. The evidence from these studies that people view nature as a one-way causal hierarchy, then, fits with the hypothesis that their understanding of causation is based on a notion of power.

Certain other features of the findings support this interpretation.

## Missing links

The animal and plant cards were organised into sub-categories representing simplified food chains. A small number of pairs chosen skipped a level in the food chain: what this means is that people are picking cards as causally related when in fact they require at least one causal intermediary *and* possible intermediaries are available among the cards given. In the first study, the total number of pairs that skip an intermediary available among the 84 cards was 85 (a mean of 3.4 per participant), and all but two people produced at least one. In fact, the number may be higher than this because I omitted from the count any that seemed at least to admit the possibility of a direct link.

Now given that the possible 'missing links' can be unequivocally identified among the other cards, we can look to see if the same participant has paired them with the cards in the pair in question. The subject could pair the missing link with the cause or with the effect. In study 1 there were 68 instances in which the missing link is paired with the cause, and five in which it was paired with the effect, and this difference is statistically significant, $t(24) = 2.05$, $p<0.05$. In study 2 fewer pairs skipping a level in the food chain were chosen, although there was a non-significant trend in the same direction.

The explanation for this, in terms of the present line of argument, is that the source of power in the generation of a chain of events lies with the first event in the chain, the initiator, the thing at the top of the causal hierarchy. If we take the chain {1–2–3}, for example, then under this view people would be likely to identify {1} as the cause of {3} because {1} is the initiator of the chain, so that the power that generates {3} is actually the power of {1}, transmitted through the causal intermediary. Thus, when people make the pair {1–3}, they are more likely also to make the pair {1–2} than the pair {2–3} because it is not the power of {2} that generates {3}, but the power of {1} transmitted through {2}. Pairs that jump intermediaries are examples of natural processes, as defined in the previous chapter. Causally, the important events in the natural process are the initiating event and the terminating event: the event that initiates the natural process is the operation of a causal power of some thing, and this is the power that drives the process, so to speak. The final event is explained by the initiating event, not by the intermediate events, which simply transmit the power of the initiating event.

### Number of effects of causes in different categories

It was also found in study 1 that individual items have more effects (within participants) if they belong to the weather and human categories than if they belong to the plant and animal categories. The mean numbers of effects per cause per subject were: weather, 2.05; human, 2.20; plant, 1.53; and animal, 1.25. The minimum possible is one. This means that those causes that have most effects on average are precisely those that are seen as not having any causal antecedents (at least among the 84 cards) – those, in other words, that are at the top of the hierarchy; and those that have the fewest effects per cause are those that are at the bottom of the hierarchy, in the sense of being primarily chosen as effect. A similar tendency was found in the second study, in which the mean number of effects per cause for each category were as follows: temperature, 3.31; water, 1.95; plant, 1.63; and animal, 1.37.

The means do not represent the likelihood of an item being chosen as a cause, because they are calculated only for those items that have been chosen as cause (hence the minimum score of one). They were calculated in this way precisely to rule out effects due to the fact that some items tend not to be chosen as causes. The trend strongly suggests, therefore, that those things at the top of the hierarchy are seen as the sources, the originators of power in the domain, and that power passes down through the levels, getting weaker (in terms of the quantity of effects it brings about) until it dissipates at or even before it reaches the bottom of the hierarchy.

### Conclusions

The evidence of these studies is consistent with a simple model of the common-sense construction of the causal order in natural processes. People do not construct cycles or loops, or a two-way causal hierarchy in the manner of the natural systems approach: instead, they understand nature as a one-way causal hierarchy in which causal chains are overwhelmingly linear and causal influence is disseminated down from the top level of the system in an anthropomorphic manner involving the action of the causal powers of things. The action of the top level is treated in a manner analogous to the exercise of free will. The top of the hierarchy consists of weather, particularly temperature changes, and the activities of human beings. The bottom of the hierarchy lies in the animal kingdom, within which causal chains are still linear and non-cyclic but with no preferred direction – findings bearing on this point are reported elsewhere (White 1992).

One cannot emphasise too strongly the provisional nature of these findings and the interpretation I have proposed: they are intended as a first approximation which will no doubt be refined, extended, or rejected in the future. But, if valid, they have significant practical consequences. In particular, if people view the world as a one-way causal hierarchy with human activities at the top, then it will seem unobjectionable to treat the world as a kind of bottomless pit into which any manner or amount of things can be dropped, with no fear of effects or consequences emerging at the human level. Teaching people new individual causal links, such as that between chlorofluorocarbons and the ozone layer, is vitally important for the future of the environment: but the present findings imply that, to achieve a global and permanent change in human interactions with the environment, it is not enough. What is needed is a profound reconstruction of the causal order of nature in common sense, from the Aristotelian model which people appear to possess at the moment perhaps to something more akin to a systems view. Adding new individual beliefs is not sufficient to achieve this. For this reason, continuing research on the causal order of nature in common sense is of both scientific and practical importance.

## THE WORLD VIEW OF COMMON SENSE

Baumer (1977) identified five 'perennial questions' in the history of ideas: these are questions which, though the range of answers on offer changes from one generation to another, have remained constant preoccupations of humankind through recorded history. Four of these are concerned with religion (in the broadest sense of the word), human nature, the nature of society, and the nature of history or time. The fifth is the question of nature, from which Baumer excluded the cultural world, and which he chose to express as follows: 'What is physical nature made of, and by what principles does it operate?' In this section I am concerned with the beliefs held by ordinary people about the latter part of this question. As I am construing it, this is the next level up from that of the causal structures considered in the previous section, and I refer to it as the world view of the psychological construction of reality.

A world view encompasses more than just causal beliefs and may be described as a general characterisation of the nature of order in the universe, subsuming all things and all types of thing. This rather inexact description becomes clearer when examples are given. In a sense, the whole of Aristotelian thought constitutes a world view, but especially the most global and general components of it. Mechanicism is a world view (Dijksterhuis 1961). There is a world view of Stoicism (Debus 1978). The global components of the natural systems approach constitute a world view. In this section I consider the particular world view of the psychological construction of reality and specifically the extent to which it resembles the Aristotelian and mechanistic world views.

If people understand nature as a one-way causal hierarchy containing linear and non-cyclic causal chains, it does not follow that the whole world view of

common sense must be Aristotelian. A one-way causal hierarchy with the top
level conceived as a causal origin is anti-mechanicist because the mechanicist
world view is fully deterministic and no event occurs without causal antecedents.
On the other hand, the findings reported in the previous section do not prove that
the top level of the hierarchy in common sense has no causal antecedents: it may
have antecedents that lie outside the range of items used in the two studies.
Moreover, linear causal chains are compatible with a mechanistic world view.
So, despite the evidence for a concept of causation as involving the causal powers
of things, it is still possible that the world view of common sense is as much
mechanistic as Aristotelian.

In order to investigate this I carried out a questionnaire study (reported in full
in White 1992). The questionnaire contained items describing components of
world views, with which participants were to agree or disagree. There were
twenty statements in all, of which ten were fillers not related to either of the world
views under test but designed to take the same global perspective (for example,
'There is almost certainly intelligent life somewhere else in the universe', 'The
universe was created by God'). Of the remaining ten statements, five described
components of the Aristotelian world view, and five described components of the
mechanicist world view.

In each case, the five were designed to be different in content but to
encompass between them the main points of the world view in question. To
ensure construct validity in the statements, each one was a quotation from or
paraphrase of a statement by a range of authors who have written about one or
both of the world views under test (Bronowski 1951; Dijksterhuis 1961;
Farrington 1944; Toulmin and Goodfield 1962; Santillana 1961). For example,
the statement 'Matter is basically inanimate, passive, and inert' was derived from
a quotation from Toulmin and Goodfield (1962: 188), describing part of the
mechanistic world view, and quoted earlier in this chapter. The statements are
accompanied below by single terms in square brackets: these were not included
in the questionnaire, but are used here as a convenient way of referring to
individual statements.

The five Aristotelian statements read as follows:

> The working of the natural world (unless interfered with by human beings)
> is like that of a state well ruled by good government. [Government]
> Living things, unless interfered with, naturally grow and develop in a way
> that is directed towards a mature form of some sort. [Mature]
> On the whole, events in the natural world tend to be constructive and fruitful
> more often than destructive and fruitless. [Constructive]
> The universe is tending to become more orderly, or at least not getting less
> so, as time goes by. [Orderly]
> Excluding the deeds of human beings, there is a kind of natural justice in the
> way things happen. [Justice]

The mechanistic statements were as follows:

The universe is like a large and complex machine. [Machine 1]

The universe is gradually running down, like a clock that will eventually unwind. [Unwinding]

Matter is basically inanimate, passive, and inert. [Inanimate]

The working of the natural world (unless interfered with by human beings) is like that of a well-oiled machine. [Machine 2]

The laws of physics (whether known or unknown at present) can ultimately explain everything that happens in the universe. [Laws]

Subjects were asked whether they agreed or disagreed with each statement. For purposes of analysis, responses were converted into numerical scores in the following way: tick = 1; blank = 0; cross = −1. For each world view, each participant therefore ends up with a score ranging from −5 (disagree with all statements) to +5 (agree with all statements). Scores for each statement are presented in Table 10.1. The mean score for the Aristotelian set across participants is +1.16, and that for the mechanistic set is −0.06. Scores were analysed with the t test for related means, and Aristotelian scores were significantly higher than mechanistic scores, $t(31) = 3.35$, $p < 0.005$.

Table 10.1 Scores for Aristotelian and mechanistic statements

| Statement | +1 | Totals 0 | −1 | Score |
|---|---|---|---|---|
| **Aristotelian statements** | | | | |
| Government[dg] | 12 | 3 | 17 | −5 |
| Mature[a] | 28 | 0 | 4 | +24 |
| Constructive[abd] | 23 | 3 | 6 | +17 |
| Orderly[g] | 2 | 14 | 16 | −14 |
| Justice[abc] | 22 | 3 | 7 | +15 |
| Total | 87 | 23 | 50 | +37 |
| **Mechanistic statements** | | | | |
| Machine 1[abcd] | 22 | 2 | 8 | +14 |
| Unwinding[fg] | 8 | 5 | 19 | −11 |
| Inanimate[bg] | 10 | 7 | 15 | −5 |
| Machine 2[bdef] | 16 | 5 | 11 | +5 |
| Laws[ceg] | 11 | 5 | 16 | −5 |
| Total | 67 | 24 | 69 | −2 |

Note: Statements are identified by the terms given in square brackets in the method section. For each statement, the possible range of scores is −32 to +32. Statements not sharing the same superscript differ by $p < 0.001$ (comparisons involve all ten statements).

These results support the hypothesis that the world view of common sense is predominantly Aristotelian. This overall result, however, masks considerable differences between statements that are apparent in Table 10.1. Further analyses were carried out using the related means t test to compare scores for individual statements across participants. Using the Bonferroni correction, the significance level for these *post hoc* tests was set at 0.001. Significant differences are depicted in Table 10.1.

This pattern of results is complex, but does show that the preference for Aristotelian statements is not without exception, and one difference runs contrary to the general trend, the score for orderly being significantly lower than those for machine 1 and machine 2. The most popular statement, mature, combines two Aristotelian concepts, the teleological concept of the directedness of development, and the concept of a 'mature' or adult form as the culmination of development, whether directed or not.

Overall, then, there is some support for the hypothesis that the world view of common sense is predominantly Aristotelian, and more Aristotelian than mechanistic. But the world view of common sense is not anti-mechanistic nor whole-heartedly Aristotelian, for two of the Aristotelian statements were disagreed with more than agreed with, and two of the mechanistic statements were agreed with more than disagreed with.

Taking the most popular statements as a guide, then, it appears that people understand the world as a large and complex machine that works smoothly and never runs down (in contradiction to the Second Law of Thermodynamics), but also one that is endowed with the anthropomorphic qualities of purposiveness, direction towards mature forms, constructiveness, and natural justice. I have termed this 'the anthropomorphic machine'.

The most general conclusion that can be drawn is that the world view of common sense is a conglomerate of elements from a number of world views to be found in the history of science: in the present studies evidence has been found for both Aristotelian and mechanistic elements, and there is evidence elsewhere that the naïve physics of motion somewhat resembles medieval impetus theories which are neither mechanistic nor Aristotelian (McCloskey 1983). Nor are other historical world views, such as the Stoic world view (Debus 1978; Santillana 1961) ruled out. The evidence of the two studies reported in the previous section does suggest, though, that there is nothing in the world view of common sense that resembles the natural systems approach; indeed, the almost ubiquitous linearity of causal chains found in those studies is in effect contrary to the systems approach. Equally, some elements of the other world views appear to be rejected: obviously, people no longer believe in the Aristotelian notion of crystalline spheres in the heavens, but in this study they also rejected his analogy with good government. People also reject the Second Law of Thermodynamics, at least in the form expressed in this questionnaire, along with the mechanistic idea that all matter is inanimate, passive, and inert.

These studies have not addressed the question of the origin of the world view of common sense. The two broad classes of origin hypothesis are historical and psychological, and it seems almost inevitable that factors of both sorts must be involved. A parallel already exists in the study of the naïve physics of motion, where errors observed in the 'falling body' problem and which resemble medieval theories of motion have been attributed to a visual illusion (Kaiser, Proffitt, and Anderson 1985; McCloskey *et al.* 1983), whereas errors in the 'curvilinear motion' problem, which also resemble medieval ideas, may represent historical influence, in default of any psychological interpretation.

Historical interpretations of psychological phenomena are not common and may have been unfairly neglected. Historical origins could no doubt be traced for many cultural beliefs, attitudes, and behavioural tendencies, and the natural tendency of psychologists to seek a psychological explanation for some phenomenon may result in pertinent historical information being overlooked.

The present findings provide a case in point. Lerner (1965; Lerner and Miller 1978) proposed that people have 'a need to believe that they live in a world where people generally get what they deserve' (Lerner and Miller 1978: 1030). The use of the term 'need' identifies this as an essentially psychological hypothesis, and Lerner's argument is that judgements are distorted by the motivation to satisfy this need, an argument based on an analogy with drive-reduction. There is considerable evidence that effects of the kind predicted under this 'just world hypothesis' do occur (Lerner and Miller 1978; Lerner and Simmons 1966).

Now consider an item from the study of world views: 'Excluding the deeds of human beings, there is a kind of natural justice in the way things happen.' This item received a score of +15, representing a high degree of agreement. The study does not elucidate the origin of this belief, of course: it is possible that the level of agreement observed reflects the same psychological tendency that underlies the derogation of the victims of misfortune observed in Lerner's experiments. But the statement gives expression to one of the central concepts in the Aristotelian world view, and it is therefore also possible that agreement with it simply reflects the survival in common sense of part of the Aristotelian way of thinking. If this is the case, then no need or motivation need be postulated. People derogate the victims of misfortune because natural justice is part of their world view, and they perceive and interpret events in accordance with that world view. This account combines historical and 'cognitive' factors, the point being that Lerner's approach may be too purely psychological. Future research should aim to discriminate between these motivational and historical/cognitive alternatives.

It is almost too easy to say that the resemblance of elements of the common-sense world view to historical antecedents can be explained in terms of historical influence. This hypothesis requires, at least, that we explain why some historical antecedents survive in or are passed down to common sense while others disappear. And it, too, must compete against psychological alternatives. One possible psychological alternative is developmental. There is evidence for widespread animistic thinking in early childhood, which gradually atrophies during development (Piaget 1930; Looft and Bartz 1969). This evidence is not free of problems of interpretation (Looft and Bartz 1969; White 1988a), but let us assume for the sake of argument that it is valid as it stands. Under this assumption, the anthropomorphic machine can be explained as a mixture of the effects of education (for example, in simple classical physics) and the vestigial residue of early childhood animism. The correct psychological explanation for animism in early childhood is not clear, but one possibility is that children begin by inferring that unobservable properties of other things resemble properties they observe in themselves, such as will, wishes, intentionality, and so on: their own experience of themselves is taken as a cue to the nature of things in the world. If they have will, then so can a tree or a piece of string. This argument has been developed in earlier chapters.

Obviously, the task of explanation has a long way to go, and the above notions are sketched out purely to illustrate the likely fact that many historical, cultural, and psychological factors interact in determining the world view of common sense. However this world view emerges and whether or not the present findings give an accurate impression of it, the likelihood is that it influences perception, causal inference, and judgement and inference of many kinds, in profound and ubiquitous ways. For this reason the world view of common sense, its origins and effects, are worthy of more investigation than they have been given in psychology hitherto.

These three chapters constitute an attempt to give theoretical structure and content to an area which has so far received little attention in psychology, and to set this in the context of psychological metaphysics. With so little in the way of research findings, any conclusions must be of the most preliminary nature. My main contention, however, is that physical causation, like causation of any other kind, is basically understood in terms of causal powers. This appears to be associated with an Aristotelian conceptualisation of causal structures, in which categories of things in nature are organised in a one-way hierarchy, the top level being the source of power that drives causal influence down through lower levels of the hierarchy. It is also associated with a world view that combines the mechanistic idea of the universe as an ideal machine with anthropomorphic characteristics that are closely associated with the notion of causal power in the Aristotelian scheme. It is to be hoped that this, together with the differentiation between individual causal connections, causal networks, causal structures, and world view, is enough to act as a basis for the development of future research in this area.

# Part 3

# Psychological metaphysics of the mind

# Chapter 11

# The concept of action

The main aim of this chapter and the next is to elucidate those things that are basic to the psychological construction of the mind. In this chapter I deal with the basic concept of action and its production. In the next I consider the idea of 'I' as an enduring substance with two capacities, consciousness and the capacity to produce action, and the issue of basic categories in the mind. In that chapter I shall also be concerned with how beliefs about the mind are formed from experience. In the remaining chapters I put this material to work in explaining some features of the common-sense understanding of the mind and how it operates.

Under the causal powers theory, people understand causation as involving some power of a thing operating to produce or generate an effect, usually if not invariably by acting upon some liability of another thing. Thus, things have two kinds of causally relevant properties – leaving aside considerations of the natures of things in which powers may be taken as grounded; Harré and Madden (1975) – powers and liabilities. Powers are active, meaning that they produce or generate effects, as in the power of a hammer to smash things, and liabilities are passive, meaning that they are acted upon in the production of effects, as in the liability of a plate to be smashed. A noteworthy feature of this concept is that the causal connection is understood as necessary (Shultz 1982b). That is, if appropriate conditions are set up for the operation of a power, the power *must* operate to produce the effect: it cannot be otherwise (unless the power is not sufficient to overcome the resistance in the object acted upon). The effect is necessitated by its cause (Shultz 1982b; Bunge 1963; Harré and Madden 1975).

In investigating the psychological metaphysics of the mind and behaviour, the first question to ask is whether this analysis of causation applies to all that people do. At first glance this may not appear such an unreasonable claim to make. If powers are causes, there seems nothing immediately objectionable about the idea that behaviours are brought about by the operation of powers of a person. It is clear, at least, that people cannot do things that they do not have the power to do: just as acid cannot turn litmus paper pink if it does not have the power to do that, so people cannot digest their food or raise their arms if they lack the power to do those things. Also, Shultz (1982b) has argued that physical and social causation are similar in that in both the causal relation is understood as generative in nature.

Thus, behaviour is produced or generated, just as physical events are produced or generated.

There is no doubt that the two categories of power and liability apply to human beings just as well as to other things. This can be seen in the examples used in Chapter 6, in the section on ascertaining the strength of a power or liability, 'John laughs at the comedian' and 'Susan passes the exam'. Success and failure were treated as involving a relation between a causal power of the person and a liability or resistance in the task. The comedian example is different: in this, the causal power is in the object (the comedian in this case, though it could just as well be an inanimate object) and the liability or resistance is in the actor. This reversal reveals two fundamental patterns in the causal interpretation of behaviour, two categories into which individual behaviours may be judged to fall: behaviours caused by the operation of causal powers of the actor, and behaviours caused by liabilities of a person being acted upon.

Empirical support for this distinction comes from research by Brown and Fish (1983). These authors used as stimulus materials sentences of the form 'Person A–verb–Person B' (for example, 'Ted likes Paul' or 'Ted helps Paul'). When subjects were asked to assign causal weights in respect of the verb used to the grammatical subject and object of the sentence, it was found that the sentences fell into two distinct categories: those in which the causal weight lay pre-dominantly with the grammatical subject, and those in which it lay pre-dominantly with the object. Brown and Fish argued for two basic types of causal schema, which they referred to as the 'agent–patient' schema and the 'stimulus–experiencer' schema. They argued that the verb alone is sufficient to evoke one of these two schemas, providing a minimal causal interpretation of the occur-rence described. Thus, 'Ted likes Paul' evokes the stimulus–experiencer schema, where the object is the stimulus and the subject is the experiencer; 'Ted helps Paul', on the other hand, evokes the agent–patient schema, where the subject is the agent and the object is the patient.

The argument here is that sentences of this type describe relations between powers of one thing or person and liabilities of another. What distinguishes them is that in the agent–patient schema the power is in the grammatical subject and the liability is in the object, and in the stimulus–experiencer schema the power is in the object and the liability in the subject. This is true of sentences referring to inanimate things, as it is of sentences referring to humans.

Apparently, then, we can talk of human causation in terms of the operation of powers and liabilities, just as for purely physical causation. Yet there is a problem. The problem is that it is far from clear that all instances of behaviour can be treated in the same way, as far as causal attribution is concerned. Consider these examples: we move our eyeballs when in REM sleep; we digest the food in our stomachs; we fall over in a faint; we raise our arms; we start running. These are all things that we do, but they do not all appear to be of the same kind. Doing something like digesting one's food does not seem to be the same kind of thing as doing something like raising one's arm. Philosophers have devoted considerable effort to defining the difference between these two things, or to defining the latter in such a way as to distinguish it from the former, and there is still profound disagreement as to how this difference is best defined. Fortunately, we do not have to delve far into this controversy to find a difference that is crucial to the present problem.

The difference is that it is, in some sense, up to me whether I raise my arm or not, but it is not up to me whether I digest the food in my stomach or not. This is not an assertion of free will (Taylor 1966, 1974). There could be deterministic accounts of its being up to me whether I raise my arm or not. Some things that I do are up to me, and others are not. As a rough guide, it is up to someone what they do if it makes sense to ask them to refrain from doing it. Thus, it makes sense to ask someone not to raise their arm (unless we know that their doing so is a tic or involuntary nervous spasm), but it does not make sense to ask someone to stop digesting the food in their stomach (Smith and Jones 1986). Another heuristic guide to the identification of action has been proposed by Taylor (1966): something counts as an action if it makes sense to use the construction 'in order to . . .' following it. Thus, it makes sense to say 'I raise my arm in order to . . .', but it does not make sense to say 'I digest the food in my stomach in order to . . .' (doubters should compare this with 'I eat in order to . . .'). Philosophers use the word 'action' to refer to a behaviour, if it is up to someone whether they do it or not, and I shall follow that usage here.

Now this characteristic of actions, which serves to mark them off as a type of behaviour, has two implications, both of which are incompatible with the basic concept of causation. The first is that it implies a denial of necessity in the causal connection. Under the causal powers theory (Harré and Madden 1975; White 1989a), if acid has the power to turn litmus paper pink and suitable releasing conditions are set up, the power operates to produce the effect as a matter of necessity. But if a person has the power to raise their arm, all sorts of suitable conditions for doing so might be set up, and yet the person might still not raise their arm. This is implied by the notion of its being up to them whether they do it or not. Thus, there is no necessity in the production of action. This feature of action is incompatible with *any* theory of causation which postulates necessity in the causal connection.

Secondly, in the case of action, powers do not cause. If powers were the causes of actions it would not be true to say that it was up to the person whether they carried out the action or not. In the case of action, powers *enable* a person to do something (Harré and Madden 1975). In the case of action, possession of a power does not determine whether something *will* happen but whether it *can* happen. Indeed, there is no philosophical theory of action in which powers are identified as causes of action.

Perhaps it could be argued that these fundamental differences between action and causation are understood only by philosophers. If that were so, then there could still be a theory of causal attribution for actions that held for anyone who was not a philosopher. Yet this seems an implausible position to maintain. If people did not believe that it was up to them how they acted, the whole basis on which social interaction is built would fall to pieces. There would be no point in asking someone not to do something if we believed that what they did was causally necessitated, because this would mean that we believed that they could not choose to refrain from doing it. The principle of deterrence in law would be regarded as useless, on the grounds that punishments could not deter someone from committing a crime if it was not up to them whether they committed it or not (Fitzgerald 1968). Examples could be multiplied indefinitely.

Similarly, people must have some appreciation of causal necessitation in the physical world, because to believe otherwise would be to believe that the world is fundamentally capricious, unpredictable, even chaotic, that even though laws might appear to govern events at present, at any moment those laws might be suspended, that rain might fall from a clear sky, or water boil at freezing point. It would be, in fact, to enter the world of radical empiricism (Hume 1739/1978). People may not understand how the world works, but it is surely undeniable that they have deep faith in its regularity and predictability, and that their actions continually demonstrate this faith. There may be instances where physical events are not thought to be causally necessitated, as in animistic beliefs (Looft and Bartz 1969) or beliefs about supernatural causation, but such beliefs, among adults in contemporary Western society, stand out as striking exceptions to the usual way of understanding physical events.

It is quite possible, as Shultz (1982b) claimed, that people understand both physical events and action as involving generative relations. It seems likely, though, that this is where the similarity between their understanding of action and their understanding of causation of physical events ends. The lack of necessity in the production of behaviour and the role of powers as enabling rather than compelling, both entailed by it being up to the actor whether they carry out the action or not, are both incompatible with the basic concept of causation. Putting this as simply as possible, people do not see action as *caused*, in the sense that they see physical events as caused. This being so, there cannot be a theory of causal attribution for action: a theory of another kind is needed to embrace people's understanding of how action originates.

The majority of causal attribution theories have been concerned with the use of regularity information, such as covariation information, to make causal attributions (Einhorn and Hogarth 1986; Forsterling 1989; Heider 1958; Hewstone 1989; Hewstone and Jaspars 1987; Hilton and Slugoski 1986; Kelley 1967, 1972a, 1972b, 1973; Shanks and Dickinson 1987). In the case of physical causation, the use of regularity information for causal inference makes fairly good sense. I have already outlined some uses for regularity information in causal inference in an earlier chapter. Consider some naïve person who wants to find out what makes it rain, for example. It would not be unreasonable for this person to make observations with the aim of discovering what is regularly associated with rain; for example, following the covariation principle, what is present when rain occurs and absent when rain does not occur. There are limits on the validity of drawing causal inferences from covariation data, as every scientist knows, but for all that the strategy is not unreasonable. What makes it reasonable is the idea of necessitation in the causal relation. Causes of physical events do not have any choice over whether to operate or not, and this lends both regularity and pre-dictability (in principle) to physical events. Although regularity does not imply causation, causation does imply regularity of some sort.

The case of action is different, however. Suppose we want to explain why John chose a roast lamb dish from the restaurant menu. What might we infer from regularity information? If we discovered, for example, that John always chose roast lamb when eating at that restaurant – high consistency in Kelley's (1967) scheme – we might infer that John liked roast lamb a lot – that is, we might infer a stable disposition in John. This is not, however, a causal attribution because inferring a disposition is not the same as inferring that that disposition was the cause of some behaviour. If we did in fact infer that the disposition was the cause of the choice, this would be to repudiate the idea that it was up to John what he chose to eat: it would be in effect to deny that what John did was an action at all. If we wish to maintain that John's choice was an action, and that it was in some sense up to him what he chose, we must refrain from inferring that his choice was caused by some disposition of his.

If we discovered that everyone chose roast lamb in that restaurant (high consensus), what would we infer? We might infer that the restaurant was famed for its lamb dishes and that people went there because of its excellence in that area. We might infer that all other dishes were off the menu, or so obviously inferior that no one could want to eat them. What we would *not* infer is that the lamb was the cause of the choice. This too would be to reject the notion that the customers' choices were actions, that it was in any sense up to them whether they chose lamb or not.

And what does high consensus tell us about John's choice, which we wanted to explain? Nothing. Since it was up to John what he chose, and it was up to everyone else what they chose, the behaviour of others is irrelevant to explaining why John made the choice he did. The reason for this is simply the lack of causal necessitation in the generation of action: nothing *made* any of them choose the way they did, therefore the fact that they all chose the same way does not help us to explain why John made the choice he made. This does not mean that every choice must be completely independent of every other choice. We might infer that John was under pressure to conform, or that he inferred from the popularity of the choice that lamb was the best thing to have, or that all the diners belonged to a Lamb Eating Society. But none of these interpretations gives causal necessity to John's choice: he could have resisted the pressure, he could have ignored the message of the dish's popularity, he could have resigned from the society.

What all of the speculative interpretations in the last three paragraphs have in common is that they give meaning to John's action. We may not know which meaning is the right one without gathering further information, but that only tells us that regularity information is limited in its usefulness. The key to the matter is this: regularity information (within limits) renders physical events causal, but it renders action (also within limits) *meaningful*. These are fundamentally different uses of regularity information, and they follow from the fundamental difference between action and physical causation.

So far I have argued that there cannot be a theory of causal attribution for actions because actions have a special feature that is incompatible with the basic concept of causation; namely, that it is in some sense up to the actor whether they do the action or not. I have also shown that this feature entails a fundamental change in the role of regularity information in the interpretation of action, in that it helps us to attribute meaning to action, instead of causation. Meaning is crucial to the understanding of action (Harré and Secord 1972), but this alone does not elucidate people's understanding of the origination of action; that is, of how action comes about. This is a major problem, perhaps the most important and neglected problem in social cognition. The first step towards this involves identifying the psychologically basic concept of action.

## THE BASIC CONCEPT OF ACTION

Discussion of action and concepts related to action is not novel in the attribution literature. One of the earliest studies related to attribution showed that people tend to describe the movements of geometrical figures in an animated film as if they were watching actors, with desires, intentions, and motives (Heider and Simmel 1944). The concept of intention figures in the work of both Heider (1958) and Jones and Davis (1965), although the latter is a theory of dispositional attribution and as such only indirectly concerned with people's understanding of the origination of behaviour.

More recently, several authors have argued for the importance of a distinction between actions and occurrences, or associated concepts. For example, Kruglanski (1975) argued that actions are explained in different ways from occurrences, and that a key distinction within actions is that between actions performed as ends in themselves or for their own sake (endogenous) and actions performed as means to other ends (exogenous). Buss (1978) and Locke and Pennington (1982) laid emphasis on the distinction between reasons and causes. Zuckerman and Feldman (1984) showed that people regard consensus information as more important for explaining occurrences than actions, and distinctiveness information as more important for explaining actions than occurrences. I (1991) reported evidence that the distinction between behaviour viewed as intentional and conscious and behaviour viewed as unintentional and non-conscious is orthogonal to the internal/external distinction used in much causal attribution research (Heider 1958; Miller *et al.* 1981).

None of these, however, counts as a sustained and thorough attack on the problem. Some idea of the unsatisfactory and piecemeal state of the attribution literature with regard to actions can be gained from the diversity of distinctions in which the literature is swimming: actions versus occurrences (Kruglanski 1975); endogenous versus exogenous actions (Kruglanski 1975); voluntary versus involuntary (also Kruglanski 1975: the distinction was used in an attempt to define actions); reasons versus causes (Buss 1978; Locke and Pennington 1982); intentional versus unintentional (Shultz 1982b; White 1991); conscious versus non-conscious (White 1991). Concepts such as purpose, desire, and need can also be found. Which of these, if any, really matters? Which is the most important? How do they relate to one another? What do they all mean? This last question is meant to point up the lack of conceptual analysis in the psychological literature. Kruglanski (1975) defined actions as voluntary behaviour, and to explicate 'voluntary' stated 'an action is commonly assumed to be determined by the actor's will' (p. 389). A glance at the philosophy of action shows this to be inadequate (Smith and Jones 1986; Moya 1990), but, more to the point, it begs the question at issue: just what concept of action do people possess?

This is a question about what is basic to action. Something counts as basic to the concept of action if its presence is both necessary and sufficient for something to be an action. That is, what is basic to the psychological concept of action is what is applied to all and only those things that people interpret as actions. Elucidation of the basic concept of action must be the starting-point for a theory of attribution for actions because everything else is a kind of optional extra, attached to the interpretation of individual actions where it is deemed appropriate and in relation to the basic concept of action. We cannot understand how people deal with these optional extras without a basic concept of action to which to relate them. Identifying what is basic to the understanding of action is therefore a way of disentangling the muddle of distinctions in the literature. To assist with this I take a look at the philosophical literature.

The philosophy of action is a lively and controversial area (see, for example, Smith and Jones 1986; Moya 1990), and it is beyond the scope of this chapter either to review the area adequately or to choose the best of the current theories of action (best as a philosophical theory, that is). There are many current proposals concerning things that differentiate action from behaviour other than action (Moya 1990; Smith and Jones 1986; Davidson 1968; White 1968; Taylor 1966, 1974; Searle 1983; Ginet 1990; Harré and Secord 1972). For present purposes I summarise some ideas concerning how action comes about, drawn mainly from Smith and Jones (1986).

It seems clear that action cannot be directly externally caused. My arm can go up as a result of someone pulling on a string to which it is attached, but this would be no action of mine. To begin with, then, it appears that action must have some kind of internal cause. But this is hardly specific enough, because watches can do things that have some internal cause, involving springs and cogs, but we would not regard the doings of a watch as actions, except metaphorically. Nervous tics are internally caused, but neither do these count as actions. At the very least, we can rule these out by saying that an action must have a cause that is both internal and mental, meaning only that one's mind has some part to play in the performance of one's actions. This is not specific enough, but it does tell us where to look for the sorts of things that might be causes of actions.

What kind of mental thing might be the cause of action? The first possibility discussed by Smith and Jones (1986) is desire: 'When you actively raise your arm, your arm goes up because you simply want it to go up . . . or because its going up is required for something else you want' (p. 122). There is an apparent problem with this, in that we do not seem to have much control over many of our desires. It is not up to us whether we feel hungry and want some food, so to say that desires are the cause of actions is apparently to deny that actions are in some sense up to us.

It seems, however, that we can deal with this problem by proposing that something intervenes between the desire and the action. Thus, when we feel desire for something, the action results from something like a decision to act on that desire, rather than from the desire itself. 'Between the desire to kiss Jill and the action comes the choice to act on that desire rather than to more wisely resist' (Smith and Jones 1986: 123). This 'choice to act' is commonly referred to as a volition or an act of will. There are several volitional theories of action, but for illustrative purposes Smith and Jones presented that of Thomas Reid (1872), which is a three-stage model: (1) desire (and appropriate belief) which influences the will but does not causally determine it; (2) the will acts (there is a volition); (3) there is the effort to produce the action (the muscles get going). Volitional theories were also advocated by Hobbes, Locke, and Berkeley.

The volitional theory seems to imply, and some of its supporters have stated, that the volition or act of will is accessible to introspection. The problem with this is that no one seems to be able to point to a volition or act of will by consulting their experience. Disagreements over what is revealed by introspection need not be fatal to the theory, however, because volitions may just be hard to pin down in experience, and it is difficult to introspect and act at the same time.

A more serious problem is that the volitional theory seeks to explain action by importing a concept that is not itself explained; namely, the volition or act of will. Worse than that, this concept appears to be of the same kind as the thing that it is used to explain, except that it is mental rather than behavioural: it is itself an act or action. The volitional theory asserts that the difference between actions and other things we do is the involvement of an act of will. If we now ask what is the difference between mental events which are actions (which include acts of will) and mental events which are just things that we undergo, it is immediately obvious that the volitional theory has no answer to this, except to embark on a potentially infinite regress. The theory merely reduplicates the same problem in a different place, which means that it takes us no nearer to understanding what action is.

Perhaps there is something of a different kind that comes between desire and action. Trying is a possibility. We all understand what trying is and we all experience trying in at least some instances of action. Smith and Jones dismissed this possibility, however, for the same reason; namely, that trying is a mental act and therefore not different in kind from volition. Moreover, they claimed, many actions do not seem to involve trying in the sense of putting in effort, so if we want to make trying the cause of every action we must change its usual meaning in some way that is not at all clear.

The next candidate is intention. Obviously this cannot be meant in the sense of prior intentions, because many actions have no prior intentions at all, and may indeed be contrary to prior intentions actually held by the actor. I may eat too much at my favourite restaurant despite the fact that I went there intending not to, and this in no way means that my eating too much was not an action, that it was not in some sense up to me how much I ate. When I make a bid at an auction I am certainly doing so on purpose, but prior to the auction I may not have intended to go quite so high in the bidding.

This being so, what is it to do something on purpose, with an intention? First, according to Smith and Jones (1986), an action is intended 'if there is an answer to the question 'why did the agent do that?' which explains the action by giving the agent's *reasons* for so acting' (p. 130, italics in original). Reasons refer to desires and beliefs: 'specifying the agent's reasons for acting is a question of mentioning a desire together with a belief to the effect that the action in question was the appropriate way of satisfying the desire' (p. 130) (except when all one desires is to perform the action, in which case no belief need be involved).

Smith and Jones argued that 'desire' does not have its everyday meaning here. For example, one can intentionally visit the dentist without having the least desire to do so. A broader, and better, term is 'pro-attitude' (Davidson 1968), which Smith and Jones characterised as an attitude which inclines one towards a certain action. It can include desires, wantings, urgings, moral views, aesthetic principles, goals, and values, so long as these conform to the characterisation in terms of inclining the actor towards a certain action. It can include permanent character traits and passing fancies. Smith and Jones argued that most desires in the broad, pro-attitude sense *are* under our control, meaning that it is up to us whether we act on them or not, though there are exceptions, such as the desire for food.

Given this, Smith and Jones suggested that 'an action is intentional only if it is done with reasons in the light of which the agent's behaviour is seen to be comprehensible. To specify reasons which make the behaviour comprehensible is to specify a relevant desire or pro-attitude, and a belief to the effect that the action done will lead to the end desired' (p. 132). In addition, the action must be done *because of* that desire and belief. One could have several sets of beliefs and desires any of which make the same action comprehensible, but it might be that the action was done only because of one set, and not because of the others.

According to Taylor (1966, 1974) all theories involving such things as volitions, acts of will, intentions, and so on, run into two intractable problems. First, many things that we would want to call actions do not seem to involve any of these things. Take intentions as an example. Many things that we would want to call actions we just do, as it were, unreflectingly, and yet they qualify as actions, not merely because that is what we wish to call them but also because it is in some sense up to us whether we do them or not. I might just raise my arm, without any intention to do so, and yet this is an action of mine because it makes sense for someone to ask me to refrain from doing it. Intentions are therefore not necessary to action, and this means that they cannot be part of the basic concept of action. The same can be said of other things that have been proposed as concepts of action, desires, acts of will, volitions, tryings, purposes, plans, choices. It is easy to think of cases in which action seems to follow a desire, or seems to be aimed at fulfilment of a plan, but it is also possible to think of actions which do not spring from any desire, or are not part of any plan.

Taylor's second argument is that, even if intentions, volitions, and so on, are present when action occurs, this does not mean that they cause or produce or initiate action. Indeed, he argued, claiming that they do so entails taking action away from the actor, saying in effect that it is not the actor that produces or initiates action but these strange mental events, and this is inadmissible.

> To speak wilfully or voluntarily or intentionally or deliberately is not first the will to speak, and then to find one's tongue and vocal apparatus carrying on from there, in response to what was thus inwardly initiated by the soul. To speak wilfully or intentionally is just to speak with a knowledge of what one is saying and why.
>
> (1966: 77)

Taylor argued that analyses of action in terms of intentions, volitions, and so on, are analyses in terms of event causation. That is, they conform to the doctrine that only an event can be a cause of another event. The reasoning behind this doctrine is that an enduring thing cannot be a cause because this would involve a denial of sufficiency in the causal relation. In simple terms, something that is there all the time cannot be a cause of something that is there only some of the time. If the effect is an event, under this doctrine the cause must be something no less transient, and that can only be another event.

Taylor rejected this in favour of a model of object causation. Object causation is, originally, an Aristotelian conception in which a cause is a being which produces certain states or events. Taylor proposed that the object that does my actions is just I, myself. 'When I believe I have done something, I do believe that it was I who caused it to be done, I who made something happen, and not merely something within me, such as one of my own subjective states, which is not identical with myself' (1974: 55). This is the most important thing about action, then, the reference to the agent: 'In my first example, we cannot say merely that my finger moved, but rather, that *I* moved it' (1966: 109, italics in original). And this is exclusive to acts. We can describe things that are not acts as if I were the cause of them, such as 'I perspired'; but in such cases it is always possible to find acceptable paraphrases that do not suggest agent causation, such as 'my hands perspired', or 'perspiration developed on my hands'. 'Nothing can be represented as a simple act of mine unless I am the initiator or originator of it' (Taylor 1966: 112).

Simply saying that I initiate or originate my own actions may sound bland, but it is important to see the claim in the light of its metaphysical foundation: (1) a concept of a self or person 'who is not merely a collection of things or events, but a substance and a self-moving being' (Taylor 1974: 55); and (2) a conception of causation according to which an agent – a substance and not an event – can be the cause of an event.

The latter, of course, represents an important point of contact between Taylor's account and the causal powers theory: both are founded on a model of object causation. From a psychological point of view this is encouraging because it would be profoundly odd for people to use a model of object causation for one type of thing and a model of event causation for another. It would also be unparsimonious to suggest such a thing. Moreover, an attractive feature of Taylor's account is its simplicity: Taylor has thrown out as much unnecessary conceptual baggage as possible, and this must surely be the right way to begin the psychological analysis of action. If it turns out through further research that more things are necessary, then the account can be amended accordingly. Better to start with too little than with too much.

The adoption into psychology of Taylor's account receives support from Piaget's (1954) investigation of causal understanding in infants. This has been reviewed in Chapter 7. Piaget's main claim was that the understanding of human causation originates in the feeling of efficacy, which can be characterised as the subjective experience of the successful production of effects, located at the juncture of effort and outcome.

Piaget's account resembles Taylor's in that it pares the concept of action down to the bare bones. The experience of efficacy occurs at a stage when infants lack most of the understanding of the world that adults take for granted: there is, for example, no appreciation of spatial relations. Most importantly, there is no differentiation of cause and effect and, consequently, there can be no idea of such things as intentions, desires, and beliefs as *causes* of actions. There is just the feeling of efficacy in the actual production of action. Piaget (1954) claimed that the differentiation of cause from effect, and the idea of desires, intentions, and so on as causes, come later.

The experience of efficacy, shorn of all other concepts, closely resembles Taylor's (1966, 1974) analysis of action, also shorn of all unnecessary concepts. I know that something is an action merely because I do it myself, rather than calling on intentions, volitions, or anything else to do it for me: the experience of efficacy gives me the sense of doing the action myself, and nothing more. It is the way in which I distinguish things done by me from things done in any other way. It might appear that Taylor's concept involves something which Piaget explicitly denied to the infant – namely, a concept of self – but this is not so. Taylor was explicit on this point: 'In saying that my acts are caused by myself, I mean *only* that I cause them or make them occur, and this is in fact inconsistent with saying that something else, to be referred to as my *self*, is the real cause of them' (1966: 135). According to Taylor, 'I' refers to a substance and a self-moving being, but it is not required of anyone that they know themselves to be such a being; that is, that they have a concept of self as such. The concept of self, therefore, is not required to be part of the concept of action.

I therefore propose that the basic concept of action, comprising all those things that are necessary and sufficient for something to be understood as an action, corresponds to Taylor's concept, and that the experience of efficacy is the psychological criterion for distinguishing one's own actions from everything else that happens. Thus, I carry out or perform my actions, I know that I am doing so inasmuch as I have the experience of efficacy in the carrying out of an action, and it is up to me what action I carry out – that is, there is no causal necessitation in action. All other concepts related to action are ancillary. I might believe that I am acting with a certain intention, or according to a certain desire, or in pursuit of a certain purpose or goal. But it is not necessary for something to be an action that I believe any of these things. Moreover, I do not believe, or have to believe, that any intention or desire or purpose that I have is a cause of my actions. These things are not causes of actions. They are things on which I may or may not choose to act, nothing more.

The notion of 'I' as an enduring substance underlying and producing action is basic to the psychological construction of the mind, and will recur frequently in the rest of this book. To distinguish it from other uses of the word 'I', I use the expression <<I>> to designate it from now on.

## DIFFERENTIATION OF THE CONCEPTS OF ACTION AND CAUSATION

Action and causation are related but different. We are now in a position to summarise the main steps in their differentiation.

1 The basic distinction between being and happening is given by the temporal integration function of iconic processing (perhaps together with similar functions in other areas of processing).
2 The experience of efficacy in the production of action yields the basic concept of action as something that <<I>> do, and the concept of the generative relation, which is common to both action and causation.
3 The differentiation of cause and effect in the production of action is the first step towards the concept of power as a cause.
4 The objectification of causation occurs through (a) the appreciation of spatial relations (yielding the idea of a releasing condition) and (b) the understanding of specificity and stability in causes (yielding the concept of a causal power). Note that *neither* of these becomes involved in the concept of action: they form no part of the experience of the production of action, but are learned from observations of occurrences involving object relations in the outside world. This is the key. Causation is differentiated from action on the basis of things learned from occurrences other than action: all that they have in common comes from the experience of the production of action.

A problem remains. The full concept of action involves a concept of <<I>> as an enduring substance. On any one occasion, <<I>> as the producer of action is unproblematic, but <<I>> as something that spans temporally separate actions is a conceptual development, and we still don't know when or how this happens. Presumably it has happened by the time the infant learns the use of 'I' as a self-referential term. More will be said about <<I>> in the next chapter.

## ISSUES FOR A THEORY OF ACTION ORIGINATION ATTRIBUTION

A concept of action, of course, is only a first step towards a theory. The construction to be erected on this conceptual foundation will be a theory, not of causal attribution but of action origination attribution. There remains a great deal of work to be done before such a theory can be proposed, but we can at least consider some of the issues that should be addressed in it. Clearly, to the extent that people see such things as intentions, desires, purposes, and so on, as involved in action, a theory must address the definition of each of these as psychological concepts. For example, how do people understand intentions? Shultz (1982b) defined an intention as 'a determination to act in a certain way or to bring about a particular state of affairs' (p. 314); other definitions can be found in philosophy (Smith and Jones 1986; Searle 1983).

A theory must also address the relation between each of these concepts and the others, and especially between each of these concepts and the basic concept of action. If intentions are not thought of as causes of action, what part do they play in the actor's performance of his or her actions? Do people understand intentions as resulting from a combination of beliefs and desires, as in the account by Smith and Jones (1986)?

These are all questions for future research to address. There are issues, however, which can be considered in more depth here.

### Releasing conditions and the timing of action

In physical causation, under the causal powers theory (Harré and Madden 1975; White 1989a) the notion of a releasing condition is bound up with the idea of necessity in the causal relation. When a suitable releasing condition is set up, the power of a thing *must* operate to produce an effect. When litmus paper is dipped into acid, the acid *must* turn it pink, so long as it has the power to do so.

In the case of action there is no causal necessitation. Powers, as we have seen, enable rather than compel. If there is anything equivalent to a releasing condition for action, it too must have a more muted role. In physical causation, releasing conditions effectively determine *when* an effect is produced. The acid has the power to turn the litmus paper pink at all times, but actually does so *when* the releasing condition is set up. In a sense, then, for action the question is one of timing: given that I do $X$, why now rather than at any other time?

It is often possible to see what seem to be releasing conditions for action. If I want to hit a tennis ball, the timing of my action depends on the path of the ball:

I must swing the racquet in this way just now, rather than then, because otherwise I would muff the shot or miss the ball. This need for timing in order to carry out one's intended action does not compel, however, because I could always choose not to hit the ball. It seems to me that I choose the timing of the shot just as I choose what shot to play: the path of the ball guides my timing rather than compels it, and guides only because I choose to use it as my guide.

If we ask what, in the concept of action, is *essential* to the timing of action, then, it appears that nothing is, except the actor's decision or determination to act *now*. In a sense, there is no releasing condition for action: I just do it, and do it now, given that now rather than then is when I choose to do it. This is all that is basic to the concept of action.

We can still consider guides to the timing of action, however. Voluntary commitment to a certain plan or intention, for example, often entails commitment to use of a certain guide to timing, as in the tennis example. People must understand action as guided in this way, and their understanding of timing and guides to timing constitutes an important part of a theory of action origination attribution.

### Reasons explanations

As already stated, causal attribution theories are theories of how behaviour is explained in terms of causes. Since action is a kind of behaviour, these theories implicitly assume that actions are explained in terms of causes. Philosophers, on the other hand, agree that actions are explained in terms of reasons, and events other than actions in terms of causes. I now examine this contrast more closely.

The first point to make is that 'reasons', in this context, has a specific meaning. It refers to the actor's reasons for acting, and this is to be differentiated from reasons of other kinds, as in 'the reason why the volcano erupted'. As such, it is a sense applicable only to actions. Here I am using the term 'reasons explanation' with this specific meaning.

The second point to make is that all philosophers agree that explanations in terms of the actor's reasons for action are proper and exclusive to actions. This does not mean that actions can only be explained in terms of the actor's reasons for action – other kinds of explanation can also be given, in some cases at least (see the next section for one kind of case) – but it does mean that everything that counts as an action has a legitimate explanation in terms of the actor's reasons for action, and nothing that does not count as an action can have an explanation of this kind. Philosophers agree on this, even though they do not agree on what goes into a reasons explanation, or on what kind of thing a reasons explanation is.

Some philosophers have argued that reasons explanations constitute a class of causal explanation (Smith and Jones 1986; Davidson 1968), whereas others have maintained that reasons explanations and causal explanations are of fundamentally different kinds (Taylor 1966, 1974; Harré and Secord 1972; Ginet 1990). The question remains unresolved. It is clear, however, that if reasons explanations are a kind of causal explanation, then the things referred to in reasons explanations must be (or be believed to be) causes of behaviour. Under the psychological concept of action postulated in this chapter, the only cause of behaviour is <<I>>, that is, the actor (Taylor 1966, 1974). Such things as intentions, purposes, and desires are not causes of behaviour but merely things in accordance with which the actor chooses to act. If these are the things referred to in reasons explanations, then, psychologically, reasons explanations are not a kind of causal explanation because the things referred to in them are not causes of behaviour.

Regardless of whether reasons explanations are a sub-class of causal explanations or a class on their own, they are categorically distinguishable from causal explanations (and from explanations of all other kinds) both by their realm of applicability (all and only actions) and by the kinds of things to which they can make reference. Although philosophers offer different accounts of what can count as a reasons explanation, there is broad agreement on the appropriateness of reference to two general types of thing.

The first type may be characterised as forward-looking and includes most commonly intentions (Smith and Jones 1986; Searle 1983; Ginet 1990) but also plans, goals, ends, and purposes (Taylor 1966, 1974; Harré and Secord 1972).

The second type is generally taken as antecedent to intentions and encompasses the actor's beliefs and desires (Smith and Jones 1986; Taylor 1966, 1974; Searle 1983). Not just any beliefs and desires will do: roughly, the desire is one which the action is intended to satisfy, and the belief is that the action in question is an appropriate way of satisfying the desire. For example, if we say that John jumped into the shop doorway because he wanted to get out of the rain, we are saying that John had the desire to get out of the rain and held the belief that jumping into the shop doorway was a way of satisfying that desire; jumping into the shop doorway was an intentional action, carried out in the light of that desire and belief. 'Desire' is to be understood in the sense of a pro-attitude, as discussed earlier.

Under the present view, the only thing that is necessary to action is that the actor carries it out. There is no kind of thing which must be referred to in a reasons explanation: such things as intentions, desires, and purposes *can* be referred to in reasons explanations, but need not be. The actor need not have had any specific intention, or any specific desire, or any specific purpose; or he or she might have had some intention but no desire, or some desire but no purpose. If there is no single kind of thing which must underlie action in such a way that it can be referred to in a reasons explanation, what is it that makes something count as a reasons explanation? More specifically, why is it that things like intentions and desires *can* be referred to in reasons explanations, and other things like reflexes and neurological conditions cannot?

Is it just that anything that is regarded as mental can be referred to in reasons explanations, and anything that is not cannot? If this were the case, then people would regard it as legitimate to refer to the unconscious or subconscious mind in a reasons explanation, and this hardly seems plausible. Example: 'Why did you raise your arm?'; 'Because I had an unconscious desire to do so'. The force of this explanation, it would appear, is to take the deed out of the realm of action altogether: it says that, in fact, it was nothing that <<I>>, the actor, did; instead it was brought about, I now realise, by this unconscious desire. It says that it was not up to the actor whether he or she did the deed or not.

This is the key point. It is a defining feature of action under any theory that it is in some sense up to the actor what to do. The things referred to in reasons explanations are, first and foremost, those things on which the actor chose to act: the actor might say, I chose to act in accordance with this consideration and not that one. What makes something count as a possible reason, therefore, is that it is the kind of thing that an actor can choose to act on or not. That is, when the actor is choosing how to act, one can imagine a field of things that the actor might take into account, and the reasons explanation for the action actually performed can make reference to those things which the actor actually did take into account.

In defining the field of possible reasons, we are defining the limits of the actor's power to choose. This serves to identify a central issue for a theory of action origination attribution: what do people believe are the limits on the actor's power to choose, on the field of possible reasons, and how do these beliefs come about? If we can take it that intentions fall within the field and unconscious desires do not, what other mental states, qualities, events, and so on do and do not, and why? Can a personality characteristic be a reason for action, as far as ordinary people are concerned?

## The description of action

A single action need not have a single correct description. An action may often be legitimately described in several ways, which may be related to one another in an orderly way. Consider the following:

He pulled the trigger.
He fired the gun.
He shot Archduke Franz Ferdinand.
He assassinated Archduke Franz Ferdinand.
He started World War I.

These are all descriptions of the same action, and are all valid as such. Furthermore, they are related in an orderly way, shown by use of the word 'by'. This order is revealed by working from the bottom up, inserting the word 'by' between each pair of sentences. Thus, it makes sense to say 'he started World War I by assassinating Archduke Franz Ferdinand', or 'he fired the gun by pulling the trigger', but it does not make sense to say 'he assassinated Archduke Franz Ferdinand by starting World War I' or 'he pulled the trigger by firing the gun'. The 'by' relation therefore helps to reveal a hierarchical order of levels of description of an action (Ginet 1990).

It is tempting to suppose that the 'by' relation signifies a causal relation, so that the ordered list of descriptors is actually a causal sequence. Although this may sometimes be the case, however, it is not necessarily so. Ginet (1990) gave an example of two descriptors, 'S's signalling at t' and 'S's extending her arm at t'. Here, 't' denotes a given time or occasion. In this case it makes sense to say that S signalled by extending her arm, but it would not be correct to say that S's extending her arm caused her signalling. The relation in this case is more akin to sign and meaning than to cause and effect.

Not all descriptions of an action describe it as an action. Consider this example, from Davidson (1968): 'I flip the switch'; 'I turn on the light'; 'I illuminate the room'; 'I alert a prowler to the fact that I am home'. These all describe the same action, and indeed form a list ordered by the 'by' relation, but the last of them does not describe the action as an action, because alerting the prowler is not something that I intended to do (let us say I was ignorant of his or her presence). This fact is important to explanations of the origination of action, as we shall see shortly.

The 'by' relation is not merely an adjunct to the philosophical analysis of action. It has been shown that people appreciate the notion of the 'by' relation and can use it to order descriptions of an action (Vallacher and Wegner 1987). That is, people can represent an action by various descriptions which are organised into what Vallacher and Wegner (1987) called an 'identity structure', and their use of the 'by' relation indicates their hierarchical ordering of the action descriptions.

Now, what counts as an explanation (of the causal or origination kind) depends on how the action is described. If I am the actor, my own understanding of my action depends upon the way in which I have described the action to myself. Thus, if I identify my action as 'turning on the light', whatever I believe myself to hold in the way of intentions, desires, purposes, and so on is attached to that description of the action. Those things that I so attach to my description of the action constitute my reasons for action. Before I can give a reasons explanation for my action to someone else, however, I must be satisfied that they have identified my action in the same way that I did.

Suppose I am the man who shot the Archduke, and that I have identified the action to myself as 'shooting the Archduke'. Suppose, further, that my reasons have to do with my desire to avenge myself upon an oppressive foreign ruler of my people, and my belief that I can fulfil this desire by shooting him. Now, if someone asks me why I fired the gun, I cannot (except elliptically) refer to my desire for revenge, because this is not my reason for firing the gun: it is my reason for shooting the Archduke. The questioner has adopted a different level of description from the one I chose myself, and for this reason my first task in explaining the action to him or her is to redescribe it: explanation by redescription. I might say 'I was shooting the Archduke', and having accomplished that redescription I might then go on to give my reasons for shooting the

Archduke. Thus, before an actor can give a reasons explanation for action, they must ensure (or assume) that the questioner understands the action *under the description to which the reason applies*.

Now, suppose the questioner asks me, 'Why did you start World War I?' The question is asked on the assumption that this is something I did intentionally. This question describes the action at a level higher (in terms of the 'by' relation) than I have described it to myself. There is an important difference between this and a question which identifies the action at a lower level. It is reasonable to say that I fired the gun intentionally, because my intention was to shoot the Archduke and I understood that I could shoot the Archduke *by* firing the gun. But I did not start World War I intentionally, because that level of description is on the wrong side of my description, in terms of the 'by' relation. It does not make sense to say 'I shot the Archduke by starting World War I'. Thus the level at which I have described the action to myself is the highest level at which the action is described as intentional. It follows that if someone asks me a question in which the action is described at a higher level than I have described it to myself, the first task of explanation is to tell the questioner that the action *under that description* was not what I intended. I might say, 'I did not mean to do that; I meant only to shoot the Archduke'. In saying this, I am saying that a reasons explanation cannot be given for the action under that description.

This is important, because there has been something of a debate in psychology as to whether actors can offer causal explanations for their own actions or not (Buss 1978, 1979; Kruglanski 1975, 1979). The present analysis offers a simple resolution of the problem. Reasons explanations apply to actions under the actor's own description of them, or to descriptions understood by the actor as coming below the actor's own description in terms of the 'by' relation. Causal explanations can be given for actions under descriptions at levels higher, in terms of the 'by' relation, than the actor has described the action to himself or herself. Thus, we could seek a causal explanation of how I started World War I, but we could not seek a reasons explanation for that, because that was not what I thought I was doing.

## The social context of action

We have already seen that action is inextricable from meaning. Identifying or describing an action (Vallacher and Wegner 1987) *is* to give meaning to an action, to say what it is. This is easy to see from the fact that the same physical movement can constitute any of several different actions. For example, in carrying out the physical movement of raising my arm, I may be hailing a taxi, attracting the attention of a friend, or making a bid at an auction. Action is not mere movement: it is, at the very least, movement plus meaning.

A theory of action origination attribution must therefore take meaning into account:

In general, social behaviour is the result of conscious self-monitoring of performance by the person himself, in the course of which he contrives to assess the meaning of the social situation in which he finds himself, and to choose amongst various rules and conventions, and to act in accordance with his choice, correcting this choice as further aspects of the situation make themselves clear to him.

(Harré and Secord 1972: 151)

According to Harré and Secord (1972) the most important part of the meaning of the social situation consists of rules, which may be loosely characterised as socially defined regularities relating different levels of identification of action to plans, on the one hand, and to the social situation, on the other. Rules guide action, but they do so not through causal necessitation, as in purely physical causation, but through the actor's awareness of the rule and what it prescribes: actors choose to be guided by a rule (or not). Thus, if we observe several people all behaving in the same way (as in high consensus – cf. Zuckerman and Feldman 1984), this is not a sign of external causation, still less of causal necessitation, but of the fact that they share knowledge of a rule and choose to be guided by it. Reference to rules is therefore an important way of explaining action.

Rules can be of many types, and have correspondingly many functions. Hargreaves (1980) distinguished four types of rule which, he claimed, reflected common usage.

1  Normative rules. These are prescriptive rules having moral force, and include social norms, institutional and organisational rules, and situational rules.
2  Implemental rules. These are technical or procedural rules, such as those involved in the exercise of a skill; for example, driving technique.
3  Probabilistic rules. These relate to regularity of conduct, to what people do usually or 'as a rule'. 'The breaking of a normative rule leads to moral disapproval and the invocation of a sanction; the breaking of a probabilistic rule leads merely to surprise at the unexpected' (Hargreaves 1980: 218).
4  Interpretive rules. These concern classifying instances (such as a certain behaviour) as of a certain kind (belonging to a certain category or concept).

Any of these kinds of rules may be referred to in explanations for action.

## Intentional, voluntary, and deliberate actions, and responsibility

There are important characteristics which people may believe some actions possess and others do not. Further conceptual analysis drawn from the philosophical literature may be of help here. First, although many, if not all, actions may be regarded as intentional, not all intentional actions are voluntary. According to White (1968),

what I do, thinking I am obliged to do it, I do not voluntarily do, since I do it thinking I have to do it. What is done to me I do not voluntarily do, since I do

not do it at all . . . To do x voluntarily is to do x with the awareness that one
has an alternative course open to one.

(White 1968: 6)

Thus we can divide intentional acts into obligatory acts and voluntary acts, as
defined by White.

This view is not shared by all authors. Smith and Jones (1986: 255) offered an
Aristotelian account of voluntary acts which is indistinguishable from their own
account of intentional acts, and indeed they stated that the Greek word which they
translated as 'voluntary' could just as well be translated as 'intentional'. Evidently, 'voluntary' as opposed to 'obligatory' is not the same as 'voluntary' as
opposed to 'involuntary'. In this section I shall reserve 'voluntary' for the sense
in which it is opposed to 'obligatory'.

Under this definition, there appear to be several classes of behaviour that do
not count as voluntary. These include behaviour under coercion or obligation,
where the action is intentional but not voluntary, muscle spasms, where the action
is neither voluntary nor intentional, and behaviour where the actor lacks control
over what he or she is doing because of lack of consciousness (Fitzgerald 1968,
who cited things done by a person asleep or because of a brain tumour or under
effects of hypoglycaemia as examples).

Under Fitzgerald's account, which is drawn from legal philosophy and practice, control is the central concept. He reported that the American Law Institute's
Penal Code excludes as not voluntary 'any bodily movements that otherwise are
not products of the effort or determination of the actor, either conscious or
habitual' (1968: 132). He concluded that 'the common minimal requirement of
the law seems to be that the accused should have had the ability to control his
movements' (p. 134). The point for legal practice is that it makes no sense to try
to deter people from committing involuntary acts, and that people are not at fault
for what they cannot help doing.

The concept of responsibility, then, is confined in application to voluntary
actions. We often hold the actions of small children and animals to be intentional,
but despite this we do not hold them responsible for what they do. According to
Aristotle we hold someone responsible for their actions when we believe that
they have the capacity for reflective deliberation (not when they actually exercise
that capacity but when we believe they could) – being capable of deliberative
choice between alternative courses of action. This, evidently, matches White's
(1968) definition of voluntary action. Thus, children and animals are not held
responsible for their actions because, or when, they are thought not to have the
capacity to reflect on their choice of action. There are various acknowledged
classes of exception to this, such as acting under duress or in ignorance. As with
most terms, though, 'responsibility' is ambiguous and can be used in different
ways (see, for example, Feinberg 1968; Searle 1983: 103).

This account enables us loosely to define deliberate action. If voluntary action
is action carried out by someone when (we believe) they have the capacity for

deliberation between alternative courses of action, then 'deliberate action' can be reserved for those instances of voluntary behaviour in which the capacity for deliberation is actually (or believed to be) exercised.

To summarise, then: not all actions are intentional. Intentional actions can be divided into voluntary actions, where the actor (believes that he or she) has a choice between alternative courses of action, and obligatory actions, where the actor (believes that he or she) has no such choice. Voluntary actions can be divided into deliberate actions, where the capacity for deliberation between alternative courses of action is actually exercised, and actions where that capacity exists but is not exercised. The concept of responsibility can be applied to any voluntary action, under the definition preferred here.

## Dispositions

In attribution, psychologists generally use the term 'disposition' to refer to stable personal characteristics such as personality traits and attitudes. This use is derived from Heider (1958), perhaps via Jones and Davis (1965). Analysis of the relevant passages from Heider's book shows that he referred to a wide variety of mental states and characteristics as dispositions, including intentions and wishes, but he emphasised stability as a key defining feature of dispositions, and perhaps because of this emphasis the term has become restricted to things more stable than intentions are usually regarded as being. This is not how the term is used in philosophy, however, and its use in this way in psychology is misleading and obfuscating. First, dispositional properties are not exclusive to persons but may be possessed by inanimate objects and perhaps even situations or circumstances. Secondly, what matters about a disposition is not its stability but its causal relevance: dispositions are things that are related in some way to the kind of behaviour that someone (or something) carries out, and the job of defining dispositions in philosophy is to find a satisfactory way of describing that relation.

There are three broad approaches to the definition of mental states in philosophy, which may be called mentalistic or Cartesian, behaviourist, and functional.

Under the mentalistic approach, mental states are definable in terms of their intrinsic qualities as states. Thus, fear, for example, would be defined in terms of the intrinsic qualities of the experience of fear, those qualities which individuate fear as an experience and distinguish it from all other kinds of state.

The prospects for a mentalistic definition of dispositions are not at all bright. For one thing, there does not seem to be any one kind of thing that a disposition has to be. When philosophers give examples of dispositions, they include not only traits such as being generous but also desires, beliefs, and acquired abilities (Smith and Jones 1986; Kenny 1989). There is no intrinsic quality that these states possess in common, other than the fact of being mental, and this does not serve to distinguish them from other mental states which happen not to be dispositions. In addition, no one has succeeded in identifying an experiential quality intrinsic to dispositionality, and this is the primary requirement for a mentalistic definition of dispositions. Furthermore, dispositions do not have to be mental: many of the examples of dispositional properties analysed by philosophers are properties of inanimate things, such as the brittleness of glass. Clearly, brittleness does not have the kinds of intrinsic qualities that mental states do, and this makes it unlikely that what marks out a disposition as such can be anything to do with its nature as an experience.

The mentalistic approach in general has been heavily criticised in recent times (Smith and Jones 1986; Kenny 1989). Philosophers of other persuasions do not deny that mental states have intrinsic qualities: they do deny, however, that such qualities have any use or importance in the analysis of mental states.

The behaviourist approach is one way of analysing mental states in terms other than qualitative, experiential ones. This approach is exemplified by Ryle (1949). In his account, a specific disposition is identified as a set of behaviours occurring under specifiable circumstances. A statement about a disposition is nothing other than a statement about how something would behave if certain conditions were realised. For example, saying that something is brittle means just that if it were firmly struck it would shatter (and so on). This definition can be used to give an analysis of mental states such as belief:

> Beliefs are to be identified . . . with dispositions or tendencies to behave in certain appropriate ways depending on the circumstances. For example, your belief that it is about to rain is nothing other than a disposition on your part to bring in the washing (in appropriate circumstances, with no distractions) [etc.].
>
> (Smith and Jones 1986: 142)

A disposition, then, is nothing other than a set of true conditional statements about behaviour. It is not a mental state as such. Having a disposition means just that certain conditional statements are true: it does not mean that dispositions are underlying mental states which make the conditional statements true.

Smith and Jones (1986) offered three arguments against Ryle's position. To give just one, if beliefs were dispositions as Ryle defined them, we could only get to know our own beliefs by observing our own behaviour under different conditions (cf. Bem 1972). Smith and Jones argued that this is wrong: 'to tell whether you yourself believe that the US budget deficit is too high, for example, you don't have to wait to catch yourself in revealing behaviour!' (p. 147). So, they concluded from this and their other two arguments, a belief as a disposition must be a mental state of some kind. They preferred Armstrong's definition of 'disposition' as 'a state of a person apt for producing certain ranges of behaviour' (p. 153). As they put it, a disposition is a causally effective state which underlies behaviour.

This definition exemplifies the third approach to the philosophy of mind, the functionalist approach. In this, mental states are defined in terms of their relation to other things, such as other mental states. A belief is still a disposition, but analysed differently. What their functionalist approach aims to do is to tell us more about a particular belief-state by telling us how it can interact with other states to produce various kinds of behaviour: in other words, it tells us about the place of one belief-state in a pattern of possible states. For example, the belief that it is about to rain is (roughly speaking) the state which combines with the desire to dry the washing and the belief that washing left out in the rain will get wetter, so as to produce the action of getting in the washing; and so on.

(Smith and Jones 1986: 154)

Clearly, there is no particular kind of mental state that a disposition must be: anything that can be said to function as an aptness for producing certain kinds of behaviour under certain circumstances qualifies as a disposition, whether it be a belief, a desire, a trait, an ability, a plan, or an intention.

What is important about the functionalist approach is that it leads us to consider how dispositions stand in relation to other kinds of mental state. For example, in Kenny's (1989) account, dispositions are identified in relation to powers or capacities and tendencies, as well as behaviour. Kenny defined the mind as a second-order capacity; that is, a capacity to acquire capacities. For instance, we could say that the mind has the capacity to learn languages. Now, if we say of someone that they have learned French, we are saying in effect that they have acquired a capacity, and this capacity functions as a particular disposition of the second-order capacity to learn languages. They might have learned Italian or Greek, but in fact they have learned French: their language-learning capacity has become disposed that way. They now have an aptness for producing French utterances under suitable circumstances, and this is what it means to say that having learned French is a disposition.

Under Kenny's view, then, dispositions fall between capacities (or powers) and actions. They are not the only thing that does, however. Kenny also identified what he called 'tendencies'. Tendencies are dispositions, but not all dispositions are tendencies. For example,

if beliefs and volitions are both dispositions, only volitions appear to be tendencies. A volition to catch a train will, in the absence of countervailing volitions, amount to a tendency to take steps to catch the train. Beliefs are not tendencies in the same way. The belief that the earth is round finds expression in saying 'the earth is round'; but it is not a tendency to say this, for even when the occasion arises to say it, one may not wish to do so and yet believe it to be true.

(Kenny 1989: 85)

Tendencies appear to direct one towards a certain kind of behaviour more strongly than do dispositions which are not tendencies. Kenny also identified habits as a sub-category of dispositions.

Clearly, theories of dispositional attribution (for example, Jones and Davis 1965) are more properly termed theories of the attribution of stable personal characteristics: whether people understand the characteristics they attribute as having the function of dispositions, and whether they see only stable personal characteristics as having that function, are different questions altogether. Moreover, a dispositional function is not the only property that a given personal characteristic might be said to have. A personality trait might function as a disposition; and it might do so on some occasions and not on others: equally, it has other characteristics, such as its intrinsic nature, which help to say what it is but which need have nothing to do with its function as a disposition. Any mental characteristic that might be referred to in an account of behaviour is so referred to in its function as a disposition, but there is more to mental characteristics than this. Theories of attribution should be mindful of these things.

## Self and other

In causal attribution research the comparison between attributions offered by people for their own actions and those proposed for the actions of others has attracted a good deal of attention (Jones and Nisbett 1972; Watson 1982; Hewstone 1989). This is an immense and complex topic, on which only a few comments can be made here, in the context of action origination attribution. It is useful, however, to distinguish three cases, not two as is more usual:

1  Explaining my action to myself.
2  Explaining my action to someone else.
3  Someone else explaining my action.

The comparison between the first and second of these serves to point up the fact that action origination attribution and causal attribution, as studied by researchers, are essentially public, social acts and as such are affected by social and interpersonal factors. Thus, an action origination attribution offered by the actor to some other person cannot be assumed to be 'scientific', in the sense of being motivated by the goals of understanding, prediction, and control (Heider 1958; Nisbett and Ross 1980). Other functions likely to be served by it include claim-backing (Antaki 1990), excuse or justification (Draper 1988; Toulmin 1970), and self-presentation (Jellison and Green 1981; Baumeister 1982): in general, such explanations are in the service of the practical concerns of the actor, whatever those may be (White 1984).

This renders the comparison with explanations given by observers problematic in the extreme. Usually, observers do not use explanations to back the claims of the actor, to excuse or justify the actor's action, or to assist the actor's self-presentation. Observers' attributions are in the service of the *observer's* practical concerns, which may differ considerably from those of the actor. There is no reason to suppose that the scientific goals of understanding, prediction, and control play any larger part in observers' attributions than they do in those of the actor.

Moreover, one fundamental part of action origination attribution is exclusive to actors' attributions as offered to observers, and that is the redescription of action. Actors and observers may both identify the actor's action to themselves, as an intrapersonal process, but the correction of a description that the actor regards as wrong or undesirable can only occur interpersonally; that is, as part or whole of the actor's explanation to an observer. For example: Observer to Oedipus, 'Why did you marry your mother?'; Oedipus, 'I didn't! I married Jocasta, who incidentally I did not believe to be my mother'. Note that Oedipus could not pose the observer's question to himself, because he had not identified his action as marrying his mother: likewise, the observer's false assumption about how Oedipus identified the action cannot be corrected without further information, as supplied by Oedipus. Of course, action redescription can also serve social and interpersonal functions such as excuse and self-presentation.

Finally, in considering case (1), we should ask whether actors ever explain their actions to themselves. Arguably, actors know what they are doing when they do it: in choosing how to act, actors act in respect of certain reasons, and this implies that those reasons must be known to them. Thus, there is no need for retrospective action origination attribution, unless an actor forgets what his or her reasons were, and has to reconstruct them, as it were, after the event. Of course, actors might come to reinterpret their action retrospectively, but this would not be to find new reasons for what they did, because that would be to imply that they had acted in respect of reasons not known to them, which amounts to a logical contradiction. Such reinterpretations could only serve to identify influences on action other than the actor's reasons – that is, causes. For example: 'At the time I thought my reason for marrying her was that I loved her, but now I see that my choice was determined by an unconscious search for a mother substitute.' Actors' explanations to themselves should not be assumed to be any more 'scientific' than explanations of any other kind: all explanations, like everything else the actor does, are in the service of the actor's practical concerns, and we can only say that intrapersonally relevant practical concerns are likely to differ from interpersonally relevant ones.

## Grey areas

This chapter might have given the impression that, as far as ordinary people are concerned, all behaviour can be divided into two kinds: actions, and behaviour other than actions. This might be correct, but it is more likely to be an over-simplification in at least three different ways.

The first way involves the problem of description, already discussed. Whether something counts as an action or not may depend on how it is described. Oedipus intended to marry Jocasta, but he did not intend to marry his mother. The former was an action of his, the latter, arguably, not. Yet they are both legitimate descriptions of the same behaviour. Given that people appreciate the possibility of different levels of identification of behaviour (Vallacher and Wegner 1987), it seems likely that they appreciate that something can count as an action under one description and not under another.

Secondly, under a given description of an action, people may include both causes and reasons in their account of its origination. We might say that Oedipus had reasons for marrying Jocasta (for example, his intention to start a family with her), but also that his marrying her was caused, in part, by an unconscious attachment to his mother, who Jocasta happened to be. Thus, people may see some actions at least as mixed in their origin, partly up to the actor, partly caused.

Thirdly, there are some identifiable kinds of borderline cases, types of behaviour which may or may not be regarded as actions. Consider behaviours that satisfy biological drives, such as eating when half-starved or drinking when parched with thirst: people might say that eating and drinking are actions, inasmuch as we can choose to do them or refrain from doing them: but do they still regard this as wholly true when the pressure from the drive becomes almost too strong to resist? What about habits? If I had a mannerism of stroking my chin whenever I thought about something, would people regard this as an action of mine? Would they if I said I was not aware of doing it, and appeared to be taken by surprise when someone asked me why I was doing it? Finally, what about behaviours performed by people in emotional states – shouting when angry, cringing when afraid, raising eyebrows when surprised, smiling when amused, and so on? Do people regard these as actions?

Clearly, a categorical distinction between actions and other behaviours is too crude. There are many questions for research to address here.

The concept of action is as basic to the psychological metaphysics of mind as the concept of cause is to the psychological metaphysics of the physical world. The chapters to follow explore some implications of this.

# Chapter 12

# Formation of beliefs about the mind

There are some perplexing mysteries in the way we look upon ourselves and our minds. We only identify ourselves with part of our minds. Why? We only feel we control part of what goes on in our minds. Why? Or, indeed, why any of it? What is this 'we', this 'I' that we feel we are, that we feel continues from one moment to the next, from one day to the next? How do we know anything about what is going on in our minds? These questions touch on the core issues of the psychological metaphysics of mind. Our concept of action, for example, rests upon an idea of <<I>> as an enduring substance, and moreover associates <<I>> distinctively with action, as opposed to behaviour of other kinds. This is basic to our understanding of ourselves and of our minds.

One might suppose that the fundamental questions about our understanding of the mind concern the repertoire of concepts we have for mental occurrences. We think of things going on in the mind as desires, intentions, thoughts, and so on, and there are some important questions to be asked about how these concepts come about, or why we have these concepts rather than others. Important though these are, they are not quite questions of psychological metaphysics. Take desire as an example. The infant does not need a concept of desire to be able to desire things. Nor does it need a concept of desire to be aware, in some sense of that perplexing word, of some mental occurrence that happens to be a desire. But it does need a concept of desire to be able to know that this mental occurrence is a desire and that one is not. One can therefore ask how the infant (and later the adult) applies a concept of desire once it has one. Indeed, this is an important question because the infant is able to formulate utterances that make appropriate use of a concept of desire by the age of 2 years (Wellman 1991), and similar skill in the use of a concept of intention has emerged by the age of 3 years (Shultz 1980). One can also ask how the infant forms a concept of desire, given that it is not born with one. This too is an important question. It is not, however, a question of psychological metaphysics. What kind of thing is a desire, as people understand it? Do people conceptualise it as an object, a state, a property? Do they see it as naturally enduring in time as objects in the physical world are thought to do? These are metaphysical questions: they are questions about basic particulars and basic categories. To put them in a more general form: what are the basic categories of mental occurrence, and what are the basic particulars, in the psychological construction of the mind?

In this chapter I propose that we construct not only the basic categories and particulars of the mind but also the very way in which we find out what is going on in our minds: that is, we construct the nature of awareness, as well as the fundamental aspects of those things of which we might be aware. One might argue that, really, there is no problem in the psychological metaphysics of the mind because we just know what the mind is like and what goes on in it, and our understanding of it reflects that incorrigible knowledge. Or, at least, if some parts of or events in the mind are hidden from us, a great deal is known beyond doubt. (Indeed, this position is not argued but just taken for granted in some areas of psychology. For example, Piaget (1954) talked of awareness of purpose, awareness of intention, awareness of desire and of effort at the stage of secondary circular reactions, as if the fact and nature of awareness of these things were unproblematic.) This argument reveals an assumption about the nature of awareness, to the effect that it gives us incorrigible knowledge of mental occurrences. In other words, that awareness is a relation of direct perception. This is only an assumption: it is not known to be true, and in fact it can be argued that it is false. But assumptions of this kind lie at the foundation of our understanding of ourselves and our minds, and elucidation of them is therefore an essential part of investigating the psychological metaphysics of the mind.

This yields the programme for this chapter: investigating the common-sense understanding of awareness (or introspection, if one prefers), elucidating what is wrong with it and providing a glimpse of a less unsatisfactory alternative conceptualisation, and through that analysis clarifying the basic categories and particulars of the psychological metaphysics of the mind.

First, a few preliminaries are in order: I need to make a terminological clarification, and to consider briefly the extreme, behaviourist claim that our understanding of the mind owes nothing to mental occurrences at all, but derives entirely from observations of behaviour and circumstances, and socialisation in the use of language.

## SINGLE AND MULTIPLE MENTAL OCCURRENCES

To begin with terminology, I use the term 'mental occurrences' to refer to any mental states, activities, or events, or indeed anything that people would regard as going on in the human mind, however they conceptualise that.

The vocabulary of mental occurrences contains an ambiguity which must be dealt with before we can make clear statements about the psychological metaphysics of the mind. Take a term such as 'deciding'. This term can be used to refer to a single act, such as just deciding to do some particular thing, or it can be used to refer to an extended activity, involving the weighing up of various courses of action, consideration of alternatives, judgements of various kinds, culminating perhaps in the choice of one of the courses of action considered. This is to point to what might be described as an 'atomic–molecular' distinction: a distinction between a single unit, which may be a single event or act or state, and a collection of units, comprising a mental activity or, in the case of a collection of states and nothing else, what may be called a mental condition. (Here 'condition' is being used in its meaning of 'state of affairs', not in its more technical sense as in 'necessary condition', 'releasing condition', and so on). An important point to note about this distinction is that a mental activity may consist of both acts and states: thus, an extended decision process may include both acts of judgement and appraisal and states of uncertainty, desire, and so on.

When using a word like 'deciding', it is important to be clear about whether we are referring to a single mental occurrence or an activity consisting of more than one occurrence. For purposes of investigating psychological metaphysics, the focus is mainly on single mental occurrences, and I use mental occurrence terms in this way unless indicated otherwise.

This ambiguity in terminology can have significant consequences. For example, Rips and Conrad (1989) investigated taxonomic judgements ($X$ is a kind of $Y$) and partonomic judgements ($X$ is a part of $Y$) concerning what they referred to as mental activities. They began by asking 15 students to list common mental activities, and in this way obtained 73 terms given by at least two people each, as well as 'idiosyncratic' terms given by only one each. The frequent terms included experiencing, feeling, having emotions, loving, imagining, dreaming, deciding, choosing, thinking, analysing, conceptualising, interpreting, reasoning, learning, figuring out, solving problems, examining, investigating, planning, questioning, and picturing. Rips and Conrad made an *ad hoc* division of the most common terms into what they called analytic and non-analytic categories, and investigated taxonomic and partonomic relations between the terms by means of a sophisticated partial ordering procedure.

The results, and several follow-up studies, showed that the term 'thinking' formed the base of the analytic taxonomy, and 'experiencing' formed the base of the non-analytic taxonomy. There is something of a conundrum in their findings, however, in that if one activity was judged to be a kind of another, the latter was judged to be a part of the former in almost all cases. For instance, conceptualising was judged to be a type of thinking, and thinking was judged to be a part of conceptualising. The atomic–molecular distinction provides a simple resolution of this conundrum. If we suppose that people use much the same vocabulary for both acts and activities, the interpretation is straightforward: the partonomic judgement relates an act to an activity (the activity of conceptualising includes acts of thinking), whereas the taxonomic judgement relates acts to acts or activities to activities (for example, the activity of conceptualising is a kind of thinking activity).

Part of the reason for discussing Rips and Conrad (1989) is that their findings on lay taxonomy could be made into a proposal about the basic categorical distinctions among mental occurrences: we could say, mental occurrences are of two kinds, analytic and non-analytic, and thinking is the basic kind of analytic occurrence, and experiencing is the basic kind of non-analytic occurrence. This is unsatisfactory in several respects, however. For one thing, it hardly seems plausible to claim that thinking does not involve experiencing: surely most people would want to say they experience the thoughts they think, that if they did not they would not know what they were thinking. Also, calling a certain category non-analytic only tells us what it is not, and does not tell us what it is. In addition, these are only categories of mental acts, and exclude what we might want to call mental states (D'Andrade 1987; Vendler 1972). I return to the issue of basic categories of mental occurrences later in the chapter.

## IS THERE ANY PATH FROM MENTAL OCCURRENCES TO BELIEFS?

The extreme view on this question has been articulated by Bem (1967, 1972). This view depends on Skinner's (1957) account of socialisation in the use of language based on operant conditioning principles. Bem noted, as Skinner did, that the socialising community faces considerable difficulty in teaching children the use of self-descriptive statements, in that they do not have access to what is going on inside the child. For teaching purposes they must therefore use cues from the child's behaviour and the circumstances in which it occurs to judge that a particular self-descriptive term is appropriate. For example, if it is past the child's usual bedtime and the child is observed yawning, an adult might infer that the child is tired. The child can then learn the use of that self-descriptive statement from the adult's use of it. Bem inferred from this that the use of self-descriptive statements might continue to be partially under the control of the public events used by the training community to infer internal states: that is, people continue to identify their own internal states by observing their own behaviour and the circumstances in which it occurs. Bem allowed that people might have some awareness of their own state of physiological arousal, but did not allow any more than that.

The challenge this poses for researchers is to show accuracy in the use of self-descriptive statements greater than that which can be achieved by any outside observer equipped with as much knowledge as the actor about the actor's behaviour and the circumstances in which it occurred. Indeed, Bem (1967) claimed that there was no need to postulate awareness of an internal state of dissonance (Festinger 1957), because in typical dissonance manipulations observers made inferences about the actor's attitudes that were similar to those made by the actors themselves.

Since then, however, evidence sufficient to disprove Bem's extreme view has been obtained. Kroll and Kellicutt (1972) ran a recall study in which they asked subjects to press a button whenever they thought they were rehearsing the material to be recalled. Correlations between amount of button-pressing and subsequent recall ranged from +0.93 to +0.97, which indicates that the button press is a virtually perfect measure of the occurrence of rehearsal. An alternative measure of rehearsal, based on observed performance on a distracter task, had a much lower correlation with subsequent recall. It seems indubitable that these subjects were aware, in some sense, of the occurrence of rehearsal. One can imagine observers pressing buttons whenever they thought the subject they were observing was engaged in rehearsal (in conditions in which the subject is not pressing a button, of course), but one cannot imagine how any such observer could achieve such a high level of accuracy in their button pressing.

A second line of evidence comes from research on the proposal by Nisbett and Wilson (1977) that people have little or no awareness of higher-order mental processes. Methodologically, this tends to reduce to a claim that people are unaware of causal influences on responses produced by higher-order processes, because experimenters can only assess influence by means of correlations between stimuli and responses. The methodological complications in this litera- ture have been reviewed elsewhere (White 1988b), and will not be repeated here. The latest study in the literature, however (White 1989c), has found evidence for report accuracy attributable to internal influence and not to the other possible sources of accuracy identified by White (1988b). If this evidence is valid, it shows an improvement in accuracy due to internal information which observers cannot infer, and this is sufficient to refute Bem's position. Other studies on this topic have also found actors' reports of superior accuracy to those made by suitably informed observers, although the reasons for this superior accuracy are not clear (White 1988b).

Even without this evidence, the extreme position would be patently absurd. Smith and Jones (1986) commented: 'to tell whether you yourself believe that the US budget deficit is too high, for example, you don't have to wait to catch yourself in revealing behaviour!' (p. 147). On this day, 2 January, I have resolved to make a change to my diet, but I have not yet engaged in any behaviour from which I or anyone else might infer such a change, nor had I verbally expressed my resolution prior to writing this; yet, clearly, I knew that I had made this resolution. Many philosophers have argued that an actor necessarily knows what his or her reasons for action are (Taylor 1966), and dissenters have had to make strenuous efforts to defend even the intelligibility of the idea of unconscious reasons for action (Young 1988).

It therefore appears indubitable that we have some knowledge or awareness, whatever that means, of particular mental occurrences and states, such as reasons for action and attitudes. Some philosophers have claimed even more. Pears (1966) argued that, in some cases, we can know beyond doubt the causes of our feelings. Three of the examples he gave are: 'I was pleased by the publication of my letter'; 'I was amused by his remark'; and 'The explosion made me jump' (p. 143). This claim, of course, has a bearing on the Nisbett/Wilson proposal, which as I have said reduces to a claim that we do not know the external causal influences on products of our higher-order mental processes. In one of the studies they carried out (1977), the dependent measure was a rating of emotional impact, which brings their claim into direct relation with Pears's argument.

The argument Pears made was that we can be mistaken about the object of our feeling in some cases (such as depression) but not in others (like amusement). (The word 'object' does not mean 'physical object' here, but just the object of reference of the feeling: thus, a remark can be an object in this sense, as can a property of a thing.) Where we cannot be mistaken about the object of a feeling, we cannot be mistaken about the cause either. Thus, one could argue that in their studies Nisbett and Wilson merely exploited cases where we can be mistaken about the object of our feeling or judgement, and that their proposal might hold good for cases of that sort but cannot hold good for cases where we *cannot* be mistaken about the object of a feeling. The word 'cannot' needs emphasis here. Nisbett and Wilson could argue that I can correctly infer that I was amused by someone's remark by applying a cultural theory about causes of amusement that happens to be correct. But this type of inference does not give indubitable knowledge because, of course, the cultural theory could have been wrong. When Pears claimed that we cannot be mistaken about the cause of a feeling, he did not mean that we could make clever inferences about it, he meant that we just know. And indeed it is hard to imagine, paraphrasing Pears, how one could know that someone had made a certain remark, and know that one was amused, and yet not know that one was amused *by* the remark. Similar comments can be made about the other two examples quoted from Pears.

Under the theory of powerful particulars (Harré and Madden 1975), such knowledge is not at all problematic. Harré and Madden claimed that one could know causal connections just as surely as one could know the shape of an object or its movement through space. For example, when a hammer smashes a plate, we observe the shape of the hammer and its movement through space, and the disintegration of the plate, and we observe the causal connection as well. There is no special problem about observing the causal connections in such cases. Of course, mistakes can be made, but these mistakes, according to Harré and Madden, are no more damaging to the claim of observability than are visual illusions: that is, they are law-like, predictable exceptions, and no more than that. The case of a feeling and its cause is just another case of a power operating to produce an effect, and under the theory of powerful particulars we can observe (figuratively if not literally) the production of the effect just as we can when a hammer smashes a plate.

Whether the Harré and Madden account goes too far or not, it seems incontestable that the extreme behaviourist view is wrong, and that there is some kind of path from at least some mental occurrences to beliefs. We do not yet know from how many or which kinds of mental occurrence the path runs. For present purposes, however, my main concern is with the nature of the path. In the next section I consider the traditional view of the nature of the path, and why this view must be wrong. Following that I explore an alternative conceptualisation of the path.

## THE TRADITIONAL VIEW

The most uncommitted view one could have of the mind (or brain, if one prefers) is just as a collection of diverse processes, functions, capacities, states, events, to some extent functionally co-ordinated, to some extent (perhaps even entirely) in the service of the survival of the organism. It takes only a moment to realise that this is not our view of our own minds: the very idea that there is a 'we' or 'I' that has a view of its own mind is enough to show that. This idea is of an enduring substance; and moreover an enduring substance that is not all that there is to the mind, for an enduring substance cannot be identified with mere events, which do not endure. Indubitably this must be the same <<I>> that is the sole cause of action according to the concept of action put forward in the previous chapter, and according to Taylor (1966). Once we draw a line between <<I>> and everything else then it becomes natural to ask how <<I>> might obtain information about other things going on in the mind. We obtain information about the outside world through perception: as people understand it, <<I>> obtains information about the inside world of the mind through conscious awareness, or introspection, if one prefers. It is also natural to ask, if <<I>> is the performer of behavioural actions, whether <<I>> might be the performer of actions in the mind as well, and indeed whether people understand much of what goes on in the mind as mental actions, performed by <<I>>. Clearly, <<I>> is of the most fundamental importance to the psychological construction of the mind, so it is necessary to begin by taking a closer look at it.

## <<I>>

As I have said, Taylor identified <<I>> as an enduring substance. This view is not without problems in philosophy. Hume (1739/1978) attempted to discover <<I>> by consulting his own experiences and found nothing more than a collection of perceptions: it has been argued, though, that this was a misguided strategy because one cannot expect to find the subject of experience by consulting the objects of experience. Ginet (1990) argued that the idea of an enduring substance causing transient events has intractable problems in that it cannot explain, for example, the timing of an action. The timing of events in physical causation is explained by Harré and Madden (1975) in terms of releasing conditions, but it is still not clear whether and how this analysis could be applied to actions.

These problems need have no relevance for psychology: people are not required to solve the problem of the timing of action before they can possess a concept of an enduring substance as the producer of action. There is a problem of a different kind, however: taking an analysis of how action is actually produced and using it as a model of how people believe it is produced means taking what is supposed to be an actual thing and turning it into a concept. In Taylor's account <<I>> is real as such: in the psychological construction of mind, <<I>> might be real, in which case we have to ask how we know about it (or whether knowing about it is a problem), or it might be a concept, in which case we have to ask how it is formed.

In the psychological construction of mind, <<I>> is the seat of consciousness and action, in Helminiak's (1984) terms 'the agent in the act . . . the seer in the seeing . . . the thinker in the thinking . . . the "understander" in the understanding' (p. 215). <<I>> is also regarded as unified, one thing, indivisible, the very seat and source of any unity that mental life may be felt to have: <<I>> has only one consciousness, one will. It has no constituents and is made of nothing other than itself. It is a basic stuff and only itself can be made of it. It has continuity: it naturally endures in time, at least until death, without alteration to its fundamental properties. 'Losing consciousness' means, to a lay person, not that the <<I>> no longer has the faculty of consciousness but that, for some reason, the faculty is temporarily 'switched off', or that <<I>> is not in a position to use it.

Where, then, does <<I>> come from? Is it necessary? Could we, perhaps, develop beliefs about consciousness and the production of action without attaching them to <<I>> or indeed to anything at all? It is tempting to assign the notion of <<I>> to the class of unarguable truths, truths which require no defence because they are self-evidently correct. Thus, <<I>> is the metaphysical foundation of the construction of the mind because there just is this thing which I have been calling <<I>>, and I cannot deny it without self-evident absurdity, without in fact doing the most extreme violence to my very notion of what it is to exist at all. So long as it is true to say that there is something it is like to be I, then <<I>> must be part if not the whole of that. If anybody seriously tries to tell me I am wrong, then I can only think that I have not succeeded in telling them what <<I>> is, and they have confused it with something else, such as a 'self' or sense of identity. This is the line taken by some thinkers (Taylor 1966; Helminiak 1984).

It might help to imagine a thought experiment in which you are asked to strip away as much of yourself as you can, until you reach a point at which you believe that to strip away any more would be to abolish yourself altogether. Because there may be many things about yourself which you would be reluctant to discard, the easiest procedure is to make forced choices between pairs of alternatives. By doing this, I can imagine myself in some sense still existing without my legs; without being able to see; without feelings; without being able to recognise formerly familiar things and people; without being able to count; without memory, though this last causes the most severe disruption to my sense of self. For me, the terminal point comes with the notion of being some kind of subject of experiences. I cannot imagine this being stripped away without feeling that I would have ceased to exist. There might be experiences, but if there were no *subject* of them then I would feel that there was no ground for saying that I was there at all. Memory, mental abilities, perceptual abilities, and so on, are all important but *ancillary*, not essential. As far as <<I>> *at the present moment* is concerned, then, the realist position appears tenable: just being <<I>> is enough, as far as knowing that to be so is concerned.

It might seem that this has occasionally been denied by sceptical philosophers. For example, Hume (1739/1978) asserted that he was nothing more than a bundle of experiences, loosely connected by the mere fact of their occurring in the same body. But Hume was committed to the philosophy of radical empiricism, and thus to the denial of the necessity of endurance in time as a natural characteristic of anything: he could not accept the literal reality of <<I>> without undermining the radical empiricist programme. More than that, though, Hume was denying not <<I>> at the present moment, but the natural persistence of <<I>> across time. He was denying that we could know that the <<I>> that is the subject of my experiences now is the same <<I>> that was the subject of experiences in my body five minutes ago. And here, he has hit upon a real problem. This is where <<I>> stops being a literal undeniable reality and becomes a concept. We literally do not know anything undeniable about the past. Our idea of <<I>> as extending into the past is a concept, a hypothesis, and as such could be wrong. So it is necessary to explain psychologically how people have as part of the basic psychological construction of the mind not just <<I>> but a concept of, indeed a profound faith in, an <<I>> that endures across time. Put this way, it is clear that we are seeking to explain the psychological construction of a primary substance, albeit one with unusual, even unique properties. I want to state clearly that I am posing this as a psychological problem, not a philosophical one. I am not concerned, for example, with the logical status of claims about the persistence of <<I>>. I am concerned with the psychological problem of how (or why) people construct a notion of the mind in which <<I>> persists across time. Now, we could say that the ways in which people distinguish things from one another, and all things that are enduring objects from all things that are not, are also the ways in which people psychologically construct the concept of <<I>>. This cannot be entirely true, however: people cannot infer identity across time in the subject of experience using those perceptual cues by which people infer identity in physical objects because no such cues are available. We do not know about <<I>> by perceiving it.

One argument might be that if people use the persistence of properties of objects to make inferences about identity of objects, then they could use the self-evident persistence of the unity of consciousness to make the inference that it is always the same consciousness: consciousness and the unity of consciousness *are* always present and self-evident so we infer from that that it is always the *same* consciousness. This may be so up to a point, but it does not explain how the inference of identity is carried across sleep (and other periods of unconsciousness), which is a kind of hiatus in consciousness. I believe I am the same <<I>> that I was yesterday, despite having apparently not been conscious while I was asleep last night. Possibly it is the continuity across the night of those things most closely associated with <<I>> that is important. For example, I could believe that I was the same <<I>> if I woke up in a different body from the one that was the point of view of all my memories. I think it would be much more difficult to believe I was the same <<I>> if all that I remembered about things that <<I>> had done (such as plans <<I>> had made for today) were different. I would certainly think this very strange, if I did not think I had somehow made the changes myself. Yet I could still believe that that apparently very different <<I>> was I.

The past is utterly inaccessible. <<I>>, my consciousness, and the unity of my consciousness may all be self-evident to me now, but their having been so for me in the past, and their having been *my* <<I>>, consciousness, and so on, cannot be self-evident at all, because the past is lost. I depend for my knowledge of how things were in the past upon memory, so I depend for my inference of the continuity of <<I>> on memory. This leads me to suggest that the continuity of <<I>> is inferred from availability of memories. But it is not just the availability of memories that leads me to appropriate them to myself. It is that the fact of being <<I>> is present in every memory I have. I remember being a subject, being conscious – it is there in all my memories – I remember being <<I>>, in fact, from the point of view of <<I>>. I remember doing things, and I have no reason to think that it was any other than <<I>> that did them. I remember experiencing things, and I have no reason to think that it was any other than <<I>> that experienced them. So there is no reason to suppose that the <<I>> in my memories was any other than I. The supposition of the continuity of <<I>>, then, is based in the evident presence of <<I>> in all of one's memories. This supposition may not be irrevocable (for example, it may be lost in some cases of schizophrenia), and it may be aided by continuities of other sorts, continuity of body, for example. But these are ancillary, not fundamental.

Whether <<I>> is a real thing or a concept of something that might or might not be a real thing, it seems uncontroversial that <<I>> is basic to our understanding of ourselves. This is not to say that all mental abilities, functions, and so forth, are existentially dependent on <<I>>. We could imagine some at least continuing if <<I>> were annihilated, but we would not imagine them as being part of ourselves, under those circumstances, for there would be no 'ourselves' to imagine them as being part of.

Under the basic concept of action proposed here, <<I>> is the producer of actions. This is, therefore, one capacity that <<I>> has – here I am using the term 'capacity' in the sense used by Kenny (1989) as referring to a collection of powers. Indeed, the actions of which <<I>> is the producer include not only behavioural actions but also mental actions such as thinking. My aim now is to explore another capacity or characteristic of <<I>>, which is, using the term loosely for the moment, consciousness.

## Consciousness[1]

Philosophers do not seem to be in any doubt that action is done consciously – this is implied by the logical truth about action that it is up to me what I do. Philosophers talk of intentions as conscious, and of actors as necessarily knowing what their reasons for action are, at least at the time at which they carry out the action in question (Smith and Jones 1986; Taylor 1966). Consciousness is there-fore a capacity, or faculty, of <<I>>: it would be regarded by most people as absurd to suggest that, when I say 'I do this' and 'I am conscious of that', I am referring to two different things, both as it were coincidentally called 'I'. The <<I>> that is the producer of action is therefore also the <<I>> that is the subject of consciousness.

But how is consciousness conceptualised in common sense? What are con-scious awareness and conscious control? We can shed some light on these issues by considering how conscious awareness has been treated in psychology.

### Conscious awareness and introspection

My usual example of this (White 1980, 1986, 1988b) has been the work of Nisbett and Wilson (1977). In the introduction I looked at their assumptions about the relation between awareness (or 'access', a term often used by them) and verbal reports, specifically 'causal reports' (White 1988b). Here I am concerned not with verbal reports but with their conceptualisation of 'access' to mental processes. One reason for choosing their work is that they appear to be denying an important feature of common-sense belief, that we do have pretty good awareness of most if not all of what goes on in our minds, but their denial is itself founded on assumptions which they *share* with common sense, and if the assumptions are removed their arguments become not wrong but meaningless. The following quotations are similar to many that can be found in their article.

we may have no direct access to higher order mental processes. (p. 232)

these investigators doubt people's ability to observe directly the workings of their own minds. (p. 232)

this would suggest that they [subjects] are not aware of the occurrence of a process. (p. 236)

a problem-solving process that is almost completely hidden from conscious view. (p. 240)

even the fact that a process is taking place is sometimes unknown to the individual prior to the point that a solution appears in consciousness. (p. 240)

Statements not fundamentally different from these can be found also in some of the replies to the Nisbett/Wilson proposal. For example, in the earliest critical response, Smith and Miller (1978) included the phrase 'perception of cognitive processes' in their title.

These statements reveal a consistent stance on the nature of awareness. First, awareness belongs to a thing or being, the person (variously referred to as 'we', 'the individual', and so on). Secondly, mental processes lie somewhere 'outside' the person, and for this reason the person has somehow to gain access to them, to find out about them. Thirdly, the means of access is conscious awareness. Fourthly, conscious awareness operates by a kind of direct perception: the phrase 'direct access to' occurs seven times in the paper by Nisbett and Wilson (1977), and the phrases 'observe directly', 'direct introspective access to', 'ability to examine directly', and 'direct introspective awareness' can also be found. The analogy with perception is revealed in phrases like 'hidden from conscious view'.

Here I would like to quote myself (1986), partly because there is a serious typographical error in the published version which I wish to correct. I pointed out that, in the common-sense Nisbett and Wilson view, <<I>> has through conscious awareness 'a privileged or "god's eye" view of mental activity' (p. 519), such that, whatever limitations there may be on the scope of conscious awareness, there is no problem or difficulty in gaining access to anything that falls within those limitations. Nisbett and Wilson took issue with common sense on the extent of the limitations, not on the means by which access is gained. (In the passage from which I quoted myself, this was supposed to be contrasted with the means of access that holds under the physicalist assumption, discussed later, but the typographical error has obscured this important difference.)

The common-sense view has been further perpetuated in theoretical work by Wilson (1985). Wilson suggested a model in which there are two mental systems, one which is non-conscious and which mediates behaviour, and one which is conscious and which attempts to verbalise and communicate mental states. The latter system may often have limited access to mental states, and then makes inferences about what these might be. The extent to which this model rests upon common-sense assumptions can be seen by asking a few questions which Wilson did not address. What is a mental system, and on what grounds should we suppose that the mind consists of two of them? What is 'access', how does it work, and how is it limited? Perhaps most importantly, how does communication *within* a system work? For example, suppose that the conscious system gains access to something in the non-conscious system: does this mean that the thing accessed is automatically freely available to *all* of the conscious system? If so, how? Consideration of the physical nature of the brain (see below) shows that these are not trivial problems, and that the assumptions in Wilson's model, and in the Nisbett/Wilson proposal, must be justified before they can be accepted. This is not to argue that Wilson's model is wrong, only that it rests upon implicit and unconsidered assumptions.

The concept revealed by the use of these implicit assumptions can be summarised as follows. <<I>> has consciousness. It is through consciousness that <<I>> can be aware of what is going on in the mind. <<I>> has the power to direct conscious awareness onto whatever mental activity it chooses to (and can) look at. The direction of conscious awareness is a mental action performed by <<I>>. The mental action of directing conscious awareness, or 'introspection', is conceived as a kind of direct perception, meaning that whatever is looked at through conscious awareness *is* the content of consciousness. Under this view there is no possibility of error in the relation between <<I>> and those things of which <<I>> is aware. Thanks to consciousness, there is absolutely no communication problem of any kind *within* the domain of <<I>>: there are only problems concerning the degree of access conscious awareness gives <<I>> to things lying outside that domain. Only <<I>> has conscious awareness: this is not a faculty possessed by any other part of or thing in the mind.

## Conscious control

Since <<I>> is both the subject of consciousness and the progenitor of action, it follows that consciousness can be involved in the direction of action: through the direction of conscious awareness upon ongoing action <<I>> can direct and control action in full knowledge of what it is doing. This is the specific meaning of the term 'conscious control': not merely the production of action but the control and direction of action informed by conscious awareness of that action.

The corollary of the association between <<I>> and conscious control is the dissociation of <<I>> from mental events and activities which seem not to be controlled. Here I can do no better than to give a personal example. While marking examination scripts, I found myself thinking 'my mind keeps wandering onto other things'. I dare say I am not the first person ever to have this thought, but why choose that form of expression? Why not, '*I* keep wandering onto other things'? The answer must be that it is interpreted as not being something that <<I>> does: it is not intended, not consciously controlled. This is one of those cases where the elusive nature of mental activity allows great latitude for the construction of interpretations that fit preconceived beliefs. There is no guarantee that we necessarily know what <<I>> does and does not do. For example, I might have decided, in some loose, unreflective sense, to think about something else, and by the time I had noticed I was no longer reading the script, I had forgotten about my decision. We rarely, if ever, have justification for feeling certain about our interpretations of what is going on in our own minds.

To summarise progress so far, I have identified what amounts to a distinct domain in the mind, the domain of <<I>>. This consists of the behavioural and mental actions of <<I>>, and *ipso facto* of those things related to action, including intentions, choices, decisions, purposes, desires, beliefs, and so on; it also consists of consciousness, incorporating conscious awareness, introspection, and conscious control. In producing action <<I>> is limited by the powers possessed by the person, but otherwise <<I>> can do anything which it is in a person's power to do at that moment. It is also worth noting at this stage that the reach of conscious control is not greater than that of conscious awareness, since it depends on conscious awareness, and that it may well be less, if <<I>> can be conscious of things which it cannot control: awareness is necessary but not sufficient for control. Powers determine what can happen, not what will happen.

What can we say about the psychological construction of the rest of the mind? Mainly that it lacks those basic capacities of <<I>> described so far. Thus, it lacks consciousness and does not produce action. In so far as things in the rest of the mind cause anything, they do so in the deterministic way of any other type of physical causation, so that effects so produced occur through the operation of causal powers under suitable releasing conditions. It does not possess the kind of unity that <<I>> possesses, though it may be regarded as functionally integrated to some extent. The usual property of necessity applies: powers determine what will happen, not what can happen.

## THE TRADITIONAL VIEW OF THE PATH FROM MENTAL OCCURRENCE TO BELIEF

We can now answer the question of how beliefs about mental occurrences are formed under the common-sense view. The basic answer is that it is <<I>> that knows about particular ongoing mental occurrences, and the way in which this happens is determined by the faculties or powers possessed by <<I>>. Those properties that are relevant to this are consciousness, including conscious awareness and conscious control, the role of <<I>> as the producer of actions, both mental and physical, and the fact that <<I>> is regarded as unitary, all one, in nature.

The immediate consequence of these properties is that there is no problem for <<I>> in forming beliefs about itself. Through its unitary nature and possession of consciousness it automatically knows itself, and there is no possibility of error in its knowledge of itself. The question how one part of it can know what another part of it is like or what goes on there never arises because it is a unitary being and all of it is conscious. This kind of knowledge is not obtained through introspection or by any other means: it is direct and given. It is given in virtue of the fact that <<I>> is the *subject* of experience, not any kind of object of awareness.

The properties of <<I>> also determine the answer to the question of how <<I>> can form beliefs about parts of or occurrences in the mind other than itself; for example mental activities, what is going on in them and how they operate, what feelings one has, and so on. For beliefs about these, <<I>> depends on the faculty of consciousness, specifically conscious awareness, and its power to direct conscious awareness onto one part of mental activity or another. <<I>> knows about those things upon which it turns conscious awareness, and does not know about those things upon which it either does not or cannot turn conscious awareness. Introspection, then, as defined under the psychological construction of the mind, is <<I>> using its power to turn conscious awareness onto some area of mental activity thereby to know what is going on there.

The word 'know' applies because of the conceptualisation of introspection as a kind of direct perception. What <<I>> discovers through conscious awareness is known directly and in a manner which precludes the possibility of error. This is not to say that what is learned in this way cannot be supplemented by inferences made by <<I>>, and the psychological construction of reality admits the possibility that such inferences, being indirect, can be mistaken. But the basic belief-forming process is the incorrigible process of introspection, gaining direct knowledge of mental occurrences. One noteworthy aspect of this is that there is no possibility of error in beliefs about consciousness. It is in the nature of consciousness as a faculty of <<I>> that <<I>> cannot be mistaken about what is conscious, what the contents of conscious awareness are, nor about what was conscious, so long as it is not too long ago.

It is important to recognise that these ideas are not restricted in application to our own minds. When we form an impression of another person, we gradually develop ideas about their individuating characteristics, their introversion, their warmth and honesty, and so on. But we do not leave these characteristics floating freely in our notion of another mind. They are firmly attached to the metaphysical assumptions we make about other minds. We assume that every other person is an <<I>>, that they have consciousness and conscious awareness, that the <<I>> in them performs the actions we see them carry out. We do not need to know anything about a person in order to attribute these things to them, other than the fact that they are a person. That is what it means to say that these things are axiomatic to our understanding of persons. Every impression we ever form of anyone is anchored in these metaphysical postulates of <<I>> as an enduring substance with its capacities of consciousness and the power to produce actions.

The fact that things seem this way to us, that we have this set of beliefs, must say something about the way the mind or brain actually is. The simplest inference is that things are as they seem, as I have just described. I now argue that this position is not tenable, because if what we are talking about is a purely physical system, then consciousness cannot do what is asked of it in the traditional approach.

## THE PHYSICALIST ASSUMPTION AND CONSCIOUSNESS

I use the term 'physicalist assumption' to refer to the assumption that what information-processing models seek to model is purely physical (Shallice 1978). Information-processing models of consciousness (Baars 1983; Hilgard 1976; Mandler 1975a, 1975b, 1984; Marcel 1983; Norman 1976; Norman and Shallice 1980; Posner and Warren 1972; Shallice 1972, 1978; Shiffrin and Schneider 1977), no matter what they take consciousness to be, therefore constitute attempts to account for or model consciousness in purely physical terms. The term I use for the thing that they are supposed to be models of is 'the system' (this presumably means the brain or parts of it if the physicalist assumption is correct).

Now, I am going to set up an arbitrary piece of the system which I shall call a belief-forming process, and I shall define this as a process that takes in information, forms a belief through some kind of operation on that information, and either holds the belief in working memory or stores it in long-term memory. For present purposes, I have no interest in the manner of operation of the process or in whether such a thing might actually exist in the system or not. It is a device which I am using to elucidate certain consequences of the physicalist assumption.

If we assume, as we must under the physicalist assumption, that the system has some kind of structure (which may or may not change over time), it follows that the belief-forming process must have some definite physical location in the system. To make this absolutely clear, I am not trying to suggest that all beliefs that ever get formed must be formed at this one definite location: there could well be other belief-forming processes elsewhere, and it makes no difference to the argument. All I am saying, really, is that there is more to the system than this belief-forming process about which I am talking now, and that we could in principle draw a boundary between this process and the rest of the system, and this much seems unobjectionable.

Now the question I wish to pose is: how does this process form a belief about something going on somewhere else in the system? The answer must be that the process depends on information coming to it through some physical channel, because under the physicalist assumption only physical channels of communication can be used. This answer immediately reveals two important things about the system.

The first is that the limit to the ability of the process to form correct beliefs is set by the physical communication channels in the system, such that (1) if there is no channel connecting some occurrence in the system with the belief-forming process, there is no way that the process can obtain information about the occurrence, and (2) if there is some channel, the process will only gain information about the occurrence if the channel is actually used; that is, if information somehow comes from the occurrence to the process, of a sort that could be described as information about the occurrence.

The second is that the information that enters the belief-forming process is very indirectly related to the occurrence in question. There can be no sense in which the process is directly acquainted with the occurrence. Instead, it depends on indirect information, information transmitted through whatever communication channels exist, with whatever attendant risk there may be of distortion, loss, translation into different codes or forms of representation, and so on.

There is nothing that can be done about these limitations: they are inescapable consequences of the physicalist assumption. Of course, if there were many belief-forming processes in lots of places then the limitations might not count for very much: but that would be a way of living with the limitations, not a way of transcending them.

Now suppose, using the traditional concepts described above, that <<I>> is conscious of some ongoing mental occurrence. What can this mean, under the physicalist assumption? It depends on where we locate <<I>>. There are three possibilities.

First, <<I>> is located at the site of the mental occurrence of which it is conscious. Now, whatever this means, whatever we might want to say about what it is for <<I>> to be conscious of something, this does not help the belief-forming process at all. That process still depends on physical channels of communication for information about the mental occurrence, and <<I>> being conscious of the occurrence, whatever that means, cannot help the process in that regard because it cannot be a means of transcending the physical limitations on communication of information, *unless* we abandon the physicalist assumption.

This is not the only problem, because stating that <<I>> is located at the site of the mental occurrence leaves us wanting to know what <<I>> is, if it is not identical with the mental occurrence. Clearly the traditional concept of <<I>> implies that <<I>> cannot be merely identical with the occurrence because <<I>> is enduring and the occurrence is transitory, and <<I>> is the subject and the occurrence is the object of experience. But if <<I>> is not identical with the occurrence then (a) what is it?, and (b) what does it mean to say that <<I>> is aware of the occurrence? How is such awareness possible? Under the physicalist assumption, if <<I>> is not identical with the occurrence then it must be some-where else in the system, even if somewhere else means right next door, and this is formally equivalent to case (2), which I shall now consider.

In the second possibility <<I>> is located at the site of the belief-forming process. In this case what it means for <<I>> to be conscious of the occurrence must be that information about the occurrence has come from the site of the occurrence through physical communication channels in the system to the belief-forming process. The presence of <<I>> at the belief-forming process can in no way enable the belief-forming process, or indeed <<I>>, to transcend depend-ence on physical communication channels, *unless* we abandon the physicalist assumption. Clearly, if what we mean by '<<I>> am conscious of that occur-rence' is that information about that occurrence has traversed physical com-munication channels to the belief-forming process, where <<I>> happens to be, then conscious awareness cannot be the kind of incorrigible direct perception that it is conceived to be in common sense. Anything could happen to the information on its way from occurrence to belief-forming process: moreover, whatever enters the belief-forming process is not the occurrence itself but information about it; so, under this case, 'acquaintance with', 'access to', or 'awareness of', whichever expression one prefers, is inevitably indirect and corrigible.

In the third case <<I>>, whatever that is (or conscious awareness, whatever that is), encompasses both the occurrence and the process. I do not know whether this case is possible under the physicalist assumption. It is not at all clear what, under the physicalist assumption, <<I>> ought to be identified as; nor is it clear what consciousness ought to be identified as. Leaving these problems aside, though, even if <<I>> encompasses both the site of the occurrence and the belief-forming process, whatever we mean by saying these things, none of this could help the belief-forming process at all: under the physicalist assumption, the belief-forming process still depends on physical communication channels for information about the occurrence.

If there is more than one belief-forming process, then they are physically isolated from one another in the sense that each depends on being connected to the others by physical communication channels in order just to have the possi-bility of finding out that there are others, or what they are doing. Moreover, if the belief-forming process has even minimal complexity, then the same kind of problem holds for the parts of the process. Suppose, for the sake of argument, that the process has a number of stages linked in a linear (temporal) chain as follows: information input–encoding–inference–storage. These are temporally and phy-sically distinct: the only sense in which we can talk of one as knowing about the other (even allowing this anthropomorphic metaphor to stand) is in the sense that information passes from one to another. In this sense, inference cannot 'know about' storage, unless somehow information about storage gets into the process and proceeds through input and encoding.

And, as I have set up the system, there is an absolute difference between occurrences in the system and the structural elements of the system. This need not be an accurate representation of reality, but if it is (it might, for example, correspond to the difference between neural impulses and the physical arrangement of neurons and synapses) then there is a profound difference between the process gaining information about occurrences in the system and the process gaining information about the structure of the system.

Perhaps the most peculiar aspect of this is that, while <<I>> may be conscious of a mental occurrence, this is not the same as having a belief that <<I>> is conscious of a mental occurrence. Forming a true belief that <<I>> is conscious of a mental occurrence depends upon a belief-forming process somewhere in the system having information to that effect, and this in turn depends on that information being communicated from wherever in the system the occurrence is to the process. Being conscious of something does not enable dependence on physical communication channels to be transcended, even to form a belief that <<I>> is conscious of something. This is deeply counter-intuitive, but under the physicalist assumption it must be true. This leaves open the logical possibility that we may believe ourselves to be conscious of something when we are not, and that we may believe that we are not conscious of something when we are. When we consider the nature of the system under the physicalist assumption, ideas about the unity of <<I>> and conscious awareness, and how these things operate, simply fall to pieces. The only way to prevent them from doing so is to reject the physicalist assumption and say that <<I>> and conscious awareness are not to be identified with any physical characteristic of, location in, or function of the system. Thus, we must reject either the physicalist assumption or the traditional concepts of <<I>> and conscious awareness. They are not compatible.

The ultimate implication of these arguments is that the psychological problem of introspection (as opposed to the philosophical problem of introspection, with which I am not concerned), the problem of how we form beliefs about what is going on in our own minds and what limitations there are on our ability to do so, is wrongly conceptualised as a relation between a subject and an object of some kind of direct perception. The limitations imposed by the physicalist assumption and discussed in the foregoing section imply a different conceptualisation in terms of information processing. Obviously this is a topic of immense complexity, not to mention methodological intractability, but at least two faltering steps can be taken towards this alternative conceptualisation without straying outside the remit of this book. First, I argue that limitations on belief-forming are set by the function of the system itself; that is, by the functional allocation of processing resources (attention). Secondly, limitations are also set by the essential transience of mental phenomena, combined with dependence upon physical communication channels within the system: the problem of introspection, under this view, is better conceptualised as a relation between occurrence and interpretation.

## THE FUNCTIONAL ALLOCATION OF ATTENTION

Any appearance of or belief or inference about things in the mind is determined in part by the allocation of attention in accordance with the needs of ongoing mental activities and actions. That is, wherever attention is allocated in accordance with functional needs, beliefs about the mind and occurrences in it will be shaped thereby. There are two versions of this hypothesis, applying to conscious awareness and causation respectively.

For conscious awareness, the functional allocation hypothesis implies that we will believe ourselves to be consciously aware of those things to which attention is allocated, those being the things information about which is available from working memory. What we take the limits on conscious awareness of mental activity to be are actually the limits imposed by functional considerations on the allocation of attention.

For causation, things not attended will not be thought of as causes of mental occurrences or behaviour. This is analogous to the idea that salience affects causal inference, such that things that are highly salient are given more weight in causal interpretations than things that are less salient (Taylor and Fiske 1975, 1978; Fiske and Taylor 1991). As an illustration, consider the position effect study by Nisbett and Wilson (1977). Here, judgements about quality of items in an array were shown to be related to the position of the item in the array. Subjects failed to report this, however, and almost invariably denied that they had been influenced by position when asked about it. Let us accept, for the purposes of the illustration, that their judgements were influenced by position (though this is contentious – see White 1988b). Under the present interpretation, subjects had no belief that their judgement was influenced by position *not* because they were not consciously aware of the process of judgement, but because they were not attending to the feature of position while looking at the stimuli. They were not attending to it because their allocation of attention was determined by the functional requirements of the process of judgement – that is, by the requirement to attend to features relevant to considerations of quality. The corollary, of course, is that those things which they should report as influential upon their judgements are those things to which they were attending in accordance with the needs of the process of judgement. These were the features of the items relevant to a judgement of quality, and therefore they should report that their judgements were influenced by quality-related features. This is indeed what Nisbett and Wilson (1977) found.

In fact, the functional allocation of attention hypothesis is even more restrictive than this, because it implies that beliefs about conscious awareness or about any mental occurrence are determined by what is available in working memory at the time at which the belief-forming process operates. If we want to form a belief about some mental occurrence that happened at some time in the past, we depend absolutely upon information about that occurrence not merely entering working memory as a result of attention being paid to it, but staying there until the time at which the belief-forming process operates. This is a severe limitation and can have drastic consequences for the accuracy of reports about mental occurrences.

An example of this comes from my reanalysis of data from Maier's (1931) problem-solving experiment (White 1985). According to my statistical analysis (Maier did not present any), Maier found that, in a problem-solving task, people who were apparently helped by a hint were more likely to report that they had not been helped by it than other people who were apparently not helped by it. Maier suggested that the appearance of the solution to the problem tends to destroy memory for immediately preceding events. If the hint is helpful, the solution is found soon after the hint is presented and therefore the appearance of the solution destroys memory for the effects of the hint. When the hint is not helpful, the solution is found a longer time after the event, and therefore does not destroy memory for events around the time of the hint, all of which show it influencing the search for a solution. From the point of view of a belief-forming (or inference-making) process occurring after appearance of the solution, in response to Maier's question, the events immediately prior to the emergence of the solution are not available and as a result there is no evidence concerning their possible influence on the finding of the solution. Causal report inaccuracy in this case is due to failure of memory, not to failure of awareness at the time of the events about which Maier was asking.

The suggestion I made on the basis of this was that the generation of the product of some process has the effect of destroying memory for the immediately antecedent process that produced it. If this happens every time, then information about the process would always have been lost from working memory before it could enter any process that might affect beliefs, and for that reason no one could ever form any beliefs about the particular mental occurrences of any process, and the process itself will inevitably appear not to have been conscious, regardless of whether it was or not. To make matters worse, one cannot attend to the process at the time it is occurring because attention is functionally allocated in accordance with the needs of the process: this means that the attempt to usurp attention for the purpose of turning it on the process necessarily disrupts the process, so that it is no longer there to be attended to. If this is the case, we literally cannot form beliefs about our own mental processes, and our processes necessarily appear not to be conscious, and this inability is due to the combination of the functional allocation of attention and the loss of memory for the process that occurs when its product emerges.

## OCCURRENCE AND INTERPRETATION

I now turn to the second of the fundamental principles governing the formation of beliefs about particular ongoing mental occurrences, and concepts of the mind and things in it. One further interesting thing about the Nisbett and Wilson (1977) hypothesis is that they make a clean distinction between 'access' and the use of beliefs such as cultural beliefs in the making of causal reports. That is, in their proposal, beliefs (or any other pre-existing cognitive structures and concepts) do not act upon information gained by 'access': they are merely a substitute for it, used to construct a causal report when no useful information is available. It is just this clean distinction that helps to reveal the common-sense concept of introspection as operating by a kind of direct perception. If we have an idea of introspection as the direct and literal apprehension of things going on in the mind, then we are virtually compelled to regard cultural beliefs, and their influence on or use in verbal reports, as *independent* of introspection, as contraposed to it: so either one can report 'genuine' introspections or one can report guesses based on cultural beliefs. One might call this the naïve realist theory of introspection.

The alternative, proposed here, is that the use of beliefs, cognitive structures, concepts, and so on, is intrinsic to the activity of interpreting mental occurrences. This can be seen in the fact that the appearance of conscious control owes something to the use of the basic concept of action. That is, in interpreting something as a consciously controlled activity, part of what we are doing is constructing an idea of it with the aid of our basic conceptual repertoire. We see it as something that <<I>> carries out, not just as a complex use of feedback in the direction of activity, because of our use of the concept of <<I>> as the producer of action.

Under this view, causal reports do not merely present appropriate-looking cultural beliefs, they present a construction made by the use of cultural beliefs (and so on) in the interpretation of available information about mental occurrences. Instead of being contraposed, the input information and the beliefs are integrated under this hypothesis. This is still independent of any hypothesis about what sort of information can be input to the constructive activity of introspection. But verbal reports, more specifically causal reports, look quite different when viewed from the standpoint of this hypothesis: inaccuracy can tell us that the beliefs involved in the construction are wrong, but it tells us nothing about the limits on the kinds of information that can be input to the constructive process of introspection.

Take as an example an overheard snatch of conversation: 'I could just *feel* the adrenalin flowing through me'. Now consider first what one might call the 'either–or' hypothesis; verbal reports *either* concern things directly apprehended through introspection (as conceived under the naïve realist theory) *or* express cultural beliefs used to make plausible but essentially uninformed guesses. Clearly the former cannot be happening in this case because the statement is uncontroversially wrong: one cannot literally feel minute amounts of chemical in the bloodstream. But the latter is not the case either, because it is hard to deny that the speaker was feeling *something* and that this something provided the occasion for the report, even if it is not clear exactly what it was. So the 'either–or' hypothesis must be wrong.

The example fits the constructive theory of introspection, because it suggests some kind of input information which is interpreted or constructed with the aid of a pre-existing belief. A defender of the naïve realist theory, however, could argue that the error arose not from introspection itself but from the construction of the verbal report: whatever the speaker learned through introspection, she learned through direct perception and therefore correctly, but deciding how to put this into words resulted in error through the introduction of a faulty belief. It is hard to be certain about the proper interpretation of a single observation. Also, the kind of thing introspected upon in this instance was presumably some sort of feeling associated with physiological arousal, and one cannot assume that this is typical of all things that can be introspected upon. Take a verbal stream of thought, for example: it seems to me that when I think verbally, not only am I directly aware of what I am thinking but also I could exactly repeat the stream of thought in speech if I chose. This seeming might or might not be illusory, but it would be wrong to assume that, if the constructive theory of introspection is valid for feelings of arousal, it is therefore valid for verbal streams of thought as well. There is no guarantee that introspection must work in the same way for everything upon which we can introspect.

Despite these caveats, it hardly seems plausible to deny that constructive processes utilising pre-existing beliefs and concepts are used upon information about mental occurrences, because there is a sound reason for thinking that they are. It is simply that mental occurrences are essentially elusive and transient. No matter how introspection works, it cannot constitute a means of pinning a mental occurrence down for inspection at leisure. If we are ever tempted to think so, this simply betrays our metaphysical assumption that there are objects in the mind that are mental analogues of physical objects: that is, that they naturally endure in time unchanged unless acted upon in some way. That this is not the case imposes the most severe limitations upon what we can usefully report, or even believe, about our own mental occurrences. Imagine describing a painting to someone who cannot see it. So long as the characteristics of the painting endure unchanged, we can take care over the choice of words for the description (although even this must involve selection and interpretation, of course). But if the characteristics of the painting keep changing, like images in a dream, the job of description is hopeless, and our attempt to describe what the painting was like a moment ago is constantly thwarted by our perception of what it is like now; and if the changes in the characteristics are somewhat influenced by our interpretations and selections and constructions of the fleeting images of a moment ago, then we cannot tell the difference between the thing we are trying to describe and our own interpretations of it.

Imagine the sequence:

Conscious mental occurrence ————→ Interpretive process ————→ Outcome

This is, apart from anything else, a temporal sequence, and by the time we have reached the end of it the original mental occurrence is in the past. This entails that we can be mistaken about it because we cannot check the outcome against the original occurrence. Accuracy in interpretation is therefore impossible to judge, and impossible to guarantee. Awareness, whatever that is, does not help at all, because we cannot be aware of something that is past.

To repeat, the essential mark of a mental occurrence is transience. Unlike physical things (probably), a mental occurrence does not naturally persist from one instant of time to the next. It is here now, meaning at this unextended instant of time, but this fact in no way guarantees its persistence to the next instant, nor that it was there, at the immediately preceding instant. It is always, and essentially, liable to change or vanish. We cannot make a mental occurrence stay. We can, however, make successive mental occurrences be exactly similar across a span of instants. This is the nearest we can get to pinning a mental occurrence down. It is, however, a feat of effortful processing. What we tend to call short-term or working memory is not really memory at all, not in any way that is similar to long-term memory. It is more nearly analogous to processes that change information: it is just another information-processing function, only its function is to hold information the same, rather than to transform it. It is, in other words, the active effort of holding something the same. Turn this off and mental occurrences are liable to change capriciously, as perhaps they do in dreams. This is an important function, of course, because many processes need some information to be held the same in order to operate upon it: inference, inspection, accurate and detailed consolidation in long-term memory, any such process that is itself extended in time.

We have an idea of our mental occurrences as much more organised and consistent than they probably are, precisely because our beliefs are limited by the difficulty of pinning down mental occurrences for inspection. Streams of fleeting mental occurrences of a constantly shifting nature pass by all the time, shifting from one idea to another, from one topic to another, with distractions, interpolations, thoughts coming apparently out of the blue, and so on: but because our attention is so involved with holding things the same for information-processing purposes, we tend not to notice. Nothing is constant in the mind but change. This way of looking at things is necessary in order to understand that the problem of introspection is not one of the relation between perceiver and object of perception, but one of the relation between occurrence and interpretation.

## BASIC CATEGORIES OF MENTAL OCCURRENCE

The strangeness of the idea that mental occurrences do not have natural persistence but are instead essentially transient helps to reveal the basic categories of mental occurrence. The basic categories in general psychological metaphysics are being and happening, the distinction between these two being defined originally by reference to iconic processing, but extending from this during development. The proposal here is that the same distinction applies to mental occurrences, so that the basic categories of mental occurrence in the psychological construction of the mind are mental 'beings' (states and so forth), and mental happenings or events.

The definition of the distinction in terms of iconic processing cannot apply literally because, of course, we do not perceive things in the mind visually. There are two ways of maintaining the distinction. One is to propose that mental occurrences are subject to temporal integration processes equivalent in function to those that operate upon visual information (Likewise, an equivalent function has been proposed for operating upon auditory information, called echoic memory; Anderson 1980). This is another occurrence–interpretation relation. We do notice change in our own minds – events, mental acts or actions, the stream of consciousness, to use a popular phrase. If there is nothing exactly analogous to iconic processing, the noticing of change in mental occurrences must involve some sort of temporal integration. Under this possibility, then, mental 'happenings' can be defined as change in the rate of change of some parameter detected by whatever processes are involved in temporal integration on short time-scales, where 'short' means comparable to the time-scale of iconic processing. For this definition it is not necessary to ascertain exactly what processes are involved or how or when they operate, although obviously one could learn a lot by doing so.

The second way is to propose that the distinction is established in the mind by a kind of generalisation. This would be equivalent to the generalisation by which the concept of event is applied to things outside the iconic time-scale, such as the fall of the Roman Empire. I have already discussed the kinds of rules and cues through which such generalisations can be made, and there seems no obvious reason why the same kinds of rules and cues could not operate in generalisation to mental occurrences. In addition to these, the being/happening distinction is reinforced by the fact that some mental occurrences are, or are taken to be, representations of physical objects. For example, if I think of a cup of tea, or specifically if I have a mental image of a cup of tea, because this represents an object in the physical world it seems to me like an object, a being rather than a happening, in my mind. If I think of a person doing something, such as running, I am able to distinguish the being of the person from the happening of the action as I imagine them: the basicity of the being/happening distinction in my understanding of the physical world imposes itself upon my images and representations of the physical world in my mind, so that the being/happening distinction appears to hold for mental occurrences also.

## 'Being' in the mind

In general psychological metaphysics, being is conceptualised in terms of primary substances with properties, as concrete material particularism. 'Being' in the mind cannot be precisely like this because mental things are not understood as concrete material particulars. Instead, they are mental particulars. Mental particulars do, however, share two of the defining features of concrete material particulars, namely boundedness in space (or in some mental analogue of space) and natural persistence. By 'natural' I mean to emphasise the special feature of being that the continuation of a thing being as it is, a particular or some property of a particular, is not normally considered worthy of explanation (unless there was a definite expectation that some change would occur). In the case of mental occurrences, these features are problematic. I have already discussed the essential transience of mental occurrences, as the reason why the assumption of natural persistence in mental 'beings' is wrong; now I consider the assumptions of natural persistence and boundedness in mental 'space' together.

Imagine that you are thinking of a word – 'Liverpool', say – and that you fix it with your attention for a few seconds so that it is continually there before you, so to speak. Or a visual image of an object or a person. Most psychologists would agree that the physical basis of the attended word or image is a sustained pattern of neural activity. We need not be more precise than that for present purposes. Those of a dualist persuasion might argue that it is instead the conscious aware-ness or representation in the mind of neural activity, but again these alternative views do not differ in any way that is important to the purposes of this section.

The problem is that this idea of a sustained pattern of neural activity does not match the properties that the word or image seems to us to have, properties that are alluded to, in fact, in the very acceptability of using terms like '*the* word' and '*the* image' to refer to them. They seem to us like plain, ordinary things: we have a clear idea of where the boundary lies between the word and everything else, or between the image and everything else; and there seems nothing explanation-worthy or unnatural about their boundedness in mental 'space' or their per-sistence in time. For many philosophers (for example, Hume 1739/1978; Salmon 1984) the persistence of material particulars is a problem to be solved, not an axiomatic truth of nature. How much more of a problem it is to explain the persistence of a pattern of neural activity, which really does seem to require to be actively sustained, which has no claim to actual independent existence, and the persistence of which no one could claim as axiomatic because it could so easily be otherwise (if our attention is distracted at the very moment the word is formed, for example).

Yet it does not *seem* at all problematic. Indeed, subjectively, although we have the impression that our attention is being actively, even effortfully, maintained on the word, we do not have the impression that the word itself is being sustained in its existence, still less that it is our attending that is causing it to exist. Rather, the impression is that the word is there, that it is there in fact whether we continue to attend to it or no, and in attending to it we are doing something essentially analogous to looking at a concrete material particular, turning our inner gaze upon it. This impression reveals the metaphysical assumption. Those things in the mind that can be attended to by us, the contents of experience, the things on which what we regard as our inner gaze can turn, are conceptualised as essenti-ally analogous to the material particulars of the physical world, in that they are regarded as naturally bounded and discrete in space and as naturally persisting through time, as having the inertia of being that is implied by the assumption of persistence. By 'naturally' I mean that these properties are for us metaphysical assumptions, things not in need of explanation. This gives us our conceptualisation of short-term or working memory: it is seen by us as a store of things. If the things in the store do not possess natural persistence, this necessitates a change in our conceptualisation of working memory, as a means of holding things the same, of imposing a kind of artificial persistence upon something that does not persist naturally.

The same metaphysical assumption is evident if we consider long-term memory. The modern view of cognitive psychology is that, not only is memory less trustworthy than people used to think, but also, whatever the nature of storage in memory, retrieval is a constructive or reconstructive activity. This is not how memory is understood in common sense. People regard or treat memory as a store of things. A thing remembered on two occasions is regarded as actually enduring in time between those two occasions, like a book on a shelf, and is so regarded because it is conceptualised as a primary substance (or as analogous to one), and the basic assumption about primary substances is that they and their properties naturally persist unless acted on in some way. Our idea of the nature of memory, then, is one of enduring primary substances, pushed around by the processes of storage and retrieval in much the way that books are stored and retrieved in libraries, naturally persisting across time. They can be lost, just as a book can, but they do not change unless acted upon in some way. Retrieval processes are thought of not as constructing things from available information, but as pulling the enduring things off the shelves on which they are stored, or possibly shining a light on them so that we can turn our inner gaze upon them just where they are.

The primary substance analogy is most easily shown in the case of things remembered because they are things the successive occurrences of which are related by people, just as successive encounters with a physical object are. In other words, we have a kind of 'object permanence' or 'object concept' with regard to things in the mind, just as we do with things in the physical world.

So, to summarise, the basic particulars of the psychological construction of mental experience are things analogous in their properties to primary substances, the basic particulars of the psychological construction of physical reality. They differ in that they are not thought to have the same *kind* of substantiality that physical primary substances have. They are made of mind-stuff, but psychological metaphysics goes no further into this than it does into sub-atomic physics. But they are the same in being thought to have the same boundedness and persistence that physical primary substances are thought to have.

One important feature of this is that it delimits the occurrence of causal processing of mental things. In the psychological metaphysics of the physical world, the basic categories are being and happening, and causal processing occurs only for happenings. The persistence of a primary substance or any of its properties is not a candidate for causal explanation. If the analogy holds, then the same should be true for the psychological metaphysics of the mind. The candidates for causal processing in mental activity are events, defined in the same way as events in the physical world are defined, and the persistence of something identified as a primary substance analogue in mental activity, whether it be a thing stored in memory or a thing held before attention, is not a candidate for causal processing. Thus, causal processing of mental activity is delimited by metaphysical assumptions about the basic particulars of mental activity. To be clear about this, the 'becoming conscious' of a mental thing is an event and therefore a candidate for causal processing, but the persistence of the thing, or its continuing to be conscious, is not an event and therefore is not a candidate for causal processing.

## Mental events

Given the distinction between being and happening as applied to mental occurrences, the only candidates for causal processing among mental occurrences are those things falling under the definition of happening. That is, causal processing can occur for mental events, but does not occur for mental 'beings'. Generally, events are understood as produced by the operation of causal powers of things under suitable releasing conditions. Usually, if not invariably, the production of effects represents an interaction between the powers of one thing and the liabilities of another. This is taken to mean that most, probably all, material particulars possess two basic types of causally relevant property, powers and liabilities. If this analysis applies to mental events, it follows (1) that mental events are conceptualised as produced by the operation of causal powers, and (2) that the mind is like concrete material particulars in possessing two basic kinds of causally relevant property, powers and liabilities.

This analysis is complicated by the proposed division of the mind into two main parts, one part consisting of <<I>> and its capacities of consciousness and the production of action, and the rest of the mind, lacking consciousness and operating in a way essentially similar to the operation of purely physical causation. This division implies two categories of mental events, distinguished by the manner in which they are brought about. One category may be called 'mental actions', which are understood as produced in the same way as behavioural actions are understood to be produced. That is, the basic concept of a mental action is that I carry out or perform my mental actions, I know that I am doing so inasmuch as I have the experience of efficacy in the carrying out of a mental action, and it is up to me what mental action I carry out – that is, there is no causal necessitation in mental action.

The other category consists of mental events believed to be produced in ways essentially similar to the ways of production of physical events, through the operation of causal powers under releasing conditions, complete with causal necessitation. One important issue for psychology is to ascertain which mental events are interpreted as falling into which category, and why.

This analysis therefore gives us three categories of mental occurrences:

1  Mental 'beings', bounded in space and naturally enduring in time, such as states.
2  Mental events interpreted as caused deterministically by the operation of powers of the mind (or conceivably, by the operation of external powers upon liabilities of the mind) under appropriate releasing conditions.
3  Mental actions, those mental events believed to be produced by <<I>>.

These categories provide the foundation for further, less basic, categorical distinctions among mental occurrences. Distinctions between concepts of desire and intention, emotion and personality trait, purpose and belief, however they are made, are made within the framework of these basic categories. Explicating these basic categories is therefore of fundamental importance to understanding the psychological construction of mental occurrences.

## NOTE

1  Although I am not concerned with the actual nature of consciousness in this section, readers might find it helpful to consult Natsoulas (1981), who usefully disambiguates the various topics treated under the general heading of consciousness. It will quickly become apparent that I am using the term rather loosely here, but this does not hamper the elucidation of the common-sense view of the relation between <<I>> and mental occurrences.

# Chapter 13

# Implications for research in causal attribution

My purpose in this chapter is to draw out some implications of the preceding chapters for research on causal attribution, by which I mean the study of people's causal explanations for behaviour, by themselves or others. Some of these implications have already been discussed in previous chapters. Most importantly, the basic conceptualisation of causation in terms of powers and releasing conditions leads to a different view of what people are doing in making causal attributions: such attributions are often automatic rather than thoughtful, and involve the application of a specific pre-existing belief rather than the use of inductive methods to identify a causal locus. I shall not cover that ground again here. The main focus here is on the basic concept of action.

Let me first recapitulate two points about action and how people explain it. First, consider again Kelley's (1967) ANOVA model of causal attribution. Someone who used Kelley's model would be relying on covariation. They would explain behaviour by looking for the thing that covaries with what they were trying to explain. Why would they do this? The answer to this is that the model assumes that behaviour is as regular and predictable as any other kind of occurrence.

Think about purely physical phenomena for a moment. Science tries to explain physical phenomena by looking for causal laws. For example, if you vary the pressure of a gas, holding everything else constant, the temperature varies in a way that is absolutely predictable. This is because there is a causal mechanism operating. A causal mechanism always operates in the same way under the same conditions. There is an exact correlation between what you do to the pressure of the gas and what happens to the temperature as a result. The covariation, in this case, is a sign of a causal mechanism at work.

Now what Kelley did was to assume that the same is true for human behaviour. His model carries the assumption that people explain human behaviour by attributing causes, and that these causes are really rather like causes in the physical world. Studies of causal attribution provide plenty of evidence of this model in operation. There is a whole series of studies that have used as their dependent measure the following question, apparently originating with Storms (1973): 'How important were the actor's personality, traits, character, personal style, attitudes, mood, and so on in causing them to behave the way they did?'

Note the presence of the word 'causing'. As I have said, people explain action not in terms of causes but in terms of reasons. It is possible to argue about whether reasons explanations are a type of causal explanation or not, but, regardless of this, what differentiates reasons explanations from (other) causal explanations is that they are invoked when it is believed to be *up to the actor* how he or she behaved. This is the mark of action.

Now here is the point. Causes compel. That is, if a certain causal mechanism is operating, then unless something actively interferes with it, the mechanism will produce its effect no matter what. If we alter the pressure of a volume of gas, the effect on temperature must follow – there is no choice in the matter. Reasons are different: they do not compel. We can say, John jumped into the shop doorway because it was raining and he wanted to stay dry, but we don't imply that he had no choice. John could have had a desire not to get wet and he could have had all the relevant beliefs, but he might still have decided to do something else instead. He might have looked around for an umbrella shop, or he might have thought, 'To hell with it, I'll put up with getting wet'. It was up to him what he chose to do. This is the important difference between causes and reasons: causes compel, reasons do not. Thus, people will not see regularity information as having the same kind of relevance to making a reasons explanation as to making a causal explanation, because when explaining action they are not seeking a causal mechanism.

The second point about action is to do with the kinds of mental occurrence and characteristic that are taken as underlying actions. Actions are understood as produced by <<I>>, and in a sense that is all there is to the causal account of an action. Reasons explanations, however, do not stop here, for this concept is taken for granted in every case of action and therefore has no explanatory value (except when the point of the explanation is to identify something as an action rather than as some other kind of thing). Reasons explanations refer to those things that <<I>> took into account when deciding how to act. Typically, these include forward-looking things such as intentions, plans, goals, and purposes; they may also include beliefs and desires, particularly beliefs that serve to identify for the person how to achieve their desires. Different philosophers give more emphasis to some of these things than to others, but there seems no reason why a reasons explanation could not refer to any or all of them.

The point of relevance for traditional theory and research on causal attribution is that personality traits are of much less importance in explaining action than they are usually taken to be (Urmson 1968). One could say that personality traits count as desires, as do many other kinds of thing (Smith and Jones 1986), or one could say that beliefs and desires and purposes are themselves to be explained in terms of the actor's personality characteristics. This latter course, though, makes personality characteristics distinctly peripheral to the explanation of action. In either case, personality characteristics do not *cause* action.

Measures used in studies of causal attribution tend to ask subjects to what extent someone's behaviour was due to their personality. The Storms measure quoted above is a good example. Five of the six kinds of personal characteristic listed are stable properties of persons, and four of them fall under the heading of personality characteristics. Intentions, purposes, desires, beliefs, and the other sorts of things that usually fall into reasons explanations, do not appear at all. The measure implies a peculiar concept of human behaviour, as *determined* by *enduring* dispositional properties of the actor, rather than as performed by the actor as a matter of choice in respect of certain reasons. Researchers do not appear to have asked whether this measure captures the common-sense conceptualisation of behaviour. If people have a concept of action as I have described it, then clearly it does not.

Since observers, if not actors, tend to give more weight to personality than situation in causal attribution (Watson 1982) this might be taken as repudiating the claim that personality characteristics are peripheral to action, and as justifying the methodological assumption that people see behaviour as internally determined by personality traits and similar personal characteristics. This, however, would be to overlook the fact that the importance of personality characteristics in an account of action depends upon the type of causal question being asked, and that causal attribution studies tend to ask a particular, and peculiar, type of question.

In the typology of causal questions set up in Chapter 6 there is a distinction between questions concerning a single occasion and questions concerning multiple occasions. Each of these comprises several types of question. These types are set up as causal questions, but we can construct an analogous typology of action questions. Thus, a single occasion single effect question would be 'Why did $X$ do that?', where $X$ is a person and 'that' refers to a single action under a description. A comparison question would be 'Why did $X$ do this now when then (one or more other occasions) he did that?' A multiple occasion occurrence question would be 'Why has $X$ done this similar thing on all of these occasions?' Now there are many personal characteristics that might be alluded to in answers to action questions: intentions, beliefs, desires, personality traits, attitudes, abilities, and so on. It is clear that the kind of characteristic that can be referred to in causal attribution depends in part on the type of causal question asked, because some types of characteristic do not meet the requirement of providing an answer to the question. Let us consider some examples.

First, an example of a single occasion single effect question.Why did John jump into the shop doorway? The answer to this may refer to anything that we suppose to have been part of John's reason for jumping into the shop doorway: this might include a desire (to stay dry), a belief (that it was raining and he could stay dry by jumping into the shop doorway), an intention, and so on. Could one refer to a personality characteristic in answer to such a question? It depends. Under the Gricean principle of co-operativeness, if one is answering a question posed by someone else, there is a requirement to tell them something that they do not already know. Thus, if the questioner knows all of John's reasons for action, the responder must supply something else and, at a loss to know what else to say (why on earth is the questioner asking me that?), a personality characteristic might suffice. But if the questioner does not know all of John's reasons for action, then the question should be interpreted as a request for reasons, and personality characteristics are not reasons, so do not count as a possible answer. One could just about get away with a personality explanation: one could say, for example, that John is very fastidious about his appearance, but this depends on the ability of the questioner to fill in a number of blanks, concerning not only John's reasons for action but also the fact that what John has done is unusual. In other words, the explanation is of a different type: it does not give John's reasons for action, but explains by individuating John, by saying how he is distinct from most other people. Under most circumstances, then, single occasion single effect questions are requests for reasons explanations, and under those circumstances reference to personality characteristics is not appropriate.

Now an example of a comparison question. Why did Jane choose ice cream this time when she has always chosen apple pie in the past? As for causal comparison questions, this question requires the responder to pick out something that differentiates this occasion from those in the comparison. Although this requirement may be met by a reasons explanation, some parts of Jane's presumed reason may not differentiate this occasion from others. Giving a desire ('she really wanted ice cream') is uninformative, not only because the want can be inferred from the choice but also because it does not explain why she did not choose ice cream on the comparison occasions. Giving a stable personal characteristic such as an attitude ('She loves ice cream') or a personality characteristic is even worse, because it implies that Jane should have chosen ice cream on at least some of the comparison occasions. Stable personal characteristics do not work as explanations in this case because the questioner specifically requires something that accounts for what is different or unusual about this occasion. There are many kinds of thing that might meet this requirement, including an occasion-specific belief or a *change* in Jane's attitude (identified as such in the answer). But an attitude or personality characteristic in itself will not do.

Now a multiple occasion occurrence question. Why does Jane always choose apple pie? Here, clearly, reference to a stable personal characteristic is not only appropriate but obligatory. Referring to an occasion-specific reason will not do because it does not explain all of the occasions in the question. Thus, in this case, reference to Jane's stable preference for apple pie is a suitable answer.

Now a single occasion multiple effect question. Why did Bill behave as he did in that conversation? As in the previous case, it is very unlikely that reference to a reason for action is appropriate in this case, because reasons are action-specific, and no single reason could explain all that Bill did. Answering a question of this sort means grappling with a difficult problem; namely, that the actor probably did many different things on the occasion in question and it is hard to find one thing that accounts for them all. The responder may have to select one or two things that carry most causal weight, or to treat the question as asking about a consistent or distinctive feature of the actor's behaviour rather than all of the things the actor did. In this case, the question is treated in effect as asking about individuating features of the actor – personality characteristics and so on. In effect, the questioner is recasting the question as a comparison question, for the sake of being able to answer it at all, and the kind of answer given depends on the kind of comparison made, or on the responder's ideas about the kind of comparison the questioner might want to be made.

There is a clear methodological implication here: the kinds of things that people refer to in causal attribution depend on the type of question they are asked, and on how they interpret it. As an illustration, consider the selected studies of actor/observer differences included in Watson's (1982) review. In Storms (1973), Galper (1976), and Moore *et al.* (1981), the question asked about the actor's behaviour during a five-minute get-acquainted conversation, and in Regan and Totten (1975) it was a seven-minute get-acquainted conversation. In Herzberger and Clore (1979) it was no actual behaviour, but behaviour in general along each of four trait dimensions. In Arkin and Duval (1975), the measure asked about a single choice between five etchings, which occurred after a four-and-a-half minute examination of the etchings.

The question posed by Herzberger and Clore (1979) is probably a multiple occasion occurrence question, but is open to other interpretations by the subject. That posed by Arkin and Duval, alone among the studies chosen, is a single occasion single effect question. The remaining studies posed single occasion multiple effect questions for their subjects. As we have seen, reasons explanations are not appropriate for these questions because reasons apply, usually, to single actions and therefore can only very rarely count as an answer to a question about multiple actions. As we have also seen, subjects have a variety of possible ways of treating these questions, which are unusually difficult ones to answer. They might, for example, treat the question as a comparison question where the experimenter is presumed to be asking about what differentiates the actor from other actors, as a way of accounting for the individual style or distinctiveness of their overall pattern of behaviour in the setting. In this case, reference to stable personality characteristics is appropriate. This possibility is encouraged by the fact that they are ostensibly having a get-acquainted conversation, which suggests to observers at least that the experimenter is interested in the impression they form of the actor's personality. There are many other possibilities.

Patterns of findings in causal attribution studies, therefore, do not reveal general tendencies in causal attribution: they reveal tendencies in how subjects deal with the particular kinds of questions they are asked. Where these questions are themselves of unusual types, little can be learned about how people normally answer questions about action. The presumed importance of personality characteristics (and other stable personal characteristics) in causal attribution may be due to the widespread use of single occasion multiple effect questions in experiments: that is, it is an incorrect impression created by a methodological bias.

The concept of action has implications for many of the topics in causal attribution. Some examples are now considered.

## THE INTERNAL/EXTERNAL DISTINCTION

Heider (1958) argued that the distinction between internal and external factors was of fundamental importance in causal attribution. Supposedly, one of the primary questions that people address in causal attribution is whether some behaviour was due to something about the person or something about the situation they were in. The issue here is not whether the internal/external distinction itself is a valid one, but whether (1) it is basic to causal attribution, as it has widely been treated as being, and (2) an attribution to an internal factor (or to an external one) has a single, unambiguous meaning. These issues are related, in that if the answer to the first is no, then the answer to the second must be no as well.

Miller *et al.* (1981) identified four problems for the internal/external distinction:

1 *The hydraulic assumption.* Heider (1958) argued that there was a hydraulic relation between internal and external causes, such that attributing more causality to one entailed attributing less causality to the other. This assumption has not been supported by research in which personal and situational attributions are measured on different scales (Solomon 1978).
2 *The category error.* The two categories cut across distinctions potentially of theoretical interest, and are so broad as to be virtually meaningless.
3 *The teleological confusion.* Miller *et al.* (1981) argued that the distinction breaks down 'whenever external cues are perceived and deliberately acted on by the person' (p. 82). This can be related to the observation by Ross (1977) that, sometimes, personal and situational attributions appear to be virtual paraphrases of each other. For example, under the coding scheme used by Nisbett *et al.* (1973), 'I want to make a lot of money' would be coded an internal attribution, and 'Chemistry is a high-paying field' would be coded external. In fact, these statements contain similar information and imply each other, as explanations for choice of career. The choice of expression does not imply that one person saw the choice as internally caused and the other saw it as externally caused.
4 *The convergent validity problem.* Herzberger and Clore (1979) found lack of convergence among various measures of personal and situational attribution, a finding repeated and extended by Miller *et al.* (1981, study 1). According to Miller *et al.*, these results indicated that 'many subjects do not think about dispositional and situational causality as theorists expect' (p. 86).

Miller *et al.* therefore set out to discover the interpretations that people make of situational and dispositional attributions. Their conclusion was that people interpret the distinction as representing acts freely chosen by the actor versus acts not freely chosen or constrained by situational factors. They argued that this is inconsistent with definitions of causality used in other areas of causal attribution research, such as actor–observer differences, 'where dispositional causality can be identified with stable traits that determine behaviour across situations' (p. 87).

The measure used by Storms (1973), and quoted earlier, exemplifies this. In this measure, four of the six categories listed refer to stable personality characteristics and the actor is the grammatical *object* of the verb 'cause'.

The solution adopted by Miller *et al.* was supposed to save the basicity of the internal/external distinction (if not its unidimensionality) by selecting a particular interpretation of it, as a chosen–not chosen distinction. Under the present theory, however, the notion that the internal/external distinction is basic to causal attribution, or that it has a single, unambiguous meaning, is abandoned. Under the present theory, the basic distinction is that between behaviour understood as action and all other kinds of behaviour. Internal and external factors have roles within each of these types, but the role depends on the type.

In the case of action, the basic concept is that <<I>> produces action. <<I>> is the only cause of action and is a causal origin. It is up to <<I>> (or, more loosely, the actor) what to do. Such things as intentions, beliefs, and desires enter into an account of the choice made by <<I>> concerning what to do. They are not, however, causes of behaviour but function more as considerations which <<I>> can take into account or ignore. Those considerations which <<I>> opted to take into account in deciding how to act constitute the actor's reasons for behaviour. Actions, therefore, are explained by reasons, and reasons include such things as intentions, purposes, desires, and beliefs.

Although the cause of action is always internal to the actor, both internal and external factors can enter into the actor's reasons for action. Beliefs have objects, as indeed do desires. When we say that John jumped into a shop doorway because he thought it was raining and wanted to stay dry, we are citing both internal and external factors as considerations relevant to John's choice of action. John has a belief (internal) about a state of affairs (external), and also a desire (internal) for a certain state of affairs to obtain (external). In fact, reasons often seem to make reference only to external factors, because stated reasons are generally elliptical, omitting those things which the explainer assumes will be taken for granted, or not regarded as necessary. Thus, we say, 'Mary bought her mother some flowers because it was her birthday', appearing to make reference only to an external factor, the birthday. We take it for granted that Mary believed it was her mother's birthday, and we do not (usually) regard it as necessary to probe any further into Mary's motivation. The explanation is not an assertion of external causation: it is merely a reference to an external factor that forms a relevant part of the account of Mary's action.

In the case of behaviours other than actions, a different and more deterministic model applies. Behaviour is caused by the deterministic operation of active or passive powers of the actor under specifiable releasing conditions: there is in principle no limit to the causal chain leading up to the behaviour, unless there is a point of origin in an action. Behaviour of this kind is not intentional and is explained by reference to causes, not reasons.

Again, both internal and external factors can enter into causal accounts of behaviour that is not action. There are two basic models. In one, behaviour is the result of some power of a thing external to the actor acting upon some liability of the actor. A simple example would be someone falling over as a direct result of being pushed, which can be technically described as the power of the pusher producing the effect of falling over by acting upon the liability of the victim to be pushed: the effect occurs because the power is greater than the resistance of the victim, which shows that both power and liability must enter into the causal account. People with greater resistance to being pushed over might have withstood the push. Thus, even where the actor appears completely passive, both internal (liability) and external (power) factors are involved in the causation of behaviour.

The second model involves some power of the actor operating to produce some effect. A simple example would be the knee-jerk reflex, which represents the operation of a power of the peripheral nervous system under the releasing condition of an appropriate kind of blow. There are two important points to note about this example. The first is that this behaviour is not an action, because the actor cannot choose whether to engage in it or not. It does, none the less, represent the operation of a power of the actor. The second is that the blow from the hammer is not sufficient as a causal account of the reflex: if it were, this would imply that similar blows would produce similar effects from any part of the body. The blow is the condition that serves to release, or bring into operation, the power of the peripheral nervous system. Technically, it is this power that is the cause, though Harré and Madden (1975) did acknowledge that it was sometimes appropriate to identify the releasing condition as the cause as well. Thus, again, the causal account makes reference to both internal (power) and external (releasing condition) factors.

It can be seen from this that our understanding of the role of both internal and external factors in producing behaviour depends fundamentally on whether we see the behaviour in question as an action or not. This is what makes the internal/external distinction ambiguous: an internal factor can be a reason underlying an actor's choice of action, or a power or liability deterministically producing behaviour. An external factor can also be a reason underlying an actor's choice of action, or a power or releasing condition (or, in fact, a liability, where the behaviour involves acting upon an object) entering into the deterministic production of behaviour. The internal/external distinction is in effect orthogonal to the distinction between action and other kinds of behaviour, and reference to an internal factor, or to an external one, makes no sense at all unless and until we have decided whether the behaviour in question is an action or not. This need to decide whether the behaviour is an action or not *before* we can make sense of any reference to an internal or external factor shows that the distinction between action and other behaviour is more basic than the internal/external distinction.

My study (White 1991) had the limited ambition of demonstrating that the distinction between action and other behaviour and the internal/external distinction were orthogonal. In the first study I used a set of sentences having the form '*X* did *Y* because *Z*'. One group of subjects was asked to judge whether the explanation given identified a reason for the actor's behaviour or a cause of it, and another group was asked whether the explanation identified something internal to the actor or something external to the actor. As predicted, these judgements were not correlated across the sentences, thus showing that the reason/cause and internal/external dimensions are independent.

The first study also served to identify four groups of sentences: internal causes, internal reasons, external causes, and external reasons. In the second study I asked subjects to judge either (1) to what extent the behaviour so explained was intentional, or (2) to what extent it was conscious. I found that the reason/cause distinction accounted for 81.4 per cent of the variance in the data, whereas the internal/external distinction accounted for only 0.02 per cent of the variance. The intentionality and consciousness judgements were almost perfectly correlated, supporting the idea that there is in effect a class of behaviour that is judged intentional and conscious and explained in terms of reasons, and a class that is judged unintentional, non-conscious, and explained in terms of causes. This is, of course, the basic distinction between actions and other behaviours, although I did not identify it as such in that publication.

The main implication of this is that asking people to make causal attributions to the person or to the situation (or to something internal or something external) is inadequate because it fails to capture the basic distinction between action, seen as intentional and conscious and explained in terms of reasons, and other behaviour, seen as not conscious or intentional and explained in terms of causes operating deterministically. The four problems with the internal/external distinction identified by Miller *et al.* (1981) can be seen as manifestations of this inadequacy.

The hydraulic assumption fails because internal and external are not opposites on a single dimension. Each subsumes more than one type of thing, and either can have the same role in some instances. For example, either can have the role of a reason for action, as in the examples discussed earlier. Giving an internal reason by no means precludes the giving of an external reason for the same action: someone could say, 'I chose chemistry because it is a high-paying field and I want to make a lot of money' without any sense of oddness or self-contradiction. I would argue, though, that the distinction between action and other behaviour does conform to a hydraulic assumption: if one sees some behaviour as action, one cannot also see it as behaviour caused deterministically. It is possible, though, that one might see part of some behaviour as action and part as not, just as one can distinguish between action as intended under one description and not intended under another, or between intended and unintended consequences of action.

The category error reflects the fact that the internal and external categories cut across the most basic distinction between action and other behaviour. There should be no category error in respect of this distinction because additional categories of theoretical interest should be subsumed under one or the other side of it.

The present theory resolves the teleological confusion by differentiating conscious and intentional acting upon what Miller *et al.* (1981: 82) called 'external causes' (things that people would refer to as reasons) from roles of situational factors in the deterministic causation of behaviour. As stated, wanting to make a lot of money and chemistry being a high-paying field would both be categorised as reasons and as belonging under the category of action, and this common categorisation reflects their implication of each other.

Finally, low convergent validity is an effect of the multiplicity of roles that personal and situational factors can have in the causation of behaviour. Measures that capture the differences between action and other behaviour should have high convergent validity.

The implication of this research is that hypotheses and studies that depend on the internal/external distinction are fatally ambiguous, and there is a consequent need to reformulate them in terms of the distinction between action and other behaviour, or to replace them with new ones. Two examples will be considered.

## THE 'FUNDAMENTAL' ATTRIBUTION ERROR

The so-called 'fundamental' attribution error was described by Ross (1977) as a 'general tendency to overestimate the importance of personal or dispositional factors relative to environmental influences' (p. 184). Fiske and Taylor (1991) described it as a tendency 'to attribute another person's behaviour to his or her own dispositional qualities, rather than to situational factors' (p. 67). Of all suspected biases and errors in the attribution process, this has been the most popular research topic, and much effort has been devoted to finding an explanation for it (Hewstone 1989; Fiske and Taylor 1991). The description of it as an error or bias also appears to be widely accepted (Fiske and Taylor 1991), although there have been dissenting voices (Hamilton 1980; Block and Funder 1986; Funder 1987).

Descriptions of the tendency by different authors (Heider 1944, 1958; Ross 1977; Nisbett and Ross 1980; Ross and Anderson 1982; Hewstone 1989; Fiske and Taylor 1991) reveal that there are three tendencies, not just one. First, a tendency in causal attribution, where the supposed error is to overestimate the extent to which the person is the cause of effects, and to underestimate the influence of situational factors. Secondly, a tendency in dispositional attribution, where the supposed error is to attribute personal characteristics to persons without adequate justification. The most commonly studied version of this is the unjustified inference of 'correspondent' personal characteristics from behaviour, as in the study by Jones and Harris (1967). Thirdly, a tendency to rely too much on attributed personal characteristics for predictions about future behaviour, or a tendency to expect behaviour to be more consistent than it actually is (Ross 1977).

Almost all research on the fundamental attribution error has been concerned with the dispositional attribution version. The only published study on the causal attribution version has been that by Kulik (1983), who found that behaviour consistent with expectations based on knowledge of the actor was causally attributed to the actor even when 'compelling situational reasons for the behaviour were present' (p. 1171). Since Kulik also found that behaviour in-consistent with such expectations was causally attributed to the situation 'even in settings normally believed to inhibit that behaviour' (p. 1171), it is doubtful whether this finding counts as support for the causal version of the fundamental attribution error: rather, it shows only that tendencies in causal attribution depend on the match between expectations and outcomes. Other studies have shown that observers tend to refer more to personal characteristics than to situational charac-teristics in causal attribution, but these do not count as support for the causal attribution version of the fundamental attribution error because they used no standard for assessing whether the tendency observed was an error or not.

The causal attribution version of the error therefore lacks any empirical support. Despite this it seems to be widely regarded as a robust tendency, as exemplified in this quotation from Fiske and Taylor (1991): 'instead of realising that there are situational forces that produce behaviour, people generally see another's behaviour as freely chosen and as representing that person's stable qualities' (p. 67). What I wish to discuss here is not so much the fact that there is no research evidence to support this claim, but the fact that the statement clearly carries an untested metaphysical assumption about the causation of behaviour. The assumption can be seen in the clause 'that there are situational forces that produce behaviour'. Is this possible? I shall show that it may be, but only in a limited sense and for a limited range of cases.

Let us first consider action. In cases of action, which cover most of the things that people do in social interaction, the idea of situational forces causing be-haviour is wrong. The reason for this is that, as already stated, it is a defining feature of action that it is up to the actor whether they carry it out or not. We can identify roughly what counts as action by considering whether it makes sense to ask someone to refrain from doing it or not. For all things falling into this category, it is false to say that situational factors cause them, and true to say that they are chosen by the actor. In the case of action the capacity for choice is always there, even if someone is holding a gun to one's head. People can always choose to ignore social norms and rules, and other situational factors. Perhaps they do not choose to do so very often, but that is beside the point and certainly does not justify the inference that social norms and rules caused their behaviour.

This is not to say that situational factors never enter into accounts of the production of action. Situational factors can be referred to in reasons explana-tions. As we have seen, when John jumps into the shop doorway he may refer to his belief (internal) that it was raining (external) as part of his reason for action. The situational factor is not here described as a cause of action, however, for the only cause of action is John himself. It has the role of a consideration that he chose to take into account in deciding how to behave.

Occasionally, situational factors enter into reasons for action in a somewhat more forceful way. For example, if I recite the National Anthem because some-one holding a gun to my head orders me to do so, it would be foolish of me to ignore this situational factor in deciding how to act. We might even want to say that I had no choice. But this is a mere figure of speech: all we mean is that no sane person would have chosen to defy the order. The capacity for choice is still there, and for this reason the situational factor is not a cause of my compliance.

If the evidence from which one infers a 'fundamental' causal attribution error is that behaviour covaries with the situation and not with the person (or a tendency in that direction), then it is necessary to reiterate that, in the case of action, covariation does not indicate causation. If everyone chooses the same dish at the restaurant, this does not justify the inference that the dish, or the situation, caused their behaviour: it only justifies the inference that they all chose the same way. Someone who attributed the choice to the chooser in the face of this evidence would not be making a mistake. Therefore, in the case of action, there can be no such thing as a 'fundamental' causal attribution error. No action is ever caused by a situational factor, and it is always up to the actor whether they do it or not.

What about behaviours other than actions? There are circumstances under which it is legitimate to talk of situational factors or things or events as causes of such behaviours. When a power of something acts on a liability of the actor to produce a certain behaviour, the operation of the power can be described as a cause in the situation. When a situational factor or event acts as a releasing condition for some behaviour, as in the knee-jerk reflex, it is also legitimate, sometimes at least, to talk of the releasing condition as a cause (Harré and Madden 1975). Nevertheless, it is hard to see how there could be such a thing as a 'fundamental' causal attribution error in respect of these things. The reason for this is that one cannot ascribe varying degrees of importance to internal and external factors in bringing about the behaviour. One cannot say that behaviour was 60 per cent caused by the situation and 40 per cent by the person, as one might be tempted to do if assigning proportions of variance to independent variables. Power, releasing condition, and liability (where there is one) are all necessary to the causation of the behaviour. The knee-jerk reflex would not occur if the right kind of blow was not struck; and it would not occur if there was a certain sort of defect in the victim's peripheral nervous system. The falling over would not occur without the push (unless there was some other cause); and it would not occur if the push was not great enough to overcome the victim's resistance to falling. One cannot assign degrees of importance to ingredients of causal accounts under the causal powers theory: one can only assign roles.

One final problem for the 'fundamental' causal attribution is of a methodo-logical nature. When explaining some behaviour, people do not generally provide a full causal account (Locke and Pennington 1982). They may, for example, omit things which they assume their questioner already knows. The account given is a selection from their full interpretation of the behaviour. For example, when asked 'Why did John jump into the shop doorway?', people may tend to say 'because he didn't want to get wet'. This would normally be coded as an internal reason (Nisbett *et al.* 1973) (even though it refers to both an internal factor, the desire, and an external one, the thing desired), and an accumulation of responses of this kind would therefore tend to give the impression of a 'fundamental' causal attribution error. To infer this would be wrong, however, because the answer given is just a selection from the full causal interpretation of the incident. We need to investigate how people make selections from causal interpretations, rather than assume that what they tell us is all they believe.

In conclusion, there is no such thing as a 'fundamental' causal attribution error. There may be a 'fundamental' dispositional attribution error, but that topic lies outside the scope of this chapter.

## ACTOR/OBSERVER DIFFERENCES

Jones and Nisbett (1972) proposed that 'there is a pervasive tendency for actors to attribute their actions to situational requirements, whereas observers tend to attribute the same actions to stable personal dispositions' (p. 80, italics removed). They argued that this tendency reflects not just motivational but also cognitive factors, and discussed the possible effects of several (such as visual orientation differences). Although research findings have been mixed (Monson and Snyder 1977), the conclusion of a recent review was that 'the basic Jones-Nisbett effect now appears to be firmly established' (Watson 1982: 698).

The problem is that, even if Watson's conclusion is correct, it is not clear just what the effect represents. The reason for this is that it is expressed in terms of the internal/external distinction, which confounds the distinction between actions and other behaviours. If we assume that actors and observers agree on whether some behaviour is an action or not, then unconfounding this distinction results in two possible actor/observer differences hypotheses:

1 For actions, actors emphasise external references in reasons explanations more, and internal references less, than observers do.
2 For other behaviours, actors emphasise external components of causation more, and internal components less, than observers do.

It is entirely possible that one of these is true and the other false. It is therefore imperative that researchers ascertain whether the behaviours about which their subjects make causal attributions are seen as actions or not.

It is also possible, however, that actors and observers do not always agree on whether some behaviour is an action or not. This complicates the range of possible interpretations to a discouraging degree. First, it opens up a new set of hypotheses concerning the fundamental distinction between actions and other behaviours. For example, one could hypothesise that actors tend to see behaviour as action more than observers do. Secondly, support for the traditionally phrased actor/observer differences hypothesis can be interpreted in a variety of ways. Here are a couple, for illustrative purposes:

1 Actors tend to see behaviour as action more than observers do, and for actions, actors emphasise external references in reasons explanations more, and internal references less, than observers do, and for other behaviours actors and

observers do not differ. This would lead to the tendency observed for evidence to support the Jones-Nisbett hypothesis.

2  Observers tend to see behaviour as action more than actors do, and for actions, actors and observers do not differ, but for behaviours other than actions, actors emphasise external components of causation more, and internal components less, than observers do. Curiously enough, this would lead to the same tendency.

No doubt readers can appreciate from these two examples that a great many interpretations fit the evidence, and this underlines the importance of ascertaining whether actors and observers agree on interpreting behaviour as action or not.

In addition, as for research on the 'fundamental' causal attribution error, it is necessary to point out that the research evidence could simply reflect subjects' decisions about what to select from a full causal interpretation. That is, actors and observers might construct the same causal interpretation of behaviour, but have reasons for selecting different parts of it to report to the experimenter. Not only that, but actors' self-attributions are affected by factors such as self-presentation (Jellison and Green 1981) which do not apply to attributions made by observers. Equally there are factors such as demand characteristics which may affect observers' attributions but do not apply, or at least not in the same way, to attributions made by actors (Block and Funder 1986). In the light of all this, it appears that the question of actor/observer differences in causal attribution is a false or illusory research problem, in terms of the typology set up in Chapter 3.

## DISCUSSION

By selecting three topics from the causal attribution literature I may be giving the impression of a piecemeal attack on isolated phenomena from the research literature. This is not the case. Heider (1958) laid down three ideas that became the collective cornerstone of all subsequent causal attribution theory and research. These were: (1) that ordinary people have a quasi-scientific concern with understanding, and use naïve versions of scientific methods in an attempt to understand events in their world; (2) that in explaining events people seek underlying stable dispositional properties; (3) that the internal/external distinction is fundamental to attribution. All of the phenomena of causal attribution tend to be interpreted in the light of these ideas.

In this book, I have set out a different set of principles. Three of these principles can be contraposed to Heider's three: (1) that causal attribution is in the service of the attributer's practical concerns, and any interest the attributer may have in scientific accuracy and understanding is subservient to that; (2) that in making causal attributions people seek only that which answers the question they have posed in the light of their practical concerns, and whether the answer refers to a stable property is incidental; (3) that the distinction between action and deterministic causation is fundamental to attribution, and the internal/external distinction is independent of this and less fundamental.

Thirty years of causal attribution research shaped and interpreted in the light of these ideas would look quite different from the existing causal attribution literature. The three examples taken in this chapter count as illustrations of the kinds of differences that would be seen.

# Chapter 14

# The battleground of the mind

To review progress so far, we have seen that the distinction between being and happening can be applied to mental occurrences just as to the physical world. The causation of mental happenings and of behaviour is basically conceptualised in terms of powers and liabilities and the generative relation, just as for other types of physical causation. In the case of mental occurrences and behaviour, however, there are two fundamentally different ways in which things are made to happen, in the psychological construction of the mind. One way resembles our understanding of physical causation in being the essentially deterministic interplay of powers, releasing conditions, and liabilities. In the other way, <<I>> is the sole cause of mental occurrences and behaviour: in producing such things, it is up to <<I>> what to do, meaning that <<I>> always has the capacity to do other than what <<I>> does, and <<I>> is also conceived as a causal origin. What <<I>> can do is limited by the powers possessed by the person. Such doings are understood as conscious and intentional, and explained in terms of reasons.

Because <<I>> is conceived as a unitary thing enduring over time, this division functions like a division of the mind into two parts: any mental occurrence or behaviour interpreted according to the deterministic, physical causation model is *ipso facto* not thought to be produced or carried out by <<I>>. The effect of this conceptualisation is that people regard the mind as if it consisted of two independent centres of causation, which may or may not act in harmony, and either of which may dominate the other. Thus, we speak of someone as giving in to an impulse or resisting temptation, or as being strong-willed or weak-willed, or having a lot of self-control or little. These expressions all suggest parts of the mind in conflict with one another. My aim in this chapter is to explore that conflict, as it is understood in common sense.

I use the term 'deterministic' in reference to the physical model of causation in the mind. This is a mere terminological convenience and is not meant to imply that people necessarily see <<I>> as possessing free will. There are two main possibilities for influence: deterministic influence on what <<I>> does, or influence from <<I>> upon deterministic causation in the mind and behaviour. I begin by considering a few illustrations of each type.

## DETERMINISTIC INFLUENCE ON WHAT <<I>> DOES

<<I>> produces action, and also formulates and adopts intentions or plans. These activities of <<I>> open up the possibility of several types of deterministic influence. For example, when an intention is held in mind for a while before being executed, there is room for deterministic influence. Such influence cannot change the intention or replace it with another one: intentions are regarded as the exclusive preserve of <<I>> and as such only <<I>> can formulate or change them. But intentions can be lost. For example, I may intend to mow the lawn this afternoon, but this intention is liable to be forgotten because of influence from my unconscious hate of mowing. Or they may be replaced by non-intended behaviour. For example, I leave home intending to drive to the dentist, but I forget what I am doing and drive to work instead. In common sense, it is not <<I>> that does these things, but instead some kind of deterministic influence disrupting what <<I>> meant to do.

There can also be deterministic interference with <<I>>'s attempt to carry out some action decided upon. Take as an example a stutter or slip of the tongue, either of which may be explained by saying 'I am [he/she is] nervous'. In common sense everything <<I>> does is seen as conscious and intentional. Mistakes such as slips of the tongue are by definition not intended, so such an occurrence is interpreted as some non-conscious and deterministic interference with the <<I>>'s control of behaviour. We might say that <<I>> put into action the plan to say whatever was intended, and the deterministic influence came between the putting into action and the actual emergence of the behaviour.

Other deterministic influences may occur prior to the formulation of intentions. For example, when Oedipus marries Jocasta, he is carrying out an action in accordance with an intention. Unknown to him, however, the considerations which he chose to take into account in deciding to marry Jocasta were themselves influenced deterministically. We might speculate, for example, that the strongest consideration for him was his love of Jocasta, and he decided to act according to this consideration. Unknown to him (that is to say, unknown to the <<I>> in Oedipus), his love for Jocasta is actually his love for his mother, who Jocasta happens to be. Note how this is interpreted in common sense: in deciding what to do, <<I>> still has the power to choose and could resist the urge to act according to the consideration of love for Jocasta. The effect of the deterministic influence is not to determine fully what <<I>> does, but to present one consideration much more forcibly than would otherwise have been the case. Thus, in cases of this sort, the deterministic influence operates at the stage prior to the formulation of an intention or the decision to act. In this case, it would still be right for Oedipus to give a reasons explanation for marrying Jocasta, referring to his love for her: he is right to do this because he still had the power to choose not to marry her. Yet it would also be right, in a sense, to say that his decision was influenced, if not actually caused, by his unconscious love for his mother, because this made love for Jocasta the strongest consideration and he chose to act in accordance with it. There may be many cases where the power of <<I>> to choose is not altogether compromised but one can still talk of influence, whether from inside or outside the mind: a state of hunger becomes increasingly hard to ignore, as do the persuasive arguments of a skilled salesperson.

## INFLUENCE FROM <<I>> UPON DETERMINISTIC CAUSATION

People also see <<I>> as having a certain degree of power to intervene in the causation of behaviour and mental events and activities, whether it be in the deterministic operation of causal powers of the actor or the evocation of liabilities of the actor. This power depends, however, on the presence of some degree of conscious awareness of what is going on. As people see it, <<I>> cannot intervene in something of which it has no awareness, except by doing something which has an unintended consequence of intervening. Although the deterministic operation of causal powers of the actor is understood as non-conscious, outcomes of such operation in behaviour can be conscious, because the person may actually perceive what he or she is doing. When this is the case, and when the evocation of a liability is understood as conscious, then this necessary condition for the capacity of <<I>> to intervene is met. When it is not, <<I>> may still attempt to intervene but such attempts are necessarily hit-or-miss, because <<I>> has no awareness of what it is attempting to intervene in. Such may be the case when some general notion of self-control is invoked.

What we are discussing here is what is commonly referred to as will-power. The operation of <<I>> is conceptualised as acting to prevent the occurrence of an effect that would otherwise follow deterministically from some antecedent: for example, 'by an effort of will he/she kept his/her temper under control'. This is ambiguous because the effort of <<I>> could act on either the state or its influence on behaviour. Thus one can keep one's cool – for example, in the face of provocation – or one can hold one's anger in, <<I>> asserting itself over the deterministic influence of the anger on behaviour.

The general theme of conflict between <<I>> and deterministic influence has a number of variations, which I now consider.

## RATIONALITY AND BIAS

The conflict between the supposedly rational, constructive tendencies of the faculty of reason and the irrational, destructive, disruptive forces of supposedly lower and more animalistic parts of the mind is an ancient and enduring theme in the history of ideas (Dawes 1976). Plato, for example, supposed that all men naturally sought virtue and justice, and that the faculty of reason, operating perfectly according to the principles of logic, was the means by which these goals are attained. But Plato also observed that people had difficulties in acting accord-ing to reason, and to explain this he developed a model of the human mind as having three basic parts (Trigg 1988).

The first part was the faculty of reason as already described. In Plato's scheme the function of this faculty is to govern the operations of the whole mind or soul, directing the person in the pursuit of virtue. The remainder of the mind consisted of the emotional elements, and Plato divided these into two main parts. In one part was what he called the 'bodily desires'. These included biological drives such as hunger, thirst, and the sex drive. The second part was termed the 'spirited' element, and this includes the passions. Plato's idea of what counted as passion was slightly different from our own, since he included here such things as ambition. But basically this was the part of the mind that housed things like anger and fear, and the passions in general.

What is particularly noteworthy about this is the absolute distinction Plato draws between reason and passion (or emotion). They belong in fundamentally different parts of the mind in Plato's scheme. Reason is the faculty by virtue of which humans aspire to the condition of gods, to all that is best in the world, to virtue and goodness and truth. The passions, on the other hand, are seen as the more animal part of our nature – they are those things in us that we share with other animal species, and which tend to drag us down, away from virtue and goodness, and towards the condition of the beasts. Thus, where reasoning processes go astray, they do so not because of any inherent defect but because of interference from such things as passions.

A similar picture can be found in the medieval world view, where the mind is organised in an even more rigid hierarchy. The important feature of the medieval world view for present purposes is the place of humankind in the great chain of being, as a separate order of creation set between the angels and the beasts. Because of this location in the scheme of things, humans are judged to have a mixed nature: a faculty of reason, which is their most nearly angelic attribute and through which they aspire to angelic standards of virtue and goodness, and more bestial characteristics such as emotions, which pull them in the opposite direction, towards the condition of the beasts (Lewis 1964; Tillyard 1943). Here we see again the categorical division between reason and such things as passion, emotion, and motivational factors, and the evaluation of reason as positive and good, and of emotion (and so forth) as destructive, negative, and reprehensible.

This traditional view of the mind continues to influence our understanding. Words such as 'bestial' and 'brutish' now have pejorative connotations (which they did not possess in the Middle Ages, when they were used simply to refer to animals) which are due to their association with what is supposedly the lowest and hence most negatively valued part of human nature. More than this, it has been argued that the traditional view has profoundly influenced theories of emotion in philosophy and psychology, at least until recent times (Averill 1974). In these, emotion tends to be conceptualised as passive (that is, we are the passive victims of emotion), as animal-like, as irrational and destructive, and is associated with supposedly primitive parts of the brain such as the thalamus (Cannon 1927; Averill 1974). Averill argued strongly that each of these features of the traditional conceptualisation of emotion is either wrong or considerably exaggerated, because of the influence of the traditional hierarchical view.

The idea that reasoning untrammelled by other influences proceeds in accordance with the principles of logic remained influential until recently in psychology (Henle 1962; Evans 1982). New ideas were proposed, however, concerning the nature of extrinsic disruptions of reasoning: for example, Henle (1962) proposed that people sometimes err on logical reasoning tasks because they comprehend the premises incorrectly. As for processes of social judgement and inference, these were also seen as open to interference from factors essentially belonging to Plato's 'spirited element'. These factors are collectively known as motivational biases. The hypothetical biases most commonly talked of as motivational in psychology include the protection or enhancement of self-esteem, the desire to create a favourable impression in others, and various 'needs' such as the need for social approval, need to believe in a just world, and need for effective control (Harvey and Weary 1984; Tetlock and Levi 1982; Zuckerman 1979). Some authors have associated motivational biases with emotion (Nisbett and Ross 1980; Hastie 1983; Harvey and Weary 1984). Nisbett and Ross (1980) associated motivational biases with emotions, passions, wishes, values, instincts, need states, and drives, and they used the broad term 'hot' to distinguish motivational biases from 'cold' cognitive biases. None the less, it is hard to find any definition of what makes something a 'motivational' bias, or any statement of what the examples listed have in common, or why any of them belongs in the 'motivational' category.

More recently, a new kind of bias has entered accounts of social inference processes. The term for this kind of bias is 'cognitive' (Miller and Ross 1975; Nisbett and Ross 1980). Under this view of bias, people retain an essentially Platonic aspiration for accurate judgement. This is part of a general conception of people as 'lay scientists'; that is, as fundamentally concerned with the scientific goals of understanding, prediction, and control (Heider 1958). People tend to be thwarted in their aspirations, however, not by intrusions from the spirited element in their nature but by imperfections in the mechanics of judgement. Specifically, people use informal, naïve versions of the tools used by professional scientists such as Bayes' theorem and analysis of variance, but their naïve versions are imperfect and hence generate inaccurate judgements on some occasions.

Superficially, this account of bias appears to have escaped from the strictures of the traditional hierarchical conceptualisation of mind, in that the source of errors in judgement is located not in some different compartment of the mind but in the very devices used to make judgements. This appearance is an illusion, however. As we have already seen, the processes by which judgements are made are regarded by researchers as not conscious, as beyond the reach of introspection (Nisbett and Wilson 1977). The evidence cited as support for this point of view is that people are unable to make accurate reports about causal influences on such judgemental processes.

If I may slip for a moment into the terminology of this book, the making of a causal report is thought to be an action carried out by <<I>>. As such, the contents of such a report can only be such things as <<I>> can be aware of.

Clearly, <<I>> cannot report something about which <<I>> knows nothing. If <<I>> does not report causal influences upon processes, then <<I>> is not aware of those influences. Despite the fact that this argument is logically fallacious, and despite the fact that a causal influence on a process is not the same as the process itself, the evidence of causal report inaccuracy was interpreted by Nisbett and Wilson (1977) as support for their hypothesis that there can be no conscious awareness of processes of social judgement and inference. Under this interpretation, then, whatever it is that has awareness and makes reports is clearly separated from processes of judgement with their intrinsic imperfections. This, coincidentally or not, perpetuates the ideology of a categorical distinction between the 'rational' part of the mind and sources of bias or disruption in reasoning and judgement.

More than that, what it shows is that the categorical distinction itself is founded on the distinction between <<I>> and deterministic influence. <<I>> is the seat of conscious awareness and action, and so <<I>> it is that produces verbal reports (which are actions) and seeks to discover what is going on in the mind through conscious awareness. The processes, which lie somewhere outside <<I>> and to which <<I>> supposedly has no 'access', operate automatically. To be more precise, they operate in a way that is not consciously controlled, because conscious control requires conscious awareness and that is what <<I>> is supposed not to have in respect of them.

This therefore yields a general explanation of the categorical distinction between reason or rationality and bias or disruption. Processes of reasoning and judgement are, like many things, understood as a battleground between <<I>> and deterministic influence. <<I>> aims to direct those processes in accordance with purposes, goals, intentions, and so on, formulated by <<I>>. This direction is achieved through conscious control, which, as stated in an earlier chapter, is conceptualised as the use of conscious awareness to gain information about what <<I>> is doing, and the consequent use of that information in the mindful direction of processes of reasoning. Such processes must therefore be understood as conscious.

Rationality is the optimal use of processes in accordance with the aim of fulfilling those purposes, and so forth, that <<I>> has at the time. It follows from this that the actions of <<I>> in directing and controlling processes of reasoning are rational, because <<I>> naturally aims them towards fulfilment of the purposes (and so on) which <<I>> has at the time. It follows in turn that sources of disruption, of irrationality, must lie somewhere outside <<I>>, because <<I>> always and necessarily knows what its current purposes are, and always acts in accordance with them: that is what it means to say that they are <<I>>'s purposes, that they are the purposes chosen by <<I>> in deciding how to act. If <<I>> chose not to act in accord with some purpose, that would mean that it was not (or no longer) <<I>>'s purpose. Being outside <<I>>, sources of irrationality must therefore be deterministic influences, operating without conscious control or awareness. Their categorical distinction from rationality, therefore, is not due merely to their location outside <<I>> but also to the profound difference in conceptualisation of their manner of operation.

The two essential marks of a source of bias or disruption of reasoning are (1) that it be of such a kind as to act against the avowed practical concerns of <<I>>, and (2) that it be seen as operating in a manner not involving conscious control. These marks can be seen in all of the ideas about sources of bias reviewed above. The case of motivational factors is particularly revealing in this respect. Such factors as the desire to protect or enhance self-esteem, to create a favourable impression on others, and to believe in a just world are identified as biases only because they are seen as operating against the fulfilment of the avowed concerns of <<I>>, which are *presumed* to be the lay scientist concerns of understanding, prediction, and control. A judgement will tend to be less accurate by the standards of science if it is affected by the desire to create a favourable impression, and it is by the assumption of that standard that the desire is called a bias.

If we change the standards to those of the practical concerns notion of rationality, then it is no longer clear whether the desire to create a favourable impression is a source of bias or not. If it is the avowed purpose of <<I>> to create a favourable impression, then that sets the standard of rationality: that is, the optimally rational judgement is the one that best contributes to the fulfilment of that goal. In such a case, the desire to create a favourable impression is *not* a source of bias. On the contrary, the desire to find the scientifically correct answer is a source of bias, if it leads to a judgement that does not optimally fulfil the avowed goal of creating a favourable impression.

If we ask why it is that the spirited element, be it passions, emotions, ambition, or motivational factors of various kinds, has so dominated the traditional concept of a bias or disrupting influence, there are two answers.

First, for much of recorded history, society has for the most part set a negative value on acting in accordance with passions, emotions, and motivational factors, especially in so far as doing so is perceived to have antisocial consequences. Thus, such things are seen as biases because (1) they tend to take behaviour away from what society judges that people *ought* to be doing, and (2) in so far as acting in accordance with such things has negative consequences for the actor (social disapproval, and so forth), to act in accordance with them is to act against one's own practical concerns, which is sufficient to regard them as biases.

Secondly, passions, emotions, and motivations are, for the most part, conceived as not consciously controlled. That is not to say that they cannot be controlled, for <<I>> can exert the force of its will over them and their potential disrupting influence, in principle at least. But this, when it occurs, is a victory for <<I>> on the battleground of the mind, and is not the natural manner of influence of passions on judgement. Their natural manner of influence is deterministic. The reasons for this probably lie in the fact that mechanisms of feedback control do not apply to internal states of the sort that count as passions.

To be influenced by passions therefore shows weakness of will, because it shows <<I>> being dominated by extrinsic, deterministic influences, and because it is to act against the presumed concern of <<I>> to gain social approval (and suchlike). Of course, people will not necessarily admit that a motivational factor was conscious or set the standard to which they were aspiring in their reasoning. If the reasoning process is seen as a kind of battleground between the powers of <<I>> and deterministic influences, then saying that the desire to preserve self-esteem was not conscious amounts to admitting weakness of will, whereas saying that it was conscious amounts to admitting prejudice or perversity. People may choose which they would prefer to admit to. Whatever people may admit to, the very existence in common sense of a distinction between rationality and bias is rooted in the basic psychological construction of the mind.

## CONSISTENCY AND INCONSISTENCY

Let me begin this section by repeating part of the previous one. Rationality is the optimal use of processes in accordance with the aim of fulfilling those purposes, and so on, that <<I>> has at the time. It follows from this that the actions of <<I>> in directing and controlling processes of reasoning are rational, because <<I>> naturally aims them towards fulfilment of the purposes (and so forth) which <<I>> has at the time. It follows in turn that sources of disruption, of irrationality, must lie somewhere outside <<I>>, because <<I>> always and necessarily knows what its current purposes are, and always acts in accordance with them: that is what it means to say that they are <<I>>'s purposes, that they are the purposes chosen by <<I>> in deciding how to act. If <<I>> chose not to act in accord with some purpose, that would mean that it was not (or no longer) <<I>>'s purpose.

This passage reveals an important feature of the psychological construction of the mind: that there is an assumption of unity of purpose in the operations of <<I>> at any one time. At any one time, if <<I>> is aiming towards the satisfaction of some particular practical concern, whatever it might be, then it cannot also be aiming away from it at the same time.

This allows that <<I>> may be seen as trying to decide which of two directions to go in, or as switching from one to another so that it has different purposes at different times. Switching of purposes, however, may be negatively interpreted as showing weakness of will, in that <<I>> appears to be influenced now by one consideration, now by another; that is, as being swayed by the deterministic influences which cause the weight of considerations to fluctuate from time to time. <<I>> is seen as bending where the breeze blows, so to speak, rather than standing firm against deterministic influence.

The assumption of unity of purpose follows from the subjective unity of <<I>>: it is one unified, self-aware thing. The same assumption is not made in the case of deterministic influences outside <<I>>: there is no unity in the conceptualisation of these influences and so they may be seen as naturally having tendencies in any number of directions at the same time. They are simply seen as independent causal forces and therefore do not necessarily tend in a common direction. Consistency, then, at least at one time, is characteristic of <<I>>, and inconsistency is characteristic of internal powers outside the subject.

This assumption of unity of purpose can be put to work in other areas of psychology. For example, it is sometimes asserted that 'inconsistency' within an individual is uncomfortable for that person and that people aim to be as consistent as possible. The best-known example of this is the theory of cognitive dissonance (Festinger 1957), in which it is stated that people seek in various ways to reduce dissonance, an unpleasant internal state brought about by the experience of 'psychological inconsistency' between cognitions. It would be too much of a digression to review the immense literature on dissonance theory, and I do not intend to take the ground away from some of the alternative interpretations that have been offered for dissonance phenomena, such as evaluation apprehension (Rosenberg 1965, 1969) or self-presentation (Baumeister 1982). But the present ideas can be used to resolve some problems with the theory.

One such problem is that the theory depends upon the fact that people try to reduce dissonance when they experience it, and Festinger (1957) originally proposed that dissonance works like a drive state, motivating people to reduce it. This has an uncomfortable taint of circularity: saying that people try to reduce dissonance because they have a drive to reduce dissonance is rather like saying that common salt makes things salty because it represents the principle of salinity (Toulmin and Goodfield 1962: 241). The unpleasantness of inconsistency can be accounted for instead by reference to the assumption of unity of purpose in <<I>>: inconsistency is incompatible with unity of purpose and therefore constitutes evidence for deterministic influence – evidence in fact that <<I>> is not fully in control of mental activity in behaviour, or is 'weak' in the sense of losing the battle for influence with those other powers. The attempt to resolve inconsistency or reduce dissonance can be interpreted as an attempt to restore belief in the command of <<I>> by regaining unity of purpose. The preferred method of dissonance reduction, therefore, is the one that alters the cognition believed to represent the operation of non-conscious powers. Alternatively, the introduction of further cognitions can be construed as an attempt to show that the inconsistency is apparent, not real, and that unity of purpose has not really been violated.

This interpretation provides a solution to the problem of defining psychological inconsistency, one of the traditional problems for cognitive dissonance theory (Aronson 1969). Psychological inconsistency is simply the simultaneous pursuit of incompatible practical concerns, where 'incompatible' means that the realisation of one acts against the realisation of the other. Thus, to take Festinger's (1957) earliest example, the cognitions 'I smoke' and 'smoking is bad for me' are psychologically inconsistent because they imply incompatible practical concerns: the concern of deriving whatever pleasure is to be had from smoking, and the concern of looking after one's physical health. 'Unity of purpose' therefore means 'compatibility of practical concerns', and this is how <<I>> is supposed to be.

Under this interpretation it makes little difference whether the discomfort is occasioned by private realisation of inconsistency or by the realisation that one's inconsistency is apparent to others. The negative evaluation of inconsistency is common to self and others, and therefore both fit into the same place in this explanatory framework.

## NORMALITY AND ABNORMALITY

It will no doubt be apparent that things associated with <<I>> in the foregoing sections, such as rationality and consistency, have generally positive evaluations, and things associated with deterministic influences, such as sources of bias, whether motivational or cognitive, and inconsistency, have generally negative evaluations. Furthermore, as discussed in the chapter on action, such things as responsibility for one's actions and self-control are believed to depend upon characteristics thought to be possessed only by <<I>>; namely, conscious awareness and the ability to choose how to act. It follows that responsibility and self-control are not thought possible for deterministic influences, which are therefore naturally seen as irresponsible and uncontrolled. These things also tend to be negatively evaluated in human behaviour.

It is arguable, though, that there is more than just positive and negative evaluation at stake here: there is a concept of normality or mental health. There have been many attempts to define mental health or normality, and at least 20 defining concepts have been proposed by various authors (White 1988c). The present theoretical perspective can be used to define a concept of normality or mental health which integrates most of these proposals – the exceptions being definition in terms of deviation from statistical norms (Atkinson *et al.* 1983), and the medical model, defining mental health in terms of freedom from gross pathology, defects, or ailments (Offer and Sabshin 1974).

I carried out a study (White 1988c) in which I sought to ascertain, by means of two questionnaire surveys, common-sense beliefs about the defining characteristics of normality (or mental health) and abnormality. The items in the questionnaire were based on 17 of the 20 defining features of mental health found in the literature (the statistical and medical definitions were excluded, as was a feature referring to a tendency to face rather than avoid conflict-provoking situations). Pairs of polar opposites were constructed (for example, 'has self-awareness' and 'lacks self-awareness'), and some fillers were added, making a questionnaire with 60 items in all. Subjects were asked to judge how normal or abnormal it would be to have each characteristic, and were instructed not to interpret 'normal' and 'abnormal' in purely statistical terms. Judgements were made on a seven-point rating scale. Two studies were carried out, one on a sample of undergraduates, the other a postal survey of a sample drawn randomly from the telephone directory. Factor analysis of the data revealed a three-factor structure, with both studies yielding similar results.

One factor consisted of most of the items rated as normal, the items with the highest loadings being: 'has feelings of well-being and high self-esteem'; 'open to new experiences'; 'behaves with respect for the rights of others'; 'flexible and able to learn from experience'; 'has self-awareness'; 'able to aspire to fulfilment of own potential'; 'independent and able to cope with reality'; 'balanced or integrated personality'; 'has will or desire to become a distinct individual'; 'has free will, able to choose behaviour from a range of options'; 'has will power'; and 'well adjusted to reality, able to get along with others'.

The second factor contained most of the items rated as abnormal, the items with the highest loadings being: 'badly adjusted to reality, unable to get along with others'; 'inflexible and unable to learn from experience'; 'lacks rational and intellectual faculties'; 'has no feeling of well-being, and has low self-esteem'; 'unbalanced or poorly integrated personality'; 'not open to new experiences'; 'not independent and unable to cope with reality'; 'lacks will power'; 'no free will, unable to choose behaviour from a range of options'; 'has no will or desire to become a distinct individual'; 'makes no distinction between right and wrong'; 'unable to aspire to fulfilment of own potential'; and 'not competent at gratifying own basic needs (food, health, love, etc.)'. A third, much smaller factor seemed to identify a concept of the responsible choice of socially approved patterns of behaviour. The first two factors together accounted for about 45 per cent of the variance in both studies, the third for an additional 5 per cent.

This research gives a strong indication that the lay concept of normality or mental health is not confined to any one or two of these items, but is instead to be found in some factor common to all of them. This factor, I propose, is that all of them depend upon the basic concept of <<I>> with its ability to choose how to act and conscious awareness, the two together making possible conscious control of mental activity and behaviour. That is, all of them are made possible only by conscious awareness and the capacity to choose how to act, integrated in a unified <<I>>. More precisely, all of them reflect the victory of <<I>> in the battle-ground of the mind. All of them show <<I>> asserting itself over the possibility of deterministic influence. The one exception, having high self-esteem, is a simple consequence for self-evaluation of the victory of <<I>>, because of the high social value attached to this. Their opposites, those things making up the factor of abnormality, show the opposite, the dominance of deterministic influence over <<I>>.

The ideal of normality or mental health in Western society is the complete domination of <<I>> in the production and control of behaviour and mental activity; and the extreme of abnormality is represented by the complete domination of deterministic influences over <<I>>. Of course, no one supposes that such an ideal is a realistic achievement, but mental health will be considered adequate, if not perfect, if <<I>> is reasonably dominant and deterministic influence is comparatively weak or confined to harmless effects. The behaviour of individuals is evaluated according to its presumed or inferred association with one or the other part of the mind. This means that types of behaviour believed only to be made possible by conscious awareness and the capacity to choose how to act will be positively valued as normal, and types of behaviour believed to represent deterministic influence will be negatively valued as abnormal. The optimum of normality, then, is the complete control of the mind and its forces by <<I>>, and complete insight into the mind through conscious awareness. The nadir of abnormality is complete control of the mind by deterministic influence and complete absence of conscious awareness (and therefore of conscious control).

This conceptualisation has significant implications for our treatment of the mentally ill, or indeed any group about which it is believed that <<I>> has lost the battle against deterministic influence. The mentally ill, that is, are an example of a group about which people believe that deterministic forces have won the battle for the mind and behaviour, temporarily or permanently, so that these people have little or no capacity for conscious control of their behaviour, and as a result possess the characteristics of the factor of abnormality. The implications hinge upon the fact that rights and privileges are accorded by society only to those individuals and groups who are considered able to exercise them in a responsible manner. Since the ability to behave in a responsible manner is seen as enabled only by the presumed capacity of <<I>> to dominate and control deterministic influences, rights and privileges will be accorded only to those individuals and groups in which <<I>> is believed to have that capacity. The implication is that the mentally ill will not be accorded those rights and privileges because, or to the extent that, people believe that deterministic influences are dominant in them. Generally, *any* individual or group will be accorded rights and privileges only to the extent that <<I>> is believed to be dominant in them, or at least to have the capacity to be dominant. Consequently, infractions of civil or human rights will be judged less unfair for individuals and groups in which deterministic influence is believed to be more dominant.

I carried out two studies to test these predictions (White 1989b). In the first, subjects were asked to judge the fairness or unfairness of certain institutional conditions under which a specified group of people was said to be living. The subjects were also asked to judge the extent to which the group was, in their belief, normal or abnormal. This was accomplished in two stages. First, the subjects estimated the percentage of people in the target group who possessed each of a number of characteristics; and, secondly, they judged how normal or abnormal it would be to have that characteristic. The characteristics were the items used in the survey of beliefs about normality or mental health. These two judgements were then correlated across characteristics for each subject, to give a correlation showing how normal or abnormal they considered the group to be.

Three target groups were used in a between-subject design: as identified to the subjects, they were elderly people suffering from senile dementia, seriously emotionally disturbed psychiatric patients, and single people working on an industrial estate. In each case the group was said to be living in some kind of residential accommodation for about 100 people. The six conditions about which fairness judgements were made were based on civil rights infractions documented as occurring in some private rest homes (Oliver 1986).

The main prediction was that, if one group was judged more abnormal on average than another, then the living conditions would be judged less unfair for the former group than for the latter. No particular order of the three groups was predicted: the hypothesis leads simply to the prediction that the order, whatever it might be, would be the same for both judgements. The results gave strong support to this prediction (White 1989b). The psychiatric group was judged most abnormal, and the rights infractions were judged least unfair for this group. Judgements for the elderly group were intermediate between the psychiatric and workers' groups. All differences were statistically significant.

One possible problem with these results is that judged normality or abnormality may be confounded with positive or negative evaluation: obviously, characteristics judged abnormal are likely to be negatively evaluated, and it is therefore possible that rights infractions were judged less unfair for the psychiatric group simply because they are believed to possess negatively valued characteristics. The second study dealt with this problem by differentiating judged abnormality from negative evaluation. With the aid of pre-ratings, descriptions of hypothetical target individuals were constructed whose characteristics were judged equally negative, but one of whom was judged more abnormal than the other. Thus, judged abnormality was varied but negative evaluation of characteristics was held constant. Results showed that rights infractions were judged much less unfair for the 'abnormal' target than for the merely negative target: indeed, ratings of unfairness for the negative target were scarcely different from ratings of unfairness for a target whose characteristics had been judged both normal and positive. This demonstrates that it is judged normality or abnormality that matters for judgements of fairness of rights infractions, not negative evaluation. The research shows, then, that the basic psychological construction of the mind has significant consequences for the treatment of certain groups in society, dependent upon the characteristics those groups are believed to possess.

## IS THERE STILL A GREAT CHAIN OF BEING?

To summarise, I have shown in this chapter that the basic psychological distinction between <<I>>, with its exclusive properties of conscious awareness and the capacity for choice, and deterministic influence, acts as the foundation for a set of opposed dichotomies in common-sense understanding of mental occurrences and behaviour: those between rationality and bias, consistency and inconsistency, and normality (or mental health) and abnormality are chief among them. The fact that these things *are* dichotomies, rather than trichotomies, continua, and so on, is also explained by reference to this basic distinction. A persistent theme of this analysis has been the evaluative connotation of this distinction: those things that are associated with <<I>> are uniformly positively evaluated, and those things associated with deterministic influence are negatively evaluated. This leads me to explore the conjecture that there is still in common sense an evaluative hierarchy of creation, with its ancestry in the medieval great chain of being (Tillyard 1943).

The medieval world picture was thoroughly and rigidly hierarchical: 'The world picture which the Middle Ages inherited was that of an ordered universe arranged in a fixed system of hierarchies but modified by man's sin and the hope of his redemption' (Tillyard 1943: 3). This order in its stability was the glory of God's creation, and the dominant metaphor of the universal order was the great chain of being, which 'stretched from the foot of God's throne to the meanest of inanimate objects. Every speck of creation was a link in the chain, and every link except those at the two extremities was simultaneously bigger and smaller than another: there could be no gap' (Tillyard 1943: 23). The chain was a moral order, not a spatial one. The chain differentiated not only species from species but also individual from individual. Tillyard (1943: 24) quoted the Elizabethan writer John Fortescue as follows: 'there is no creature which does not differ in some respect from all other creatures and by which it is in some respect superior or inferior to the rest'. Moreover, within each class of creation there was a highest member: Tillyard quoted the medieval writer Sebonde as nominating the dolphin among fishes (sic), the eagle among birds, the lion among beasts, the emperor among men, the sun among stars, justice among the virtues, and the head among the body's members. The resonances of this way of thinking have yet to die away: most people will have heard the lion referred to as the king of beasts, even if they no longer quite believe it, and even if they no longer believe that the king is the best of men.

Humanity occupied a place in the hierarchy below the lowest of the angels and above the highest of the animals. The reason for this location was basically humanity's possession of a rational soul, by virtue of which humanity is said to possess a faculty of reason, the function of which is to draw us towards better things and good behaviour. We resemble animals in all respects except in our possession of a rational soul, which places the meanest man above the noblest beast in the chain, and we resemble angels to some extent through our possession of a rational soul (I say to some extent because angels do not require a faculty of reason, being possessed of clear understanding, but they do share with us possession of free will) and fall below the lowest angels in the chain. As Sebonde said, the emperor or monarch is traditionally the highest human member of the chain.

It is sometimes asserted that the basis of the medieval world view, the idea of order, has been superseded not only in science but in common sense by a new basis in the idea of causal laws, originating in the Scientific Revolution (Bronowski 1951). It seems more likely, though, that elements of the medieval way of thinking survive in common sense. Studies of the naïve physics of motion show that people understand motion in ways that resemble some medieval theories (McCloskey 1983), though whether by coincidence or by historical influence is not clear. I have shown earlier that common-sense understanding of causal processes in nature to some extent resembles an Aristotelian causal hierarchy. And the familiarity of ideas such as the lion being the king of beasts testifies to the power of ancient ideas to persist in common ways of thinking.

It is also undeniable that other elements of medieval thought have disappeared entirely from common sense. No one nowadays thinks of the solar system as a set of crystalline spheres in which the planets are rigidly set, for example, and the complex hierarchy of angels familiar to the Elizabethan world (Tillyard 1943) is perhaps known to few today. This raises a question of the most profound importance to the study of common sense – important specifically to the study of that part of common sense that comprises explicit, verbalisable beliefs (Fletcher 1984): is it possible to explain and predict why some ideas survive and others do not, specifically in this case why some ideas have survived from medieval times to the present day and others have not?

There may be many factors governing the survival of ideas, but here I wish to propose one that may account for the survival of tendencies towards a hierarchical conceptualisation of creation, and perhaps for other ideas as well. This is that an idea will survive to the extent that it is grounded in psychological metaphysics. There are two parts to this, which may or may not be complementary. First, an idea is well grounded in psychological metaphysics if it is directly implied by the most basic metaphysical assumptions of the psychological construction of reality. Secondly, an idea is well grounded in proportion to the number of other beliefs that are existentially dependent upon it. As stated in Chapter 3, the more beliefs are existentially dependent upon some proposition, the more resistant to change that proposition is. The second part has less predictive value in the long term, because more superficial beliefs are more apt to change and therefore the number of beliefs that are existentially dependent upon a proposition is liable to change over time, *ipso facto* altering its resistance to change.

The specific hypothesis I propose here relates to the first part of the grounding hypothesis: those elements of the medieval world view that survive in common sense today are those which are most directly implied by the basic assumptions in the psychological construction of the mind. One of those basic assumptions is the distinction between <<I>>, with its properties of the capacity to choose and conscious awareness, and deterministic influence. This assumption directly implies an evaluative hierarchy of creation, based on the attribution of <<I>> and its exclusive properties to different individuals and species. This hierarchy is organised in two related ways. First, individuals and species may be believed to have <<I>> or not to have it. Those who are believed to have it are *ipso facto* higher up the hierarchy than those who are not. Secondly, within the realm of those individuals and species who are believed to have <<I>>, the hierarchical arrangement is determined by the relative dominance of <<I>> over deterministic influence. Thus, the hypothetical optimum of normality, an individual possessing, through <<I>>, complete control of his or her own mental activity and behaviour, and complete conscious awareness of mental activity, would be the apex of the hierarchy. Groups such as those used as targets in the research discussed earlier, psychiatric patients and elderly people suffering senile dementia, fall below normal adult human beings in the hierarchy.

The evaluative connotations of the distinction between <<I>> and deterministic forces suggest further that attributions based on the distinction may play a considerable role in social dynamics such as intergroup discrimination and prejudice. In principle, dominance of <<I>> over deterministic forces implies greater responsibility and self-control. Therefore, in the case of intergroup comparison and discrimination, people might reason as follows: 'I, and members of my group, have greater responsibility (or will-power or self-control, or other relevant properties associated with dominance of <<I>>) than those people in that group, therefore it is fair that we should have a greater say in the allocation of resources, because we will make decisions in a more responsible way than they would.' Or people might reason: 'I (and people like me) have the strength of will (and so on) to resist the effects of watching violent television, but they (or that group) do not have such great strength of will and therefore are more easily influenced by violent television into behaving more aggressively, therefore there is a need for censorship of violence to protect us from its effects on those weak-willed people.'

What is important about this is that discriminative behaviours, judgements, and beliefs are not necessarily negative in an undifferentiated way. Not just any kind of social comparison will do. The beliefs that make the difference are specifically those that relate closely to the battle between <<I>> and deterministic influence: moreover, these beliefs make the difference because they are at a relatively basic level of the psychological construction of the mind.

This has implications for beliefs about society and ideology. There is a tendency in the history of ideas for liberal political beliefs to be associated with an optimistic view of human nature, in which people are seen as basically good or co-operative, and for more authoritarian beliefs to be associated with a more negative view of human nature in which people are basically selfish, greedy, or irrational (Baumer 1977). I would hypothesise that similar tendencies can be found in common-sense belief. Thus, people in whose view of human nature <<I>> tends to be dominant over deterministic influence should be likely to favour a libertarian approach, basically on the grounds that the good of society is adequately served by allowing people to behave in accordance with their own judgement. They should also tend to favour the retributive theory of punishment, on the grounds that people are basically responsible for their own actions, rather than driven deterministically by forces over which they have no control (Berry 1986). Those who see <<I>> as relatively weak compared to deterministic influence in human beings in general should be likely to favour a more authoritarian system in which the interests of society are preserved by enforceable rules, basically on the grounds that external controls are necessary to hold the deterministic forces in check, given that the will of <<I>> is not strong enough.

Similarly, for groups, sub-groups, and individuals within society, people should favour authoritarian, rule-based control of those in whom <<I>> is judged to be weak, but more liberal systems for those in whom <<I>> is judged to be relatively strong. Thus, returning to the example just used, rule-based censorship of television may be deemed appropriate for people judged to be susceptible to its influence through weakness of will, but not appropriate for people judged to have the strength of will to resist. It is the view one takes on the relative dominance of <<I>> and deterministic influences that counts: thus, if one knows what someone believes on this in respect of a certain individual, group, or society as a whole, then it should be possible to predict their preference for liberal or authoritarian systems in respect of that individual, group, or society.

To summarise, there is still a great chain of being in common sense, even if the detailed arrangement of its members has changed, and the chain owes its survival to the fact of being rooted in the psychological metaphysics of the mind.

# Chapter 15

# Judgement and feelings

The aim of this chapter is to reconstruct the study of lay judgement from the perspective of the practical concerns orientation. It is claimed that the study of lay judgement under the lay scientist analogy, while not wholly wrong, has obscured the issue by treating judgement out of its natural context and by using unrepresentative types of problem and categorisation of lay judgement. Judgement should be considered from the point of view of its function, not that of its scientific accuracy, or the degree to which judgemental processes succeed in modelling normative scientific procedures. The main role of judgement is to assess the extent to which some state of affairs, course of action, or decision, real or hypothetical, satisfies some standard set by the practical concerns of the judge at the time of judgement, thus acting as a guide to behaviour or decisions aimed towards satisfying that standard. It is wrong to assume that lay judgement either does or should have any resemblance to scientific judgement.

## THE LAY SCIENTIST ANALOGY AND THE PRACTICAL CONCERNS MODEL APPLIED TO LAY JUDGEMENT

The study of lay judgement under the lay scientist analogy has a number of characteristic features. First, the goal of judgement is presumed to be accuracy. The goals of judgement and inference for lay people have sometimes been claimed to be understanding, prediction, and control (Heider 1958; Nisbett and Ross 1980), but the presumption is that understanding – that is to say, judgemental accuracy and correctness – is the key, the prerequisite for prediction and control.

Secondly, the ways in which people are presumed to make judgements are effectively mechanical procedures, analogous to the use of statistical rules of inference such as Bayes' theorem, and the statistical techniques for treating data from controlled experimental designs, such as analysis of variance. 'Feelings' have been extirpated from these hypothetical processes. Even errors and biases in judgement are commonly regarded as consequences of defects in the mechanisms of judgement, such as use of a simple rule that does not work as well as some normative statistical rule. Errors and biases formerly regarded as motivational in origin have been reinterpreted as 'cognitive' or mechanical (Miller and Ross

1975; Nisbett and Ross 1980), although the contest between cognitive and motivational interpretations is still on (Harvey and Weary 1984; Tetlock and Levi 1982; Zuckerman 1979).

Thirdly, the judgemental tasks set for subjects in research studies tend to be those for which normative scientific and statistical procedures generate standards against which the quality of lay judgement can be assessed. I have already argued that this begs the question of whether people are actually aiming for accuracy by the scientific standard at all costs; but it also begs the question of representativeness. That is, those judgemental problems for which clear, agreed scientific standards of comparison can be established are a sub-set, possibly a small one, of all judgemental problems. No one has sought to discover whether they differ from the judgemental problems for which no clear scientific standard of correctness can be established. If they do, then they are not representative of judgemental problems and results from studies of them will be of low generalisability.

Fourthly, the typology of lay judgement reflects the assumption of the lay scientist analogy: that is, it is a typology of judgements in science merely applied to lay judgement. The typology is explicit in the layout of the influential book by Nisbett and Ross (1980), which considers lay judgement under a series of chapter headings that reflect types of scientific judgement: 'characterizing the datum, sample, and population'; 'assessment of covariation'; 'causal analysis'; 'prediction'; and 'theory maintenance and theory change' (chs 4 to 8).

I have already argued that the lay scientist analogy is false, and that the standards of judgement to which lay people aspire are those set by the practical concerns that pertain for them at the time of judgement. This argument leads to a number of counter-propositions.

The first is that the goal of judgement is the optimal satisfaction of the practical concerns, whatever they are, in respect of which and because of which judgement is taking place. The job of judgement is to be functional, not to be accurate: accuracy only matters when it is in the service of practical concerns.

The second is that the model carries no prescription for the making of judgements. It does state, however, that factors that can be called motivational in nature, or feelings, are not biases and do not lead to errors. Such factors are or relate to practical concerns and as such their influence on judgement is legitimate. There may still be 'cognitive' biases in judgement, but these can only be assessed against the standards set by the judge's practical concerns at the time of judgement, not against normative scientific standards. Under the practical concerns notion of rationality, not only may feelings enter into judgemental processes but it may be right and proper for them to do so. That is, for lay people, behaving in accordance with one's feelings may often be the best way of satisfying relevant practical concerns.

The third counter-proposition is that there are a number of reasons related to practical concerns why judgemental tasks set in the laboratory are not representative of lay judgement in general. First, the dominant practical concerns for subjects in experiments are specific to the experimental setting, or nearly so: for example, evaluation apprehension, gaining a course credit, helping the experimenter fulfil the scientific goals of the study with minimum effort, and so on. Clearly, how people behave under the thrall of these concerns cannot be assumed to predict how they behave when these concerns are absent.

Secondly, the dominant practical concerns of the person outside the laboratory are absent or in abeyance inside it: the laboratory task has no place of importance in the subject's life, and therefore tells us nothing about how people make judgements on matters that *are* important to them. These are, moreover, likely to be judgements for which science provides no normative standards of correctness, for which there is no known optimal procedure or rule. Some years ago, Brickman (1980) made a plea for the study of fundamental human concerns, and listed such things as justice, love, power, freedom, happiness, work, and play. People depend on judgements to sort out these fundamental concerns as best they can: surely no one can say that the way in which people approach a pencil-and-paper problem about the numbers of babies born in two hypothetical hospitals tells us anything about that.

The fourth counter-proposition is that a typology of judgement based on types of scientific judgement is inappropriate. Having said that, the practical concerns model does not provide a ready-made typology of judgement, and some investigation of common practical concerns would be necessary to construct one. Such an investigation has yet to be carried out, and it is not unlikely that the list of concerns would be too extensive to be of much use for a typology of judgement. A more empirical approach can be adopted, however, and an exploratory step into this approach is reported here.

Some years ago I asked two groups of 20 and 18 volunteers respectively to write essays about themselves. They were instructed to write for as long as they wished, and to write about anything they wished so long as it was about themselves. The latter group also, on a different occasion, wrote a similar essay about some person well known to them, making a total of 56 essays. These essays are used throughout this chapter to elucidate aspects of lay judgement and feelings. The essays were consulted for instances of judgement in which some kind of context was given: that is, the writer described something that followed judgement, something perhaps that judgement was in aid of. Several examples were found, and are worth considering individually.

1  'It makes me very sad to feel that I am being carried along by events and if I feel this at any time I try to change things, either the events or my approach to them.' The sequence of events here described is: (a) perception or judgement of a state of affairs (I am being carried along by events); (b) evaluation (in this case described as negative affect); (c) action. That is, she perceives that something is the case or is happening, this is negatively evaluated, and the consequence of the negative evaluation is action specifically aimed at changing the state of affairs in a direction that would presumably be more positively evaluated.

2  This is a narrative of almost 1,000 words, but the basic steps are as follows. Things began with a novel perception, of conflict between the values held by various friends and family of the writer. The writer felt 'disturbed' by this, because she didn't know which friends to relate to in her mind: that is, at different times she had been relating to different friends, and what disturbed her about the conflict was the impossibility of adopting all of the values. The effect was a decision to 'start from the very beginning' to re-establish friends and values by making positive choices rather than by passively accepting. The sequence is similar to that in (1): judgement of state of affairs; negative evaluation; action aimed at changing what was judged negative about the prior state of affairs.

3  'I couldn't give in to them entirely and try to conform to their idea of what I should be like – it would never have worked – so I decided I had to make a stand and show them what I was really like.' The initial step is a judgement, but of a different kind which may be called 'hypothesising on conditionals' – judging that if $X$ happens then $Y$ will follow. The judgement is again negatively evaluated and the consequence is action which avoids or precludes the occurrence of the conditional.

4  Here the action is dropping out of medical school, for which the following explanation is given. 'I am convinced that the doctor/patient relationship is (or should be) more important than the mechanics of treatment . . . . [As a doctor] I would have failed those seeking help because I would not myself have been sane enough to recognise their personality, including the illness, in its wholeness.' This follows a similar pattern to (3), with the addition that the evaluation is made by comparison with a criterion or standard, in this case a statement of values.

5  'I don't feel mentally stretched at all now so I'm determined to do an Open University course just to start my brain working again.' Here the evaluation is implicit, and the effect is just a decision or statement of intention, rather than the actual action.

6  'This is perhaps another reason why I can never get down to writing or painting. I feel that the effort required to put down what I really believe, to express myself to my own satisfaction, would (a) give me little time for my friends, and (b) I would become very critical of them and drive them away perhaps.' This is similar to (4).

7  'At the age of 12 my eldest sister left [the village school] as my parents felt she was getting too tomboyish.' This is similar to (1) and (2).

In some places a similar sequence can be seen in the writer's efforts to construct the essay itself.

8  'I am desperately trying to think of something positive to say as the tone of this piece strikes me as rather maungy.'

9  'Convinced this inward-looking stuff leading round in a circle and shall try another theme.'

10 'I don't feel I'm getting anywhere with this. I'll try again from more recent events.'

Each quotation comes from a different writer, but in each case the writer has stopped to judge and evaluate what has been written, and the negative evaluation leads to a decision to try a different approach.

These ten instances can be seen to share a common pattern. In each case there is a sequence of judgement, followed or accompanied by evaluation (sometimes these two are inextricable because one word serves both functions), followed by the formulation of an intention, the making of a decision, or the description of some action or inaction presumably in accordance with some implicit intention or decision. Moreover, the decision or action has an invariable aim, which is to correct or improve upon (where the thing judged is present or past) or avoid or preclude (where it is future or hypothetical) whatever it is that has been negatively evaluated. The individual sequences can be imagined as extracts from series in which the person continually acts (or decides, or avoids), judges and evaluates (the action or some consequence of it), and corrects or improves or decides again. Ideally, a sequence stops when no more positive evaluation is thought possible: in practice, it is more likely to stop when other practical concerns become more pressing. For the sake of simplicity I shall refer to an individual sequence as a JEA sequence (judgement–evaluation–action).

The sequence is not invariable, as the following examples show.

11 'I realised by this time that I couldn't really explain, so I just let things go.' No evaluation is reported here. For some judgements no evaluation is necessary for a decision to be taken, and a judgement of impossibility is one: if a course of action is impossible, or the goal at which it is aimed cannot be achieved, there is no point in trying.

12 'He never gets worked up about *anything* – which drives me to fury when I feel he *should* be emphatically on one side or the other.' Here the evaluation is based on an explicit mismatch between a real or hypothetical state of affairs and a standard, as in (4). The effect, however, is not a decision or an action but a *reaction*, an affective state. The difference seems to be related to perceived controllability. When the evaluation concerns something over which one believes oneself to have control, the JEA sequence applies: when it concerns something over which one believes oneself to have little or no control, the consequence is an affective state or affective behaviour, or both. I shall call this the JER sequence, and I hypothesise that perception of controllability is the factor that determines whether the sequence is JEA or JER. Affective reactions are not precluded from JEA sequences, but it is noticeable that they are not mentioned in any of the examples of JEA sequences to be found in the essays.

13 'I have no real friends because I regard the one I have in my wife as enough.' Here the evaluation is positive: the state of affairs judged to exist is deemed satisfactory, and the consequence is that no particular action is taken – that is, in this case no definite effort is made to make new friends.

There are many examples of judgement in the essays, but only a few give explicit clues to the function of the judgement: of these, none unambiguously violates the patterns exemplified in the cases given. These various sequences can be summarised diagrammatically, as in Figure 15.1.

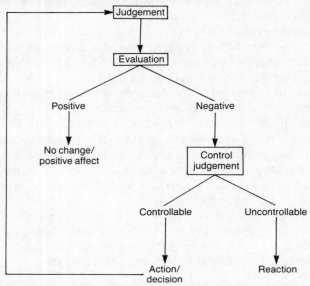

*Figure 15.1* Schematic diagram of types of judgemental sequence

In two of the examples, (4) and (12), an explicit criterion or standard for evaluation can be found. In other parts of the essays general or abstract criteria, as guides to evaluation and action, are reported, though not as attached to particular sequences:

'I've learned to recognise when a person or experience is good for me – by comparison against other possible feelings I've gradually become able to rate it for myself.'

'I'd be happier doing what *I* felt' (that is, rather than following the advice of others).

'If I did not see eye to eye with my husband I should have stuck to principles I felt deeply were right.'

'With people for me the important thing is what you perceive in yourself when you're with them – you're either high or low and that's the criterion.'

'If in doubt as to what decision has to be made, which may not be easy, I think of what my parents or grandparents or even great-grandparents would have done, and what action they would have taken in similar circumstances.'

These quotations exemplify a considerable range of possible standards: principles, values, feelings, paragons. Three points are worth making about them. First, they are designed for use in evaluations and decisions to which the normative standards of science cannot be applied. Secondly, the rightness or wrongness of these as standards can only be assessed in relation to the practical concerns of the person in question. Essentially, they are imperfect if and when reliance on them results in less than optimal satisfaction of the practical concerns in respect of which they were used, and this will be signalled by negative evaluation of the judged consequences. Thirdly, in all except the last, feelings are prominent.

This exploration has revealed a number of topics to be considered in more detail. What are the types of judgement? What are feelings and what roles do they play in JEA and JER sequences? What is the logic of the JEA sequence? Each will be considered in turn.

## TYPES OF JUDGEMENT

The essays already referred to in this chapter were consulted for mentions of instances of judgement. The main problem was identifying judgements as such: a decision was made to use linguistic criteria, specifically the writer's use of such clauses as 'it strikes me', 'I suppose', 'I'm sure', and 'it seems to me' – that is, expressions which explicitly indicate an activity of judgement. This means of course that things which were actually judgements but which were not marked by these linguistic tags were excluded from the sample, and it is impossible to say how many there were. In this way 279 examples of judgement were found. These were studied to see whether they fell into recognisable types. What follows is not being proposed as a formal typology because the categories have not been submitted to a reliability check. The intention is to set up typology of lay judgement as a topic for research, and to provide some initial hypotheses about what might go into such a typology. The following are the rough types found, with some examples of each. Numbers in parentheses are the numbers of instances classified under each category. These add up to more than 279 because an instance could be classified in more than one way. For example, 'I think the chief characteristics that have affected my life are idleness, lack of ambition, (etc.)' was classified under both causal judgement and judgement of self.

1   *Judgement of matter of fact, present or past*
    1a Perception or judgement of other person (53)
        '. . . who, I am fairly sure, little realised the tension I was under.'
        'I know that he could not get on without my mother.'
        'When I thought about these home-friends, their values conflicted with one another and with those of my parents.'
        Only five of these were unambiguous trait ascriptions: others concerned other people's intentions, feelings, attitudes, needs, values, reactions, and states of knowledge.

1b Abstract, general judgements of what people are like, of the course of one's life, of the state of life, of the nature of things or the world in general (25).

'I think students here are very limited.'

'Then came what was the turning-point for me, I think.'

'I have always thought selflessness to be as selfish as anything else.'

1c Judgements about self (92)

'I do think I am very hard-working.'

'I should think that by birth and by training I am relatively good at observing.'

'I think I have found it relatively easy to get used to retirement.'

'I don't think I ever loved him.'

The popularity of this category is likely to be an artefact of the task.

1d Judgement of interpersonal relation or dynamic either involving self or not (36)

'I don't think my sisters and I helped him much.'

'I think part of the attraction for us both was to do with this: our similar reactions to stress.'

'I knew that the people I was travelling with would not get on with any of my home friends or my parents.'

1e Characteristics of situation or state of affairs or strategy of living (23)

'I can't help feeling that something is going to burst soon.'

'[I think I] have to achieve some amazing things to spite the essential horror.'

2 *Judgement of cause, reason, or blame (43)*

'I think the illness has affected me by making me try and understand people if I can.'

'I should say the experiences of a world war between the ages of 9 and 13 probably did a considerable amount of harm on many counts.'

3 *Prediction (11)*

'I can see it lasting way into the future or falling amicably apart.'

'I think he will be a "good-looker" in his teenage years.'

4 *Hypothesising on conditionals (14)*

'I always feel, if we had a bigger garden [etc.] then I'd be a better mother.'

'If I could overcome this lack [of confidence] I feel I would be capable of creating a far better life for myself.'

5 *Judgements of likelihood or probability (16)*

'Probably they're very nice people.'

'Ideally I can see myself living in a small cottage by the sea . . . Not very likely, I think.'

As the examples show, this category is problematic because in naturally occurring judgements the decision as to whether something is a likelihood or probability judgement has to be made by linguistic criteria: 11 of the 16 examples in this category were placed here because of the use of the word 'probably'. This begs the two questions of whether 'probably' does indicate a judgement of likelihood or serves some other function, such as a rhetorical one, and whether other judgements may actually be judgements of likelihood or probability but carry no linguistic marker that enables them to be identified as such.

6  *Judgements of frequency (3)*

'I think many people find me a bit uninteresting.'

Analogous comments can be made about this category.

An additional category of judgements of covariation was set up a priori, but no examples of this were found. This does not mean that people do not make judgements of covariation, of course, and indeed some of the other judgements they make may depend upon judged covariation; all one can say is that there is no explicit judgement of covariation to be found in the essays.

Because of the problems already discussed, the frequencies of occurrence of these different categories in the essays cannot be taken as representative of their relative frequencies of occurrence in real life. It is clear, however, that the majority of instances found in the essays are judgements of matters of fact: that is, actual (or supposedly actual) single events or states of affairs, as opposed to multiple events, likelihoods, or causal relations. It could be argued that judgements of this kind are actually disguised judgements of likelihood and can be modelled in terms of judgemental heuristics such as representativeness. One of the examples used by Kahneman and Tversky (1973) in their studies of representativeness concerns the likelihood that a hypothetical person has a certain occupation (for example, librarian), and this is a judgement about a simple matter of fact: Tom W. either is or is not a librarian. The peculiar feature of this judgement, though, is that there is a kind of base rate information (the proportions of people in the population actually falling into each occupation) that is relevant to the judgement. This can hardly be said to be the case for the matters of fact about which judgements are made in the essays. For example: 'After a while I sensed more and more her disapproval', or 'Then came what was the turning-point for me, I think.' Perhaps it could be argued that there are base rate occurrences of disapproval and turning-points, but they have no conceivable relevance to, and there is no normative way to use them in the making of, these judgements.

If people don't use base rate information it isn't because they are using the representativeness heuristic: they may be doing so, but this begs the question why they should use this heuristic. It is because almost all of the judgements they make are judgements for which there is no relevant base rate information, and they therefore have to proceed in ways that do not involve utilisation of base rate information. Since there is no clear means of discriminating judgements for which there is relevant base rate information from those for which there is none, people will tend to continue with their judgemental routines effectively automatically, and this is why they neglect base rate in judgemental problems for which it should normatively be used.

As to how people actually make judgements of the kinds illustrated here, almost nothing is known about that. There are many reasons for this, but one overriding reason should be mentioned: it is that people's judgemental activities and abilities are studied by putting them in unfamiliar territory. In person perception, people judge characteristics of hypothetical individuals or strangers; in judgement under uncertainty, abstract and hypothetical problems with unfamiliar subject-matter. Let me take an analogy. Territorial animals such as jays and owls reap enormous benefits from having a patch of ground in which they live for long periods and with which they become familiar. Jays, for example, store large numbers of nuts for winter food and are able to remember where they have placed a high proportion of nuts because they orient themselves with the aid of a kind of cognitive map of their territory. Owls navigate on the wing in pitch darkness in the same way, needing only the faintest of visual cues which they can interpret in terms of their cognitive map of their patch. Either bird, taken from its own territory and placed in strange surroundings, would appear to be far more inept at storing and finding nuts, and navigating in darkness, respectively, until it had time to build up a map of its new surroundings. All of the judgements in the essays are to do with aspects of the writer's own territory, so to speak – themselves, their family and friends, the course of their life, and so on: all of the judgements subjects are asked to make in research studies, on the other hand, are judgements about unfamiliar territory, and therefore likely to underestimate people's judgemental abilities. Use of the representativeness heuristic may be a fallback, a strategy to be used with unfamiliar circumstances where one's usual ways of making judgements, which depend on intimate knowledge of one's own territory, cannot be applied.

## FEELINGS

In ordinary discourse we frequently use the language of feeling. 'I feel like bacon for tea tonight.' 'I feel like seeing a good film.' 'I feel something is wrong with John and Susan's marriage.' Assuming that uses of the words 'feel' and 'feeling' are not random, they are presumably being used as a marker of some kind of mental state and/or activity. In order to investigate the role of feelings in judgement, it is necessary to unravel the common-sense understanding of the nature of feelings.

People regard feelings as of great personal importance. I carried out an exploratory study to discover what people regarded as the most essential features of themselves. I assembled a list of 16 possible features, including: feelings; ability to distinguish between right and wrong; ability to understand what other people are saying; ability to get on with other people; ability to walk; balanced or well-integrated personality; plans for the future; ability to think; competence at gratifying own basic needs (food, health, love, and so on); ability to learn from experience; conscious awareness; high self-esteem; openness to new experiences; free will; ability to use language; and ability to remember own past life. Some of these describe basic psychological and physical capacities; others are taken from the literature on concepts of normality and mental health discussed in the previous chapter. I asked 39 first-year psychology undergraduates to rate each one on a scale consisting of seven verbal alternatives, from 'impossible to imagine myself without this' (scored 1), through 'almost impossible . . . ', 'very hard . . . ', 'fairly hard . . . ', 'fairly easy . . . ', 'very easy . . . ', to 'I don't have this characteristic' (scored 7).

On this scale, the mean of 38 ratings of 'feelings' (one respondent left a blank) was 1.39. The second-ranked item was 'ability to think' (mean 1.67) and the third-ranked item (competence) had a mean of 2.22. 'Free will' had a mean of 2.24, and 'conscious awareness' 2.52 (rank eighth). Why did feelings emerge as the top-ranked item from this set, and why did respondents consistently find themselves unable to imagine themselves without feelings?

According to the scheme worked out earlier, feelings are within the 'mental being' category of mental occurrences, things of which <<I>> is consciously aware but which <<I>> does not consciously control, and not analogous to objects in the physical world (in the way that a visual image is, for example).

While this serves to locate feelings in the psychological metaphysics of mind, it is not sufficient to define feelings as understood by ordinary people, nor to pin down just how feelings are involved, or thought to be involved, in mental activity. There are at least two distinct meanings of the word 'feel' in ordinary discourse. One refers to the experience of emotional states, such as 'feeling sad', and presumably has the connotations of passivity and involuntariness that attach to emotional states in general (Averill 1974). The other refers to sensory experiences, as in feeling something with your hand. The 'feel' of leather or fur is a tactile sensation, and in this sense feeling is an active kind of perceiving, arguably more active than looking, exploring the properties of things with the hands (or other parts of the body). It is also understood as more direct, in that the hand is actually in contact with the thing felt, whereas the eye is distant from the thing seen, the ear from the thing heard.

I sampled from the essays all expressions in which the word 'feel' and words having 'feel' as their root were used. There were 121 such expressions in all, 108 of which were feelings attributed to the person writing the essay. A minority of these (18) were recognisable 'emotional' feelings such as 'feel very sad', and 'felt sorry'. The rest were less obviously emotional in nature and covered a wide range of states and experiences. Here are some examples, each from a different writer:

'I feel I ought to be doing more different, "interesting" things.'

'Now I feel that unless one has an irresistible compulsion to write, better not.'

'I feel I must have some courage to go on facing myself.'

'I feel that some of my self-confidence has transmitted itself to him.'

'I feel I would be capable of creating a far better life for myself.'

'I feel I know him very well sometimes.'

'I feel myself getting emotional.'

It is evident that these are not mere affective states: even the last one expresses something more akin to perception of an emotional state rather than actually being one. They all assert propositions, the content of the proposition being the thing felt: stable personal characteristics of the writer or others; transient mental events or states of the writer or others, relations between others and the writer; states of affairs or events in the world; hypothetical statements such as counter-factual conditionals; possible courses of action. Is there anything that marks these sorts of feelings, or things felt, off as a category in common sense from, for example, thinking, or things thought?

In an attempt to answer this question, I sampled from the same essays all uses of the word 'think' and words having 'think' as their root. In the investigation by Rips and Conrad (1989), 14 out of 15 people asked to list common mental activities included 'thinking' in their list, and thinking was found to form the base of the taxonomy of 'analytic' mental activities. It is probably therefore sufficiently important in common sense to make a suitable comparison case. There were 129 uses of 'think' and so on in the essays, and it was clear that 'think' was used in ways very similar to 'feel', as in the following examples:

'I think many people find me a bit uninteresting.'

'I think our personalities can't stand being near each other for too long.'

'I don't think I hold enough firm opinions.'

'I think my attitudes, outlook, and character have adapted themselves to the various circumstances.'

'At present I think it is almost immoral to spend vast sums on clothes.'

Substituting 'think' for 'feel' in the first list, and 'feel' for 'think' in the second, does not seem obviously wrong. In fact, in two cases this overlap is explicit:

'It is impossible to say why I think so, but I feel he will develop into a very good man.'

'At present I think it is almost immoral to spend vast sums on clothes. What I don't know is whether I would feel the same if I had vast sums.'

But the overlap is only partial. 'Think' is never used to refer to emotional states, and substituting 'think' for 'feel' in 'I feel very sad' immediately appears absurd. 'Think' is also used as a generic term for various kinds of mental activity. Consider the following examples: 'I can't think of any good stories;' 'I do not think much about the past;' 'As soon as I began to think in this way [difficult circumstances in life give a challenge] things began to alter.' Substituting 'feel' for 'think' in these sentences does not seem appropriate, or at least considerably changes the meaning. These sentences illustrate types of mental activity that people regard as specific types of thinking (Rips and Conrad 1989): reasoning, interpreting, retrieving things from memory, deciding, planning (and, I would add, conjecturing, as in 'There are times when I think what I might have done'). The word 'feel' cannot be used as a substitute for any of these specific kinds of thinking.

In addition, both 'think' and 'feel' can carry connotations of uncertainty. Compare, for example, 'I believe Madrid is the capital of Spain', 'I think Madrid is the capital of Spain', and 'I feel Madrid is the capital of Spain.' In the case of 'feel', the metaphor of feeling one's way, as one of the ways in which the sense of touch can be used, is appropriate.

## History

Let me take another dip into the medieval world view. For many centuries, the faculty of reason was regarded as the highest attribute of human beings, the feature by virtue of which humans were superior to the beasts. Originating in ancient Greece (for example, it can be found in Plato), by the Middle Ages this idea had become amalgamated with Christian beliefs about souls and angels. The mind was considered to be an ordered hierarchy of parts: vegetable soul (shared with animals and plants and responsible for all unconscious and involuntary processes such as growth and digestion); sensitive soul (shared with animals but not plants and including the five outward senses and five inward senses such as memory and imagination); and the rational soul, which animals were believed not to possess, and by virtue of which humanity fell between the beasts and the angels in the chain of being.

The rational soul was thought to have two parts, called ratio and intellectus. Ratio corresponds approximately to our modern notion of reasoning. For example, 'we are exercising ratio when we proceed step by step to prove a truth which is not self-evident' (Lewis 1964: 157). Intellectus, however, is the higher and more nearly angelic faculty. For example, 'we are enjoying intellectus when we 'just see' a self-evident truth' (Lewis 1964: 157). Intellectus is more nearly angelic than ratio because angels were presumed to apprehend truths directly, that is by intellectus, and to have no need of the comparatively cumbersome and indirect devices of reasoning. Intellectus, not reasoning as we understand the term now, was the highest human faculty.

Just as ratio is the epitome of thinking, being its most rigorously logical form, so intellectus is the epitome of feeling, being its most clear, immediate, and trustworthy form. Here we see something of the subjective importance of feelings: the concept of the rational soul and the hierarchy of faculties may have disappeared from common sense, but the apparent immediacy of feelings as a guide to reality is reminiscent of the directness and incorrigibility of intellectus. Intuition, perhaps, is the closest modern relative of intellectus.

## Characteristics of feeling

To summarise, the characteristics of feeling all resemble or are analogous to the main characteristics of perceptual feeling.

First, just as perceptual feeling is believed to be more direct and immediate than seeing or hearing, by virtue of the fact that one is in physical contact with the thing felt, so feeling is more direct and immediate than any kind of thinking.

Secondly, just as perceptual feeling is actively directed by the perceiver (as in the use of the hand), so feeling is an activity directed by <<I>> except that conscious control is not required because of the sureness, swiftness, and immediacy of the activity.

Thirdly, just as perceptual feeling is directed in a way that is expressive of the person's individuality; for instance, in choosing to stroke the fur of a cat because one likes the feel of it, so feeling involves and expresses the individuality and sensitivity of the person, in that one does not expect others to feel as one does. Different people can see the same thing at the same time, and one expects them to agree on what they see once allowance is made for point of view; but different people are unlikely to feel the same thing at the same time because they must be in actual physical contact with different things or different parts of a thing.

Fourthly, just as perceptual feeling can be used for things for which other faculties would normally be used but cannot for some reason (as in feeling one's way because it is too dark to see), so feeling can be used with connotations of uncertainty for judgements which would normally be made in other ways (for example, consulting an encyclopaedia) but which for some reason cannot be made that way.

## The nature of feeling

Thinking and feeling can both be kinds of judgement, in the broadest sense of the term. Indeed, they denote what are, in common sense at least, the most basic forms of judgement. Why two basic forms, and why is the effortful, time-consuming, and indirect appearance of one contrasted with the effortless, swift, and direct appearance of the other?

I argued earlier that a basic distinction can be made between automatic and controlled causal processing. I now argue that the same distinction can be drawn in respect of all kinds of judgement. Automatic judgements are those made by stable, well learned routines not dependent upon attention and not confined by the limited capacity of short-term memory. Controlled judgements are those made in ways that are not well learned, that is on problems to which well-learned routines cannot be or are not applied, and subject to the limited capacity of short-term memory. My hypothesis is that people apply the concept and term of 'thinking' to any activity of controlled judgement, and the concept and term of 'feeling' to any activity of automatic judgement. As for the things called feelings, they are products of judgemental processes, but not only of automatic processes of judgement. Outcomes of judgement can be stored in memory and retrieved on later occasions, when the process or activity of which they were the product is either forgotten or not retrieved: so the noun 'feeling' can be used for any outcome of judgement retrieved from memory, so long as information about how it was generated is either not available or not retrieved.

The overlap between feeling and thinking, the plausibility of substituting one term for the other in some expressions, is therefore a consequence of the fact that feeling and thinking denote different ways of doing the same thing – namely, making a judgement. The fact that 'feel' cannot be substituted for 'think' in some expressions reflects the fact that information is available about the activity of judgement which precludes the possibility of its being an outcome of feeling. That is, if there is enough information available for it to be identified as a specific type of thinking, then there is enough for it to fall outside the definition of feeling. For example, availability of information about a process of reasoning, such as a series of intermediate products, is incompatible with the definition of feeling as direct, and so the term 'feeling' would not be used under such circumstances. How the automatic processes identified as feeling actually operate is of no relevance for present purposes: it is the fact of their automaticity, and what that implies about speed of execution and lack of involvement of attention, that matters.

The hypothesis about feelings explains some of the subjective properties of feelings. They are believed not to be consciously controlled because automatic judgement is in fact not carried out attentively. Feelings are characterised as relatively direct or intuitive in relation to the relevant part of reality because (1) the speed of automatic processing means that the product of the judgemental process emerges very quickly after the input of the relevant information and (2) the fact that the processing is not attentive means that there appears, from the point of view of any process that might form beliefs about what is going on, to be little or nothing intervening between information and judgement, and the person is not able to specify criteria (and so on) used in the judgemental process. They may be able to identify (correctly or incorrectly) reasons and other information relevant to the feeling, but not how input information is converted into a judgement, except possibly by some sort of *post hoc* rationalisation, such as the use of cultural beliefs as hypothesised by Nisbett and Wilson (1977). The same feature, the appearance that there is nothing much going on, explains the occasional connotation of uncertainty: one knows how one knows something when one consults an encyclopaedia, but one doesn't know how one knows something when relying on feelings, in the sense of feeling one's way, instead, because of the unavailability of information about the process.

One of the main differences between thinking and feeling, under this hypothesis, is the apparent directness of the latter, which the former does not appear to possess. It is this which leads people to place greater trust in things felt than in things worked out through the kinds of thinking. Thinking is less trustworthy because it seems to be further removed from reality, not so constrained by it. Feeling is direct, so must represent how things actually are. This leads me to suggest that people distrust mechanical procedures such as computer diagnosis and prediction from regression equations because they take the feeling out of judgement.

## FEELINGS AND JEA SEQUENCES

It is apparent so far that feelings can belong, along with other forms of judgement, in the judgement stage of a JEA sequence. There is more that differentiates feelings from thoughts and types of thinking, however, than automaticity. Feelings can have an evaluative component, and in fact most feeling statements imply, if not stating directly, evaluation as good or bad, pleasant or unpleasant, right or wrong, by their use of words with those connotations. Strictly speaking, 'I usually feel out of place at social gatherings of any size' is a judgement of a matter of fact, or perhaps a judgement of frequency; in fact, everyone recognises the negative evaluative connotation of the statement.

Feelings, and in particular their evaluative component, are taken as indicators of how one is doing with regard to one's practical concerns. Thus, bad or negative or unpleasant feelings or feelings of wrongness show something going wrong with practical concerns, and good feelings show that things are going right, or that attempts to get things right are going well. The propositional content of feelings is important because it is the means by which people can relate different feelings and practical concerns to each other. Thus, 'I usually feel out of place at social gatherings of any size' is a specific assertion, the propositional content of which is necessary if the writer is to make use of it in relation to, say, a decision about whether to attend a party or not; but the influence of it on this decision is in accordance with the criterion of avoiding bad feelings, so that it effectively reduces the likelihood that the writer will decide to attend the party. There are three main roles that feelings play with respect to judgement, decisions about behaviour, and so on.

First, feelings initiate judgemental activities. As stated, bad feelings are taken as indicators that something has gone wrong with respect to one's practical concerns, and as a result activities are initiated to try to set things right – judgemental processes aiming at the practical concerns criterion. Examples from the essays are as follows:

> 'It makes me very sad to feel that I am being carried along by events and if I feel this at any time I try to change things.'

> 'I don't feel I'm getting anywhere with this. I'll try again from recent events.'

Secondly, feelings can be used as criteria for judgement. A good judgement, by the practical concerns criterion, is one that is in accordance with feelings one already has. For example, 'I usually feel out of place in a social gathering of any size' is a feeling that may be taken into account when deciding whether to attend a social occasion or not. If this is the only relevant feeling and there are no other relevant practical concerns, then the optimally rational judgement is the judgement in accordance with the feeling, presumably in this case that it would be better not to attend the party.

In most cases it is likely that more than one feeling is relevant (I shall ignore practical concerns other than feelings for convenience), and it may not be possible to judge in accordance with all feelings. For example, 'I usually feel out of place at a social gathering of any size' may conflict with another feeling 'I'd feel worse about myself if I chickened out again.' The process of judgement can then be described as a contest between these feelings, in which the stronger one wins out. This is a simplification because the strength of a feeling need not be fixed, and can change if the person concerned ponders about it. But, basically, one judges in accordance with the stronger feeling or set of feelings. The aim in such cases is to produce or preserve feelings that are subjectively experienced as good or positive, and to avoid or terminate those that are subjectively experienced as bad or negative. Here I am using the term 'feeling' in its broad sense to encompass not only products of judgemental processes that have evaluative loadings but also the 'emotional' side of feeling, since the evaluative dimension is prominent in relation to these. Three of the five examples of abstract criteria for evaluation given earlier make explicit reference to feelings:

'I've learned to recognise when a person or experience is good for me – by comparison against other possible feelings I've gradually become able to rate it for myself.'

'I'd be happier doing what *I* felt' (that is, rather than following the advice of others).

'If I did not see eye to eye with my husband I should have stuck to principles I felt deeply were right.'

Thirdly, feelings are used as retrospective evaluations of judgements or decisions made, acts committed, and so on. By the practical concerns standard, a good judgement is one that brings about good feelings, feelings of rightness, and so on, and a bad judgement one that brings about bad feelings. This is to propose that the activity of feeling, an automatic process, a routine which once put into operation proceeds rapidly and without the involvement of attention, can be used to check or evaluate judgemental outcomes. The activity is optional and its occurrence is determined primarily by the individual's practical concerns at the time. Also optional after a feeling of not-rightness has emerged is some kind of search for an explanation for the feeling; and in this way the activity of judgement continues. Feelings are how to tell whether the practical concerns in respect of which the judgement or decision was made were optimally satisfied or not: they are the lay person's equivalent of the normative standards of science.

'I feel I was irresponsible in marrying as I did.'

'I felt absolutely no guilt at all, and still don't, and no regrets.'

'I felt strengthened and calmed as I hadn't felt for years.'

Readers may regret the appearance of vagueness in these accounts. One major merit of a theory such as Kelley's (1967) ANOVA model of causal attribution is that it is relatively precise and ubiquitous: under that theory, people always make causal attributions in a set way and using the same types of information. Under the present theory things are not always the same, and the activity of judgement is permeated by choice points in which people may or may not do certain things, according to the practical concerns that prevail for them at the time; and the range of possible processes is much wider, in accordance with the variability not only of practical concerns but also of the types of information that people may have to handle. The rigorous sampling procedures that make exact and invariable techniques possible for science are not feasible for ordinary people. The same problem, and given the same information, may still legitimately be handled in different ways by different people, according to differences in their practical concerns at the time of judgement. The termination of a judgemental activity comes when the judge decides that the outcome thus far is adequate to satisfy practical concerns: checking outcomes against practical concerns may occur frequently during the course of a judgemental activity.

Although I have used the term 'strength' in relation to feelings, it is not easy to define this. Strength is basically the evaluative weighting of a feeling, but this may be modified by other factors such as the certainty that the thing felt is correct. I suspect that strength is the relation between a feeling and practical concerns. This covers both the positive/negative loading and the definiteness of the place of the feeling in practical concerns. A thing strongly felt is a thing both strongly positive or negative and a thing with definite, undoubted relevance to practical concerns.

This chapter is avowedly exploratory. I have attempted to show that lay judgement needs to be reconceptualised in terms of the judge's practical concerns; that feelings are important rational contributers to judgemental activities; that the activity of judgement needs to be studied *in vivo* if we are to avoid engendering a misleading representation of lay judgemental competence, not to mention the purpose of lay judgement. Studying lay judgement as it should be studied is very much more difficult than studying it as it has been studied: but we fail our scientific concerns if we ignore the shortcomings of our scientific procedures.

# Summary and comments

## SUMMARY

The whole set of beliefs which people possess about the world and everything in it, including themselves, is an organised construction, grounded in things that function as axioms, the metaphysical assumptions which depend on nothing but on which all else in the construction depends. This book therefore has set out to elucidate and explain the metaphysical assumptions in the psychological construction of reality, focusing on a set of key questions.

1  What are the metaphysical assumptions and how do they originate (Chapters 4–7 and 11–12), and what are they there for (Chapter 2)?
2  What is it for something to be basic in the psychological construction of reality; or, what is the main organising principle of that construction (Chapter 3)?
3  How are the observable phenomena of social cognition and social psychology in general grounded in psychological metaphysics (Chapters 8–10 and 13–15)?

In social cognition the traditional view of function has been that the primary aims of inference, judgement, and attribution are understanding, prediction, and control, understanding being the most important of these, qualified by the need for economy of effort and time in the face of heavy demands on processing capacity. The view put forward here is that the primary aim of inference, and so on, is to serve the practical concerns of the judge at the time of judgement, whatever they may be, and that any desire for understanding is strictly subsidiary to this. People will not aim for understanding or accuracy in judgement where it is not in the service of their practical concerns to do so.

Basicity is defined in terms of imaginary existential dependence. This is the main structural principle defining the organisation of beliefs in the construction of reality. The metaphysical assumptions at the base of the construction are existentially dependent on nothing except one another, and that is what it means to say they are basic. The more things are existentially dependent on some element, the more resistance to change that element possesses. This is because, when an element changes, every element that is existentially dependent on it must change as well. Thus, people hold onto elements not because of the weight of evidence that supports them but because of the weight of elements that they support. People prefer changes in elements that entail the fewest changes to the construction of reality.

The basic categories in the psychological construction of reality are being and happening. Being is understood in terms of primary substances with properties: the prototypical being is solid, self-contained, distinct, passively maintained (as opposed to the active maintenance of natural systems), and possesses natural inertia, meaning that its natural persistence does not require explanation. Happening is defined as a sudden change in the amount or type of change occurring in some property of a substance, and 'sudden' is defined in terms of the temporal integration function of iconic processing. This marks the distinction between being and happening. The definition of happening broadens during development.

Happening relates to causation. The basic concept of causation is as a generative relation in which a causal power of a primary substance operates to produce an effect under some suitable releasing condition. Reference may also be made to the liability of the thing acted upon. Causal inferences and attributions are made through either automatic or controlled processing, by applying specific acquired beliefs about the causal powers of things. In controlled causal processing, a causal inference can be viewed as an answer to an implicit or explicit question. The type of information preferred for inferential purposes is information about the occasion or occasions implicit or explicit in the question, and the aim is to answer the question posed. Thus, types of regularity information are preferred for corresponding types of question about multiple occasions. Regularity information may also be used to answer questions about single occasions when preferred types of information are not available, and is also useful when ascertaining the relative strength of a power or liability.

The origin of the basic concept of causation lies in infancy. The earliest instance of causal processing may occur in perception of launching effect stimuli, but these stimuli can give rise only to a concept of causation based on transfer of properties, and perhaps the idea of releasing conditions, through the necessity of physical contact in the launching effect. The concept of a generative relation is thought to originate in the experience of efficacy in the production of action (Piaget); the concept of power from the differentiation of cause from effect followed by the development of understanding of specificity and stability in causes; the concept of a releasing condition from the acquisition of spatial relations, if not already from the launching effect. These concepts are all generalised beyond their source during the course of development, but do not change in themselves.

It is convenient to regard the construction of the physical world as organised at a number of hierarchical levels from individual occurrences through to an overall world view. People understand the world and happenings in it as possessing natural lawful order and stability.

At the level of individual occurrences a number of topics can be distinguished, including mechanical and qualitative causation, possible differences in the conceptualisation of causes internal and external to things, and causation in the natural and artificial realms. Individual causal relations are linked by natural processes, defined as change in at least one property of at least one thing and in which there are either no events or only events that are wholly automatically causally processed.

At a higher level, beliefs about causal relations are organised into chains and hierarchies. There is evidence that causal beliefs relating categories in the natural world are arranged in a unidirectional (Aristotelian) causal hierarchy, and this tendency can be explained in terms of the causal powers theory. Chains of causal beliefs tend to be linear, as opposed to feedback loops and cycles. The world view of common sense resembles what I have termed the anthropomorphic machine: people understand the world as a large and complex machine that works smoothly and never runs down, but also one that is endowed with the anthropomorphic qualities of purposiveness, direction towards mature forms, constructiveness, and natural justice.

The psychological construction of reality embodies a strong metaphysical distinction between the physical world and the mind, under which the mind possesses unique properties. The third part of the book considers these. First, action is distinguished from all other types of happening in that people understand it as being up to the actor what he or she does in cases of action. The basic concept of action is simply that the actor, or <<I>>, performs or carries out action, where <<I>> is understood as an enduring substance. The experience of efficacy is the identifier of action, and the origin of the concept of action: action and causation are differentiated during development as the concepts of power and generative relations are applied to occurrences not accompanied by the experience of efficacy.

I then consider how people form beliefs about the mind, their own or the mind in general. Under the traditional view, <<I>> uses its capacities of consciousness and the ability to produce actions to turn conscious awareness onto whatever of mental activity it chooses to 'look at'. The means of access of <<I>> to mental activity, conscious awareness, operates by analogy with perception, except that it is direct (that is, incorrigible, unmediated) perception. <<I>> forms beliefs unproblematically from that to which it gains access. Consideration of the consequences of the physicalist assumption, however, shows that this view cannot be correct.

The view proposed here is that the problem of information availability is not one of a relation between perceiver and object of perception but one of a relation between occurrence and interpretation, thanks to the essential transience of mental occurrences. Availability of information to belief-forming processes is determined by the functional allocation of attention in mental activity. Beliefs are formed by processes of construction from available information, using cultural beliefs, personal beliefs, analogies, and so on, in the interpretation of that information.

This analysis reveals the metaphysical bases of the psychological construction of the mind. <<I>> is conceptualised as an enduring substance. <<I>> has as capacities consciousness and the ability to produce actions, which together enable conscious awareness, conscious control, and self-awareness. The basic categories of mental occurrence are being and happening, constructed by analogy with being and happening as understood in the physical world. Causal processing of mental occurrences occurs only for those occurrences interpreted as happenings. Happening is divided into mental actions, understood as produced in the way that behavioural actions are understood as produced except for the fact of being mental, and other mental events, understood as caused in the way that physical events are understood as caused, again except for the fact of being mental.

The psychological metaphysics of the mind has implications for all topics in social cognition and social psychology, some of which are considered in the final three chapters.

In the case of action, personality characteristics are peripheral to action and do not cause it. Explanations for the origination of action tend to refer to such things as intentions, purposes, desires, and beliefs, and personality is less important than it is traditionally regarded as being in causal attribution research. The kind of personal characteristic referred to in causal attribution also depends on the kind of question asked about action. The internal/external distinction, proposed by Heider as basic to causal attribution, is not basic because it confounds the distinction between action and other forms of behaviour, both of which may include reference to either internal or external factors in explanations. This analysis also has implications for the study of actor/observer differences in causal attribution. In addition, there can be no such thing as a 'fundamental' causal attribution error in the case of action, because no action is caused by any external thing or factor.

As far as the mind and behaviour are concerned, people see two possible ways of producing behaviour and mental events, one involving <<I>> and consciousness producing behavioural or mental actions, and the other involving the deterministic, non-conscious operation of powers of the mind. These two sources of behaviour and mental events can come into conflict, and the idea of a conflict of this sort is used to interpret notions of rationality and bias, and consistency and inconsistency. It is further shown that mental health or normality tends to be defined in terms of the dominance of <<I>> over other sources of mental events and behaviour. These ideas are associated with a hierarchical conceptualisation of nature, and evidence for the survival of some elements of this chain of being in common sense is reviewed.

The final chapter presents a reconsideration of judgement from the perspective of this book. Judgement is seen as contributing to the practical concerns of the judge and a simple model of the place of judgement in practical concerns, based on analysis of extracts from self-report essays, is proposed. Feelings are analysed as products of automatic processes of judgement conceptualised by analogy with tactile perception. Feelings, in their role as judgements, are indicators of how the judge is doing with regard to his or her practical concerns. They initiate judgemental activity, are used as criteria for judgement, and as retrospective evaluations; for example, of actions undertaken.

## COMMENTS

### Content and social function of the construction of reality

I have talked very little about the contents of the psychological construction of reality. I have said that these are elements, and that an element can have either or both of two kinds of attitude attached to it, a truth value (relating to the true/false dimension) or an evaluation (relating to the good/bad dimension) Attitudes of both kinds may qualify the resistance to change of elements. An element with a strong attitude of belief attached to it, independent of its place in the construction, may thereby be more resistant to change than an element with a weaker attitude of belief or no attitude of belief at all, other things being equal. An element with a strong feeling attached to it, perhaps especially of a positive character, may thereby be more resistant to change than an element with just as much existentially dependent on it but without strong feeling attached to it.

For an element to survive in the construction, it is not necessary that the person should believe it to be true. What holds a stereotype in the construction of reality, for example, is not just that it is believed to be true – it may not be believed to be true at all – but the fact that it has existentially dependent upon it a whole lot of things which the person who holds it finds useful. For a start, the stereotype provides a basis for communication with others: a set of shared stereotypes helps us to communicate by giving us a common construction of reality to inhabit, the elements of which can be left implicit in social discourse because it is understood that everyone shares them. Secondly, the stereotype serves social functions. For example, a person may have a stored record of jokes about the stereotype by using which they may make a contribution to social occasions. The jokes are existentially dependent upon the stereotype and thereby increase its resistance to change, even though the person may not believe the stereotype to be true. Likewise, the features in the stereotype help that person to understand jokes told by others.

Stereotypes, and indeed any elements of the construction of reality, do not exist primarily to serve cognitive or information processing functions. They exist primarily to serve social functions, and it is these that anchor them in the construction of reality. If they ignore these social functions, social cognition researchers will never understand why stereotypes do not change in response to contradictory evidence.

In the chapter on basicity I included a hypothetical model of a construction of reality with no particular content. In this book I have been concerned with one particular type of content, that of universal metaphysical assumptions about being and happening. However, in principle, anything could go in. To bar any kind of content would be to make a metaphysical assumption of my own, and at present I see no good reason for this. Consider an example. A metaphysical axiom could be 'the world is an unsafe place'. Note that this assumption is (probably) not universal. Note also that there is nothing intrinsic to the proposition that compels it to function as an axiom. It could be installed anywhere in the construction of reality. But there is nothing, a priori, to bar it from functioning as a metaphysical assumption. It is perhaps more likely to function as an axiom if it is acquired early in development, but this is an empirical question.

Now the point about this is that, precisely because it is not universal, this axiom can be characterised not just as an element in a psychological construction of reality, but as a *personality* characteristic, an individuating factor. Moreover, because it lies deep in the construction of reality it is likely to be very resistant to change, thus constituting a stable influence on its possessor's outlook on reality. For the same reason, it is likely that there will be many elements in that individual's construction of reality that are existentially dependent upon it – elements concerning judgements of and beliefs about risk, for example. Many instances of judgement may involve implicit application of the proposition in its function as an axiom just as many instances of judgement involve application of the basic concept of causation.

This is not intended as a complete account of personality. No doubt much of personality is made up of things that do not belong to the construction of reality at all: degree of extroversion/introversion may be one such, for example. But it does seem plausible that personality, considered as a stable orientation upon reality, incorporates elements from deep within the psychological construction of reality, elements upon which many of the individual's beliefs, feelings, judgements, and tendencies in action may be existentially dependent.

I have emphasised that the metaphysical axioms tend to be laid down early in life and to remain unchanged through development. This appears to contradict Piaget's idea of stages in cognitive development, such that the whole structure of knowledge is transformed in the transition from one stage to the next. The contradiction is not real, however. First, Piaget also held that much of what is learnt during the sensorimotor period continues unchanged through development: this applies to the appreciation of spatial relations, for example, which is a condition for the acquisition of later knowledge of the properties of objects and processes. Secondly, the construction of reality changes continually through development, but most changes are to elements which have little or nothing dependent on them. Elements deeper down have greater resistance to change, therefore change less often. But every now and then one such does change, and this change, with concomitant change in every element that is existentially dependent upon it, corresponds to a transition from one Piagetian stage to the next. This does not explain how such transitions come about, of course: it is only to argue that there is nothing implausible about modelling such changes as changes at deep levels of the construction of reality.

## Mental faculties

There can be little doubt that this book has not uncovered the whole range of topics to be found in psychological metaphysics. The basic distinction between mind with its exclusive properties and everything else, how that distinction originates and develops, how mind and various of its properties are attributed to other things or not, these constitute a set of topics in psychological metaphysics of the most fundamental importance. The notion of a 'theory of mind' as it is currently being conceptualised in psychology, is only the tip of the iceberg.

Within the mind, I have distinguished powers and liabilities, being and happening, action and consciousness, associated through being regarded as capacities of <<I>>, other behaviour and mental occurrences. Are these the complete set of fundamental categorical distinctions that people make in reference to the mind? One can find, both in common sense and in the philosophical and psychological literature, frequent references to distinctions between reason and emotion, intellect and will, belief and desire, cognition and affect (or motivation, particularly as contrasted sources of bias in processes of judgement and inference). These distinctions have a kind of family resemblance, and they are used so commonly that we must consider whether they serve to identify some fundamental distinction between faculties of the mind, whether independent of or related to those already considered.

The idea of distinct natural faculties within the mind has a long history, and is indeed one of the main themes in theories of human nature (Trigg 1988; Stephenson 1981). One of the most ancient and influential theories of the structure of the mind is that of Plato (Trigg 1988). Plato distinguished three parts to the human mind. One part was the faculty of reason, the remainder consisted of the emotional elements, comprising the bodily desires (hunger, thirst, and so on) and the spirited element (the passions). Thus Plato made a fundamental categorical distinction between reason and the passions. Through reason we aspire to virtue, to the condition of the gods; through passion we tend to be dragged down towards the condition of the beasts. Passion disrupts the otherwise perfect rationality of the faculty of reason.

This established a theme which runs through the whole course of the history of ideas. By medieval times the structure of the mind had become much more elaborate, but retained the Platonic notion of an absolute distinction between reason and emotion, with reason at a higher, more positively valued hierarchical level in the mind (Lewis 1964; Curry 1960; Tillyard 1943). The faculty of reason was marked out as uniquely human, the attribute by virtue of which humans fall between angels and beasts in the chain of being: other animals have passions, memory, and imagination, but do not have the capacity to reason.

Modern accounts of the structure of the mind lack the hierarchical ordering and implicit or explicit value judgements of these older ideas, but in other respects look similar. For example Kenny (1989) divided the mind into intellect and will. This division, like the medieval version, excludes such things as the senses, memory, and imagination. Kenny defined the mind as the capacity to acquire capacities (this is a functional definition), and the capacities which it can acquire are of two basic kinds, cognitive and volitional. He offered a heuristic guide for differentiating intellect and will: 'Those states and activities which can be evaluated on the true/false scale belong to the cognitive side of the mind [intellect]; those states and activities which are evaluated on the good/evil scale belong to the affective, volitional side of the soul [will]' (p. 75). Under the intellect come cognition and cognitive activities, beliefs, concepts, and judgement. Cognition comprises such things as awareness, expectation, certainty, and knowledge. Under the will come affect, meaning, and wants, which comprise desire and volition. Indeed, I have applied this scheme myself in claiming that elements in the construction of reality have two kinds of attitude, truth value and positive or negative evaluation.

This consistent theme in the history of ideas, whatever its sources or justification in fact, has exerted great influence not only on common sense but also on psychological theory. This was made apparent by Averill (1974) in his analysis of theories of emotion. Averill (1974) traced the dichotomy between reason and emotion back as far as Anaxagoras (500 BC) and showed that the tendency to ascribe opposed properties to emotion and reason has been a consistent feature of theories of emotion since that time. He argued that all such theories in psychology, at least until the 1960s, shared certain characteristics which could be traced to these long-established ideas about the structure of the mind. These characteristics are passivity, irrationality, involuntariness, and animality. These can all be contrasted with traditional ideas about the faculty of reason, which is characterised as active, rational, voluntary, and divine or angelic.

A somewhat similar dichotomy can be found in the field of social inference, between 'cognitive' and 'motivational' biases in judgement. I have discussed these elsewhere in this book. Briefly, cognitive biases refer to supposed defects and shortcomings in the processes of judgement: that is, the judge attempts to make an accurate judgement, but goes astray because of imperfections in the mechanics of the judgemental process (Miller and Ross 1975; Nisbett and Ross 1980). Motivational biases, on the other hand, refer to ways in which needs and motivational states can supposedly disrupt judgement. These include such things as the desire to protect or enhance self-esteem, or the need for belief in a just world (Nisbett and Ross 1980; Zuckerman 1979; Harvey and Weary 1984).

Although a considerable variety of things falls into either class (Nisbett and Ross 1980; Tetlock and Levi 1982), they have been consistently treated as distinct, to the extent that there was at one time a debate in social cognition as to whether shortcomings of social judgement might be either all cognitive or all motivational. Throughout this debate, the validity of the distinction between them does not appear to have been questioned. The distinction was interestingly characterised by Nisbett and Ross (1980) as 'cold' (cognitive) versus 'hot' (motivational).

It is hard to escape from some kind of distinction between cognition and volition: as philosophers have said before, without volition we would never do anything and without cognition we would never know what to do. On the other hand, without an empirical investigation of some kind it is equally hard to know just how the mind is divided in common sense: that is, how mental occurrence terms fall into different categories.

Research on lay judgement and inference has been profoundly influenced by the idea of the ordinary person as a naïve scientist. As we have seen, this idea has even affected the kinds of judgement that people are thought to engage in. These include such things as covariation assessment, causal inference, prediction, and theory maintenance (Nisbett and Ross 1980). A glance at these categories suffices to show that they are purely intellectual categories of judgement. Volition, as we have seen, is considered only as a source of bias (motivational factors). In Kenny's terms, this would mean that the only evaluative criteria applicable to judgements are those based on truth and falsity.

This is an error of immense proportions. It could only have been made because of the fact that research isolates individual instances of judgement from their natural context in the mental life of the person who makes them, and employs purely intellectual criteria of the sort used in science to assess them. It must surely be the case that intellect and volition are in continual mutual interaction; that, for example, the evaluative criteria used on judgemental outcomes by ordinary people are often, if not always, volitional rather than intellectual. This would be a strange assertion to make if the categories of judgement were indeed the quasi-scientific categories of the account by Nisbett and Ross (1980); but it is not at all strange if we start to look at the categories of judgement from the perspective of the practical concerns orientation. Here, affective criteria are the primary indicators of whether a judgement satisfies practical concerns or not. I have explored this topic earlier in the book; and it appears that common-sense notions of mental faculties, derived perhaps from the long-established traditions of thought summarised here, may have an important part to play in this. This is by way of saying that the ideas presented here are only a beginning, opening up a new field rich with possibilities.

## Constructing a causal interpretation

Here I would like to lay emphasis on a theme mentioned in passing earlier in the book. Making a causal attribution does not involve merely observing some behaviour and inferring a cause of it. Observers (and actors) construct causal interpretations of greatly varying complexity, and explicit causal attributions, answers to explicit or implicit causal questions, are selections made from this causal interpretation.

Let me take a hypothetical example. John leaps into a shop doorway. One possible causal interpretation of this might run as follows. John's behaviour was an action carried out by <<I>> (namely, John) in accordance with a conscious intention formulated by <<I>>. Evidently, John has the causal power to act in this way and the intention was formulated with full knowledge or presumption of this power. It is raining; the doorway is the nearest place of shelter; it appears to be unoccupied. Presumably these facts were apparent to John as they are to the attributer. Presumably, for John the practical concern of avoiding getting wet was predominant in his formulation of the plan of jumping into the doorway. Perhaps in turn this reflects a stable disposition of not liking to get wet. As it happens, John bumps into someone coming out of the shop. This is an unintended consequence of his action.

Much of this causal interpretation is likely to be constructed automatically – that is, it is a highly skilled activity. There may be little deliberation. But it serves to identify a number of research issues for causal attribution.

1 How do people decide that behaviour was action or not? Further, how do they judge whether it was consciously controlled action or not?
2 How do people distinguish intended from unintended consequences of actions?
3 How do people attribute reasons (that is, practical concerns or facts or states of affairs relevant to practical concerns)?

These questions are quite separate from the problem of how people answer a particular causal question. Arguably, they have been neglected. Researchers have concentrated on how people answer causal questions (that is, make explicit causal attributions) and have ignored how people construct the causal interpretation from which the answer to the causal question is produced.

There has so far been little relevant research, but let me offer a few conjectures as to how people distinguish actions from other behaviours. Langer (1978) argued that people assume that their own and others' behaviour is carried out under full conscious awareness, in a deliberative manner. The thrust of her research was to show that much ordinary social behaviour was not carried out in a thoughtful manner, by inducing people to do things that they would recognise as absurd if they thought about it. Her arguments and findings support the contention that people assume that behaviour is action (that is, done consciously by <<I>>) under normal circumstances. This is a kind of default assumption, suspended only in the face of evidence that behaviour was not conscious and intended. I would suggest at least four circumstances under which this happens.

1 In the case of errors such as slips of the tongue, tripping, mis-hits at tennis, and so forth. This begs the question of how observers identify errors, which must involve the use of contextual cues and general knowledge (such as knowing that you cannot win a point at tennis by serving the ball into the net).
2 By the actor's responses (for example, saying, 'I didn't mean to do that', responding in a manner interpreted as expressing embarrassment, attempting a correction such as repeating an utterance without the parapraxis it contained the first time).
3 By speed of reaction. The idea of conscious, intentional behaviour implies the involvement of a certain amount of time – appraising the situation or events,

constructing a plan, and putting it into operation – and people may identify as non-conscious responses which clearly occur more quickly than the amount of time they believe to be involved in this. Thus, one can hear tennis commentators calling some shots 'instinctive', which can be interpreted to mean that they were skilled but none the less too quick to be actions performed by <<I>>.

4  Behaviours interpreted as representing the evocation of liabilities. Liabilities, as already argued, are not seen as involving conscious control because they are evoked by other things, usually if not always external to the actor. While <<I>> may be deemed to have been consciously aware of the response, <<I>> will therefore not be deemed to have produced it. Which behaviours are interpreted in this way is an empirical question, but it might include such things as startle or surprise responses, and some kinds of facial expression.

## Nature and culture, science and the history of ideas

There are two steps in the theory of psychological metaphysics presented here. In the first, causal processing and higher-order mental processes such as processes of judgement and inference are explained in terms of psychological metaphysics: that is, they are explained as constructions erected on foundations consisting of things that work as metaphysical assumptions. The job of culture, society, and all other factors in the environment is to shape the extension and construction of the person's understanding of reality from and upon these metaphysical assumptions. In the second step, those metaphysical assumptions are explained in terms of simple basic psychological facts, basic in the sense that they are present and operative (albeit unsophisticated) from the start or near the start of life. The metaphysical bases *never change*: change, such as abolition of one belief, process, way of thinking, and so on and replacement by a different one, is always at a less basic level.

Much research on judgement and inference has tended to explain the phenomena of judgement in terms of processes. For example, Kelley's ANOVA model, although not a precise description of processes, none the less seeks to explain causal attribution in terms of a set procedure for transforming a certain kind of input information (about covariation along each of three particular dimensions) into a judgement of causal locus. The representativeness heuristic (Kahneman and Tversky 1972, 1973) is a process which takes a certain kind of input information (about salient characteristics of a sample), compares it with other information (the corresponding characteristics of a population) in such a way as to produce a judgement of similarity between the two, and transforms the similarity judgement into a judgement of likelihood that the sample was drawn from the population.

The representativeness heuristic, to take one example, is probably not unreasonable as it stands: what is good about it, if the supporting research findings are valid, is that it subsumes a variety of judgemental phenomena under a common explanatory device. The problem, however, is that it (and other process models) carry a spurious appearance of explanatory power. We can say, people exhibit certain predictable judgemental tendencies because they are using the representativeness heuristic and not using relevant information such as base rate information: but why are they using a representativeness heuristic and not, say, a base rate information heuristic? Where does the heuristic come from? Why do other possible heuristics not come from there? Something that is arbitrary, set up by fiat, or 'just wired up that way' does not really explain. What determines the particular processes, routines, judgemental devices, and so on, that people actually possess?

My answer to this is that processes and so forth reflect and conform to fundamental assumptions: that the process is, in fact, merely a way to get from assumptions to judgements, and people will use *any* process that enables them to do that – any process, in other words, that does not violate their fundamental assumptions. Some assumptions are given by culture, some by nature, and it is the latter that are truly fundamental, the axioms of the system. An example of the latter would be the temporal integration function of iconic processing, proposed here as the source of the conceptual distinction between being and happening.

The effect of these foundations is to delimit a range of possible belief-systems, judgemental devices, processes, and so on. The range actually possessed by an individual is further delimited by culture (as well as by the capacity of individuals and groups to develop new ideas, belief-systems, processes, and so forth).

The point about culture is worth pursuing. Because we are surrounded by people who share our culture and our ways of thought to a large extent, it is difficult to falsify the notion that these ways of thought are universal, or even part of human nature. For example, we think of people as consisting of (among other things) more or less stable personality characteristics that act as dispositions in shaping behaviour, expressing the individuality of their possessors, and rendering their behaviour roughly predictable. We have hundreds of trait descriptors – Norman (1967) studied 2,800 – and the whole literature on impression formation is devoted almost exclusively to personality traits and behaviour descriptors, ignoring the place in impressions of attitudes, beliefs, feelings, thoughts, values, temperament, and other classes of individuating factor, considering how these traits are organised into coherent representations of individuality. By contrast, consider what passed for individuating characteristics to the medieval mind, and the implications for explanations of behaviour.

The medieval world was a comprehensive hierarchy of being in which individual things were identified largely in terms of their place in the hierarchical order. Human beings were below angels and above animals, and were distinguished from the latter by virtue of their possession of a rational soul, seat of the faculty of reason (Lewis 1964; Tillyard 1943). Indeed, the mind itself was regarded as a hierarchy of faculties, in which the lowest faculties were those that humans shared with plants, such as growth and nutrition, and the faculty of reason was highest because of its exclusive association with humanity.

Although all humans possessed all human faculties, humans differed one from another in various respects. Just as nature was a fixed hierarchical order, so was society, and individuals had places in the social order that were as fixed, as natural, and as hierarchically constrained, as the places of things in nature. Thus place in the social order gave people such identity as they possessed: 'Man in feudal society is corporate man. In greater or lesser degree, he seeks integration in the group to which he belongs, adopting its standards, its ideals and its values, its ways of thought, its patterns of behaviour and the symbolism which imbues it' (Gurevich 1985: 298). Life on Earth is in the service of God, and that service is best executed by fitting into one's place as exactly as possible – by being one's type. This positively discourages individuality, which is viewed pejoratively as imperfection or deviation from one's proper type.

Personality trait labels were hardly used, and never in the way that they are used now. The original meaning of 'persona' was 'mask', as in a theatrical mask, and in the Middle Ages people only had personalities to the extent that they exemplified a 'type', the personification of a role or a value. There were, however, other ideas about individuating characteristics, coming from several sources.

1 *The four temperaments.* In medieval science there were four fundamental and opposing Constancies: hot, cold, wet, and dry. These combined in pairs to produce, in nature, the four elements, and in human physiology the four humours: melancholic (cold and dry); phlegmatic (cold and wet); sanguine (hot and wet); and choleric (hot and dry). In the ideal man (Christ) these four are in balance, but in most people one or another humour predominates, giving the person a corresponding temperament. The symbolism of the four humours was widely understood in the Middle Ages, and is superbly illustrated in the analysis of Bosch's 'Christ crowned with thorns' by Foster and Tudor-Craig (1986).
2 *Planetary influence.* In the medieval world view, the spheres of the planets transmit to Earth what are called Influences. These affect events, plants, minerals, and human psychology. According to Aquinas, the influence of the spheres is confined to the body, leaving the rational soul (reason and will) free. The will can be affected by the body and therefore indirectly by the spheres, but such influences can be resisted by the will (Lewis 1964).
3 *Physiognomic theories.* There was in the Middle Ages an extensive lore on physiognomy, concerning the ways in which one's character was indicated by one's physical features. These amount to physiognomic stereotypes, in that a type of character is identified by a type of feature. Thus, readers of Chaucer could obtain a detailed impression of a character from Chaucer's descriptions of that character's physiognomy (Curry 1960). The familiar association between red hair and quick temper is an example of a surviving remnant of this lore.

All this might give the impression that medieval people did have a view of personality or individuating characteristics basically similar to our own, and that they just had some strange ideas about determinants and indicators of personality characteristics. According to Gurevich (1985), however, there is a profound difference.

> Medieval man had a clear concept of the human personality: this personality is answerable to God and it possesses an indestructible metaphysical core – the soul; but it is not an individuality in our sense of the word. The insistence on what is common to all, typical, on the universal, on deconcretisation, militated against the formulation of any clear idea of human individuality.
>
> (Gurevich 1985: 308)

And:

> When the hero does something, it is not his personality as a whole that is acting but an aggregate of uncoordinated qualities and forces acting independently. Medieval realism personified vices and virtues . . . and conferred independent status on them. Thus, for the ecclesiastical chronicler it is a man's several attributes that take turns to act, not one integrated self.
>
> (Gurevich 1985: 304)

And:

> As a rule, medieval man did not see himself as the centre, as the coordinating agent at the core of actions affecting other persons. The inner life of the medieval individual did not 'jell' as an autonomous entity.
>
> (Gurevich 1985: 301)

And:

> Various forces [i.e., vices and virtues] struggle for supremacy in man's soul, but they are not activated or called into play by the personality. Hence, these forces or moral qualities are themselves impersonal, and vices and virtues are general concepts. They take on no individual colouring from the individual in whom they are housed; on the contrary, it is their presence in him that determines his mental condition and conduct.
>
> (Gurevich 1985: 304)

The last quotation in particular indicates the kind of causal attribution that might have made sense to the medieval mind: attribution to a characteristic that is internal but not part of the person – in a sense, the person is not responsible for conduct attributable to a quality housed within them. Even this, however, overlooks the fact that explanation meant something quite different then from what it means now. 'The world as a whole, as medieval man saw it, was not subject to the principles of causality. Events are linked not horizontally (in terms of "cause–effect", "action–reaction") but vertically through a hierarchy' (Gurevich 1985: 293). In simplest terms, to explain something was not to say how it came about but to identify its location in the general scheme, in the ordered hierarchy of the world. This is not to say that there was no concept of cause. The notion of the causal relation as involving power is an ancient one (and can be seen in the foregoing quotations – for example, in the references to moral qualities as 'forces', and in the idea of a battle for control of action between the will and planetary influences), and the Aristotelian concepts of efficient cause and final cause, and of natural development and interference, were commonplace. But they did not have the same place in the lay construction of reality as they have now.

The point of this is to warn against taking cognitive processes, such as processes of causal attribution, as universal, or absolute. To a large extent such processes should be viewed as cultural artefacts, as selections from the range allowed by the natural features of the system made in the light of experience gained during development. Thus, postulating a causal attribution process as an explanation for a range of causal attribution phenomena is only the first step. The process should be rooted in a cultural and historical account: it is only this that enables us to place limits on the generalisability of the phenomenon and the underlying process across cultures and historical periods. Equally important is to separate the natural features of the system from features acquired as a result of experience: this has been a major part of the aims of the present book. The metaphysical axioms of the psychological construction of reality are those things given as a direct consequence of the natural features of the system, those things that provide the foundations of the construction of reality in any time or culture (subject to evolutionary changes in the natural features of the system). What is built upon them is constrained by them and shaped by time and culture. Thus, social psychology is part science and part history, and the explanatory force of social psychological hypotheses can only be reduced if either of these aspects is ignored.

Relating this back to the representativeness heuristic, the kind of further explanatory step one could take is to say that people use the representativeness heuristic because it conforms to an assumption or theory relating similarity to likelihood; and they don't use processes that incorporate base rate information (such as a naïve version of Bayes' theorem) because they have either no assumptions or theories relating base rate information to likelihood or none that they know how to use (and again the gap between knowing that and knowing how may be crucial).

Research has not altogether neglected supposedly basic assumptions. For example, Wrightsman (1974) has investigated lay beliefs about human nature. According to Furnham (1988), studies of basic assumptions have generally had little success in predicting behaviour, but there are probably two reasons for this. First, beliefs about human nature are of a very general nature whereas behavioural measures are comparatively specific, and it is well known from attitude research that verbal and behavioural measures at different levels of specificity tend to be poor predictors of each other (Heberlein and Black 1976; Ajzen and Fishbein 1977; Jaccard *et al.* 1977). A measure of beliefs about human nature having greater correspondence with a behavioural measure might show better predictive power.

Secondly, questionnaires inevitably treat assumptions about human nature as part of a conceptual system – knowing *that*, rather than knowing how. I have stressed at intervals throughout this book that the axioms of common sense are practically orientated – belonging in the realm of knowing how. People's thoughtfully worked out beliefs as revealed by questionnaire studies have a life quite independent not only of behaviour but also of the axioms that guide and constrain behaviour. People may think that chairs are made of atoms, but this in no way prevents their actual behaviour towards chairs from being founded on a solid matter primary substance metaphysics. Likewise, people may think that others are unselfish but this would in no way prevent their behaviour towards others from being founded on a basic assumption of selfishness in others.

This emphasis on culture is not meant to indicate a preference for historical determinism. Innovations occur, ideas change and develop. Biddiss (1977) has expressed the matter very clearly:

> To see society as moulded overwhelmingly by mind is no more helpful than to regard intellect as some mere side-effect of dominant material conditions. There is a vastly more complex and fluctuating dialectic between given social circumstances and man himself, who perceives them so variously and strives to transform them according to a wealth of competing aspirations.
>
> (Biddiss 1977: 13)

He also referred to 'the intricate nexus between thought as a social symptom and ideas as creative influences upon society' (p. 13). It happens that the focus of social psychological research on judgemental phenomena that are general across people militates against the elucidation of individual creativity in judgemental processes. This is a bias, which perhaps owes a good deal to our desire to discover laws of human behaviour.

A process, then, is not an inviolable mechanism. Only biologically determined processes may be unalterable: those processes that are constructed culturally or intra-individually may be modified in the same ways. Thinking of the phenomena of judgement as due to fixed mechanisms the operation of which is driven by stimuli is inadequate, in that it ignores both the choice of processes from a repertoire of possibilities on any particular occasion, and the ways in which processes are constructed and modified by both cultural influence and the individual's use of acquired beliefs about mental activity.

Historical explanations have not been popular in social psychology. When Gergen (1973) proposed that social psychology was history, the flurry of critical responses may have been partly motivated by a feeling that Gergen's arguments threatened the status of social psychology as a science. This feeling is misplaced: historical explanations are not favoured in physics, for the good reason that physics seeks laws that are omnispatial and omnitemporal in application; but they are respectable and proper in many other scientific disciplines, such as geology and palaeontology, and there seems no good reason why social psychology should take physics as its model, rather than either of these. Indeed, history itself can be called a science, in so far as it shares the scientific aims of knowledge, understanding, explanation, and so on. The theme of this book, of course, implies that social psychology is not *just* history: but it is, in a sense, history grounded in psychological metaphysics, and social psychology can only lose by failing to accord historical explanations their proper place.


## Psychology and the perennial questions

According to Baumer (1977), there are five perennial questions in the history of ideas. These questions are raised, with differences of formulation and different favoured answers, throughout history, though one or another may be predominant in any given age.

1 *The question of God, but not just God, still less the Christian God.* The question 'delves into first and last things. It asks whether naturalistic categories alone can explain the world and man; whether there is not also a transcendental or "extra" dimension to human life' (Baumer 1977: 12).
2 *Nature.* 'What is physical nature made of, and by what principles does it operate?' (Baumer 1977: 13).
3 *Human nature.* Baumer listed a number of subsidiary questions under this heading, including: 'not only the reaches of human cognition . . . but also the extent of man's freedom, his moral propensities, ultimately his power to change his own destiny' (Baumer 1977: 14); and 'Assuming some sort of raw human nature, what is its chief mark? Is it reason or unreason, spirit, will, love, aggression, sin, sex, the death wish – or freedom?' (Baumer 1977: 14).
4 *Society.* This question 'asks how society, or the state, should be conceived in the first place' (Baumer 1977: 15). For example, 'Is society static or dynamic? . . . Is it more like a machine or an organism?' (Baumer 1977: 15).
5 *History.* This is concerned with the future as well as with the past. For example: 'Does history move in any visible direction? . . . Does it appear . . . to have some sort of design, to be subject to law?' (Baumer 1977: 16).

Work in psychology has a definite place in the mainstream of the history of ideas. Though psychological research can contribute to any of the perennial questions in some way, its most obvious place is in the debate over human nature. Over the centuries there have been many proposals about human nature: humans are basically distinguished by their possession of a rational soul or faculty of reason (Aristotle, Descartes, medieval world view); humans are basically irrational or ruled by passions rather than by reason (Freud, Hume); humans are basically selfish and competitive (Hobbes); humans are basically social and co-operative (Locke, Rousseau); humans have free will (Aquinas, Butler); humans do not have free will (La Mettrie, Hobbes); humans are basically good and strive for virtue (Plato); humans are basically sinful (the New Testament). In the twentieth century there has been something of a revolt against the postulation of absolutes in human nature. As Baumer (1977) put it, we have moved from a view of human nature as being (static, absolute, universal) to one of human nature as becoming (dynamic, relative, variable).

This is an important shift, but it has come about because everyone seems to have shared a restrictive conceptualisation of how human nature might be characterised. What all of the foregoing points of view share is the postulation of what we usually regard as some stable individuating characteristic as being shared by, and basic to, all human beings. In contemporary psychology these things tend to be treated as individual differences: one person may be more competitive than another, one may be ruled by passion more than another, and so on. Perhaps cultures and historical periods may tend to differ from one another in these respects also. So long as we conceptualise the question of human nature in terms of stable traits of character it is hard to contest the view that there is no basic universal constant in human nature, because the evidence that things of this sort vary is all around us.

One move from within psychology that could be taken as changing the perspective on the question of human nature is the postulation, not of particular traits, but of trait dimensions, as basic. For example, Eysenck (1953) claimed that the two basic dimensions of human personality were introversion–extroversion and stability–instability. Thus, individuals differ in the extent to which they are introverted or extroverted, but the respect in which they do not differ is that of the basicity of the dimension. What makes the dimension basic is the fact that it is founded in a feature of the central nervous system (capacity for cortical arousal in the case of introversion–extroversion), together with the fact that it underlies more specific traits and habitual responses (Eysenck 1953). Eysenck's two dimensions – together with his later addition of psychoticism as a third basic dimension (1975) – illustrate a shift towards postulating personality trait dimensions as basic, as opposed to mental faculties such as the faculty of reason. Although Eysenck has related his two dimensions to the four temperaments, the idea that such things could be basic to human nature would probably have appeared absurd to the medieval mind: the four temperaments were minor imperfections, deviations from the individual's true type, utterly superficial compared to the faculty of reason, and not intimate parts of the person as such at all (Gurevich 1985). None the less, the idea of replacing characteristics with dimensions could be a viable means of preserving the notion that something related to personality is basic and universal and thus serves to define human nature.

Arguably, however, people have been looking for constants in the wrong place. A more radical solution which psychology can provide is to claim that the universal constants that define human nature are basic psychological functions, constraints, and capacities. These include, I would propose, the fundamental assumptions of the psychological construction of reality, together with the psychological features which give rise to them. This is almost certainly not exhaustive as an account of human nature, nor does it serve the function of differentiating human beings from other species. It does, however, serve to indicate the direction in which psychology can take the issue of human nature. A faculty of reason, if we have one, works within the framework of assumptions in the psychological construction of reality: although the specifics of how it works may vary from person to person, culture to culture, and time to time, they never violate the axioms of the construction. Feelings and emotions are aspects of responsiveness to interpretations of reality which may vary from person to person, culture to culture, and time to time, but again without violating the basic assumptions that make such interpretations possible in the first place. Perhaps only in such severe disorders of mental function as take place in schizophrenic illness are these basic assumptions violated or suspended: otherwise, they are universal features of human psychology.

## How to give a complete account of social judgement

Aristotle proposed four types of cause: material, formal, efficient, and final. These were not just four assorted ways in which things might happen, but together constituted an attempt to specify all that was necessary for a complete account of the being of a primary substance (White 1990). Taking an oak tree as an example of a primary substance, the four causes were supposed to cover everything that was necessary to explain the tree, from germination of the acorn to death of the aged oak. The aim was completeness of explanation. This leads me to ask, by analogy, what would it be to give a *complete* explanatory account of some judgement, inference, or attribution? That is, what *kinds* of thing would we have to include in an explanatory account, if we wanted to make it complete? At present, and duly admitting the provisional nature of these views, I see six kinds of thing.

1  *Metaphysics.* What is the foundation of the judgement in psychological metaphysics, the basic assumptions on which it depends, the basic concepts in terms of which it is constructed?
2  *Function.* What is it for, what does the judgement do for the person who makes it? (I do not mean to imply that the answer to this must refer to some purpose or goal. One can find non-teleological answers to questions such as what birds have feathers for, and so it may be for social cognition too.)
3  *Development.* How does the making of this sort of judgement originate and develop in the individual?
4  *Culture.* What is the contribution to judgement of culture, history, socialisation processes?
5  *Process.* How does it work, how is the judgement actually made, and are the same processes used for different instances of judgement?
6  *Taxonomy.* What kind of judgement is it? What are the natural kinds of judgement, and what makes them distinct as kinds?

These questions are interrelated to such a degree that we cannot hope to understand the answers to any one of them without setting it in context with all the others. I have the impression that research into judgement, inference, and attribution is at present unbalanced in that comparatively little attention is being given to metaphysics, function, development, culture, and taxonomy. When I look at models and hypotheses of judgement and so on, I see processes floating in the air. Although metaphysics is my main concern in this book, I have tried not to neglect these other kinds of thing, because I cannot see that an investigation of psychological metaphysics could make sense without them. As everything in this final chapter is intended to emphasise, much remains to be done.

# References

Abelson, R. P. and Lalljee, M. (1988) 'Knowledge structures and causal explanation', in D. J. Hilton (ed.), *Contemporary Science and Natural Explanation: Commonsense Conceptions of Causality*. Brighton: Harvester Press.

Adelson, E. H. (1983) 'What is iconic storage good for?', *The Behavioural and Brain Sciences*, 6, 11–12.

Ajzen, I. and Fishbein, M. (1977) 'Attitude–behaviour relations: a theoretical analysis and review of empirical research', *Psychological Bulletin*, 84, 888–918.

Anderson, J. R. (1980) *Cognitive Psychology and its Implications*. San Francisco: Freeman.

Antaki, C. A. (1990) 'Explaining events or explaining oneself?', in M. J. Cody and M. L. McLaughlin (eds), *The Psychology of Tactical Communication*. Bristol: Multilingual Matters.

Aristotle (1963) *Categories and De Interpretatione* (J. L. Ackrill, trans.). Oxford: Oxford University Press.

Aristotle (1965) 'Substance', in C. A. Baylis (ed.), *Metaphysics* (pp. 63–4). New York: Macmillan.

Arkin, R. M. and Duval, S. (1975) 'Focus of attention and causal attribution of actors and observers', *Journal of Experimental Social Psychology*, 11, 427–38.

Aronson, E. (1969) 'The theory of cognitive dissonance: a current perspective', in L. Berkowtiz (ed.), *Advances in Experimental Social Psychology*, vol. 4, pp. 1–34. New York: Academic Press.

Asch, S. E. (1952) *Social Psychology*. New York: Prentice-Hall.

Atkinson, R. L., Atkinson, R. H., and Hilgard, E. R. (1983) *Introduction to Psychology*, 8th edn. New York: Harcourt Brace Jovanovich.

Averill, J. R. (1974) 'An analysis of psychophysiological symbolism and its influence on theories of emotion', *Journal for the Theory of Social Behaviour*, 4, 147–90.

Ayer, A. J. (1956) *The Problem of Knowledge*. Harmondsworth: Penguin.

Baars, B. J. (1983) 'Conscious contents provide the nervous system with coherent, global information', in R. J. Davidson, G. E. Schwartz, and D. Shapiro (eds), *Consciousness and Self-regulation*, vol. 3. New York: Plenum.

Ball, W. A. (1973) 'The perception of causality in the infant' (Report No. 37). Ann Arbor: University of Michigan, Department of Psychology, Developmental Program.

Bassili, J. N. (1976) 'Temporal and spatial contingencies in the perception of social events', *Journal of Personality and Social Psychology*, 33, 680–5.

Baumeister, R. F. (1982) 'A self-presentational view of social phenomena', *Psychological Bulletin*, 91, 3–26.

Baumer, F. L. (1977) *Modern European Thought: Continuity and Change in Ideas 1600–1950*. London: Collier Macmillan.

Beasley, N. E. (1968) 'The extent of individual differences in the perception of causality', *Canadian Journal of Psychology*, 22, 399–407.
Beauchamp, T. L. (ed.) (1974) *Philosophical Problems of Causation*. Encino, CA: Dickenson.
Bem, D. J. (1967) 'Self-perception: an alternative interpretation of cognitive dissonance phenomena', *Psychological Review*, 74, 188–200.
Bem, D. J. (1972) 'Self-perception theory', in L. Berkowitz (ed.), *Advances in Experimental Social Psychology*, vol. 6, pp. 1–62. New York: Academic Press.
Berry, C. J. (1986) *Human Nature*. London: Macmillan.
Berzonsky, M. D. (1971) 'The role of familiarity in children's explanations of physical causality', *Child Development*, 42, 705–15.
Bhaskar, R. (1975) *A Realist Theory of Science*. Leeds: Leeds Books Ltd.
Biddiss, M. D. (1977) *The Age of the Masses: Ideas and Society in Europe since 1870*. Hassocks: Harvester Press.
Block, J. and Funder, D. C. (1986) 'Social roles and social perception: individual differences in attribution and "error"', *Journal of Personality and Social Psychology*, 51, 1200–7.
Boas, M. (1962) *The Scientific Renaissance, 1450–1630*. London: Collins.
Borton, R. W. (1979) 'The perception of causality in infants', Paper presented at the meeting of the Society for Research in Child Development, San Francisco.
Boyle, D. G. (1960) 'A contribution to the study of phenomenal causality', *Quarterly Journal of Experimental Psychology*, 12, 171–9.
Brickman, P. (1980) 'A social psychology of human concerns', in R. M. Gilmour and S. Duck (eds), *The Development of Social Psychology*. London: Academic Press.
Brickman, P., Ryan, K., and Wortman, C. B. (1975) 'Causal chains: attribution of responsibility as a function of immediate and prior causes', *Journal of Personality and Social Psychology*, 32, 1060–7.
Bridgeman, B. and Mayer, M. (1983) 'Iconic storage and saccadic eye movements', *The Behavioural and Brain Sciences*, 6, 16–17.
Bronowski, J. (1951) *The Common Sense of Science*. London: Heinemann.
Brown, R. and Fish, D. (1983) 'The psychological causality implicit in language', *Cognition*, 14, 237–73.
Bunge, M. (1963) *Causality: The Place of the Causal Principle in Modern Science*. Cambridge, MA: Harvard University Press.
Buss, A. R. (1978) 'Causes and reasons in attribution theory: a conceptual critique', *Journal of Personality and Social Psychology*, 36, 1311–21.
Buss, A. R. (1979) 'On the relationship between causes and reasons', *Journal of Personality and Social Psychology*, 37, 1458–61.
Campbell, K. (1976) *Metaphysics: An Introduction*. Encino, CA: Dickenson.
Cannon, W. B. (1927) 'The James-Lange theory of emotion: a critical examination and an alternative theory', *American Journal of Psychology*, 39, 106–24.
Carr, B. (1987) *Metaphysics: An Introduction*. London: Macmillan.
Chapman, L. J. (1967) 'Illusory correlation in observational report', *Journal of Verbal Learning and Verbal Behaviour*, 6, 151–5.
Cheng, P. W. and Novick, L. R. (1990) 'A probabilistic contrast model of causal induction', *Journal of Personality and Social Psychology*, 58, 545–67.
Collingwood, R. G. (1940) *An Essay on Metaphysics*. Oxford: Clarendon Press.
Collingwood, R. G. (1945) *The Idea of Nature*. Oxford: Oxford University Press.
Curry, W. C. (1960) *Chaucer and the Medieval Sciences*. London: George Allen & Unwin (originally published 1926).
D'Andrade, R. (1987) 'A folk model of the mind', in D. Holland and N. Quinn (eds),

*Cultural Models in Language and Thought* (pp. 112–48). Cambridge: Cambridge University Press.

Davidson, D. (1968) 'Actions, reasons, and causes', in A. R. White (ed.), *The Philosophy of Action* (pp. 79–94). Oxford: Oxford University Press.

Dawes, R. M. (1976) 'Shallow psychology', in J. S. Carroll and J. W. Payne (eds), *Cognition and Social Behaviour*. Hillsdale, NJ: Erlbaum.

Debus, A. G. (1978) *Man and Nature in the Renaissance*. Cambridge: Cambridge University Press.

Dijksterhuis, E. J. (1961) *The Mechanization of the World-Picture* (C. Dijkshoorn, trans.) Oxford: Clarendon Press.

Doise, W. (1986) *Levels of Explanation in Social Psychology*. Cambridge: Cambridge University Press.

Draper, S. W. (1988) 'What's going on in everyday explanation?', in C. Antaki (ed.), *Analysing Everyday Explanation: A Casebook of Methods* (pp. 15–31). London: Sage.

Einhorn, H. J. and Hogarth, R. M. (1986) 'Judging probable cause', *Psychological Bulletin*, 99, 3–19.

Emmet, D. (1984) *The Effectiveness of Causes*. London: Macmillan.

Evans, J. St B. T. (1982) *The Psychology of Deductive Reasoning*. London: Routledge & Kegan Paul.

Eysenck, H. J. (1953) *The Structure of Human Personality*. New York: Wiley.

Eysenck, H. J. (1975) *The Inequality of Man*. San Diego, CA: EDITS.

Farrington, B. (1944) *Greek Science: I. Thales to Aristotle*. Harmondsworth: Penguin.

Farrington, B. (1969) *Science in Antiquity*, 2nd edn. Oxford: Oxford University Press.

Feinberg, J. (1968) 'Action and responsibility', in A. R. White (ed.), *The Philosophy of Action* (pp. 95–120). Oxford: Oxford University Press.

Festinger, L. (1957) *A Theory of Cognitive Dissonance*. Evanston, IL: Row, Peterson.

Fincham, F. D. (1983) 'Developmental aspects of attribution theory', in J. Jaspars, F. D. Fincham, and M. Hewstone (eds), *Attribution Theory and Research: Conceptual, Developmental, and Social Dimensions* (pp. 117–64). London: Academic Press.

Fincham, F. D. and Jaspars, J. (1980) 'Attribution of responsibility: from man the scientist to man-as-lawyer', in L. Berkowitz (ed.), *Advances in Experimental Social Psychology*, vol. 13. New York: Academic Press.

Fiske, S. T. and Taylor, S. E. (1991) *Social Cognition*. New York: McGraw-Hill.

Fitzgerald, P. J. (1968) 'Voluntary and involuntary acts', in A. R. White (ed.), *The Philosophy of Action* (pp. 120–43). Oxford: Oxford University Press.

Fletcher, G. J. O. (1984) 'Psychology and common sense', *American Psychologist*, 39, 203–13.

Forsterling, F. (1989) 'Models of covariation and attribution: how do they relate to the analogy of analysis of variance?', *Journal of Personality and Social Psychology*, 53, 615–25.

Foster, R. and Tudor-Craig, P. (1986) *The Secret Life of Paintings*. Woodbridge: Boydell.

Funder, D. C. (1987) 'Errors and mistakes: evaluating the accuracy of social judgement', *Psychological Bulletin*, 101, 75–90.

Furnham, A. F. (1988) *Lay Theories: Everyday Understanding of Problems in the Social Sciences*. Oxford: Pergamon Press.

Galper, R. E. (1976) 'Turning observers into actors: differential causal attributions as a function of "empathy"', *Journal of Research in Personality*, 10, 328–35.

Garcia, J. and Koelling, R. A. (1966) 'The relation of cue to consequence in avoidance learning', *Psychonomic Science*, 4, 123–4.

Garcia, J., McGowan, B., Ervin, F.R., and Koelling, R. (1968) 'Cues: their relative effectiveness as reinforcers', *Science*, 160, 794–5.

Gelman, S. A. and Kremer, K. E. (1992) 'Understanding natural cause: children's explanations of how objects and their properties originate', *Child Development*, 62, 396–414.

Gentner, D. and Gentner, P. R. (1983) 'Flowing waters or teeming crowds: mental models of electricity', in D Gentner and A. Steven (eds), *Mental Models* (pp. 199–230). Hillsdale, NJ: Erlbaum.

Gergen, K. (1973) 'Social psychology as history', *Journal of Personality and Social Psychology*, 26, 309–20.

Gick, M. L. and Holyoak, K. J. (1980) 'Analogical problem solving', *Cognitive Psychology*, 12, 306–55.

Gick, M. L. and Holyoak, K. J. (1983) 'Schema induction and analogical transfer', *Cognitive Psychology*, 15, 1–38.

Ginet, C. (1990) *On Action*. Cambridge: Cambridge University Press.

Gorovitz, S. (1965) 'Causal judgements and causal explanations', *Journal of Philosophy*, 62, 695–711.

Gurevich, A. J. (1985) *Categories of Medieval Culture* (G. L. Campbell, trans.). London: Routledge & Kegan Paul.

Haber, R. N. (1983a) 'The icon is finally dead', *The Behavioural and Brain Sciences*, 6, 43–54.

Haber, R. N. (1983b) 'The impending demise of the icon: a critique of the concept of iconic storage in visual information processing', *The Behavioural and Brain Sciences*, 6, 1–11.

Hamilton, D. L. (1979) 'A cognitive-attributional analysis of stereotyping', in L. Berkowitz (ed.), *Advances in Experimental Social Psychology*, vol. 12, pp. 53–84. New York: Academic Press.

Hamilton, V. L. (1980) 'Intuitive psychologist or intuitive lawyer? Alternative models of the attribution process', *Journal of Personality and Social Psychology*, 39, 767–72.

Hankins, T. L. (1985) *Science and the Enlightenment*. Cambridge: Cambridge University Press.

Hansen, R. D. (1980) 'Commonsense attribution', *Journal of Personality and Social Psychology*, 39, 996–1009.

Hargreaves, D. H. (1980) 'Common-sense models of action', in A. J. Chapman and D. M. Jones (eds), *Models of Man*. Leicester: British Psychological Society.

Harré, R. and Madden, E. H. (1975) *Causal Powers: A Theory of Natural Necessity*. Oxford: Blackwell.

Harré, R. and Secord, P. F. (1972) *The Explanation of Social Behaviour*. Oxford: Blackwell.

Hart, H. L. A. and Honoré, A. M. (1959) *Causation in the Law*. Oxford: Clarendon Press.

Hart, H. L. A. and Honoré, A. M. (1974) 'The analysis of causal concepts', in T. L. Beauchamp (ed.), *Philosophical Problems of Causation*. Encino, CA: Dickenson.

Harvey, J. H. and Weary, G. (1984) 'Current issues in attribution theory and research', *Annual Review of Psychology*, 35, 427–59.

Hastie, R. (1983) 'Social inference', *Annual Review of Psychology*, 34, 511–42.

Heberlein, T. A. and Black, J. S. (1976) 'Attitudinal specificity and the prediction of behaviour in a field setting', *Journal of Personality and Social Psychology*, 33, 474–9.

Heider, F. (1944) 'Social perception and phenomenal causality', *Psychological Review*, 51, 358–74.

Heider, F. (1958) *The Psychology of Interpersonal Relations*. New York: Wiley.

Heider, F. and Simmel, M. (1944) 'An experimental study of apparent behaviour', *American Journal of Psychology*, 57, 243–9.

Helminiak, D. A. (1984) 'Consciousness as a subject-matter', *Journal for the Theory of Social Behaviour*, 14, 211–30.

Henle, M. (1962) 'On the relation between logic and thinking', *Psychological Review*, 69, 366–78.

Herzberger, S. D. and Clore, G. L. (1979) 'Actor–observer attributions in a multitrait-multimethod matrix', *Journal of Research in Personality*, 13, 1–15.

Hesslow, G. (1988) 'The problem of causal selection', in D. J. Hilton (ed.), *Contemporary Science and Natural Explanation: Commonsense Conceptions of Causality* (pp. 11–32). Brighton: Harvester Press.

Hewstone, M. (1989) *Causal Attribution: From Cognitive Processes to Collective Beliefs*. Oxford: Blackwell.

Hewstone, M. and Jaspars, J. (1987) 'Covariation and causal attribution: a logical model of the intuitive analysis of variance', *Journal of Personality and Social Psychology*, 53, 663–72.

Hilgard, E. R. (1976) 'Neodissociation theory of multiple cognitive control systems', in G. E. Schwartz and D. Shapiro (eds), *Consciousness and Self-regulation*, vol. 2. New York: Plenum.

Hilton, D. J. and Slugoski, B. (1986) 'Knowledge-based causal attribution: the abnormal conditions focus model', *Psychological Review*, 93, 75–88.

Hume, D. (1978) *A Treatise of Human Nature*. Oxford: Oxford University Press (originally published 1739).

Jaccard, J., King, G. W., and Pomazal, R. (1977) 'Attitudes and behaviour: an analysis of specificity of attitudinal predictors', *Human Relations*, 30, 817–24.

Jellison, J. M. and Green, J. (1981) 'A self-presentation approach to the fundamental attribution error: the norm of internality', *Journal of Personality and Social Psychology*, 40, 643–9.

Johnson, W. E. (1921) *Logic*. Cambridge: Cambridge University Press.

Johnston, L. and Hewstone, M. (1992) 'Cognitive models of stereotype change: 3. Subtyping and the perceived typicality of disconfirming group members', *Journal of Experimental Social Psychology*, 28, 360–86.

Jones, E. E. and Davis, K. E. (1965) 'From acts to dispositions: the attribution process in person perception', in L. Berkowitz (ed.), *Advances in Experimental Social Psychology*, vol. 2, pp. 219–66. New York: Academic Press.

Jones, E. E. and Harris, V. A. (1967) 'The attribution of attitudes', *Journal of Experimental Social Psychology*, 3, 1–24.

Jones, E. E. and Nisbett, R. E. (1972) 'The actor and the observer: divergent perceptions of the causes of behaviour', in E. E. Jones, D. Kanouse, H. H. Kelley, R. E. Nisbett, S. Valins, and B. Weiner (eds), *Attribution: Perceiving the Causes of Behaviour*. Morristown, NJ: General Learning Press.

Kahneman, D. (1991) 'Judgement and decision making: a personal view', *Psychological Science*, 2, 142–5.

Kahneman, D., Slovic, P., and Tversky, A. (eds) (1982) *Judgment under Uncertainty: Heuristics and Biases*. Cambridge: Cambridge University Press.

Kahneman, D. and Tversky, A. (1972) 'Subjective probability: a judgement of representativeness', *Cognitive Psychology*, 3, 430–54.

Kahneman, D. and Tversky, A. (1973) 'On the psychology of prediction', *Psychological Review*, 80, 237–51.

Kaiser, M. K., Jonides, J., and Alexander, J. (1986) 'Intuitive reasoning about abstract and familiar physics problems', *Memory and Cognition*, 14, 308–12.

Kaiser, M. K., Proffitt, D. R., and Anderson, K. (1985) 'Judgments of natural and anomalous trajectories in the presence and absence of motion', *Journal of Experimental Psychology: Learning, Memory, and Cognition*, 11, 795–803.

Kaiser, M. K., Proffitt, D. R., and McCloskey, M. (1985) 'The development of beliefs about falling objects', *Perception and Psychophysics*, 38, 533–9.

Karmiloff-Smith, A. (1988) 'The child is a theoretician, not an inductivist', *Mind and Language*, 3, 1–13.

Kassin, S. M. and Baron, R. M. (1985) 'Basic determinants of attribution and social perception', in J. H. Harvey and G. Weary (eds), *Attribution: Basic Issues and Applications*. London: Academic Press.

Kassin, S. M. and Pryor, J. B. (1985) 'The development of attribution processes', in J. B. Pryor and J. D. Day (eds), *The Development of Social Cognition*. New York: Springer-Verlag.

Kelley, H. H. (1967) 'Attribution in social psychology', in D. Levine (ed.), *Nebraska Symposium on Motivation*, vol. 15, pp. 192–238. Lincoln, NB: University of Nebraska Press.

Kelley, H. H. (1972a) 'Attribution in social interaction', in E. E. Jones, D. Kanouse, H. H. Kelley, R. E. Nisbett, S. Valins, and B. Weiner (eds), *Attribution: Perceiving the Causes of Behaviour* (pp. 1–26). Morristown, NJ: General Learning Press.

Kelley, H. H. (1972b) 'Causal schemata and the attribution process', in E. E. Jones, D. Kanouse, H. H. Kelley, R. E. Nisbett, S. Valins, and B. Weiner (eds), *Attribution: Perceiving the Causes of Behaviour* (pp. 151–74). Morristown, NJ: General Learning Press.

Kelley, H. H. (1973) 'The processes of causal attribution', *American Psychologist*, 28, 107–28.

Kelley, H. H. (1983) 'Perceived causal structures', in J. Jaspars, F. D. Fincham, and M. Hewstone (eds), *Attribution Theory and Research: Conceptual, Developmental, and Social Dimensions* (pp. 343–69). London: Academic Press.

Kellman, P. and Spelke, E., (1983) 'Perception of partly occluded objects in infancy', *Cognitive Psychology*, 15, 483–524.

Kellman, P., Spelke, E., and Short, K. R. (1986) 'Infant perception of object unity from translating motion in depth and vertical translation', *Child Development*, 57, 72–86.

Kelly, G. (1955) *The Psychology of Personal Constructs*, 2 vols. New York: Norton.

Kenny, A. (1989) *The Metaphysics of Mind*. Oxford: Clarendon Press.

Kintsch, W. (1970) *Learning, Memory, and Conceptual Processes*. London: Wiley.

Klahr, D. and Dunbar, K. (1988) 'Dual space search during scientific reasoning', *Cognitive Science*, 12, 1–48.

Klatzky, R. L. (1983) 'The icon is dead: long live the icon', *The Behavioural and Brain Sciences*, 6, 27–8.

Klingensmith, S. W. (1953) 'Child animism', *Child Development*, 24, 51–61.

Kroll, N. E. A. and Kellicutt, M. H. (1972) 'Short-term recall as a function of concept rehearsal and of intervening task', *Journal of Verbal Learning and Verbal Behaviour*, 11, 196–204.

Kruglanski, A. W. (1975) 'The endogenous–exogenous partition in attribution theory', *Psychological Review*, 82, 387–406.

Kruglanski, A. W. (1979) 'Causal explanation, teleological explanation: on radical particularism in attribution theory', *Journal of Personality and Social Psychology*, 37, 1447–57.

Kuhn, D. (1989) 'Children and adults as intuitive scientists', *Psychological Review*, 96, 674–89.

Kuhn, D., Amsel, E., and O'Laughlin, M. (1988) *The Development of Scientific Thinking Skills*. Orlando, FL: Academic Press.

Kulik, J. A. (1983) 'Confirmatory attribution and the perpetuation of social beliefs', *Journal of Personality and Social Psychology*, 44, 1171–81.

Lalljee, M., Lamb, R., Furnham, A., and Jaspars, J. (1984) 'Explanations and information search: inductive and hypothesis-testing approaches to arriving at an explanation', *British Journal of Social Psychology*, 23, 201–12.

Langer, E. J. (1978) 'Rethinking the role of thought in social interaction', in J. H. Harvey, W. I. Ickes, and R. F. Kidd (eds), *New Directions in Attribution Research*, vol. 2, pp. 35–58. Hillsdale, NJ: Erlbaum.

Laszlo, E. (1972) *The Systems View of the World*. Oxford: Blackwell.

Lerner, M. J. (1965) 'Evaluation of performance as a function of performer's reward and attractiveness', *Journal of Personality and Social Psychology*, 1, 355–60.

Lerner, M. J. and Miller, D. T. (1978) 'Just world research and the attribution process: looking back and ahead', *Psychological Bulletin*, 85, 1030–51.

Lerner, M. J. and Simmons, C. H. (1966) 'The observer's reaction to the "innocent victim": compassion or rejection?', *Journal of Personality and Social Psychology*, 4, 203–10.

Leslie, A. M. (1982) 'The perception of causality in infants', *Perception*, 11, 173–86.

Leslie, A. M. (1984) 'Spatiotemporal contiguity and the perception of causality in infants', *Perception*, 13, 287–305.

Leslie, A. M. and Keeble, S. (1987) 'Do six-month-old infants perceive causality?', *Cognition*, 25, 265–88.

Lesser, H. (1977) 'The growth of perceived causality in children', *Journal of Genetic Psychology*, 130, 145–52.

Lewis, C. S. (1964) *The Discarded Image: An Introduction to Medieval and Renaissance Literature*. Cambridge: Cambridge University Press.

Locke, D. and Pennington, D. (1982) 'Reasons and other causes: their role in the attribution process', *Journal of Personality and Social Psychology*, 42, 212–23.

Looft, W. R. and Bartz, W. H. (1969) 'Animism revived', *Psychological Bulletin*, 71, 1–19.

McArthur, L. Z. (1972) 'The how and what of why: some determinants and consequences of causal attribution', *Journal of Personality and Social Psychology*, 22, 171–93.

McCloskey, M. (1983) 'Intuitive physics', *Scientific American*, 248, 395–400.

McCloskey, M., Caramazza, A., and Green, B. (1980) 'Curvilinear motion in the absence of external forces', *Science*, 210, 1139–41.

McCloskey, M., Washburn, A., and Felch, L. (1983) 'Intuitive physics: the straight-down belief and its origin', *Journal of Experimental Psychology: Learning, Memory, and Cognition*, 9, 636–49.

Mace, W. M. and Turvey, M. T. (1983) 'The implications of occlusion for perceiving persistence', *The Behavioural and Brain Sciences*, 6, 29–31.

McGill, A. L. (1989) 'Context effects in judgements of causation', *Journal of Personality and Social Psychology*, 57, 189–200.

Mackie, J. L. (1965) 'Causes and conditions', *American Philosophical Quarterly*, 2, 245–64.

Mackie, J. L. (1974) *The Cement of the Universe: A Study of Causation*. Oxford: Clarendon Press.

Mackie, J. L. (1975) 'Causes and conditionals', in E. Sosa (ed.), *Causation and Conditionals*. Oxford: Oxford University Press.

Madden, E. H. and Humber, J. (1974) 'Nonlogical necessity and C. J. Ducasse', in T. L. Beauchamp (ed.), *Philosophical Problems of Causation*. Encino, CA: Dickenson.

Maier, N. R. F. (1931) 'Reasoning in humans. II. The solution of a problem and its appearance in consciousness', *Journal of Comparative and Physiological Psychology*, 12, 181–94.

Mandler, G. A. (1975a) 'Consciousness: respectable, useful, and probably necessary', in R. Solso (ed.), *Information Processing and Cognition: The Loyola Symposium*. Hillsdale, NJ: Erlbaum.

Mandler, G. A. (1975b) *Mind and Emotion*. New York: Wiley.

Mandler, G. A. (1984) *Mind and Body: Psychology of Emotion*. New York: Norton.

Marcel, A. J. (1983) 'Conscious and unconscious perception: an approach to the relations between phenomenal experience and perceptual processes', *Cognitive Psychology*, 15, 238–300.

Mendelson, R. and Shultz, T. R. (1976) 'Covariation and temporal contiguity as principles of causal inference in young children', *Journal of Experimental Child Psychology*, 22, 408–12.

Michotte, A. (1963) *The Perception of Causality*. New York: Basic Books.

Mill, J. S. (1967) *A System of Logic Ratiocinative and Inductive*. London: Longman (Originally published 1843).

Miller, D. T. and Ross, M. (1975) 'Self-serving biases in the attribution of causality: fact or fiction?', *Psychological Bulletin*, 82, 213–25.

Miller, F. D., Smith, E. R., and Uleman, J. (1981) 'Measurement and interpretation of situational and dispositional attributions', *Journal of Experimental Social Psychology*, 17, 80–95.

Monson, T. C. and Snyder, M. (1977) 'Actors, observers, and the attribution process: toward a reconceptualization', *Journal of Experimental Social Psychology*, 13, 89–111.

Moore, B. S., Sherrod, D. R., Liu, T. J., and Underwood, B. (1981) 'The dispositional shift in attribution over time', *Journal of Experimental Social Psychology*, 15, 553–69.

Moya, C. J. (1990) *The Philosophy of Action: An Introduction*. Cambridge: Polity Press.

Munn, N. L. (1965) *The Evolution and Growth of Human Behaviour*, 2nd edn. Boston: Houghton Mifflin.

Natsoulas, T. (1981) 'Basic problems of consciousness', *Journal of Personality and Social Psychology*, 41, 132–78.

Neunaber, D. J. and Wasserman, E. A. (1986) 'The effects of unidirectional versus bidirectional rating procedures on college students' judgements of response-outcome contingency', *Learning and Motivation*, 17, 162–79.

Nisbett, R. E., Caputo, C., Legant, P., and Maracek, J. (1973) 'Behaviour as seen by the actor and as seen by the observer', *Journal of Personality and Social Psychology*, 27, 154–65.

Nisbett, R. E. and Ross, L. (1980) *Human Inference: Strategies and Shortcomings of Social Judgment*. Englewood Cliffs, NJ: Prentice-Hall.

Nisbett, R. E. and Wilson, T. D. (1977) 'Telling more than we can know: verbal reports on mental processes', *Psychological Review*, 84, 231–59.

Norman, D. A. (1976) *Memory and Attention*. New York: Wiley.

Norman, D. A. and Shallice, T. (1980) 'Attention and action: willed and automatic control of behaviour', Unpublished paper. Centre for Human Information Processing. University of California, San Diego, La Jolla, CA.

Norman, W. T. (1967) '2800 personality trait descriptors: normative operating characteristics for a university population', Unpublished manuscript, University of Michigan.

Offer, D. and Sabshin, M. (1974) *Normality: Theoretical and Clinical Concepts of Mental Health* (revised edn). New York: Basic Books.

Oliver, P. (1986) 'Rest home accommodation for the elderly: a civil rights perspective', *Community Mental Health in New Zealand*, 3, 74–91.

Orvis, B. R., Cunningham, J. D., and Kelley, H. H. (1975) 'A closer examination of causal inference: the roles of consensus, distinctiveness, and consistency information', *Journal of Personality and Social Psychology*, 32, 605–16.

Pears, D. F. (1966) 'Causes and objects of some feelings and psychological reactions', in S. Hampshire (ed.), *Philosophy of Mind* (pp. 143–69). New York: Harper & Row.

Philips, W. A. (1983) 'Change perception needs sensory storage', *The Behavioural and Brain Sciences*, 6, 35–6.

Piaget, J. (1930) *The Child's Conception of Physical Causality*. London: Routledge & Kegan Paul.

Piaget, J. (1954) *The Construction of Reality in the Child*. New York: Basic Books.

Piaget, J. (1977) *Understanding Causality*. New York: Norton.

Piaget, J. and Inhelder, B. (1969) *The Psychology of the Child*. London: Routledge & Kegan Paul.

Posner, M. and Warren, R. E. (1972) 'Traces, concepts, and conscious constructions', in A. W. Melton and E. Martin (eds), *Coding Processes in Human Memory*. Washington, D.C.: Winston.

Reid, T. (1872) *The Works of Thomas Reid*, W. Hamilton, ed., 7th edn. London: Longman.

Regan, D. T. and Totten, J. (1975) 'Empathy and attribution: turning observers into actors', *Journal of Personality and Social Psychology*, 32, 850–6.

Richards, G. (1989) *On Psychological Language and the Physiomorphic Basis of Human Nature*. London: Routledge.

Rips, L. J. and Conrad, F. G. (1989) 'Folk psychology of mental activities', *Psychological Review*, 96, 187–207.

Rosenberg, M. J. (1965) 'When dissonance fails: on eliminating evaluation apprehension from attitude measurement', *Journal of Personality and Social Psychology*, 1, 28–42.

Rosenberg, M. J. (1969) 'The conditions and consequences of evaluation apprehension', in R. Rosenthal and R. L. Rosnow (eds), *Artifact in Behavioural Research*. London: Academic Press.

Ross, L. (1977) 'The intuitive psychologist and his shortcomings: distortions in the attribution process', in L. Berkowitz (ed.), *Advances in Experimental Social Psychology*, vol. 10, pp. 174–220. New York: Academic Press.

Ross, L. and Anderson, C. (1982) 'Shortcomings in the attribution process: on the origins and maintenance of erroneous social assessments', in D. Kahneman, P. Slovic, and A. Tversky (eds), *Judgement under Uncertainty: Heuristics and Biases* (pp. 129–52). Cambridge: Cambridge University Press.

Ross, M. and Fletcher, G. J. O. (1985) 'Attribution and social perception', in G. Lindzey and E. Aronson (eds), *Handbook of Social Psychology*, 3rd edn. New York: Random House.

Ruble, D. N. and Rholes, W. S. (1981) 'The development of children's perceptions and attributions about their social world', in J. H. Harvey, W. Ickes, and R. F. Kidd (eds), *New Directions in Attribution Research*, vol. 3, pp. 3–36. Hillsdale, NJ: Erlbaum.

Ryle, G. (1949) *The Concept of Mind*. London: Hutchinson.

Sacks, O. (1973) *Awakenings*. London: Duckworth.

Salmon, W. C. (1984) *Scientific Explanation and the Causal Structure of the World*. Princeton, NJ: Princeton University Press.

Santillana, G. de (1961) *The Origins of Scientific Thought: From Anaximander to Proclus, 600 BC to 300 AD*. London: Weidenfeld & Nicolson.

Schaffer, S. (1987) 'Godly men and mechanical philosophers: souls and spirits in Restoration natural philosophy', *Science in Context*, 1, 55–85.

Schuberth, R. E. (1983) 'The infant's search for objects: alternatives to Piaget's theory of object concept development', *Advances in Infancy Research*, 2, 137–82.

Schustack, M. W. and Sternberg, R. J. (1981) 'Evaluation of evidence in causal inference', *Journal of Experimental Psychology: General*, 110, 101–20.

Searle, J. R. (1983) *Intentionality: An Essay in the Philosophy of Mind*. Cambridge: Cambridge University Press.

Sedlak, A. J. and Kurtz, S. T. (1981) 'A review of children's use of causal inference principles', *Child Development*, 52, 759–84.

Shaklee, H. and Mims, M. (1981) 'Development of rule use in judgments of covariation between events', *Child Development*, 52, 317–25.

Shallice, T. (1972) 'Dual functions of consciousness', *Psychological Review*, 78, 383–93.

Shallice, T. (1978) 'The dominant action system: an information processing approach to consciousness', in K. S. Pope and J. L. Singer (eds), *The Stream of Consciousness: Scientific Investigations into the Flow of Human Experience*. New York: Plenum.

Shanker, S. (1991) 'Automatic actions and the "cognitive unconscious"', Unpublished manuscript, York University, Ontario, Canada.

Shanks, D. R. and Dickinson, A. (1987) 'Associative accounts of causality judgement', in G. H. Bower (ed.), *The Psychology of Learning and Motivation*, vol. 21, pp. 229–61. New York: Academic Press.

Shanon, B. (1976) 'Aristotelianism, Newtonianism, and the physics of the layman', *Perception*, 5, 241–3.

Shiffrin, R. M. and Schneider, W. (1977) 'Controlled and automatic human information processing: II. Perceptual learning, automatic attending, and a general theory', *Psychological Review*, 84, 127–90.

Shultz, T. R. (1980) 'Development of the concept of intention', in W. A. Collins (ed.), *The Minnesota Symposium on Child Psychology*, vol. 13. Hillsdale, NJ: Erlbaum.

Shultz, T. R. (1982a) 'Rules of causal attribution', *Monographs of the Society for Research in Child Development*, 47, 1–51.

Shultz, T. R. (1982b) 'Causal reasoning in the social and non-social realms', *Canadian Journal of Behavioural Science*, 14, 307–22.

Shultz, T. R., Altmann, E., and Asselin, J. (1986) 'Judging causal priority', *British Journal of Developmental Psychology*, 4, 67–74.

Shultz, T. R., Fisher, G. W., Pratt, C. C., and Rulf, S. (1986) 'Selection of causal rules', *Child Development*, 57, 143–52.

Shultz, T. R. and Kestenbaum, N. R. (1985) 'Causal reasoning in children', in G. Whitehurst (ed.), *Annals of Child Development*, vol. 2, pp. 195–249. Greenwich, CT: JAI Press.

Shultz, T. R. and Mendelson, R. (1975) 'The use of covariation as a principle of causal inference', *Child Development*, 46, 394–9.

Shultz, T. R. and Ravinsky, R. B. (1977) 'Similarity as a principle of causal inference', *Child Development*, 48, 1552–8.

Shultz, T. R., Schleifer, M., and Altman, I. (1981) 'Judgements of causation, responsibility and punishment in cases of harm-doing', *Canadian Journal of Behavioural Science*, 13, 238–53.

Siegler, R. S. (1975) 'Defining the locus of developmental differences in children's causal reasoning', *Journal of Experimental Child Psychology*, 20, 512–25.

Siegler, R. S. and Liebert, R. M. (1974) 'Effects of contiguity, regularity, and age on children's causal inferences', *Developmental Psychology*, 10, 574–9.

Skinner, B. F. (1957) *Verbal Behaviour*. New York: Appleton-Century-Crofts.

Smith, E. R. and Miller, F. D. (1978) 'Limits on perception of cognitive processes: a reply to Nisbett and Wilson', *Psychological Review*, 85, 355–62.

Smith, P. and Jones, O. R. (1986) *The Philosophy of Mind: An Introduction*. Cambridge: Cambridge University Press.

Solomon, S. (1978) 'Measuring dispositional and situational attributions', *Personality and Social Psychology Bulletin*, 4, 589–94.

Sophian, C. and Huber, A. (1984) 'Early developments in children's causal judgements', *Child Development*, 55, 512–26.

Sosa, E. (ed.) (1975) *Causation and Conditionals*. Oxford: Oxford University Press.

Sperling. G. A. (1960) 'The information available in brief visual presentations', *Psychological Monographs*, 74 (whole no. 498).

Stephenson, L. (1981) *The Study of Human Nature: Readings*. Oxford: Oxford University Press.

Storms, M. D. (1973) 'Videotape and the attribution process: reversing actors' and observers' points of view', *Journal of Personality and Social Psychology*, 27, 165–75.

Suppes, P. (1970) *A Probabilistic Theory of Causality*. Amsterdam: North Holland Publishing Co.

Tagiuri, R. (1960) 'Movement as a cue in person perception', in H. P. David and J. C. Brengelman (eds), *Perspective in Personality Research*. New York: Springer Publishing.

Taylor, R. (1966) *Action and Purpose*. Englewood Cliffs, NJ: Prentice-Hall.

Taylor, R. (1974) *Metaphysics*, 2nd edn. Englewood Cliffs, NJ: Prentice-Hall.

Taylor, S. E. (1981) 'The interface of cognitive and social psychology', in J. H. Harvey (ed.), *Cognition, Social Behaviour, and the Environment* (pp. 189–211). Hillsdale, NJ: Erlbaum.

Taylor, S. E. and Fiske, S. T. (1975) 'Point of view and perceptions of causality', *Journal of Personality and Social Psychology*, 32, 439–45.

Taylor, S. E. and Fiske, S. T. (1978) 'Salience, attention, and attribution: top of the head phenomena', in L. Berkowitz (ed.), *Advances in Experimental Social Psychology*, vol. 11, pp. 249–88. New York: Academic Press.

Tetlock, P. E. and Levi, A. (1982) 'Attribution bias: on the inconclusiveness of the cognition-motivation debate', *Journal of Experimental Social Psychology*, 18, 68–88.

Tillyard, E. M. W. (1943) *The Elizabethan World Picture*. London: Chatto & Windus.

Toulmin, S. (1970) 'Reasons and causes', in R. Borger and F. Cioffi (eds), *Explanation in the Behavioural Sciences* (pp. 1–26). Cambridge: Cambridge University Press.

Toulmin, S. and Goodfield, J. (1961) *The Fabric of the Heavens*. London: Hutchinson.

Toulmin, S. and Goodfield, J. (1962) *The Architecture of Matter*. London: Hutchinson.

Trigg, R. (1988) *Ideas of Human Nature: An Historical Introduction*. Oxford: Blackwell.

Tversky, A. and Kahneman, D. (1973) 'Availability: a heuristic for judging frequency and probability', *Cognitive Psychology*, 5, 207–32.

Urmson, J. D. (1968) 'Motives and causes', in A. R. White (ed.), *The Philosophy of Action* (pp. 153–65). Oxford: Oxford University Press.

Uzgiris, I. C. (1984) 'Development in causal understanding', in R. M. Golinkoff (ed.), *The Development of Causality in Infancy: A Symposium. Advances in Infancy Research*, 3, 125–65.

Vallacher, R. R. and Wegner, D. M. (1987) 'What do people think they're doing? Action identification and human behaviour', *Psychological Review*, 94, 3–15.

Vendler, Z. (1972) *Res cogitans: An Essay in Rational Psychology*. Ithaca, NY: Cornell University Press.

Watson, D. (1982) 'The actor and the observer: how are their perceptions of causality divergent?', *Psychological Bulletin*, 92, 682–700.

Watson, J. S. (1984) 'Bases of causal inference in infancy: time, space, and sensory relations', in R. M. Golinkoff (ed.), *The Development of Causality in Infancy: A Symposium. Advances in Infancy Research*, 3, 125–65.

Weiskrantz, L., Warrington, E. K., Sanders, M. D., and Marshall, J. (1974) 'Visual capacity in the hemianopic field following a restricted occipital ablation', *Brain*, 97, 709–28.

Wellman, H. M. (1991) 'From desires to beliefs: acquisition of a theory of mind', in A. Whiten (ed.), *Natural Theories of Mind: Evolution, Development, and Simulation of Everyday Mindreading* (pp. 19–38). Oxford: Blackwell.

White, A. R. (1968) 'Introduction', in A. R. White (ed.), *The Philosophy of Action* (pp. 1–18). Oxford: Oxford University Press.

White, P. A. (1980) 'Limitations on verbal reports of internal events: a refutation of Nisbett and Wilson and of Bem', *Psychological Review*, 87, 105–12.

White, P. A. (1984) 'A model of the layperson as pragmatist', *Personality and Social Psychology Bulletin*, 10, 333–48.

White, P. A. (1985) 'The awareness issue and memorial influences upon the accuracy of verbal reports: a re-examination of some data', *Psychological Reports*, 57, 312–14.

White, P. A. (1986) 'On consciousness and beliefs about consciousness; consequences of the physicalist assumption for models of consciousness', *Journal of Social Behaviour and Personality*, 1, 505–24.

White, P. A. (1988a) 'Causal processing: origins and development', *Psychological Bulletin*, 104, 36–52.

White, P. A. (1988b) 'Knowing more about what we can tell: "introspective access" and causal report accuracy ten years later', *British Journal of Psychology*, 79, 13–45.

White, P. A. (1988c) 'Common sense beliefs about the defining characteristics of normality and abnormality', Unpublished paper, Department of Psychology, University of Auckland, New Zealand.

White, P. A. (1989a) 'A theory of causal processing', *British Journal of Psychology*, 80, 431–54.

White, P. A. (1989b) 'Judgements of abnormality and their consequences for judgements of infractions of human and civil rights', *Community Mental Health in New Zealand*, 4, 72–86.

White, P. A. (1989c) 'Evidence for the use of information about internal events to improve the accuracy of causal reports', *British Journal of Psychology*, 80, 375–82.

White, P. A. (1990) 'Ideas about causation in philosophy and in psychology', *Psychological Bulletin*, 108, 3–18.

White, P. A. (1991) 'Ambiguity in the internal/external distinction in causal attribution', *Journal of Experimental Social Psychology*, 27, 259–70.

White, P. A. (1992) 'The anthropomorphic machine: causal order in nature and the world view of common sense', *British Journal of Psychology*, 83, 61–96.

Wilson, J. T. L. (1983) 'A function for iconic storage: perception of rapid change', *The Behavioural and Brain Sciences*, 6, 42–3.

Wilson, T. D. (1985) 'Strangers to ourselves: the origins and accuracy of beliefs about one's own mental states', in J. H. Harvey and G. Weary (eds), *Attribution: Basic Issues and Applications*. New York: Academic Press.

Wrightsman, L. (1974) *Assumptions about Human Nature: A Social-Psychological Approach*. Monterey, CA: Brooks/Cole.

Wyer, R. S., Jr. and Srull, T. K. (1984) *Handbook of Social Cognition*, 3 vols. Hillsdale, NJ: Erlbaum.

Young, J. (1988) 'Is Schopenhauer an irrationalist?', *Schopenhauer Jahrbuch*, 69, 85–100.

Zuckerman, M. (1979) 'Attribution of success and failure revisited, or: the motivational bias is alive and well in attribution theory', *Journal of Personality*, 47, 245–87.

Zuckerman, M. and Feldman, L. S. (1984) 'Actions and occurrences in attribution theory', *Journal of Personality and Social Psychology*, 46, 541–50.

# Name index

# Subject index